DHARMA

THAT EVERY BUDDHIST
MUST FOLLOW

DHARMA
THAT EVERY BUDDHIST
MUST FOLLOW

AMANG NOPU PAMU

Translated by
BODI WENTU RINPOCHE

WORLD DHARMA VOICE, INC.
2111 N. SAN GABRIEL BLVD., SUITE F
ROSEMEAD, CALIFORNIA 91770

First edition published 2001

ISBN 1-892727-23-4

Designed and Typeset by SG Graphic Design Group
South Pasadena, California

☞ *How to Treat This Sacred Dharma Book* ☜

THIS BOOK, AS WELL AS other books that contain the correct Buddha Dharma, is sacred and should be treated with the utmost respect. Therefore, it should be kept off the floor and any type of seat. It should not be taken into the bathroom or any other unseemly place. The reader should wash his hands before touching this book and should not sully his hands during the time of reading. This book should be kept in a high, clean place, and no other objects should be placed on top of it. The more respectfully one treats any sacred Dharma book, the greater the likelihood that one will benefit from it.

Table of Contents

⁓ DHARMA ⁓
THAT EVERY BUDDHIST
MUST FOLLOW

Part One
INTRODUCTORY PORTION

⌐ *Translator's Introduction* ⌐

IT IS MY HONOR TO have had the opportunity to translate this great book on Buddhism from Chinese into English. I would like to thank Dharma Kings Yangwo Yisinubu and Amang Nopu Pamu for their magnificent teachings. I would also like to express my sincere appreciation to all of the people who assisted me in this project.

This book contains much English and non-English Buddhist terminology. The reader is advised to consult the glossary when coming across unfamiliar terms. For those readers not versed in Buddhist terminology, reviewing the glossary before reading the book would be extremely helpful. The glossary and all endnotes are the work of the translator for which the author is not responsible.

Whether a beginning or advanced practitioner of Buddhism, I am confident that the reader will find this book to be a true Buddhist treasure. May this book benefit many living beings and lead them to enlightenment. I dedicate the merit of my translation to the happiness and liberation of all living beings.

— *Bodi Wentu Rinpoche*

≈ Publisher's Introduction ≈

WE WERE FORTUNATE TO have been able to view the videotape that contains the entire process of Dharma King Amang Nopu's[1] practice of the Dharma to have the Buddhas bestow nectar.[2] It was incomparably magnificent and wonderful. As far as we are concerned, it was an unprecedented event.

Many people think that magical events, such as making the Statue of Liberty disappear, are mysterious. They think that David Copperfield's flying through the air is mysterious, that Krisha Lawar's walking through concrete walls is mysterious, or that UFO's are mysterious. However, that which is in fact magnificently mysterious is Amang Nopu Pamu's ability to draw nectar from the realm of the Buddhas to this world. We believe that this is a sacred mystery, not just an ordinary mystery.

Although we saw the entire process of Pamu's[3] practice of the Dharma to have the Buddhas bestow true nectar, we regrettably were only able to obtain videotapes that contain a portion of the entire Dharma Assembly. However, even though it was only a portion, we were able to clearly see that the nectar came from nothingness. It was not an object of this human world. We were able to see the nectar shaking, expanding, and contracting in the bowl, as if it were a living object. Its celestial construction, unpredictable changes, and natural structure definitely cannot be compared with any other object that one may find in this world.

The ability to make nectar descend proves that Pamu has attained the state of realization of a Holy One. It is most important that we study and practice that which is contained in the commentaries and Buddhist books written by Amang Nopu Pamu. This is fundamental for accomplishment and liberation from the cycle of birth and death.

We greatly revere Pamu's supreme realization and her selfless actions. In this world, we have yet to see any other Dharma King, Rinpoche, or Dharma Teacher who does not accept any offerings and who has taken a vow not to do so for his or her entire life. She cares only about benefiting others. She never considers herself. She selflessly contributes to living beings. Wherever she goes, she tells people, "I am an ordinary person, equal to any one of you." Although this is Pamu's attitude, nevertheless, we at World Dharma Voice Inc., along with so many eminent personages within Buddhism, all think that she is a true Mahasattva who is present in our world.

As the publisher, we would like to sincerely and respectfully thank the most honored Dharma King Amang Nopu Pamu for her great, compassionate wish to have our publishing company print and distribute this series of most precious Buddhist books. Through these books, one may increase one's good fortune and wisdom and end the cycle of birth and death. These books will benefit living beings in all of the Dharma realms and will cause the correct Dharma of the Tathagata to shine once again. We would also like to respectfully thank Great Rinpoche Ge Sang Ga Ma Yang Zong and the other eleven Great Rinpoches who participated in the Nectar Dharma Assembly for having sincerely attested to what they saw. They did this for the benefit of living beings in all of the Dharma realms, thus proving the true magnificence of the Buddha Dharma.

— *World Dharma Voice, Inc.*

Sacred Occurrences at the Dharma Assembly

I AM ZHUO MA RINPOCHE. I and nearly 100 Rinpoches, Geshés, Khenpos, and Dharma Teachers participated in the Great Nectar Dharma Assembly conducted by Pamu. At the Dharma Assembly, I saw sacred occurrences that I had never seen before in my life. Pamu was seated on the Dharma King dais. Part of her discourse was as follows:

> **Everybody look clearly. This is a pure gold, empty Dharma bowl that has just been washed by a Rinpoche. There is nothing in it. Nobody is allowed to approach it.**
>
> **The video camera is not allowed to move during the entire videotaping today. The scene shot by the video camera will not change. Your eyes and the video camera will be used to keep watch on the bowl so as to see how this nectar arrives. Of course, it will be bestowed by the Buddhas themselves!**
>
> **Although I am now living overseas, I know how difficult it is for many Chinese people and other practitioners of Buddhism who do not understand the Tibetan language to learn Vajrayana Buddhism. Additionally, the entire practice of the Dharma today is the result of the ripening of conditions for there to be a great Buddha Dharma event in the land of the Chinese people. I will, therefore, solely use the Chinese language to give a discourse on the Dharma and to practice the Dharma.**

In the middle of the Dharma Assembly, it seemed as if my entire body was filled with a warm current. It was incomparably wonderful. It was not as if I had entered samadhi, yet it was not as if I had not entered samadhi. I truly do not know the reason why. The sky was changing. The earth was changing. There were numerous sacred sights at the Buddhist altar area.[4] I can truthfully say that this is the first time I saw the Buddhas and Bodhisattvas come to the human realm. The empowerment that those virtuous ones in attendance received cannot be described in words.

At the Dharma Assembly, specifically for the Great Perfection Rainbow Body Accomplishment Dharma Initiation, Pamu practiced the Dharma for invoking the bestowal of the Most Precious Nectar. This nectar is indispensable for such initiation. The Most Precious Nectar can also be made into Most Precious Pills. It is the highest level of nectar. With just one taste of it, one will definitely have no obstacles in this lifetime in attaining accomplishment. At the time the nectar descended, the Buddhas also bestowed more than 1,000 yellow, white, and black shariras[5] into the gold bowl.

At the Dharma Assembly, Pamu practiced the Dharma to have five types of nectar bestowed. Each type of nectar was of a separate grade. There was Long Life Nectar. It can extend one's life span, increase one's merit, deepen one's state of realization, and help one develop supernormal powers.

There was also the Crystal Body Nectar bestowed by Aksobhya Buddha. Its luster was much more captivating than that of any precious gem. After being initiated with this type of nectar, one can successfully practice the Dharma to achieve the Transparent Crystal Reward Body. With just one taste of this nectar, one can immediately go through walls and have other miraculous powers.

With just one taste of the silver-gray nectar bestowed by the Long Life Buddha, one's life span will increase to over 120 years. With two tastes, one's life span will increase to over 150 years. There is also the Red Bodhi Nectar. This was bestowed by Amitabha, the first leader of the Vajrayana. This nectar is specially used in the highest and most sacred initiation within Vajrayana Buddhism: The Great Perfection Rainbow Body Dharma.

We Rinpoches who were in attendance also saw that the nectar did not have the slightest semblance of anything which was made by man. The different types of nectar could not possibly have been objects made by an ordinary person! Each type of nectar had a mysterious and natural structure and seemed to be alive.

When the Dharma Assembly was about to end, Pamu gave the following instructions:

Whoever saw the Buddhas descending from the sky and the bestowing of nectar into the Buddhist altar area must attest here today to what they saw in order to uphold the correct view for living beings.

Those of you who did not see these things and who falsely attest will receive karmic retribution.

Those Rinpoches and Great Virtuous Ones in attendance all attested to what they saw. The descending of nectar enabled all of us to understand the true tantra[6] and especially enabled us to understand the magnificence of Pamu's Buddha Dharma. I do not need to say what type of Holy One Pamu is, since everyone already knows. What else can I say at this point? I can only say the following words: Maintain a heart of humility, cultivate yourself well, and save living beings everywhere.

— Disciple Zhuo Ma
True Words Respectfully Written

☞ *Lessons Induced From Nectar* ☜

PAMU GAVE A DISCOURSE as follows:

The live videotape of the Buddhas bestowing nectar and the scenes of myself and Buddhist disciples cannot be shown to those who do not understand the Buddha Dharma. This is because outsiders would not recognize or understand the wonderful states concerned with unworldly Dharma. Of course, those practitioners of Buddhism who are Great Rinpoches and those who have deep roots of kindness[7] may view the videotape.

You have requested numerous times that proof of the truth of the Buddha Dharma be provided. You can use real photographs of my practicing the nectar Dharma. You can also use the attestations of the Great Rinpoches that they personally participated in the Dharma Assembly and that they personally saw the Buddhas bestow nectar. However, one must use only group scenes. I am not qualified to claim personal merit or engage in self-acclamation. As long as living beings are benefited, that is enough.

The Buddhas have bestowed nectar in response to the ripening of conditions of good fortune of those of you who were able to partake of the nectar. I think that the Buddhas' bestowing of nectar must have been due to a Great Virtuous One among our disciples here who was helping me practice the Dharma. I am just a humble person. How could I have such great abilities? I and all of you practitioners of Buddhism seated here today, including Great Bodhisattvas, should constantly maintain a heart of humility. You must remember what I say. I will never accept any offerings from anyone. This is because we are practitioners of Buddhism who maintain a heart of humility. We have come to this world to benefit living beings, not to covet and accept the money and property of others.

One of my disciples said that those false Rinpoches will hate me. I said that this is exactly the law or principle of cause and effect. This is because whoever is a false Rinpoche does not understand the Buddha Dharma. Such people are ordinary beings with ignorance, defilements,[8] anger, and hatred.

They are not able to obtain the true nectar of the Buddhas, are not able to experience true empowerment, and do not possess the qualifications to receive Supreme Division initiations. They must accept many disciples and rely upon the offerings of such disciples.

I do not accept many disciples. I only teach several dozen people of noble character. Anyone else who wants to learn the Buddha Dharma from me can only learn from the books I have written. Through learning from the books I have written, one can in the same manner obtain great fortune and end the cycle of birth and death. I do not have time to receive more disciples. Unlike those false Rinpoches, I do not accept any offerings.

If they did not hate me, whom would they hate? In previous times, were Sakyamuni Buddha, Master Padmasambhava, and Master Marpa not despised by false Rinpoches and followers of erroneous ways? If any of you who are my disciples meet up with evil people who defame me, you must not become angry or hateful. You must not use your supernormal powers to kill them. On the contrary, you must have great compassion for them and must be concerned for them. You must vow to bring them good fortune. You must vow to enable them to receive the correct Dharma as soon as possible. You must not give rise to even the slightest harmful thought, since we are living in this world to benefit and save living beings.

There is another point I would like to especially remind those Rinpoches and Dharma Teachers here today to convey to all other practitioners of Buddhism. Under no circumstances should one, upon seeing a Rinpoche, think of beseeching him or her to practice the Dharma to have true nectar bestowed. It could be said that this is impossible. Even those Rinpoches who are at the level of Dharma King may not have attained such realization. Practicing such Dharma is only for true Holy Ones who are Great Dharma Kings.

As for myself, if the conditions for all of you in attendance here today to receive the blessing of nectar were not mature, and if there was not a Holy Dharma King among you practicing the Dharma whom I do not have the ability to see, then I would not have been able to cause you to taste true nectar bestowed by the Buddhas! Thus, you disciples of mine who are Rinpoches and Great Virtuous Ones should tell your students not to make unrealistic demands upon other Rinpoches. As long as they are truly Great Virtuous Ones who actually propagate the correct Dharma of the Tathagata and are not false Rinpoches, we should be respectful toward them.

☙ *Preface* ❧

Dorje Losang, a name given to me by my Master,[9] is who I am. People ask me how old I am. I do not know. At the temple, it is said that I am over 100. My government documents indicate that I am 91. Let us just say that I am 91.

I am a Lama. Monks and nuns say that I am the incarnation of Vimalaprabha. Because of this, I was pushed on to the Dharma King dais at an early age. What could I do? I still think of myself as just a monk with a heart of humility.

Many sutra teachers taught me to read the sutras. I learned the Tripitaka and the ten sets of scriptures of Vajrayana Buddhism. I also followed some Great Dharma Kings and learned mudras and mantras. The Elder Dharma King at the Zong Sa Temple is my Master. Chi Ming Chi Song De Zhen is also my Master. He taught me the Long Qin Spirit-Body Great Perfection Dharma. I also followed Master Pabongka and learned the Kalachakra Vajra Dharma. I received over 1,000 tantric initiations.

There are some Great Rinpoches and Dharma Kings who call me Dharma King Master. As soon as I hear people call me this, I get goose bumps. I am just one with a heart of humility. What qualifications do I have to be called a Dharma King Master? Could it be that those people in society who say of themselves, "I am a Dharma King," or "I am a Great Rinpoche," are the real Dharma Kings? Empty titles are of no use. They cannot liberate one from the cycle of birth and death. If you are a Dharma King or Great Rinpoche, then show people some of your skills. Invoke the Buddhas to bestow some nectar. Unfortunately, those people are far from being capable of such a thing. They speak empty words and cheat the unknowing.

I often transmit the Dharma to Rinpoches. Have you heard of Dharma King Dilgo of Nyingma school?[10] I conferred upon him an initiation. They all respect me. If you believe this, fine. If not, it is also fine. This year, an organization with a name something like *The World Buddhism Association* issued to me a piece of paper. The paper said that it was decided by the judging panel that Dorje Losang was a noble monk on the level of an international Dharma King. It also said that I was an Elder Dharma King. My attendant read it aloud to me. The attendant and my disciples all said that it was rather authoritative and that such piece of paper was worth a high price. I asked what price it was worth. They answered that it was worth a good deal of gold. I said, "Put it away. Let's get a good price and sell it." When my disciples heard this, they laughed heartily. Afterwards, I don't know which person took that paper away. Maybe it was sold for money.

These types of things have no use. Everything is impermanent. I only have a Dharma bowl, a tattered robe, and a worn-out rush cushion. I have no family property. If you say that I am poor, well, to others it might appear that I am poor and have an uneasy mind. If you say that I am rich, well, there are few Rinpoches who can compare with me. There have been Great Rinpoches who came to see me. From outside the door, they walked in kneeling. If you gathered together all of the money and property that they offered to me, such money and property could not be moved by even 30 people.

I view gold and dirt as having no difference. To me, silver and pieces of plaster are the same. Precious gems are like pearls of dew on the grass. I never accepted any of those valuable things. My respected Master, Great Dharma King Yangwo Yisinubu, said, "Even the Dharma should not be clung to, let alone that which is not the Dharma." I accept this saying. Only the Dharma that my Master transmitted to me is truly precious! I practice it day and night. For the past few years, I have not known what is meant by the word *sleep*. My eyes have remained wide open for even a one-month period. My body is as large as the sky. It is without limits. These are honest words. My valuable asset is having become one with the Dharma.

Some Great Rinpoches ask me to write prefaces for the books they have written. They want me to write complimentary words. My hands can lift Buddhist books and Dharma objects, but they cannot lift such a pen. Therefore, I am unable to write such prefaces.

There were a few authors for whom I would like to have written prefaces. However, they are no longer on this earth. I thus cannot write for them. They were those who wrote *The Hetu-Vidya Treatise*, *The Mulamadhyamaka-karira Treatise*, *The Prajna Treatise*, *The Precepts and Discipline Treatise*, *The Abhidharmakosa Treatise*, and *The Treatise on the Stages of the Path to Enlightenment*. If you ask who such people were, they were Master Padmasambhava,

Master Marpa, Venerable Atisha, Master Tsongkhapa, Nagarjuna, Kana-deva, Asanga, Vasubandhu, Dignaga, Chandrakirti, Samkara-svamin, Silabhadra, Dharmakirti, and Xuan Zhuang. There are also Great Dharma King Yangwo Yisinubu and Great Dharma King Amang Nopu Pamu, who are alive.

They are all true Buddhas and Bodhisattvas, true Dharma Kings. Their commentaries are so good, and their Buddha Dharma is so correct. They are so great! They really have something to show to people. Do you Rinpoches have their knowledge, talents, wisdom, miraculous powers, and depth of realization? For me to write a preface in your books would not be right. Think about it. In just one of your chapters, there are 30 or 40 mistakes. How can this be called a Buddhist book? How can I lift my pen?

The book *Dharma That Every Buddhist Must Follow* was written by the Holy Mother, Amang Nopu. I read every sentence in it from beginning to end. My hand lifted a pen. Nobody wanted me to write a preface, but I could not put the pen down, as if it were glued to my hand. You must be asking what pleasant words this old man Dorje can say with his old, dry, toothless mouth. In cultivating oneself, it is important to let go of the concept of self. Do not underestimate me. Although I am old, I still have saliva. My words may be a little unrefined. It is not good, however, when writing is too refined and cannot be understood. Although I might be as old as rotten boards, if I had not learned real Dharma, I could not be pushed on to the Dharma King dais. I want to speak on the main subject now. Listen:[11]

I remember the beginning of heaven and earth when there was the state of impermanence and chaos. At that time, the six great elements united through the maturing of conditions. The three karmas of body, speech, and mind arose, which constitute complicated causes. Living beings, acting foolishly through their momentarily changing thoughts, began creating karma. They were born into the six realms due to shameful, selfish desires. One could see clearly their accumulated karma, which caused them to revolve in the cycle of reincarnation since beginningless time.

Alas! I groan and weep over such a tragic situation. How can a Holy Virtuous One bear to ignore such a situation? All Holy Ones and Bodhisattvas act to save living beings. When appearing in this earthly realm in response to the needs of living beings, each Holy One and Bodhisattva brings his best Buddha Dharma.[12] They compassionately provide a boat to ferry living beings across the sea of misery. But living beings are extremely difficult to save because of the two attachments,[13] which are so prevalent in the world.

One type of living being learns erroneous ways, such as fortune telling, astrology, feng shui (geomancy), and religions other than Buddhism. They do not believe in the Buddha Dharma. They do not believe in any deities or they believe in evil deities.

Another type of living being says that leading a happy life is just a matter of obtaining wealth, high position, and honor. Their hearts have been covered with clouds of desire from beginningless time. They say, "Buddhist books could be piled up to form a mountain, but where is the truth of such books manifested?"

How pitiful! How sad! Have they not heard of the most exalted Amang Nopu, the Holy Mother? She often manifests the Dharma in the world. Are such manifestations not Dharma states? Nectar descends from the sky. Her accumulated merit is seen by all. Is this not manifestation of the Dharma? The awesome Buddha power caused the Vajra hair between my eyebrows and the hair of my beard to grow again. How did this happen? Was this not the manifestation of awesome Dharma power by the holy Buddhas and Bodhisattvas? When will such ignorant and doubting children wake up from their delusions and dreams? How long will they wait before being saved by learning the Buddha Dharma?

I now take up my brush to write this preface so as to respectfully send you the Dharma of the Buddha Mother, Amang Nopu, who is truly a Great Virtuous One! Listen carefully. Books written by the Holy Mother, Amang Nopu, are most sacred. All of them are precious Dharma treasures. You must respectfully and diligently put into practice all of the principles contained in such books. By doing so, you will be walking on the correct path! I am a humble monk with a heart of humility and bow my head to the Holy Mother.

I made a vow to come into this world to save living beings. This earthly realm is so vast. Of all those whom I recognized as my Master, eight or nine out of ten could be called lofty ones. How could any of those in today's world who are truly ordinary, but who call themselves holy, compare with such Masters? In this time of the five turbidities[14] when the karma of living beings is heavy and evil ways have almost become common practice, even those who can be called great moral ones find it difficult to subdue the strong negative karma of living beings.

Therefore, I will concentrate on cultivating my own mind. It cannot be helped. Hence, guarding my heart of humility, I have lived alone in a mountain cave for a long time, waiting for the right time, waiting for the conditions to mature. When that time comes, I will raise the banner of the true Dharma. I will propagate the supreme Dharma contained in *The Mahamudra of Liberation* written by my respected Master of great power, Dharma King Yangwo Yisinubu.

While I was waiting and during a state of deep samadhi, I suddenly heard that the discourses entitled *Dharma That Every Buddhist Must Follow* had been given to benefit the world. I then realized that the Holy Mother Master, out of great kindness, had empowered this ignorant child, Losang. My beard, which had basically stopped growing, grew again rapidly. This was manifestation of the true Dharma. In this entire earthly realm, how could there be any other holy Dakinis who are higher than the supreme Amang Nopu?

In a state of deep samadhi, I visited the sacred realms to inquire into how high Amang Nopu really is. The answers I received verified my view. Those in the sacred realms all praised the Holy Mother Amang as the most exalted. They praised her numerous writings as containing the essence of Buddhism. They praised her for having met the seven criteria of a Dakini as described in *Know The True Doctrines*. They praised her as truly being the foremost among all Holy Mothers in the history of Buddhism. They praised *Dharma That Every Buddhist Must Follow* as a most precious treasure for leading living beings to liberation. Even Arhats and Bodhisattvas should practice its principles. Therefore, this book will provide limitless benefit to all living beings in the three spheres of existence.

Although I am a Dharma King, in truth I am a poor monk with a heart of humility, an ignorant child of Amang Nopu. My writing skills are poor, and I have sullied this book with my preface. I hope Amang Nopu will forgive my poor writing and will magnanimously empower this ignorant child. I, Dorje Losang, take up my brush to write this preface today for the sake of living beings. No matter what I write, I am unable to adequately praise the supreme enlightenment and wonderful purity of Amang Nopu. In honor of Amang Nopu, I kowtow four times, wishing that her Dharma teachings will forever exist. Wo Ba Mei.

— *Dharma King Dorje Losang*
respectfully offers this preface

The Beginning of Awakening

As soon as one mentions Amang Nopu Pamu, everyone knows that she is the one who saves living beings, who does not accept any offerings, and who is infinitely compassionate. She is a Buddha Mother with extraordinary realization, a great Mahasattva. She is the true Vajravarahi Great Mahasattva, who is on the same level as Selfless Mother Great Mahasattva and Kuan Yin Great Mahasattva! Her position, depth of realization, and the solemnness and fullness of her appearance show that in the Buddha Dharma realms of the present age, she is truly foremost among female yidams! She is one of the three great female Dharma Kings in the history of Buddhism!

Research of the history of Buddhism from ancient times until the present shows that there have been many Dakinis in the Buddha Dharma realms throughout history. There have not been any Dakinis who can match her magnificent and outstanding manifestation of the Dharma. Not only did she master the entire Tripitaka at the age of 20, she also wrote five commentaries of her own and other Buddhist books. Who would have thought that when Pamu wrote the *Commentary on the Hetu-Vidya Treatise*, she was only eight years old? Although it is the work of an eight-year-old, due to its classical grammatical style and the depth of its literary language, even graduate students and those with Ph.D. degrees cannot fully comprehend it within a short period of time. It is clear that Pamu's talents cannot be found in others throughout history!

After Pamu's Master, **Mahavairocana Great Dharma King Zun Sheng**, taught her the Dharma for only five months, she joined her palms in front of her heart and said to her Master, "Buddha Master, please do not teach me the Dharma for the next six months. Also, do not make me engage in daily meditation. During my meditation, I have seen and understood that the views of Buddhist practitioners in the world have become slanted. These practitioners have already lost the standard by which to judge what is correct knowledge and practice. Therefore, I want to use this time to write a commentary on *The Hetu-Vidya Treatise* in order to allow people of later generations to identify what the correct understanding of the Buddha Dharma is."

When those Arhats and ordinary Bodhisattvas who were her fellow disciples heard her say this, they truly felt that her taking on such a project was ridiculous. They thought, "How could a child who has entered the Esoteric Dharma Institute only five months and who does not understand any Inner-Institute Dharma go so far as to want to write a commentary on *The Hetu-Vidya Treatise*? Even those of us who have followed the Master for 20 or 30 years would not dare be so presumptuous. Her words are truly the crazy words of a child. She does not realize that there are those who are wiser than she. What a huge joke this is! Furthermore, we are each reincarnations of Great Rinpoches and Great Dharma Teachers. What does this child know?"

At that time, the Buddha Dharma King Master fully saw through the hearts of everybody and said, "Amang Nopu is the incarnation of Vajravarahi, and she has come to this world in response to its needs. Do not look down upon her for having studied the Dharma only six months. After you debate with her on topics of the sutras, you will naturally understand." Other fellow disciples then began to ask her questions about *The Hetu-Vidya Treatise*.

Who would have thought that the young Pamu covered the essence of the treatise in just a few words! Her pithy words moved the hearts of those holy fellow disciples. Each Arhat and Bodhisattva fellow disciple was stupified. No one thought that such a gentle child could be so great. They were all struck dumb with astonishment. Each stared speechlessly at the others. All of them then joined their palms in front of their hearts, knelt before her, and praised her profusely! With great reverence, they actually prostrated themselves before Pamu!

There is another astonishing and true event that I would like to relate to everybody. Any true Great Rinpoche knows that there is a certain Dharma. This is the loftiest Dharma within the entire Buddha Dharma. It is called the king of initiations. It is the Ati Yoga Heart Essence Wu Xiu Natural Vision of Wisdom – the Buddhas Bestowing Nectar Supreme Perfection Dharma. By performing this initiation, one is manifesting the highest state of realization and the greatest supernormal powers. When it comes to empowerments and initiations, it is the supreme king of all Dharma. It is the Dharma that must be practiced in initiations relating to transforming into a rainbow body and attaining a transparent body. There are no other initiations in Vajrayana

Buddhism that are as high as this. Whoever is able to perform this Dharma must be an incarnation of a Buddha or twelfth-stage Bodhisattva. Only they would have the qualifications and depth of realization to perform this Dharma. Otherwise, the performer of this Dharma would not be able to commune with the Buddhas. In such case, it would not be possible to successfully invoke true nectar!

One can study the history of Buddhism to understand that, other than Sakyamuni Buddha, one must be a first class Great Dharma King in order to have the depth of realization to perform this Dharma, which calls for inviting the Buddhas to bestow nectar from the sky in front of those in attendance. Research of the past and present ages indicates that the following four Holy Ones had or have the depth of realization to successfully invoke nectar: Great Dharma King Chi Ming Chi Song De Zhen of the Nyingma school (who has passed away), Elder Dharma King Zong Sa Jiang Yang Qin Zhe of the Sakya school (who has passed away), Great Dharma King Pabongka of the Gelug school (who has passed away), and Great Dharma King Yangwo Yisinubu of Vajrayana Buddhism. Other than these four, I have yet to learn of any other great noble one who wore or wears the Dharma King crown and who had or has the depth of merit and realization to successfully invoke true nectar from the Buddhas.

Maybe there are others who are hiding their skills or whom I do not know about for other reasons! Ordinary Rinpoches cannot possibly reach such a true Dharma state. Hence, we often see that the nectar of Rinpoches is composed of medicine, water, or the five ingredients. Added to this is sharira. It is then empowered by the chanting of mantras and called nectar. Of course, such nectar has its aspect of empowerment, but it is absolutely not true nectar from the land of the Buddhas!

It is even more rare for those who are holy Bodhisattva female Dakinis to be able to successfully invoke nectar and thoroughly master the Dharma. There have been only three holy female Mahasattvas who have successfully invoked true nectar from the Buddhas. They are Great Dharma King Selfless Mother, Great Dharma King Kuan Yin,[15] and Great Dharma King Amang Nopu. Why do these female Holy Ones have the title of Dharma King? Because what they practice is already in the category of a Dharma King.

For example, when practicing the supreme, great Dharma to invoke nectar from the Buddhas, one must chant the holy mantras of a Dharma King, must put one's hands in the mudra of a Dharma King, must use the robe and bowl of a Dharma King, and must sit upon the throne of a Dharma King. These are the four holy things that a Dharma King must be qualified to do. Not a single one can be omitted. Those who successfully practice the Dharma to invoke nectar must be qualified to do all of these four things, which can only be done by a Dharma King. Then and only then can they successfully invoke the Buddhas and Bodhisattvas, who appear in the sky, to bestow nectar. I have not been able to find any female Bodhisattvas who can successfully invoke true nectar from the Buddhas besides those three holy female Dharma Kings.

I would like to point out to everybody that what I mean by Dharma King is not a position that people have the right to confer upon someone else. Dharma King is not a position that someone can attain through the recommendations of other people. The position of true Dharma King is conferred and prophesied by the Buddhas. Only such Dharma Kings possess the true depth of realization to be a Dharma King. What is meant by Dharma King is also not someone who is selected by people as a reincarnation of a previous Dharma King and who then succeeds to the old position of Dharma King in this lifetime. Of course, the right ones are chosen sometimes, such as the child Panchen Tulku now living in Tibet and the child Tulku selected as the second incarnation of Kalu Rinpoche now living in the United States. However, such right selections are extremely rare!

On the day of September 8, 1997, a gold Dharma bowl was washed clean in front of almost 100 Rinpoches, Geshés, and Khenpos. There were also female Rinpoches. The empty bowl was placed upon the Dharma platform. Pamu began to practice the Dharma. At the time, the sky was full of dark clouds, as if a great storm was on the horizon. Pamu then shouted out the mantra-order *Pei*, and immediately the clouds dispersed. The sun came out, and a colorful rainbow appeared. Within ten minutes, the Dharma Protectors, Dakinis, Dakas, yidams, and Buddhas all appeared in the sky. Each was moving about in its own way, bestowing great empowerment.

At this time, the Rinpoches and others in attendance all saw that the red body of the Long Life Buddha was sparkling more than 100 times stronger than any precious gem. From its precious vase, the Long Life Buddha bestowed silver nectar, which fell like flakes of snow. It appeared like a silver pillar whose circumference was the size of a bowl. When the nectar fell to about 20 meters from the ground, it suddenly turned into a flash of red light, which slowly descended. When this light was about five meters above the Dharma bowl, it suddenly and directly entered the bowl by going right through the lid of the bowl, causing several flashes of light to appear.

Pamu then ordered us to view the inside of the bowl. Indeed, nectar had descended to fill the once empty bowl. The nectar truly did not have the shape of anything in this human world! At this time, there were only tears of joy and the marveling of those in attendance over such an eye-opening experience. In order to prove to those practitioners of Buddhism who were not in attendance that this was a true Dharma state, those Rinpoches and other Buddhist practitioners in attendance attested that they personally participated in this Dharma Assembly and that they saw the Buddhas bestow nectar.

I remember that when Pamu sat on her Dharma King throne on the Dharma King dais, her throne immediately rose 50 centimeters high, hanging there in midair. The Dharma Wheel on her chest was emitting mysterious golden flames. Pamu's gold Dharma bowl, handed down to her through generations, transformed into the two wheels of the sun and the moon. Pamu's left palm transformed into three palms.

The photographs we see in this book are photographs copied from the live videotape of Pamu practicing the nectar Dharma. Included is a photograph of female Rinpoches and other Buddhist practitioners standing in line to attest before the Buddhas and Bodhisattvas. Out of respect for the wishes of those who attested, their names were not written down in the book. They are identified by the particular numbers given to them in the photographs.

During the Dharma Assembly, in front of everybody, Dharma King Pamu performed nectar empowerment for the Rinpoches, Geshés, Khenpos, and Dharma Teachers in attendance. After tasting the nectar, there were those in attendance who immediately obtained miraculous powers, who attained great wisdom, who became enlightened, and who, after thoroughly repenting their past mistakes, became holy people. Ulcers and strange ailments of those in attendance disappeared on the spot within three minutes.

This shows the difference between true nectar bestowed by the Buddhas and nectar made from ordinary objects that have been empowered. Even true nectar bestowed by the Buddhas retains only five percent of its original power when mixed with ordinary objects and made into pills. Nectar made from ordinary objects has, at the very most, only one percent of the power of true nectar.

There was a Rinpoche in attendance from China who had lived in the United States for 27 years. He had been paralyzed for 18 years and could not walk at all. In less than two minutes after he tasted the true nectar that Dharma King Pamu invoked the Buddhas to bestow, one could hear the bones in his body crackle. From his seat, he suddenly flew more than one meter into the air. He then exhibited the 27 movements of Vajra Kong Xin Fist in straight sequence. That Rinpoche said, "I am truly very moved. I can only use this Buddha Dharma as an offering to Master Dharma King Pamu!" All of those in attendance were extremely touched, telling each other that this man does not appear to be one who has been paralyzed and seriously ill for 18 years. He looked like a veteran athlete!

Another example is a Buddhist layman in Hong Kong whose last name is Chen. He lost more than 70 million Hong Kong dollars when his hotel business failed. At the time Pamu was practicing the Dharma to invoke the Buddhas and Bodhisattvas to bestow nectar, he happened to be right out- side the building. Since participation in that Dharma Assembly was limited to Rinpoches and the like, he was unable to enter the building. After the Dharma Assembly, he made every possible effort to use his connections to convince Pamu to receive him.

Finally, he was able to meet with Great Rinpoche Ga Ma Yang Zong, who is a close disciple of Pamu. He asked her if he could see Pamu in order to request empowerment. Yang Zong Rinpoche politely refused his request. However, in view of his disastrous, painful, and tragic predicament, she imme- diately asked and obtained the consent of Pamu to empower him. Yang Zong Rinpoche gave him a little bit of true nectar bestowed from the sky by Prabhuta-ratna Buddha. She also gave him the following warning: "From now on, you must strictly abide by the precepts. You may not again harm any life. You must live according to the four limitless states of mind and must act with a heart of awareness. If you are able to do all of this, within one month after you taste the nectar, the money that you lost will come back to you twofold.

"I will give you a real example of this. Three years ago, the supreme leader of Vajrayana Buddhism, Great Dharma King Yangwo, was in Hong Kong. His lay disciple, Mr. Liu, offered him 50 million Hong Kong dollars. The Great Dharma King refused to accept it, saying, 'I only save living beings. I do not accept offerings.' But Mr. Liu steadfastly refused to take back the money. No matter how the Great Dharma King declined the offering, Mr. Liu would not comply.

"Seeing no other way, the Great Dharma King gathered together his disciples in Hong Kong and told them to use this money to operate a foundation that would benefit people. Since Mr. Liu's pure heart in offering such money moved the Great Dharma King and the Buddhas and Bodhisattvas, the Great Dharma King practiced the Dharma to invoke the Buddhas to bestow nectar in order to empower him. At the time, the Great Dharma King told him, 'The merit you have earned from offering money to benefit people is great. I will empower you so that the money you offered will come back to you several dozenfold to one hundredfold. At that time, you will have several billion Hong Kong dollars worth of property.'

"Today, the worth of Mr. Liu's property in fact has increased to several billion Hong Kong dollars. I would not lie to you or deceive you. If I made up this story involving the Great Dharma King Yangwo and Mr. Liu in order to deceive living beings, then I would descend into the Vajra Hell or would become a hungry ghost or an animal. If what I said is true – that on the day Mr. Liu made his offering, the Great Dharma King Yangwo really did instruct that this money be used to operate a foundation to benefit people, that the Great Dharma King did tell Mr. Liu that he would empower him so that his money would multiply between several dozenfold to one hundredfold, that the Great Dharma King already practiced the Dharma to invoke the Buddhas to bestow nectar to empower Mr. Liu, and that the worth of Mr. Liu's property has now truly increased to several billion dollars – then may I receive good luck and prosperity, and may I soon realize the supreme awareness. (Great Rinpoche Ga Ma Yang Zong said that she could not remember the exact words spoken by the Great Dharma King. She said that she could only recall that he generally spoke the above-quoted words and did the above-described things. She stated that what she recounted actually occurred.)

"I am not giving a discourse to you. Rather, I am making a vow to you and also a vow to all living beings. Despite having received so much empowerment, Mr. Liu must bear something in mind. Although the Great Dharma King blessed him with such great fortune, except for his own limited personal use, if he does not use his money to further Buddhist affairs, from now on all of his wealth will dissipate.

"Do not worry! The nectar from Pamu's practice of the Dharma also contains the same merit. However, you must act according to what I just told you in order for the nectar to be of use. Otherwise, it will be of no help."

After tasting the nectar, Mr. Chen, in accordance with the Dharma, upheld the precepts, carried out the four limitless states of mind, and maintained a sacred heart of awareness. In less than ten days, the profits from his businesses, when calculated in total, increased by several times the original amount. The stock from one of his businesses increased in value by more than eight times the original worth. On the 23rd day after he tasted the nectar, after deducting costs and expenses, the combined profit he earned from all of his businesses amounted to more than 183,400,000 Hong Kong dollars.

He was greatly moved and brought for Pamu a check in the amount of 20 million Hong Kong dollars as an offering. He also asked if he could again be empowered with a few particles of nectar. Representing Pamu, Great Rinpoche Ga Ma Yang Zong said to him, "Pamu has never accepted offerings. In the future, she will also not accept offerings." She thus returned to him the check and gave him the following instructions: "There is no end to people's greed, as you have just shown. It is truly quite pitiful! From now on, do not continue to be bogged down in the business world. Do not continue to crave money; otherwise, you will lose the money you presently have. These things are impermanent. Make the best use of your time to study well the series of books and the discourses written by Pamu. Only then will you experience the fullest happiness." Mr. Chen was so moved that he did not know exactly what to say. He repeatedly uttered, "Amitabha! Amitabha! I will do as you say. I will do as you say!"

There have been so many magnificent things done by Pamu. I will not go into them here. In summary, she meets the criteria of a Great Bodhisattva laid down in *Know the True Doctrines*! The beards of Elder Dharma King Dorje Losang and Henghsing Gyatso Rinpoche had basically not grown for years. Nectar Dharma water offered by Pamu was then sprinkled on their beards. Their beards started to grow again, which is in complete accordance with the Dharma laid out in *Know the True Doctrines*. She perfectly meets the criteria of all of the Seven Branches.

The disciples of Pamu are either Dharma Kings or Rinpoches. All practitioners who have been taught by Pamu have attained great supernormal powers, very deep Dharma powers, and increased wisdom. They are people of morality and realization. Take, for example, Great Rinpoche Ga Ma Yang Zong, Na Mo Rinpoche, and Great Rinpoche Yang Zong Da Wa. Ordinary Rinpoches definitely cannot match the depth of their realization. Their miraculous powers, wisdom, and morality are all extraordinary and on the level of a Holy One.

We can say that throughout the history of Buddhism until today, no Dakini can compare with the loftiness and magnificence of Pamu. In the entire history of Buddhism, Amang Nopu Pamu is the foremost among female yidams! There have been instances of Buddhist books that she wrote emitting a bright light when worshipped at the Buddhist altar or when respectfully studied. Other manifestations of her miraculous powers have frequently occurred. It is just because of this that Dharma Teacher Shi Yan Hui broke the precepts by printing Pamu's books without her permission. This created quite a great stir in Taiwan and throughout the world.

It is the holy desire of Mahavairocana Buddha that this book, *Dharma That Every Buddhist Must Follow,* be published and distributed. This book, written by Pamu, contains instructions given specially to Rinpoches and Great Virtuous Ones! This Buddhist book contains the essence of the practice of Buddhism. It contains the supreme Dharma, which is hard to come by in even countless eons. It is a supreme Dharma treasure that is indispensable for all practitioners of Buddhism.

Pamu stated that the Dharma contained in this book must be practiced by all practitioners of Buddhism no matter whether they practice great Dharma or small Dharma, no matter whether they practice exoteric or esoteric Dharma,[16] and no matter what sect they belong to. Otherwise, it will definitely be difficult to attain liberation. Some people might ask the following question: Since this book has just been published, how did the great noble ones of the past attain liberation? The ones of great accomplishment in prior generations attained such accomplishment by following the essence of the Dharma contained in this book. Thus, one can easily understand that *Dharma That Every Buddhist Must Follow* is the mother of the mother of all Dharma. It is not simply a question of being the mother. It is the mother of the mother.

Finally, I would like to reiterate that Pamu has throughout her life propagated the Dharma and benefited living beings without ever accepting any offerings. The disciples she teaches are Great Rinpoches, Great Dharma Teachers, and Dharma Kings. She does not teach the Dharma to ordinary practitioners of Buddhism. She once said, "In fact, I am an ordinary practitioner of Buddhism with a heart of humility. All that I can do is act in accordance with Buddhism. If all of you act in accordance with Buddhism and seriously study the Dharma books I have written, you will certainly attain liberation from the cycle of birth and death. You need not worry! Of course, although I am very ordinary, my Master is Mahavairocana Zun Sheng Dharma King. Therefore, I, being an ordinary person with a heart of humility, am able to teach those who are Dharma Kings and Great Rinpoches the theory and practice of the Dharma!"

The supreme loftiness of Pamu cannot be described in writing. Because of the ripening of certain conditions, we are able today to read this Dharma treasure book she has written. From this book, we can learn the Dharma of this true Vajravarahi Mahasattva and can attain great accomplishment. This is truly the result of good merit accumulated through eons of time!

— Losang Ga Dan Luo Bu

⤳ Confessions of a Rinpoche ⤳

A FAMOUS RINPOCHE OF THE Nyingma school said the following: "When Dharma King Pamu conducted the Nectar Dharma Assembly, I was in Seattle. I truly planned to rush over to Washington D.C. to attend, but there were always some doubts in my mind. I was not able to vanquish such doubts. I was not able to rush over to the Dharma Assembly.

"In our minds, Pamu is, of course, a Holy Mother. Her realization is truly foremost. She is pre-eminent among female yidams at the highest level. At the age of eight, she was able to write a penetrating commentary on logical reasoning. No other person in this world has been able to do that. Furthermore, she mastered the entire Tripitaka at the age of 20. She also wrote five commentaries, such as *The Prajna of Ultimate Reality* and *Entering the Door of the Dharma*, along with other Buddhist books. Throughout the history of Buddhism, it is truly difficult to find such a Holy One. In our hearts, Pamu is truly the most revered one on whom we can rely.

"As a Rinpoche who has reached a rather high state of realization, I do not have any doubt whatsoever about the Buddha Dharma. I practice the Dharma every day and have seen many supernormal states. I transmit the Dharma to others to save them and have many disciples. These are the duties of those of us who are Rinpoches. However, the doubt that I have is as follows: Is there really such a thing as the Buddhas bestowing nectar from the sky? I have seen the magnificent Buddhas during my meditation. However, I have never seen a state where the Buddhas transform themselves and appear in this world, where they appear live in our real world right before us.

"Because of various causes and conditions, I was not able to personally attend the Nectar Dharma Assembly conducted by Pamu. This is something that I regret most of all. It was only after I saw the live videotape of the Buddhas bestowing nectar, along with the photographs, that I realized I was like an immature, ignorant, and pitiful child!

"According to mundane logical thinking, it is impossible for such a mysterious thing to have occurred in this world. However, it truly did occur in this world in front of a number of people! I would like to say that I do not know how to explain this. Ordinary language, high-tech principles, or the most advanced scientific theories cannot explain such a thing. This mysterious thing simply cannot be explained. It is truly wonderful, magnificent, and unbelievable!"

The true feelings expressed by that Rinpoche were also the feelings I had 30 years ago. When I was a boy, I was acknowledged as the reincarnation of a Holy One, as a Rinpoche. Thus, I have always been extremely loyal to the Buddha Dharma, and I respectfully learned the Buddha Dharma. I can be called a devout Buddhist disciple. However, with respect to the Buddhas and Bodhisattvas taking away a piece of paper on the spot[17] or the Buddhas themselves bestowing nectar from clouds in the sky, I always harbored some doubts, which I could not overcome. This is the reason why I never personally encountered, experienced, or saw such things.

Thirty years later, I extricated myself from that diabolical state of doubt when I received the Inner-Tantric Initiation. Because I was able to remove the shackles of doubt, I experienced many wonderful benefits. My supernormal skills and depth of realization increased dramatically. I also believe that my having had the good fortune to participate in the great Buddhas Bestowing Nectar Dharma Assembly conducted by Amang Nopu Pamu, thereby obtaining firsthand experience, was probably due to the fact that I finally overcame those diabolical doubts. It was probably connected with the fact that the Buddhas and Bodhisattvas, seeing in my mind that those doubts were overcome, bestowed upon me this good fortune.

I saw the entire Buddhas Bestowing Nectar Dharma Assembly conducted by Dharma King Pamu and the incomparably wonderful states that appeared on the ground and in the air. I personally saw no fewer than 1,000 Buddhas and Bodhisattvas. I saw the Long Life Buddha bestow nectar. When thinking of how ignorant I was 30 years ago, I feel deeply disgusted with myself and deeply remorseful. When I think about those who are ignorant, pitiful Rinpoches, I think of those practitioners who have not seen true Buddha Dharma states. I believe that not seeing such states is due to their ignorance and foolishness. Maybe even after they see photographs of true nectar, they will still harbor doubts about its genuineness.

In order to prevent other practitioners of Buddhism from taking the tortuous and sinful route that I took, as a Rinpoche with a heart of humility and as one who has been through it before, I must remind and warn those who harbor such doubts that if you continue to give rise to such doubts, you will definitely be guilty of a huge sin! You ought to step back and consider the mysteriously natural structure of the nectar. Other than the Buddhas and Bodhisattvas, who could construct such a wonderful and mysterious structure? What skilled craftsman or master artisan in the world could do so? In the entire world, there is no such skilled craftsman or master artisan!

What is even more important is that the Rinpoches and other Buddhist practitioners in attendance all attested to their personal participation in the assembly and what they personally saw. If they spoke falsely, they would naturally descend into the Vajra Hell realm! Is it really possible that these Rinpoches do not know the incomparable suffering of hell? Is it really possible that these Rinpoches and other practitioners of Buddhism are willing to falsely attest and descend into hell?

Every sentence that I have written here is from the bottom of my heart. I would like to earnestly tell all of those ignorant people who still harbor doubts that they must definitely not follow in my ignorant footsteps of 30 years ago!

— *Ga Du*

Attestations of Great Rinpoches
Who Participated in the Nectar Dharma Assembly

On September 8, 1997, many Rinpoches participated in various segments of a Nectar Dharma Assembly. Great Rinpoche Ga Ma Yang Zong, Ah Kou Na Mo Rinpoche, and others participated in that Dharma Assembly. The following attestations were recorded as originally spoken.

(1) I am disciple Ge Sang Ga Ma Yang Zong. Today, I attest in front of the Buddhas and Bodhisattvas. During today's Dharma Assembly, I personally saw Amang Nopu Pamu successfully invoke the Buddhas in the sky to bestow true nectar from the Buddha realm. The form of the nectar was truly not of this human world. This wonderful scene, which I saw, was real. I vow that if what I just said is false, I am willing to descend into the Vajra Hell realm. If what I just said is true, I am willing to dedicate all of the merit to my respected and beloved Great Jewel Vajra Master, Dorje Pamu. I wish that the Master's Dharma teachings will forever exist, that she will forever live in this world, and that she will save countless living beings. May all living beings receive good fortune and realize enlightenment. May I soon attain perfect good fortune and wisdom. May I attain great merit and the supreme enlightenment. May I follow Master Pamu in saving all living beings throughout all of the Dharma realms! Wo Ba Mei!

—Dharma Princess: Ge Sang Ga Ma Yang Zong

(2) The nectar was totally bestowed by the Buddhas in the sky. Today, I personally participated and personally saw this. I am a Rinpoche and disciple of Pamu. If what I just said is false, I am willing to descend into

the Vajra Hell realm. If what I just said is true, may it bring limitless merit to myself and all living beings.

(3) Today, I saw the most magnificent Pamu successfully invoke the Buddhas to bestow nectar from the sky. It came into being from the sky. I am a disciple of Pamu. I am a Rinpoche. I verify in front of the Buddhas and Bodhisattvas that if what I just said is false, I will descend into the Vajra Hell realm. If what I just said is true, I dedicate all of the merit to all living beings.

(4) I am a disciple of Pamu. What I am about to say is true. The nectar that I saw today was bestowed by the Buddhas in the sky. What I say is true. If what I just said is false, I am willing to enter the Vajra Hell realm. If what I just said is true, may my Dharma power and merit be limitless, and may the merit of all living beings be limitless.

(5) The nectar bestowed by the Buddhas today was real. I saw it personally. I am not saying anything false at all. If what I just said is false, I am willing to descend into the Vajra Hell realm. If what I just said is true, I dedicate all of the merit to all living beings in the six realms within the three spheres. May they have limitless merit and attain great accomplishment.

(6) The nectar bestowed by the Buddhas today, which I myself saw, was the result of Pamu's practice of the Dharma. What I just said is true. If I spoke falsely, I am willing to descend into hell. If what I just said is true, may all living beings in the six realms have limitless merit and good fortune!

(7) I personally saw the Buddhas bestow nectar from the sky into the empty Dharma bowl. I saw this with my own eyes. It was real. If what I just said is false, I am willing to descend into the hell of uninterrupted suffering. If what I just said is true, may I attain limitless merit and great supernormal powers so as to save all living beings in the six realms.

(8) I was fortunate to be able to participate in the Buddhas Bestowing Nectar Great Dharma Assembly. I personally saw that the sacred nectar in the Dharma bowl was bestowed by the Buddhas and Bodhisattvas in

the sky. This sacred object in the once empty bowl came from nothingness. It was incredibly wonderful, and there are no words to describe it. I attest that what I saw was real. If what I just said is false, may I descend into the hell of uninterrupted suffering. If what I just said is true, I beseech the Buddhas and Bodhisattvas to immediately empower me so as to increase my wisdom and attain great accomplishment in order that I may save all living beings. May I and all living beings in all of the Dharma realms together receive limitless Dharma benefits.

(9) Today, I received great empowerment from Pamu and the Buddhas and Bodhisattvas. I personally washed the Dharma bowl and put on its lid. The Buddhas bestowed true white nectar from the sky. The Dharma platform and gold bowl emitted very strong light of various colors. The Buddhas descended from the sky. At this time, my body received great empowerment. It became tingly and expansive. A hot current traveled up to the crown of my head. I am a Rinpoche. If what I just said is false, may I descend into the hell realm. If what I just said is true, may I attain limitless merit.

(10) I was fortunate to have been able to participate in the Buddhas Bestowing Nectar Great Dharma Assembly. I personally saw the Buddhas bestow nectar into the Dharma bowl. If what I just said is false, I am willing to descend into the Vajra Hell realm. If what I just said is true, may I attain limitless good fortune and wisdom, may I successfully practice great Dharmas, and may I soon attain great accomplishment and realize Buddhahood. Furthermore, may this also cause my relatives and all living beings in the six realms of existence to avoid suffering and experience happiness, and may we together realize enlightenment.

(11) Under the watchful stare of our open eyes, the crystal pillars that held up the Dharma bowl emitted thin lines of light several times. I do not know how it happened, but nectar came out of nothingness to fill up the Dharma bowl. This nectar is a white solid material. Nothing with material form in this world has such a mysterious structure. Every word and sentence that I just spoke is true. If I said anything that is false, I will naturally descend into the hell of uninterrupted suffering without ever being able to be raised therefrom. If what I just said is true, may

my learning of Buddhism result in great accomplishment in this lifetime. May I also be able to use the correct Dharma of the Tathagata to save living beings everywhere.

(12) I personally participated in the Buddhas Bestowing Nectar Great Dharma Assembly. I personally saw the Buddhas bestow true nectar into the Dharma bowl. This nectar came out of nothingness. Nothing else in this world has its form. If what I just said is false, I am willing to receive all karmic retribution. If what I just said is true, may I realize in this lifetime the Three Bodies. May I forever follow the Master in saving all living beings, and may all living beings in the six realms of existence, who are all my dear relatives, attain liberation.

Elder Dharma King Dorje Losang Asks the Great Dharma King for Clarification

THE ELDER DHARMA KING ASKS: Living beings have certain questions, which I would like to ask on their behalf. Great Dharma King and respected Master who is supreme, would you instruct us?

The Great Dharma King answers: If you have any questions, then raise them.

Q: What types of practitioners of Buddhism have the ability to successfully invoke nectar?

A: Those Holy Ones and Great Dharma Kings who have reached the level of a Buddha or Mahasattva.

Q: According to what the Great Dharma King just said, do all Dharma Kings within Vajrayana Buddhism have the ability to successfully invoke the Buddhas to bestow nectar?

A: Not all of them are able.

Q: Why are not all of them able?

A: It is not necessarily true that all Dharma Kings are able to successfully invoke nectar.

Q: What is the reason for this?

A: Since there are those who are Dharma Kings in name but who have not attained the realization of a Dharma King, they are, therefore, not true Dharma Kings. Naturally, they are unable to commune with the Buddhas. How, then, could nectar be bestowed?

Q: Can the present Dalai Lama successfully invoke the Buddhas to bestow nectar?

A: I have not heard it said that he has such ability.

Q: What is nectar?

A: Holy food that corresponds with the miraculous powers and great wisdom of the Buddhas and Bodhisattvas.

Q: What is the function of nectar?

A: To plant the holy seeds of Vajra in order to realize enlightenment. It can eliminate all karma one produced in this world. Ending the cycle of birth and death becomes as easy as turning one's hand.

Q: How big is the difference in power between true nectar and the five types of nectar in this earthly world?

A: As big as the difference between the great ocean and a drop of water, between 10,000 miles and a small step. There is no comparison.

Q: What is the reason for this?

A: Those five types of nectar are called nectar. In fact, they are ordinary things of this world that are empowered by mantras. True nectar bestowed by the Buddhas is something sacred that has come from the realm of the Holy Ones and Buddhas. There is a world of difference. It is the difference between the ordinary and the sacred. How could they be mentioned in the same breath?

Q: Have there been any ordinary Rinpoches who have successfully practiced the nectar Dharma?

A: Throughout Buddhist history until the present, there has not been one.

Q: You are the Great Dharma King and Holy Master in our world. Could you invoke some nectar to empower everybody?

A: When certain causes and conditions of living beings mature, nectar will fall naturally. If the Buddhist practitioner does not possess enough merit, there will be no nectar. I am an ordinary practitioner of Buddhism. I do not have the ability to successfully invoke nectar.

Q: Then why did I personally see you successfully invoke the Buddhas to bestow nectar?

A: That was due to the fullness of merit of those who were able to partake of the nectar. I alone do not have the depth of realization to successfully invoke the Buddhas to bestow nectar.

Q: In this world, how many Rinpoches are able to successfully practice the Dharma of invoking the Buddhas to bestow true nectar?

A: All of those who have attained the realization of a true Dharma King can successfully practice it. Furthermore, they must practice it.

Q: Is it unacceptable not to practice it?

A: It is unacceptable.

Q: Why is that?

A: With respect to the highest Dharma within Vajrayana Buddhism,

the initiation of Ati Yoga, Great Perfection of the Vajra division, nectar is an indispensable holy element for cleansing one's negative karma and is the resource for planting the seeds of Vajra. If the true nectar Dharma is not practiced, then it is an ordinary initiation.

Q: The level of realization of Amang Nopu Pamu is extremely high. She is also able to successfully invoke nectar. Is she a Dharma King?

A: In order to successfully invoke the Buddhas to bestow true nectar, one must recite the holy mantras of a Dharma King, must put one's hands in the mudra of a Dharma King, and must ascend to the throne of a Dharma King.

Q: I would like to ask if the Great Dharma King's Buddha Dharma is any different from her Buddha Dharma?

A: The Buddha Dharma is the same. It is all passed down from the ancient Buddhas.

Q: Does the Great Dharma King study the Buddha Dharma with Pamu?

A: I have not seen her yet in this lifetime. Until now, I have not yet spoken to her. The Buddha Dharma is not the study of Buddhism. It does not contain the element of study. Only ordinary people of the world study it.

Q: Generally speaking, what is the Buddha Dharma?

A: It is cultivating yourself to live in accord with the law of cause and effect or karma. It is that simple. It is the same with nectar.

Q: What is the reason for that?

A: No reason. For example, you, Dorje Losang, have attained the position of an Elder Dharma King. However, your realization deepened and your beard grew only after you received empowerment from Pamu. This is cause and effect.

Q: Can the Eight Great Rinpoches of Tibetan Tantric Buddhism successfully invoke the Buddhas to bestow nectar?

A: Even the Four Great Dharma Princes[18] do not have such power.

Q: Why does each and every Rinpoche in today's world have nectar pills?

A: This is correct, but such pills are ordinary things of this world, such as medicine or other things, that are empowered by adding sharira and chanting mantras. After such empowerment, they are called nectar or the five great pills.

Q: Thus, can 100 out of 10,000 Rinpoches successfully invoke nectar?

A: It would not be a disappointing result if there were only 1 out of 10,000 Rinpoches who can successfully invoke nectar.

Q: If there are so few, how can they save living beings?

A: All 84,000 Dharma methods can be used to save living beings. As long as any method is the Buddha Dharma, it can be used to save living beings.

Q: Which Dharma is the best and easiest method for attaining liberation?

A: It is best to learn the Dharma spoken by Sakyamuni Buddha and the Dharma of true Great Dharma Kings. In today's world, the Buddha Dharma that can liberate living beings most easily can be found in Buddhist books which are composed of commentary and instruction by Amang Nopu Pamu!

Q: Is there any usefulness in being initiated without real nectar?

A: There is usefulness in being initiated by ordinary Rinpoches. As long as it is the correct Buddha Dharma, accomplishment can be achieved.

Q: If accomplishment can be achieved through both real nectar and ordinary nectar, then why distinguish between real nectar bestowed by the Buddhas and nectar made from ordinary objects that have been empowered?

A: The difference lies in whether the accomplishment is great or small and the time it takes for such accomplishment. If one cultivates oneself according to the Dharma after having been initiated with real nectar, then one day of such cultivation would be better than 10 years, or even 20 or 30 years, of cultivation after having been initiated with ordinary nectar of this world. After having been initiated with real nectar, one can achieve in this lifetime the Three Bodies.

Q: Why are the initiations performed by many Rinpoches not called nectar initiations?

A: Nectar is the basic ingredient used in any initiation. This basic ingredient of nectar is then mixed with other things according to different tantra. Therefore, there are different names for various initiations.

Q: Are those who were able to receive an ordinary initiation also able to receive a true nectar initiation or a true nectar empowerment?

A: If one devotedly practices the Buddha Dharma and lives in accordance with Buddhism, then this will be clearly known by the Buddhas and Bodhisattvas. When one has accumulated enough merit, a Great Dharma King will initiate such person with nectar bestowed by the Buddhas! I already told you. Everything is cause and effect.

What Is Meant By Nectar

ALTHOUGH I AM AN ORDINARY RINPOCHE without any deep realization, nevertheless, I am very fortunate to have visited many Rinpoches. I have sought instruction from Great Dharma King Yangwo Yisinubu and from famous Rinpoches, such as Panchen Lama, Dalai Lama, Karmapa, Bo Mi Qiang Ba Luo Zhu, Dorje Losang, Dilgo Khyentse, Jiang Gong Kang Qin, Jiang Gong Kang Ce, Ga Wang, Zong Nan Jia Chu, Chuang Gu, Xia Ma, Hsi Jao, Bei Lu Qin Zhe, Tai Xi Du, Heng Sheng, Jia Cha, and Kalu. Especially with respect to nectar, I have a detailed understanding.

In general, nectar can be divided into five types: Most Precious Nectar, Great Precious Nectar, Long Life Nectar, Vajra Nectar, and Bodhi Nectar. These different types of nectar can also be divided into two different types: nectar that comes from sacred Dharma practice and nectar that comes from exoteric Dharma practice. There are several different types of nectar within the category of nectar that comes from sacred Dharma practice, depending upon the different manifestations of Dharma by each Buddha.

Nectar resulting from exoteric practices is most prevalent in contemporary Vajrayana Buddhism. Basically, any Rinpoche can practice the Dharma to produce such nectar. Medicine or food is mostly used. Added to and mixed together with the medicine or food is sharira or a Dharma object that has been empowered. This is then made into powder to make pills. This powder is then empowered through practice of the Dharma and the recitation of mantras to become various types of nectar. Nectar that comes from exoteric Dharma practice is mostly used for empowerment, curing illnesses, and other reasons.

Nectar that comes from sacred Dharma practice is totally different from nectar that comes from exoteric, ordinary Dharma practice. The degree of empowerment from nectar that comes from sacred Dharma practice as compared with nectar that comes from exoteric Dharma practice is as different as ten thousand miles and one footstep. No words could adequately praise the nectar that comes from sacred Dharma practice. Ordinary Rinpoches and ordinary Dharma Kings who have been conferred such titles by the world cannot successfully practice the sacred Dharma to invoke nectar. Only those who are true Buddhas, or incarnations or transformations of Great Bodhisattvas, can successfully practice such Dharma.

In the sacred Dharma practice to invoke nectar, the Dharma King conducting the practice will assemble over 100 Rinpoches to form a mandala. Gold, silver, and other precious items will be burnt as offerings. The Great Dharma King will then practice the holy Inner-Tantric Dharma to invoke the Buddhas and Bodhisattvas to bestow nectar from the realm of the Buddhas. The Buddhas will assemble in the sky or will enter the mandala area. This holy scene will be seen by all of the more than 100 Rinpoches in attendance.

At this time, the Buddha who corresponds to the particular nectar that is being invoked will descend. The appearance of that particular Buddha and its bestowing of nectar can be seen. There will be the emission of light and the manifestation of supernormal states when the nectar descends into the bowl. This Dharma bowl must first be thoroughly washed and must be empty.

There is absolutely nothing in this world which has the mysterious and changeable shape of the nectar that descends into the bowl. It is exactly as what is described in the book *Know the True Doctrines*. According to people of great virtue, only this type of sacred nectar is true nectar. According to Tibetan tantra, nectar is the holy material used for initiations. No matter what type of initiation is performed, nectar must be used. Especially for the supreme yoga initiations, true nectar is an absolutely indispensable material for the initiation Dharma water.

True nectar represents the causative factor that raises one from the ordinary world to the realm of the Buddhas. If true nectar is not used as the basis for an initiation, such as when man-made nectar created from medicine is used to empower, then such initiation is not an Inner-Tantric Sacred Dharma Initiation. Therefore, according to tantra, nectar is fundamental for liberation.

Determining whether a Dharma King is the incarnation of a Buddha or Great Bodhisattva mostly depends upon whether he or she has the depth of realization to successfully practice the nectar Dharma. Can he or she commune with the Buddhas and successfully invoke them to bestow nectar? Any explanation other than this, no matter how many times said, is merely empty talk. This includes explanations such as, "I am the heir to a certain spiritual legacy....Since childhood, I have been officially recognized as a Holy One and have been so for many lives....I am a Dharma King recognized by a certain Great Rinpoche....I am the head of a certain great temple." This only proves that they are Rinpoches according to worldly regulations and teachings. Of course, they can save living beings. However, such explanations definitely do not prove that they are able to represent the sacred essence of the supreme tantra. Nevertheless, one cannot dismiss such people. They are persons of great virtue. It is simply a matter of different levels of attainment.

When visiting Rinpoches, I would speak of this matter of the Buddhas bestowing true nectar. Some Rinpoches who do not have the ability to successfully invoke true nectar become quite unhappy when this subject is raised. I think that this is not a big problem. If you think that you are a Great and Holy Dharma King or a Great Rinpoche, then conduct a Nectar Dharma Assembly in order to prove that you are someone whom living beings can fall back upon. Let everybody see that you have the Buddha Dharma within you and that the Buddha Dharma is true. This is saving living beings! Otherwise, use empowered medicine as nectar and save living beings while cultivating yourself with a heart of humility!

I would like to raise the following question for everybody's consideration. Are the Dharma Kings who successfully invoke the Buddhas to bestow nectar in front of everybody able to represent the Buddhas and Bodhisattvas or are the Dharma Kings who only speak empty words able to represent the Buddhas and Bodhisattvas? This question is worthy of deep consideration! I and many people of great virtue believe that those who can commune with the Buddhas and Bodhisattvas are definitely Great Dharma Kings. Those who can only reach ordinary states are ordinary Rinpoches!

— *Henghsing Gyatso*

❧ Preface ❧

(Excerpted from the book *The Dharma of Concentration and Visualization Essential for Enlightenment*)

PAMU HAS BEEN SERIOUSLY sick now for three months. She is often in a state of unconsciousness, with sores all over her body. Since she can only intake a small amount of liquid food, her body is as dry and thin as rattan. Her once youthful and solemn face has already become like that of a 100-year-old lady, with spots and deep wrinkles. She often says, "Time does not wait for anyone. Everything is changing. Everything is in a state of impermanence. You should use this as a lesson. After you have read the books I have written, you should put into practice the principles contained in those books. Otherwise, you will not be able to end the cycle of birth and death."

We used all kinds of medicine and thought of all kinds of methods. We still could not cure her illness. Thus, on March 29 of this year, Sang Ba Kun Jue Rinpoche and I returned to Lalong-gegan. On the fifth day after our return to our country, we made our way to Lhasa. We went to the Zu Pu Temple to worship, make offerings, and pray for Pamu's swift recovery. Because of time constraints, we only stayed there three days and then rushed back to our meditation cells.

Sang Ba Kun Jue and I together practiced the Wu Xiu Yoga Samadhi. We decided to go to the Tusita Heaven to ask Maitreya Bodhisattva to save Pamu. In my state of concentration, I arrived at the inner palace of the Tusita Heaven and paid my respects to Maitreya Bodhisattva. After I prostrated myself, I suddenly saw Vajrasattva and Pamu each sitting on a lotus throne discussing the Dharma with Maitreya Bodhisattva.

At this time, Maitreya Bodhisattva said to me, "Yang Zong Da Wa, go back and tell those good men and women that Amang Nopu Pamu is the magnificent Buddha Mother of wisdom." I joined my palms in front of my heart and asked the Bodhisattva, "If people ask me how it is that she is magnificent, how should I answer them?" Maitreya Bodhisattva said, "When looking at the history of Buddhism in the human realm, which Buddha

Mother in the earthly world has been able to master the Tripitaka and write so many commentaries by the age of 20? Her Dharma water can cause a beard that has stopped growing to grow again rapidly. This is the true Vajravarahi. Have you seen any Buddha Mother who simply saves living beings without accepting any offerings? Her magnificence fills the infinite space and cannot be completely expressed to living beings with words. You should quickly go back. Your Pamu will at once return to the earthly world to preach *The Dharma of Concentration and Visualization Essential For Enlightenment.* If you do not quickly leave, then you will miss this class."

I again joined my palms in respect and said to Maitreya Bodhisattva, "Greatly Honored Maitreya Mahasattva, Pamu is now ill. Why is she here with you? I will go back together with Pamu." Maitreya Bodhisattva smiled but did not speak. At this time, Vajrasattva said, "Do not say anything more. Such deep Dharma is so seldom heard in the world. Quickly go back to the human realm." I hurriedly prostrated before Pamu, Vajrasattva, and Maitreya Bodhisattva and bid farewell to them. Through my state of samadhi, I returned to the human realm.

After I came out of my state of concentration, three months and six days had already passed. Without even thinking about washing myself, I hurriedly went to pay my respects to Pamu. When I saw Pamu, she still looked so old. She was in the sacred state of having only a faint breath of life left. Pamu said, "You entered that state of concentration for a few months. I was waiting for you to return. I will soon give discourses on the essential Dharma for practicing concentration and visualization."

Representing all living beings, I hurriedly prostrated myself before Pamu, joined my palms in respect and asked, "Most kind Pamu, when did you return?" Pamu replied, "Return from where? With such a serious illness, I did not go anywhere." I said, "I clearly saw you in the inner palace of the Tusita Heaven." Pamu rejoined, "This is what you viewed in your state. Do not speak nonsense. Things of the world are all impermanent. One must make the best use of one's time to benefit living beings."

As soon as we obtained Pamu's kind approval, we then and there took a few photographs of Pamu's virtuous face. After the film was developed, one photograph showed a young, solemn appearance and one photograph showed an aged appearance. These two photographs were taken within a few seconds of each other but were totally different. This is truly unbelievable. We immediately took the photographs to Pamu and asked her to explain the causative factors surrounding this. As soon as we entered the door, everybody was startled. Pamu could hardly speak. Her face was shriveled up and had no color. The Great Rinpoches all began to cry.

The next day, when everybody was terribly sad and hopeless, Pamu got up from her seat. My heavens! After only one night, she who was sitting before us was not an old lady about to die, but our young and solemn Pamu! All of those who witnessed this were stupefied. At this time, the sound of crying mixed together with the sound of laughing. Pamu then said, "Do you all think that I really can mysteriously change myself? In fact, you are mistaken! You were not able to see clearly since there was medicine on my face and I was under the lamp light. I only have a heart of humility. How could I have such great skills? You should not become distracted with this. You must realize that everything is impermanent and always changing." She then swiftly walked out of the cave palace. Her old face symbolizing impermanence disappeared overnight, and she spoke of it in only a few plain words. Such occurrences can only make us sincerely surrender ourselves to her great, pure heart – the heart of a Buddha or Bodhisattva.

The next day, Pamu formally ascended to her throne to give us a discourse. A group of Great Virtuous Ones and I together heard all of her Dharma discourses. The subject was that which everybody is learning today, namely, the Dharma of concentration and visualization (the discourses of Pamu that Maitreya Bodhisattva told me to quickly return to hear).

With utmost sincerity, I am telling everybody that this is the transcription of the discourses of Amang Nopu Pamu Rinpoche, the greatest and most outstanding Holy Mother in the history of Buddhism. Why can Pamu be called the supreme Holy Buddha Mother in the history of Buddhism in the earthly realm?

At this point, I would like to make a comparison. I am sure that everybody knows that the Buddha Mothers of the great Master Padmasambhava – Yeshe Tsogyal and Mandarava, especially Yeshe Tsogyal – could be rated as the most outstanding of all Buddha Mothers of that time within Tibetan Tantric Buddhism. The Buddha Mother Tsogyal received initiation for the first time when she was 20 years old. She was still studying the sutras and sastras when she was 21 years old. It was only at the age of 70 when she gave rise to a heart of enlightenment. However, Pamu is totally different from Buddha Mother Tsogyal. Because of Pamu's innate knowledge, at the age of 20 she mastered the Tripitaka and had already written several commentaries. Even if one carefully studies the chapters of Buddhist history, one will not find any Buddha Mother with such merit and skills!

I will give one ordinary example of something that none of those Great Rinpoches of the present age could do. Since Pamu descended to this earthly realm, from the time she began to propagate the Dharma and benefit living beings until the present, she has never accepted any offerings. Whether it be gold, silver or other valuables, whether it be as many as tens of millions of dollars or as little as one cent, she herself does not accept any of it. She also does not accept any offerings in the name of building temples or doing charitable work. Such unspoiled virtue is truly something that cannot be said of contemporary Great Rinpoches or Great Dharma Teachers. She is totally unselfish, silently contributing to the benefit of living beings throughout the three spheres of existence.

This lesson of the Dharma practice of concentration and visualization is composed of the discourses of Pamu given to the foremost great sastra masters and Great Rinpoches when she was 21 years old. These discourses were given after she completed her great samadhi state of concentration and returned from the inner palace of the Tusita Heaven. In the history of Buddhism in this world, no other Buddha Mother or Dakini can compare with Pamu's loftiness or match her magnificence. In order that others may have a general understanding of Pamu, I am presenting here for your consideration my feelings, which are contained in the prefaces from the books *Entering the Door of the Dharma* and *The Prajna of Ultimate Reality*.

This book should have been published a few years ago. However, since the Dharma conditions were not ripe for living beings to accept this Dharma, its publication was postponed until the present, when Pamu just recently allowed its distribution. This is truly due to the merit of countless living beings. Thus, we should join our palms in front of our hearts, prostrate ourselves before and feel grateful to the Great Jewel Amang Nopu Rinpoche Holy Mother. We should also appreciate the empowerment of the Buddhas and Bodhisattvas abiding in the ten directions.

— *Yang Zong Da Wa*

⁓ *Part Two* ⁓

DISCOURSES OF
AMANG NOPU PAMU

Chapter One

INITIAL DISCOURSE

I WILL NOW FORMALLY begin to speak of the Dharma. Everybody must listen carefully. When I am giving a discourse, nobody is permitted to make any sound. This applies no matter whether you are a Great Rinpoche or a Great Dharma Teacher. Of course, this rule applies to all pagers and cellular phones.

A few days ago, I finished giving discourses entitled *The Dharma of Concentration and Visualization Essential for Enlightenment*. I already told my attendants to immediately organize such discourses into a book in order to benefit living beings everywhere. This is a task of top priority! It is under special circumstances that such book will come into being. It can be said that if Buddhist practitioners do not practice the contents of that book, then it will not be possible for them to end the cycle of birth and death.

You know that *The Dharma of Concentration and Visualization Essential for Enlightenment* is Dharma that was revealed under rare and special circumstances. However, today I would like to clearly tell all of you good Buddhist practitioners that besides the need to practice *The Dharma of Concentration and Visualization Essential for Enlightenment*, you definitely must also study *Entering the Door of the Dharma*, *The Prajna of Ultimate Reality*, and other books that I have written.

Why must you read the books that I have written? Because I am very clear about their quality. In short, they can surely liberate some living beings! Otherwise, these books would not emit light and exhibit holy states. Otherwise, the Buddhas would not bestow nectar for us and would not allow such books to serve as important learning material for Great Rinpoches to study.

Other than the need to learn the Dharma that I just mentioned, something that is indispensable in one's practice is Dharma which I have entitled *Dharma That Every Buddhist Must Follow*! These lessons are also given under special circumstances. It is such Dharma on which I will give discourses today to you Dharma Kings, Rinpoches, and Geshés.

All of you Buddhist practitioners seated here have deep roots of goodness and are models for others to emulate. As teachers, if you do not look within yourselves and correct your behavior according to the discourses I am about to give, then you will undoubtedly be servants of Mara, the Evil One! Although such words are not pleasant to hear, nevertheless, this is the reality of cause and effect. What use would there be for me to speak pleasant words?

Therefore, today I am telling all of you that you must strictly practice this Dharma and must teach it to your disciples. Only then will it be of use to you. Everyone must now attentively listen to my discourses!

I will not tell everybody what special circumstances underlie these discourses. According to tantra, there are rules prohibiting certain public announcements! We have decided to use the preface from the future book *The Dharma of Concentration and Visualization Essential for Enlightenment* for everybody's study. That preface describes the great underlying circumstances of that book. Therefore, you should not look down upon the discourses given over the next few days, since the circumstances underlying such discourses are just as special as those underlying the discourses entitled *The Dharma of Concentration and Visualization Essential for Enlightenment*!

Everybody must attentively listen to the discourses. Your consciousness should not wander. It should not roam to Hawaii to eat papaya. If your thoughts leave this discourse hall, I will not continue to give the discourses. In such case, I would not be refusing to give the discourses. You would be refusing to listen. It would not be that I did not want you to follow my instructions. It would be that you did not want to follow my instructions.

Cultivation is as follows. No matter how many teachings are spoken by a Buddha or a Master, only if you put into practice such teachings can it be called cultivation. Otherwise, no matter how many times I say something, it will be of no use to you.

Why do I want to give discourses on *Dharma That Every Buddhist Must Follow*? It is due to the ripening of conditions that have been maturing throughout countless eons! Since it is the wish of Mahavairocana Buddha that these discourses be given, you should put into practice their lessons. Everybody must attach special importance to these discourses! It would be best if you memorize and put into practice the substance of each lesson.

Some people have studied *Entering the Door of the Dharma* and also have exerted themselves in learning *The Dharma of Concentration and Visualization Essential for Enlightenment*. However, they are still unable to go deep into the ninth stage of meditation. I think that there may be some people who cannot even enter the fifth or sixth stage! Why is this? It is because they have not learned and practiced the Dharma according to those books. At most, they have learned such Dharma but could not put it into practice! Those books are also Dharma treasures.

In response to the maturing of conditions relating to this major event, today I will give discourses to everybody on the perfect, wonderful, supreme, great Dharma, which is both ordinary and deep, common and of general significance. Why is it the supreme, great Dharma? It truly is supreme! This is because it will be futile to practice most great Dharma if such practice deviates from *Dharma That Every Buddhist Must Follow*. After understanding this principle, can you say that it is not great Dharma? Of course it is great. Those who say it is not great are undoubtedly demons.

Dharma That Every Buddhist Must Follow is different from *The Mahamudra of Liberation* written by Great Dharma King Yangwo Yisinubu in terms of the depth of the Dharma body state within the Great Perfection. However, in terms of its Dharma significance to those walking on the Bodhisattva path, *Dharma That Every Buddhist Must Follow* can be likened to an airplane rather than a rickshaw. One can easily see the rapid speed with which one can obtain liberation. I, therefore, think that this Dharma is an indispensable aid in the practice of any other Dharma! I believe my Buddha Master would agree with my viewpoint!

What is meant by *Dharma That Every Buddhist Must Follow*? The Chinese character 子 means seed, like a mother who has the function of perpetuating. It also means the successors of the Buddhas. Thus, the word *disciple* in the term *Buddhist disciple* contains the Chinese character 子. The word *disciple* in the term *disciple of the Master* also contains the Chinese character 子. *Dharma That Every Buddhist Must Follow* contains the supreme principles that Buddhist disciples must rely upon and study. It contains true teachings, which must be put into practice.

Dharma That Every Buddhist Must Follow is very deep Buddha Dharma, which must be relied upon and applied by teachers and disciples. Because of such conditions, if one does not rely upon, does not study, and does not practice *Dharma That Every Buddhist Must Follow*, then no matter what

Dharma one practices, one cannot attain liberation from the cycle of birth and death. To hope for such an attainment would be simply daydreaming. It would be impossible to become accomplished.

Everybody knows that *Essential Yoga Dharma* is the mother of all Dharmas. I think that *Dharma That Every Buddhist Must Follow* is the mother of the mother of all Dharmas. It is, therefore, even more indispensable. *Essential Yoga Dharma* was transmitted by my Buddha Master, but *Dharma That Every Buddhist Must Follow* is even more important! My Master agrees with my viewpoint. Therefore, Buddhist disciples can easily understand its importance.

⌒ *Chapter Two* ⌒

DISCOVERING ONE'S CONSCIENCE

THE LION'S ROAR BUDDHA SAID, "Upon recognizing one's wrong conduct, one should repent and rely on the Master in order to reach the other shore."[19] This was spoken by Great Dharma King Yangwo Yisinubu, the future Lion's Roar Buddha, to those engaged in cultivation. In cultivating oneself, one must recognize the various shortcomings in one's behavior. As soon as one understands and recognizes them, one should immediately repent and live according to the teachings of the Master. One should cultivate oneself according to the teachings and precepts expounded by the Buddhas. If one is able to do this, then one will naturally attain liberation and accomplishment.

The word *conscience* and the term *having a conscience* are not unfamiliar to people of the world. Their meaning is also not difficult to understand. We might say that their original meaning is the good heart of people. It is treating people and handling things fairly. It is having a sincere and good heart, a heart that is neither biased nor evil, a heart that is magnanimous and loving. Ultimately, it is that which one relies upon to correctly understand and correctly judge what is right and wrong, good and evil, beautiful and ugly, good and bad, true and false, etc., with respect to everything around oneself.

Of course, having a conscience can be applied to different circumstances, such as those involving very old people or those involving little children. Some say that one who does not look after his elderly relatives truly has no conscience. Some say that one who requites kindness with enmity has no conscience. Some say that one who bullies and humiliates other people has no conscience. With respect to children, one can also say that a child who, without reason, constantly grabs things for himself has no conscience.

From all of these examples, it is clear that people of the world use having a conscience as a basis for measuring right and wrong and the extent of one's morality. It is the standard used to discern whether someone is good or bad. Whoever has a conscience is a good person. Thus, it is the yardstick by which we judge who is right and who is wrong!

However, practitioners of Buddhism use an entirely different yardstick – one that is not as simple and shallow – to gauge whether one's morality is high or not. This yardstick is composed of the precepts and discipline contained in the Buddha Dharma! Whoever violates this yardstick by breaking the precepts or discipline is thus not a good person. Such a person might even become a bad person. To a certain extent, one can say that a person who is recognized by the world as being a good person with a conscience would not necessarily be considered a good person if judged according to the truth of Buddhism.

In most cases, those who learn Buddhism and cultivate themselves, especially those who are devout, have rather deep roots of goodness, which were planted in their previous lives stretching over eons of time. This is the essential prerequisite that enables them to learn and practice the Buddha Dharma. With respect to this point, using mundane language, one can say that such people very much have a conscience. In learning Buddhism and cultivating oneself, can one be called a good Buddhist disciple, a good practitioner of Buddhism, by simply having a conscience? Not necessarily.

For example, there are some Buddhist disciples who, due to wonderful conditions resulting from many previous lives, have the good fortune of following Great Virtuous Ones and eminent monks in learning and practicing the Buddha Dharma. Of course, they are also able to receive empowerment or even special initiations. If their three karmas correspond with the teachings of their Vajra Master, they will receive great benefits. They will increase their good fortune and merit. However, disciples who can truly do this are few and far between.

When receiving empowerment or when being initiated at the Buddhist altar, most practitioners of Buddhism are extremely devout and extraordinarily moved. For the most part, their minds are able to give rise to correct understanding. They are very respectful toward their Master, bowing their heads and joining their palms in front of their hearts. They worship their Master by prostrating. At such time, one can say that they have an incomparably pure heart. They abide by all of the precepts and rules transmitted by the Master. They view each word of the Master's discourse as a gem and each sentence as gold or jade.

It is as if they experience a sudden awareness of the Dharma. They see through the vanity of worldly life. They are moved to cry bitter tears, to burst into loud sobs over fear of the future. At that time, there are those who are remorseful, brokenhearted, or in bitter pain. They might solemnly vow to abide by the precepts and discipline. They might firmly affirm that they will act in accordance with the Buddha Dharma. They might wholeheartedly promise to do things in furtherance of Buddhism. Their reactions are too numerous to mention.

It cannot be denied that at such time these practitioners can truly be called real practitioners of Buddhism. Even if they were ordinary people previously, at that time they are not ordinary. They are practitioners with a totally pure inner heart. If each of them would sincerely practice in such manner, how would it be difficult for them to attain liberation? Therefore, the Buddha said, "If one could continue to practice Buddhism just as one did in the beginning, then one could attain liberation."

However, it is such a pity that this type of rare and precious pure heart sooner or later is either killed or abandoned, bringing it to an early demise. It is like a newly born child in swaddling clothes whose parents cut off its food before it grows and matures and then totally abandon it, leaving it exposed to the elements in barren land. Its parents do not ask about it or pity it. How could such a child survive? As time goes on, the parents even forget about the birth of their child. How could it possibly continue to grow?

If there were such cruel-hearted parents in this world, it would surely arouse the passions of people to attack them. Newspapers and magazines would all issue calls to attack them. Righteous indignation and words of condemnation would spring up everywhere, like bamboo shoots after a springtime rain. People would carry banners and shout loudly. They would wave flags and sharply denounce this kind of behavior. There would be many who would vow to catch such heartless, unrighteous, cowardly parents so as to cut them open to see whether they have a conscience!

After these parents undergo such punishment and criticism, maybe they would gradually repent or maybe they would suddenly be moved by their conscience and feel anguished and ashamed. They would then be touched by their deep emotions, would clutch their wrists and stamp their feet in regret, and would experience endless distress. People would then be falling over each other to sympathize with them, sighing, "At least they have a little bit of a conscience and can be considered as human beings. This is fortunate. They are not like rotten wood. They can still...." The attacks against them would be called off, and this matter would quickly disappear.

Since they found their conscience, the people's anger would be relieved, and the people's hearts would be comforted. Everybody would be happy that the parents can turn over a new leaf! Some matters of the world are handled in such a manner, resulting in a seemingly satisfactory conclusion.

There are quite a large number of Buddhist disciples who treat the Buddha Dharma in the same casual manner, hoping all the while to reach great perfection and realize great accomplishment. They have a heart intent upon liberation at the time they are at the Buddhist altar, which I just described. After they leave the Buddhist altar, maybe they can maintain this heart for four to six hours. Maybe they can maintain it for one or two days. Maybe they can maintain it somewhat longer – for three to five days or even half a month. Those disciples who can maintain the same heart they had at the Buddhist altar for up to one month can truly be called practitioners with superior innate faculties and deep roots of goodness.

Those who strictly abide by the teachings of the Vajra Acarya Master,[20] who abide by the precepts transmitted to them, who understand and correct their errors, and who have pure karma are truly few and far between, like the morning stars. There might not be even one or two in one hundred or one thousand!

We can, therefore, understand why there are so few who realize enlightenment even though there are so many who learn Buddhism. We should reflect upon the fact that this is due to people losing the heart they had when they first began walking the Buddhist path.

When they are at the Buddhist altar receiving the precepts, many practitioners truly give rise to a heart that understands impermanence and fears horrible states. They make up their minds to leave this fire-wheel, that is, these six realms of constant suffering and dissatisfaction. Thus, in front of the Vajra Master, they are repentant and vow to thoroughly rectify their faults!

After leaving the Buddhist altar for no more than a moment, some people give rise to egocentric thoughts and wild, selfish desires. They then stir up trouble, quarrel, contend, or speak sarcastically. Some even engage in physical fighting, which results in the spilling of blood or the loss of life. At such time, how could such people be called those who engage in cultivation? How could it be said that they remember the vows they just made at the Buddhist altar?

They have totally cast aside the earnest counsel of the Vajra Master and have totally forgotten the precepts and rules. All of the good states of mind at the Buddhist altar lasted so briefly. In an instant, such states were totally and forever wiped out by negative karma and bad practices accumulated over many lives. How could this type of practitioner be one who engages in cultivation?

At the Buddhist altar, the Vajra Master admonished them to practice enduring insults, since such practice can lead one to accomplish the supreme nirvana. However, after leaving the Buddhist altar, when they hear something unpleasant, they feel resentful. If such words directly insult them, they feel even more unable to endure them. They might immediately jump up and respond with even more insulting language. They might even slap the other person across the face to show how tough they are so that such person will not dare scold or insult them again.

The Vajra Master told them to treat people generously. However, when they are mistreated by someone, they exclaim, "I will avenge this wrong even if it takes ten years. You wait and see!" Afterwards, they secretly cause their wrongdoers trouble.

The Vajra Master told them that they should practice the four limitless states of mind: limitless loving-kindness, compassion, sympathetic joy and equanimity. Through this practice, they could achieve limitless merit. When somebody unintentionally bumps them slightly, however, they immediately give a contemptuous look and say, "Are you blind? You forgot to take your eyeballs with you when you began walking. Next time, remember your eyeballs, all right? Huh!" If the other person's response is unsatisfactory, they will immediately become enraged, like a man-eating tiger, and stare at such person with angry, wide-open eyes!

The Vajra Master admonished them not to kill living beings. This, they remember. They think that they can easily comply with such precept, saying to themselves, "I will not kill, but others can kill!" Thus, as soon as they walk into a restaurant, they say to others, "Prepare a live, fresh fish to eat! But don't let me know about it. I do not kill living beings." Then, very pleased with themselves, they say, "Anyway, I did not raise my hand to kill it. Thus, I am not killing living beings!"

The Vajra Master admonished them to treat people in an amiable manner. The Vajra Master told them that fellow disciples should get along in a harmonious and friendly manner. However, when they discover the slightest thing wrong with someone else, some improper attribute, they immediately ridicule and insult such people, yelling, "How can you be so stupid? You are like a pig. You have no brain. You don't use your mind. In all of the world, it is impossible to find one stupider than you!"

The Vajra Master told them to meditate every day. They meditate one day and put it aside for the next several days, performing this responsibility in a perfunctory manner! If they think about it, they will do it. If they do not think about it, they will not do it. If today they are weary from dancing, they will not do it. If tomorrow they are too tired from work, they will consider doing it the next day. If the next day they are too busy discussing business with customers, they might make time for it some other day.

The Vajra Master admonished them not to lie to the Master or deceive the Buddhas and Bodhisattvas. However, in their hearts, they secretly desire to compete with the Master to see who is more wise, talented, and clever. They want to match wits and debate views. Thus, they tell many lies. They are secretly pleased with themselves, gloating, "Maybe the Master does not know. The Master is just mediocre. You see, I pulled one over on the Master. I told him lies and he did not even know. It seems that if I do something in the future which violates the Buddha Dharma, it won't be important. Anyway, the Master would not know."

Occasionally, they banter with friends who also violate the Dharma. Feeling apprehensive, they encourage each other by saying, "The Master probably doesn't know about this! You and I are in a similar position. Our friendship is close. I won't tell the Master. You also should not tell the Master. Let's both keep our mouths shut!"

The Vajra Master said that those who cultivate themselves and learn Buddhism must love living beings and pray for world peace! However, when they see others fighting, they laugh and become elated. If they discover that war has broken out in certain places, they become so excited they dance with joy. They repeatedly say, "They are fighting well. It is exhilarating when opposing guns and canons meet each other! Only then do things become interesting. As for human beings, this type of thing is inevitable. It is very normal! It is not even exciting enough. It would be best if a world war erupted. That would really be fun!"

The Vajra Master said that Buddhist disciples must have correct understanding and must clearly believe in cause and effect and karmic retribution. One must not fall into ignorance, must not give rise to evil views, and must not practice evil ways, as this will make it impossible for one to attain liberation. However, they harbor evil views all day long, cheating people wherever they go. Under the pretense of acting on behalf of the Master, they speak nonsense. They praise themselves as being a favorite and close disciple of the Master, having received all of the Master's true Dharma. They even boast of themselves as being an heir to their sect's spiritual legacy, saying that from now on, other disciples can either obey what they say or obey what the Master says since they have complete authority to speak on behalf of the Master!

The Master is a Buddha. Each of them thinks that he is also a Buddha. The Master is a Dharma King. Each of them thinks that he is also a Dharma King. The Master is a Rinpoche. Each of them thinks that he is also a Rinpoche. The Master is a Dharma Teacher. Each of them thinks that he is also a Dharma Teacher. In short, they think that they are disciples of the Master by direct line. If the Master is a Buddha, each of them will even go so far as to say that he can give himself a shake and change into a super-Buddha. One can easily understand the true underlying meaning of their words. It is that the disciple is superior to the teacher, that the disciple has surpassed even a Buddha!

It is even more bemusing when today they claim to be Buddhas, tomorrow they claim to be Rinpoches, and the next day they feel that the Buddhist path is no good and change into great fortune tellers. Two days later, they become great experts in feng-shui (geomancy). They boast that they have vast supernormal powers, that they possess unlimited Dharma powers, that they can do whatever they want, that there is nothing they cannot do, that they are the reincarnation of Zhang Guo Lao....[21]

These types of examples are numerous. Today, I am telling you frankly that people like these are pitiful living beings who are all standing in line waiting to descend into hell! Yet, they think that they can sleep in comfort the rest of their lives, after having cheated people out of their money. After they dupe people out of their money or property at a certain place, they go somewhere else to play the same old tricks on others, cheating pitiable people out of their hard-earned money. Is this not digging a tunnel for oneself that leads directly to hell? The more one deceives oneself and others, the closer the tunnel approaches the ultimate destination of hell and the faster one descends.

To speak in common terms, this is digging a tunnel that leads to one's grave! Can those Buddhist disciples who treat the Buddha Dharma and precepts with contempt, who treat the principles of the Buddha Dharma as trifling matters, possibly be proud of themselves? Can those who are ignorant worldlings possibly be proud of themselves?

There is a Chinese phrase, "As if one were waking from a dream." It basically describes those people who have taken the wrong path, who have been duped, or who have suffered losses. After other people give them correct direction or after the true facts come out, they realize their previous mistakes in judgment. When these people finally wake up and realize how heavy their losses are, they often fall into deep remorse and overwhelming sorrow. They feel as if they just awoke from a nightmare. Thus, the above mentioned Chinese phrase has a negative connotation. Of course, when it is used to describe such worldly situations and such people, it is an accurate simile.

However, with respect to those practitioners who violate the teachings of the Master, who know the precepts but who violate the precepts, such as in the examples I gave above, by the time they finally discover their ignorant mentality, there is often no more time or opportunity for them to turn over a new leaf. For some of them, their time in this world is about to end and their karmic retribution is about to befall them. At such time, some will have already been expelled from their Master's group and will not have the opportunity to be saved again. As for those with deep and heavy negative karma, the suffering they will then experience cannot nearly be described with the phrase, "As if one were waking from a dream." This is because the law of impermanence will not keep them in this world. They will not remain by the Master's side!

It is the same for those practitioners who make vows at the Buddhist altar but who, after leaving the altar, do things that are entirely contrary to the Buddha Dharma they heard at the altar. Sooner or later, they completely forget about the vows they made at the altar! Those who previously killed living beings continue to kill living beings. Those who previously engaged in sexual misconduct continue to engage in sexual misconduct. Those who previously harmed others continue to harm others. Those who previously were greedy continue to be greedy. Those who previously lied continue to lie. They hardly have any misgivings and are still indifferent to it all, thinking that as long as the Master does not know, everything will be fine!

It seems they are under the illusion that as long as the Master does not know, all of their sins simply never existed and all of their offenses were never perpetrated! Naturally, they believe no negative karmic retribution could ensue since it is as if nothing whatsoever occurred. Of course, in such case, they feel justified in intentionally or unintentionally perpetrating all kinds of wrongs and breaking all of the precepts they received. This is because, to them, it all never existed!

Are these people actually cultivating themselves for the Master? Are they cultivating themselves to attain liberation from the cycle of birth and death? Could it be that the Master really does not know? Not necessarily. I am afraid that it is more appropriate to say that they are deluding themselves and others!

Some disciples, pretending to be serious, say, "I know that if the Master heard about this, he would be disappointed. Therefore, in order not to sadden the Master, I did not tell him!" Some rationalize, "I still have not done it completely. Therefore, I have not reported it to the Master!"

Such pretexts sound so dignified and noble. Such explanations sound so reasonable. Come to think of it, they should win an award for such pretexts! It seems as if they have more of a conscience than anybody else and that they show more solicitude for the Vajra Master than anyone else! However, even a three-year-old immature child knows that things which the Master tells one not to do, one should not do. Even such a child knows that the Master naturally will be saddened if one does not obey his instructions.

Can the Master sleep peacefully, without a sad heart, when there are those who play these types of tricks on him? Is this a matter of one's conscience coming to the fore or simply a matter of using farfetched pretexts to console oneself? Those who engage in such conduct should be more clear about this than anyone else! Of course, this does not exclude the possibility of people acting in a state where their minds are covered with sheer ignorance.

There is another type of person. They are extremely devout and completely respectful toward the Master. They sincerely believe in the words and teachings of the Master. They prostrate themselves before the Master in admiration of his miraculous powers! They think that the Master is a Tathagata in this world, the reincarnation of the Buddha! Their faces beam with joy and their hearts are happy!

They think, "The Master has such great abilities. What do I have to worry about? What do I have to fear? There is nothing more to worry about. In the future, I will do whatever I want to do. Even if I commit a few wrongs, it won't be serious. Anyway, the Master is so compassionate and has such great abilities. He has the heart of a Buddha or Bodhisattva. Even if I create some negative karma, do a few bad things, receive some karmic retribution, it won't matter. The Master will definitely save me. The Master is like a protective umbrella over my head. The Master is my protective talisman. I previously feared receiving some karmic retribution. Now I don't fear anything! I will just go ahead and do it without hesitation."

After thinking such thoughts, they secretly feel happy. When the Master assigns them a task or tells them something, their response is to prevaricate or hem and haw. The Master's words go in one ear and out the other. Sometimes, the words do not even enter their ears! They are content with the present situation and do not worry about anything. They feel that they do not have to do their daily meditation taught to them by the Master. They feel that it does not matter if they engage in sexual misconduct. They feel that the Master's instructions to carry out the four limitless states of mind have nothing to do with them. They do not even care about their own parents. They even feel that the presence of their parents in the family shrine room sullies the room, since they are old and their bodies are smelly. Their heart of awareness has long since left, not to mention any determination they might have had to fulfill the vows they took! The vows they previously made are later broken!

As before, they persist in their old ways without any concern. When they make money, they are jubilant. They engage in feasting and revelry, spending money lavishly. They engage in sexual misconduct. At this time, it is of no concern to them who and where the Master is. If they experience some difficulty, such as loss of capital in their business that causes them to pace about in an agitated state of mind, then and only then do they recall the Master, who is their protective talisman and protective umbrella. They then urgently search for the Master everywhere so as to beseech the Master to empower them, eliminate their difficulties, help them through their rough times, and remove their disasters.

As soon as they extricate themselves from their difficulties, they hurriedly thank the Master and then completely disappear from his sight without leaving a trace. There is no word of them for a few months or even half a year. They have disappeared.

Could it be said that such disciples are disrespectful? According to what they say, they are very respectful. They think that they venerate the Master as a Buddha or Bodhisattva and look upon the Master as a supreme Holy One. They prostrate themselves before and worship the Master. It seems as if they very much respect the Master. However, they in fact regard the Master as a Dharma treasure who enables them to be free of worry, someone they can rely upon to help them do whatever they please.

To put it a bit more clearly, they view the Master as being their trump card and a tool to make money! As such, they think they can defeat anyone. They think they can overcome any adversary in the business world! We can clearly see what kind of practitioners these people really are.

Are they, in the end, engaging in true or false cultivation? Are they true practitioners or only superficial practitioners without any substance? Are they learning and practicing the Buddha Dharma in order to liberate themselves from the cycle of birth and death or are they practicing the Buddha Dharma in order to use the Master to make money and lead a life of peace? Are they Buddhist disciples? Today I will clearly tell all of you good people: These people do not even have the prerequisites to give rise to a conscience. They are most pitiable!

There are those who are even worse. Some people, under the pretense of the Master's name, issue orders so as to receive offerings or assistance from other believers or fellow disciples. They cheat their way into money and position. They set up a network of people in order to make money and fulfill their greed. They think that as long as they can convince others that they are acting for the benefit of living beings, of course it is all right.

As such, the hearts they had when they began to learn the Buddha Dharma, hearts that were intent upon liberation from the cycle of birth and death, have completely changed. How could such people not descend into lower realms? How could this not be the Dharma-Ending Age? How could the circles of Buddhism in society not be in utter confusion? How could this state of affairs not spell an end to people's wisdom and cut off the roots of their kindness?

One day, while they are at the Master's side listening carefully to his discourse on the principles of the Dharma, the Master will use his limitless power to bless them, educate them, and guide them so that they may quickly awaken to the Dharma. At that time, if they look within themselves and if their wisdom opens up, such education and guidance might change them. They would then feel and experience sadness and remorse.

In other words, the repeated teachings of the Master might touch the bottom of their hearts, stirring their consciences, which were not totally extinguished, and their souls, which were not totally degenerated! Therefore, at such time, they might feel the pangs of contrition. They might think thoughts of remorse. Thus, they might tearfully confess to the Master that they have totally, or almost totally, broken the precepts transmitted to them by the Master.

They violate almost all of the principles they should hold fast to, principles on which the Master gives discourses and instruction, such as doing good deeds, giving to others, the four limitless states of mind, and good karma relating to body, speech, and mind (not killing, not harming living beings, not engaging in sexual misconduct, not lying, not speaking harshly, not using profane or flowery language, not speaking words that sow discord or cause rifts among people, not giving rise to anger or hatred, not drinking liquor, etc.). They ignore the instruction of the Master to do certain deeds. Instead, they do all of the things that the Master instructs them not to do.

After receiving the Eight Precepts, they break them all. They break each of the Ten Precepts they received as well. Without any qualms, they break the Hinayana precepts. They fully and delightfully break the Bodhisattva Precepts! One can imagine whether they hold fast to the vows they made at the Buddhist altar!

Not only do they not hold fast to their vows, some of them even go around sowing discord. This is not enough for them. Some even go further and organize a team of fellow disciples in order to attack other specific people. If their efforts are of no use with the Master, then they go to one of the elders for help. Some even plan to come to my place to complain against others. Could it be said that this type of fabrication of groundless rumors, this type of ignorant bias, is a manifestation of their four limitless states of mind?

They are not even as good as a virtuous ordinary person! When a virtuous ordinary person sees what the evil conduct of these people has wreaked, he will endeavor to put an end to it. At the very least, he is able to keep himself morally clean and pure.

There are even followers of evil who malign the Vajra Master, who disparage the Master as being worthless. They attack him as being good for nothing and insult him viciously. They recklessly distort his words. They suspiciously analyze what the Master said. What significance could the words of the Master possibly have to them? As far as they are concerned, such words are nothing more than floating smoke or passing clouds, which disappear in an instant. To put it in more unpleasant terms, hearing the discourses of the Master gives them an opportunity to spin a cocoon around their ears!

When these disciples sit down below the seat of the Master and receive his earnest instruction, their consciences make them feel uneasy. They may feel that they have turned their backs on the teachings of the Master, given so tirelessly and patiently. They may feel that they truly have gone a bit too far. They may feel remorse over having broken the precepts. Since they know that the karmic retribution for one who knows the precepts yet breaks the precepts is surely descending into hell or one of the three evil realms, at this time they begin to cry bitterly in fear of their future. They quickly beg the Master to save them, telling him that they must be empowered, that from now on they will definitely and resolutely correct their ways and will never break the precepts again! If they ever break the precepts again, they say, then they are willing to descend into hell! All of those who see this scene are deeply touched, and all of those who hear this are moved to cry their hearts out!

Often, the compassionate Vajra Master will dedicate his own merit to them to greatly empower them or will himself bear their karmic retribution. He will instruct them repeatedly, admonishing them to use this as a lesson and never break the precepts again. Each one of them solemnly promises to comply. If they really do keep their promises, then the efforts of the Master will not have been in vain. However, what ultimately happens?

Those who can keep their promises do so for no more than a few days. For a very short period, they still have a certain trepidation and act very scrupulously, often calling to mind the instructions of the Master. Occasionally, they forget such instructions. When they recall them, they still have feelings of fear and anxiety. They often worry about breaking the precepts. At this stage, they are still vigilant.

After a few more days, their self-discipline loosens. At this time, their thoughts of vigilance have no real meaning. The bad habits and karma that they have accumulated throughout previous lives led to their undisciplined minds and affect their current lives. The obstructions of bad habits and karma overwhelm them. At this stage, these people still do not understand. Rather, they think that their thoughts are meritorious. It seems to them that they are progressing a bit.

After a while, they completely revert back to their old ways. Their vigilant minds have gradually become apathetic. Their whole thought process has become indifferent and careless. When others, out of kindness, try to help them by reminding them of their mistakes, they do not feel any of the pangs of conscience they felt when they previously listened to the live or taped discourses of the Master! They respond by simply snorting or slightly knitting their brows. In an instant, their thoughts have floated far away on to something else.

In a rather indifferent, mocking tone, they might say the following exquisite words: "My negative karma is deep and heavy!" They will then turn around and swiftly leave, walking with a very exquisite gait. They might show a light and unemotional smile and then casually say in passing, "Thank you for reminding me!" In their hearts, however, they harbor animosity. Later on, just as before, they continue with their original course of conduct, persisting in their old ways no matter what others say. They do not think that they are doing anything egregious and take great exception to any constructive criticism.

There are even those who become angry from embarrassment. They are quick to show their strength by ridiculing the other person, saying, "You are educating me? Who do you think you are? You must think you are the Master! What qualifications do you have to criticize me? Who do you think you are to lecture to me? Only the Master has the qualifications to say such things. You're scolding me? It is true that I have some deep negative habitual tendencies, but are you awesome? What type of person are you? How much better are you than I? Remember when you on such and such a day went out with that certain person and fooled around? Remember when you did such and such a thing at such and such a time? You think that I don't know about those things? We'll talk about me after you are able to take care of yourself well. This is the way I am. If I have faults, then it is a matter for the Master. The Master will tell me about them. You do not have to worry about them! Have you not heard the expression, 'Each one sweeps the snow from his own doorsteps and does not bother about the frost on his neighbor's roof'?"

Thus does such person reprove his friend to his face. Not only do such people not reflect on their own faults, after reproving their friends, they even feel proud of themselves, thinking that they avenged a wrong and can thus hold their heads up high. In fact, in the end, they are simply adding to their own negative karma!

After the gradual passage of time and the fading of memory, all of the experiences at the Vajra Buddhist altar lose their freshness. All of the Master's painstaking support, teaching, words of persuasion, and admonitions become more and more obscure with the passage of time. In the end, they are all buried without a trace under the activities of dancing, going to nightclubs and bars, talking business, going to movies, gambling, playing the slot machines, playing cards, discussing politics, running around handling business matters, playing mahjong, eating and drinking, making money, being promiscuous with beautiful women, etc.

Monks and nuns are no exception. If they are not forming cliques to serve their own selfish interests, then they are scheming in private to increase their power. Today, they want to become head of the temple. Tomorrow, they want to be supervisor of the temple. They think that if they have the opportunity to put on makeup and go outside to have a good time, why not do it?

What have been buried are not only the Vajra Master's painstaking efforts. I am afraid that what have been prematurely consumed are the merit accumulated over many lives and eons; blessings and wisdom that could have been obtained; the reward body of good karma that could have been experienced in this life and future lives; and one's own good fortune and the good fortune of one's close relatives, the causes and conditions for which resulted from cultivation spanning over countless eons.

They have wandered around in this vast net of karma woven out of manifold worldly selfish desires. After almost completely exhausting their previously accumulated merit because of attachment, they might have a moment of reflective silence wherein their thoughts of deceiving themselves and others are totally overcome by their feelings of uncertainty and fear over what may occur in their lives and after they die. At that time, these practitioners might recall the admonitions of the Master. They will then immediately leaf through Buddhist books or listen to Dharma tapes. At such time, it appears as if their minds have given rise to a bit of awareness and that their consciences have been moved to some extent. They also feel some slight distress. When they recall the vows they previously made and count all of the precepts they broke, they break out into a heavy sweat even though there may be cold winds blowing. They feel great remorse!

They then again rush over to see the Master, whom they have not seen for a long time, and cry their hearts out before him. They show contrition, ask for help, feel sad, confess, make vows, and make a big scene. Once the Master again forgives them, they resume their same old patterns, which I just described. At that point in time, when such disciples stop to analyze themselves, they will use a rather deep Buddha Dharma phrase. They will use the following elegant, diplomatic language to perfectly express themselves: "My negative karma is truly too deep and heavy....Alas!...I don't know why my negative karma is so deep and heavy....Alas!...That my negative karma is so deep shows that my innate faculties are not as good as other fellow disciples.... Alas!..."

Their faces will then become perfectly serene. No more than a few minutes later, however, they will be talking cheerfully and humorously just as before.

Could you not feel sad after hearing their brilliant explanation? In just a few sentences, they totally absolved themselves from all responsibility. Not a single trace of responsibility remains! Their response reached the point of perfection!

As far as the Vajra Master is concerned, practitioners such as these are especially frightening. To put it accurately, these so-called practitioners are most pitiful! Their entire spirit has already become numb. To use a simile, such disciples are like a rotten piece of wood. To carve such wood into the sacred likeness of Sakyamuni Buddha would be much harder than walking the difficult passages of Sichuan.[22]

As a popular saying goes, "It is difficult to walk the passage to heaven. The difficulty in walking the passages of Sichuan is almost as difficult as ascending to heaven." I can see no chance for these practitioners to ascend to the Western Paradise! This truly makes one feel heartbroken!

If an ordinary person of the world is unmoved by the teachings of the Buddha Dharma and reacts to such teachings with indifference, it can be considered as excusable. This is because nobody ever taught such person the principles of karma and the Buddha Dharma. That such person regards the Buddha Dharma and the precepts as nothing special at all can be expected.

However, it is truly difficult to understand why a Buddhist disciple who has practiced the Buddha Dharma for a long time, after discovering that he has broken the precepts laid down by Sakyamuni Buddha together with his own vows, still acts indifferently, as if nothing ever happened, as if such things have nothing to do with him. This type of behavior calls for deep thought. Of course, they do not always have such a reaction. On extremely rare occasions when the Master's Dharma talk, like a steel whip, forcibly scourges their hearts and spirits, they feel great pain and deeply look within themselves!

These types of disciples and these types of occurrences are not few. On the contrary, such disciples and occurrences are many!

Is this not so? When first taking up Buddhism, many practitioners follow the Master and practice the Buddha Dharma with the motivation to end the cycle of birth and death, to leave the six realms of samsara. There are also those who, after seeing the limitless Dharma power of the Master, take up Buddhism in order to seek familial peace and happiness. Later on, they are influenced by the Master and understand the Buddha Dharma principle of cause and effect. They understand that everything in this world is but an illusion, a dream. They then truly become those who engage in cultivation. With determination, they vow to study and practice the Buddha Dharma in order to leave the six realms of samsara.

No matter which type of practitioner, as long as he gives rise to a heart intent upon leaving samsara and as long as he gives rise to awareness, then he will wholeheartedly devote himself to the practice of Buddhism. However, a heart that is intent upon leaving samsara is difficult to maintain for a long time. During the process of practicing and learning the Buddha Dharma, this type of heart gradually disappears due to various worldly concerns and fetters. Thus, as far as most disciples are concerned, the desire to liberate themselves from the cycle of birth and death that they first had when they took up Buddhism and acknowledged the Master as their teacher, gradually turns into seeking money, profit, and position, fighting over power, being unwilling to make the smallest sacrifice, and scheming against others. Such selfishness grows with time to the point where such people are continually seeking more and more in order to fill their insatiable desires. They slowly but surely walk toward the abyss of degeneration. They become more degenerate than they were before they took up Buddhism.

The most important thing is that at the time they are degenerating, they do not know that they are moving farther and farther from the path of liberation, that the difference in conduct between them and a true Buddhist disciple is becoming greater and greater. They continue to think that they are practicing Buddhism, just like before. They even think that they are not just ordinary practitioners.

In the end, when other disciples have overcome various obstacles and difficulties to attain great accomplishment, greed has already pulled these degenerating disciples to the doorsteps of the hungry ghost realm or the realm of hell! Only then do they repent. However, it is already too late to repent!

This is definitely not alarmist talk. It is, however, the result of the law of cause and effect! What is so ironic is that a disciple who practices and learns Buddhism is the very person who should know that the chief culprit causing living beings to revolve in the six realms of samsara is greed.[23]

Could it be that they do not understand this principle? Each of them understands! It is simply that they have become intoxicated by their day-dreams of false things, which are more enticing and attractive to them due to deeply ingrained worldly desires and greed.

They did not pass the test. They do not know that demonic obstructions always appear when the disciple who engages in cultivation is about to realize great accomplishment! The principles that they previously learned from books and the teachings and discourses of the Master are all relegated to the back of their minds when the demonic obscurations come to hinder them. The old patterns of selfishness, greed, possessiveness, and ignorance endlessly grow in their minds. In the end, such old patterns, like a ball of flames, devour and burn them up.

Thus, fellow disciples fight fiercely over the most trifling things. If something involves personal profit, then they will rack their brains to benefit themselves and will fight over every little thing. Each tries to cheat the other, fearing that they will lose some profit or be taken advantage of.

In order to maintain their face and their gains, they are willing to raise a big uproar and rebuke others. Some turn their backs on the Master and secretly engage in disputes over the most trifling advantages. Of course, this type of conduct is not as bad as it could get, since they still have some consideration for the Master. In their hearts, they still have a trace of good thoughts relating to the Buddha Dharma.

However, there are certain disciples who simply make one's hair stand on end. When they contend with people over gain, they go so far as to openly revile and wrangle with others at the Vajra Buddhist altar in front of the Vajra Master and the Buddhas and Bodhisattvas.

At such time, one can hear the sounds of crying, heated arguing, and sharp reproach. It is quite a sight. Their words are indiscreet. They stamp their feet and quake with rage. All kinds of ugly scenes appear. Their negative karma grows and grows! Those who feel they have been aggrieved even yell at the Master, asking him to be the judge of who is right. Those who have taken advantage of others still loudly argue to justify their points of view. Examples of this type of conduct are endless. Such wrongdoings are too numerous to be listed!

Do these people know what it is to endure insults? Do they know what it is to be a Buddhist disciple? These are the same Buddhist disciples who, when they first took up Buddhism, said in a voice choking with tears that they wanted to study and practice Buddhism and vowed to save living beings! These are the same Buddhist disciples who repeatedly say that one should practice enduring insults! Are they the same students who say, "I very much follow whatever the Master says. When the Master tells me to do something, I do it."? Are they the same practitioners who constantly say that they engage in serious cultivation and abide by the teachings of the Buddhas and Bodhisattvas?

In seeking personal worldly gain, they deepen their old odious patterns of behavior carried over from many previous lives. In satisfying their vanity and pride, they give no consideration whatsoever to the sacredness and solemnity of the Vajra Buddhist altar. They totally ignore the Vajra Master's most respected position. They even stop going to group cultivation sessions to learn from the Master's teachings just because of a minor misunderstanding between them and other fellow disciples. Their pretext is, "Since my three karmas correspond with the teachings of the Master, I won't be together with all of you." This is truly a case of causing oneself to descend into hell, although they still do not understand this. They do not understand that by acting in such manner they in fact do not care at all about the Buddhas and Bodhisattvas, and they have no respect at all for the Vajra Master!

According to their way of thinking, the Vajra Buddhist altar is a place to argue and bicker, like a market. They view their fellow disciples as sellers and buyers of goods and the Master as the manager of the market who mediates disputes!

Presently, this is the attitude that certain practitioners have toward the Buddha Dharma. In the depths of their minds, this is their understanding of the Buddha Dharma! In this world, there are disciples of some Rinpoches who are like this. I really want to use the Five Thunder Correct Dharma Palm to finish them off with a flash of rainbow light. But I see that they are truly so pitiful. Because of their merit from having introduced some people into Buddhism, I will forgo using the Five Thunder Correct Dharma Palm.

These practitioners treat the Vajra Master in such a careless manner. They engage in internal strife with their fellow disciples, treating them coldly or even not communicating with them. One can imagine the attitude they have in treating those who are not fellow disciples. It surely is one of arrogance, conceit, and unreasonableness. They frequently unleash a torrent of abuse on others. Some even get into physical fights or secretly cause trouble for others. If someone even slightly offends them in some way, they give rise to hatred and rack their brains to think of ways to get even.

It can be said that these people cannot even save themselves. How could they possibly save others? Such conduct only causes others to experience suffering and vexation. There are no benefits arising from such conduct!

They are even much worse than some ordinary worldly people. Their basic qualities and morals and their cultivation are not even as good as those of a good worldly person. They could hardly be called people who have successfully cultivated themselves. Because of such lack of cultivation, they have caused some people to give up Buddhism. They have also caused quite a large number of good people to lack the faith to take up Buddhism. Almost the majority of practitioners are like this. They do not model their conduct after Sakyamuni Buddha. Rather, their conduct is diametrically opposed to the Buddha Dharma, the teachings of the Master, and the precepts.

These people profane the Buddha Dharma. They are not propagating the Buddha Dharma. They are creating negative karma and breaking the precepts. They are not cultivating themselves and seeking truth. They assume the appearance of those who engage in cultivation. However, in their heart of hearts, they are clearly selfish.

They constantly talk about cultivating the four limitless states of mind. In fact, some of their odious conduct has even caused ordinary worldly people to feel quite disappointed.

Of course, these people who appear to be cultivating themselves for the Master, but who are only cheating themselves and others, will undoubtedly end up eating the bitter fruits of their own making! This is due to the natural law of cause and effect. It is a scientific inevitability. No emotional pleas can change this natural law one bit!

The law of cause and effect and karmic retribution work as follows. If what you put forth is false, then what you receive in turn will also be false. If what you put forth is goodness, then the reward you receive will also be goodness. If what you put forth is vicious conduct, then you will definitely receive the punishment of vicious conduct. If you do not sincerely believe in the Buddha Dharma law of cause and effect, you will definitely fall into ignorance. If you are utterly devoid of conscience, you will definitely have a full record of crimes and misdeeds. If you act for the good of others, you will definitely command public respect and support.

There is no room for any falseness within the law of cause and effect! Thus, those who treat the Buddha Dharma, the Master, and other living beings with an impure heart must be very careful. Their odious behavior will certainly bring about further and more painful karmic retribution. This is because another name for karma is science!

Therefore, we describe the types of practitioners I enumerated above as people who repeatedly find their conscience, and we describe their frequent remorseful expressions as recurrent discovery of conscience. However, there is no real meaning to their constantly seeking out the Master. Of course, this type of cyclical offensive conduct and remorse is merely labeled as being moved by one's conscience. One cannot say that such people are progressing or that they give rise to true awareness in their hearts. This is because it can be said that they treat repentance as a daily perfunctory procedure. Thus, such repentance does not give rise to true awareness in their hearts. Sometimes they are distressed. However, this distress only lasts momentarily, like the taste of a delicious meal, which soon fades away. This is precisely why they are unable to maintain a vigilant mind.

When they are occasionally moved by their conscience, they feel unhappy and have the impulse to repent. However, when they become entangled in worldly matters, this evanescent "conscience" totally disappears. If this is not recurrent discovery of conscience, what is it? Could there be a more appropriate phrase to describe the ways of such practitioners?

However, practitioners who treat the compassion of the Master as merely a Dharma treasure to lean upon and who treat each event of repentance as a trifling matter are undoubtedly falling into degeneration at the same time that other practitioners are exerting great efforts in their cultivation and realizing wonderful accomplishments. When the time comes, these practitioners who fell into degeneration will be like moths who throw themselves into a fire to be burned up! This is because they time and time again wrapped themselves up in their own cocoon and refused to realize their errors. How can they blame anyone else?

What I have described above is not only referring to ordinary practitioners. Even some low-level Rinpoches engage in such conduct!

Therefore, when you feel repentant, or suddenly come to awareness while listening to a discourse of the Master, or are moved by a certain situation that makes you look within yourself and feel sad, you might then and there vow to be a true practitioner who abides by the precepts and Dharma and whose three karmas correspond with the teachings of the Master. At such time, you should remember to practice Buddhism as you originally intended when you first took up Buddhism. That is, you should always remember the scene when you first took up Buddhism. You should never change your original mind-set! If you can truly do this, I, Pamu, guarantee that you will become accomplished with room to spare. Therefore, I deeply hope that all practitioners will be careful and strictly adhere to their original mindset!

Rinpoches and Dharma Teachers who hear my discourses or those practitioners who read these transcribed discourses must pay special attention to the following. I previously stated the importance of disciples following the teachings of the Master. However, you must not misunderstand this to mean that you should follow the teachings of anyone who calls himself a master. By doing so, you would be falling into a state of ignorance, since most people who call themselves Rinpoches or masters are just ordinary people. The Master that I am referring to is one who is a Vajra Master according to the Dharma of Vajrayana Buddhism – namely, one who is the reincarnation of a true Buddha or Bodhisattva, who has mastered both exoteric and esoteric Dharma, who has perfected the Five Sciences, and who can perform the Inner-Tantric Initiations. I am not referring to those who are ordinary people yet who call themselves masters.

However, you must also bear in mind that we should be respectful toward those ordinary masters who are not proficient in exoteric and esoteric Dharma and who have not perfected the Five Sciences, but who nevertheless carefully uphold the precepts, cultivate themselves according to the Dharma, and spread the Dharma according to Buddhist tenets. We should learn from their good qualities. I, therefore, want to point out to everyone that one can only rely upon the teachings of a correctly selected Master. Otherwise, there will be no end to the trouble one experiences in the future.

⬱ *Chapter Three* ⬱

THE TEN SUPERFICIALITIES OF PRACTITIONERS

MASTER PADMASAMBHAVA SAID, "A great many people fall into superficialities in their practice of the Dharma."

This means that for many practitioners, the practice of Buddhism has become a mere formality. They do not truly practice. Rather, their practice is totally superficial. They even give people the false impression of being truly engaged in cultivation. They maintain an extremely irreverent attitude toward practice of the Buddha Dharma. Their "practice" is perfunctory, and they treat the Master, Buddhas, and Bodhisattvas in a careless, insincere manner!

Of course, it is impossible for such practice to result in any accomplishment or real benefit. On the contrary, superficial practice that has become perfunctory will only cause such practitioners to move in the direction of degeneration. Now then, what are the ten types of superficiality? The first superficiality is as follows:

1. The Superficiality of Reciting Passages Without Belief

What is meant by the superficiality of reciting passages without belief? Without belief means not believing that the principle of cause and effect never errs, not believing in the teachings contained in the sutras, not believing in the wonderful religious doctrine of the Buddha Dharma, and not believing in the words of Sakyamuni Buddha. Reciting passages means reciting passages from the sutras and commentaries. The meaning of the entire phrase is that if someone who practices Buddhism does not clearly believe in the scientific nature of the law of cause and effect, karmic retribution, and the Buddha Dharma, then even if such person recites passages from the sutras or reads

Buddhist books and commentaries, that person's practice will become perfunctory and will produce no real benefits.

The practice of the person who lacks this clear belief is actually a superficial practice. Their practice is analogous to drawing water with a bamboo basket – nothing is achieved. They are far from accomplishment. Such practice could even cause them to descend into the three lower realms. Naturally, these practitioners are not true practitioners.

On the surface, they appear just like genuine practitioners. Genuine practitioners practice Buddhism. These non-genuine practitioners also practice Buddhism. Genuine practitioners recite passages. These non-genuine practitioners also recite passages. Genuine practitioners go to temples, light incense, and worship the Buddha. These non-genuine practitioners also follow along and worship. Genuine practitioners meditate. These non-genuine practitioners also meditate. Genuine practitioners practice the four limitless states of mind and do good deeds, thus increasing their Buddhist resources[24] and merit. These non-genuine practitioners also follow along and join in the fun.

Can one say that these non-genuine practitioners are not practicing Buddhism? Along with others, they handle various Buddhist matters and take care of various chores. Can one say that they are practicing Buddhism? In fact, they do not sincerely believe in cause and effect and are not really practicing the Buddha Dharma.

In their hearts, they do not think that they must liberate themselves from the cycle of birth and death in order to obtain true, eternal happiness. On the contrary, they feel that this human world sometimes has a certain kind of happiness of its own. To them, cultivation is just a term spoken by the Master, something that the Master demands of his disciples. It really does not have much to do with them. To them, learning Buddhism is just a matter of following the general trend, following the crowd. They figure that if they follow along, it will not hurt them. In fact, they think, it will be good. They can join in the fun. If disasters or difficulties occur, they think that they can rely on the Master for relief. Thus, it does not matter to them whether they truly cultivate themselves or not. However, they think that they must still perform the superficial formalities. At any rate, they feel that they are still half-practitioners.

In a word, this type of person is not studying and practicing the Buddha Dharma in order to end the cycle of birth and death.

This type of person includes both monastic and lay practitioners. As for monks and nuns, genuine monastics chant the name Amitabha. Non-genuine monastics likewise chant the name Amitabha. Yet, when genuine monastics chant the name Amitabha, they do so with a focused and devout mind. Their minds do not leave the image of Amitabha Buddha, and their thoughts are concentrated on their voice. However, when non-genuine monastics chant the name Amitabha, although their mouths are chanting, their thoughts have flown away somewhere and are floating around in some distant corner of the world.

As for laypersons, those who are genuine lay practitioners seek out the Master in order to learn the Dharma. Those who are non-genuine lay practitioners also seek out the Master. The genuine lay practitioners truly desire to end the cycle of birth and death. The non-genuine lay practitioners, however, seek out the Master to bless and protect them so that they can attain promotion and wealth. They have an indifferent attitude toward cause and effect and karmic retribution as taught by the Master. They pay even less heed to the Master's instructions concerning what they should do in their worldly affairs. To them, such instructions could be followed or not followed.

It would be nice if they could attain the state as implied in my name, *nonexistence of tiny things*. There is not even the tiniest thing. Naturally, huge things also do not exist. When one understands that there is nothing huge or tiny, one can comprehend the meaning of emptiness.

But this is not how they think. They think that it is not as serious as the Master says. When the Master tells them not to do something or warns them of the possible future results of their conduct, they do not believe him. They think that the Master is making up such things in order to scare them into not doing bad things. When one has fallen into such viewpoints, how is it possible even to discuss becoming accomplished? Their solemnity toward the Buddha Dharma and their understanding of the Buddha Dharma are limited to the superficial repetition of "yes, yes, yes" in front of the Master and superficial prostrating and worshipping. In their heart of hearts, they have no concern whatsoever for the Buddha Dharma, the precepts, the doctrines, and the rites. How could they be called those who truly engage in cultivation?

Thus, these practitioners cannot be considered as true cultivators. Their cultivation is only superficial cultivation, since they do not understand at all the true meaning of cultivation. Their practice is merely perfunctory.

There is another type of disciple. In their heart of hearts, they think that they are devout Buddhists. When they enter temples or stupas, they burn incense and make offerings. They also seek out the Master and study the Buddha Dharma under the Master. However, nothing can change their bad habit of killing and harming living beings. They do not believe in the law of cause and effect. They do not believe that killing living beings is breaking the precepts and that they will have to shoulder the karmic consequences of such conduct. On the contrary, they think that killing living beings is natural. Because they want to eat meat, they might think of certain excuses that appear to be quite reasonable in order to kill living beings.

From their perspective, obeying the instructions of the Master, on the one hand, and having respect for the Master, the Buddhas, and the Bodhisattvas, on the other hand, are two totally different matters. They ignore the admonitions of the Master and do not care about the rules of the Buddhas and Bodhisattvas. However, they feel that they are very respectful toward the Master. They ignore the doctrine of the Buddha Dharma. However, this does not affect the image they have of themselves. They fully believe that they are Buddhist disciples.

Having such a self-image is merely an extremely ignorant way of thinking on their part. They cannot be considered as Buddhist disciples! This is because their deviation from the teachings of Sakyamuni Buddha is too great. They are extremely ignorant and do not have the slightest correct understanding and correct views.

With respect to such pitiful people, one could at best say that they are simply outsiders who believe in Buddhism. Even if belief in Buddhism has been ingrained into the deepest part of their spirit and has become their spiritual support or sustenance, and even though they are nominally following the Master, none of this will change the fact that they will ultimately descend into hell or another one of the three evil realms.

This is due to the inevitable efficacy of the law of cause and effect. The inevitable result of killing living beings is descending into hell. Those who do not clearly believe in the law of cause and effect and who do not believe in the Buddha Dharma will fall into ignorance and will descend into the animal realm. Even though the Master has the power to save the most desperate situation, even though the Buddhas have limitless compassion, they cannot contravene the law of cause and effect. This is the Buddha Dharma principle that the law of cause and effect never errs!

Those practitioners who do not believe in cause and effect and karmic retribution are making futile efforts that will result in no merit. On the contrary, they will bring upon themselves limitless suffering. This being so, what is the difference between them, who are engaging in this type of superficial cultivation, and worldlings who have no understanding at all of the Buddha Dharma, who drift along in a muddle-headed way, and who are constantly manipulated by the karmic consequences they produce?

In summary, when one does not clearly believe in the law of cause and effect, cultivation and recitation of passages from the sutras are merely acts of an ordinary, common person. Practicing Buddhism as a mere formality is creating negative karma for oneself and is of no use!

This is the first type of superficiality of practitioners.

2. The Superficiality of Speaking About Benefiting Others When One Does Not Have Great Compassion

What is meant by benefiting others? In general, it refers to all conduct and states of mind that benefit others. It includes speech, action, thought, and even personal habits and dispositions. As long as it helps other living beings, no matter whether the help is large or small, it can be called conduct that benefits others.

All people will engage in some kind of conduct that benefits others. Examples of conduct that greatly benefits others are making charitable donations, repairing bridges, paving roads, operating schools, providing disaster relief, aiding the poor, building stupas and temples, etc. Minor examples of conduct that benefits others are the hard work of parents in providing the basic necessities of life for their children, some words of care, sympathy, and concern spoken to another, an understanding smile, or some small and simple act of assistance. All of these are acts that benefit others.

Now then, what is the relationship between benefiting others and practicing Buddhism? Why do I say that practitioners who engage in conduct beneficial to others, but who do not have a heart of great compassion, are only practicing in a superficial manner?

It can be stated as follows. A true practitioner is one who benefits others out of a heart of great compassion. Of course, one who is not a true practitioner might also be a person who benefits others. However, this type of benefiting others is totally different from benefiting others out of great compassion. The two cannot be spoken of in the same breath.

This is because one who is not a true practitioner does not understand the relationship between benefiting others and the real practice of Buddhism. Such person does not know that beneficial conduct not based upon a heart of great compassion is only beneficial conduct in the mundane sense. However, conduct that benefits others based upon a heart of great compassion is a true manifestation of bodhicitta. This is beneficial conduct in the wonderful sense!

Why do I say this? It is very simple. A true practitioner certainly acts in accordance with the teachings of Sakyamuni Buddha. Such person is a Buddhist disciple who strictly adheres to the principles of the Buddha Dharma. Practice of the correct Dharma is beneficial to living beings in all of the Dharma realms.

Although the practice of the Buddha Dharma is divided into the Great Vehicle, the Middle Vehicle, and the Small Vehicle,[25] practitioners of each Vehicle have as their primary goal ending the cycle of birth and death. Even practitioners of the Great Vehicle must also seek this goal. Only then can they save other living beings. One is able to save others only after one is able to save oneself. If one cannot even save oneself, is it not meaningless to speak of saving others?

Practitioners of the Small Vehicle and Middle Vehicle only seek the state of realization of an Arhat or a Pratyeka Buddha so as to save themselves. They do not arouse bodhicitta[26] so as to save others. They only strive for their own complete compliance with the precepts and their own perfect practice of the Dharma. They are attached to the state of realization associated with the Small Vehicle or Middle Vehicle. Even so, they also practice the four limitless states of mind in order to accumulate merit and thereby realize good fortune and wisdom.

Thus, no matter what Vehicle, all include conduct that benefits others. This is all the more true for those who cultivate the four limitless states of mind. They must first calmly reflect upon their own mistakes. Before bringing benefit to others, they themselves must first fully adhere to the precepts. Their practice must be strict. They absolutely cannot harm other people. Not harming others is actually benefiting others. This will definitely lessen the harm done to others.

Thus, it is the nature of one who is a true practitioner to benefit, make happy, and help all sentient beings. However, during one's real practice, worldly desires and greed frequently gain the upper hand. This causes simple Buddhist matters to become complicated. What was originally a holy and pure mind intent on benefiting others becomes covered with impurities. Conduct arising from this impure mindset is beneficial to others only in the worldly sense.

For example, many practitioners arouse Mahayana bodhicitta. Under the Master, they study and practice the Buddha Dharma. They vow to save sentient beings. Each one wants to be a Bodhisattva, not just an Arhat. They sometimes walk the Bodhisattva path and perform some acts that benefit others. For example, together with the Master they free captive animals, help other living beings according to the wishes of the Master, introduce people or other living beings into Buddhism so that they can learn and practice the Buddha Dharma under the Master, assist in propagating the Dharma, etc. Undoubtedly, to perform such acts is walking the Bodhisattva path. Such is the conduct of a Bodhisattva.

However, when some practitioners perform such Buddhist acts, they are not guided by great compassion that springs from bodhicitta. The basis of their conduct is to enjoy and covet things of this world. Their underlying motivation in vowing to walk the Bodhisattva path is to further their own vital interests or protect the interests of a few other people (such as their close friends, their own relatives in this lifetime, their children, etc.).

They have not decided to selflessly contribute to the lives of sentient beings. They are not willing to renounce everything they have for the benefit of all living beings in all of the Dharma realms. They are not willing to give up their lives rather than disregard the Dharma. They are not willing to personally feel pain rather than have other living beings feel pain. They are not willing to personally descend into hell rather than have other living beings descend into hell. They have not sincerely vowed to definitely save all living beings. One who, unlike them, is willing to do such things is the model of a Holy One. If one carries out such acts, then one is engaging in true Bodhisattva conduct.

Thus, it can be said that the acts they perform to benefit others do not emanate from the bodhicitta vows they previously made. The acts and the vows are two separate matters. This being the case, the acts themselves go against their vow to reach enlightenment for the sake of others. They vow in one way and act in another!

All practitioners know that it is useless to make empty vows that are not actually performed. It is useless to go about practicing the Buddha Dharma in such a manner. Furthermore, it is clear that they will often violate the law of cause and effect! Thus, this type of superficial practice will cause them much harm and will be of no benefit. It will be totally ineffective.

Likewise, when certain countries or regions experience natural disasters, many Buddhist disciples will lend a helping hand by contributing goods and materials, money, clothes, etc. If these beneficial acts truly emanate from a heart of great compassion and sympathy, then the resulting merit will be limitless in the wonderful sense. In such case, these acts would be in accord with the Dharma, would be worthy of emulating, and should be respected.

Regretfully, quite often things are not that simple! Some of these Buddhist disciples, to a greater or lesser extent, harbor selfish motives. Some of them seek to make a name for themselves from their relief efforts and raise their level of fame. Some want to win a good reputation for themselves in the world so that others will know what wonderful and good people they are. Some want to win the favor of certain other people. They want to be in good graces with certain important people. Some want to flaunt how well-off they are and reveal their wealth for all to see. Some want to use this as an opportunity to contribute a large sum of money so as to exhibit their financial power. In this way, other people's confidence in their business will increase and they can thus do more business with people. Some are forced to contribute. They painfully give up their property because they are forced by others to do so or because others constantly entreat them to do so. Some contribute in order to spread the name of their company. In short, these people rack their brains and act with all kinds of motives. It is something that is incredible.

These are all examples of conduct that, in form, is beneficial to others. Of course, one cannot deny that in fact such conduct is beneficial to others. Other people actually derive benefit to some extent. However, such conduct is only beneficial in the worldly sense! At least one can say that this type of beneficial conduct emanates from an impure heart. It will, therefore, not produce pure karmic results. It can only be considered as worldly beneficial conduct. One can never mention in the same breath such conduct, on the one hand, and completely pure conduct emanating from a heart of great compassion that has aroused bodhicitta, on the other hand!

No matter who the practitioner is, all of the Buddhist acts that he performs and all of the practices that he upholds must be based upon a most devout motivation. Otherwise, he is not truly practicing Buddhism; he is merely a worldly good person who does good and makes donations. He is just moving further and further from the goal of accomplishment. In the end, just like ordinary worldly people, they will not be able to liberate themselves from the cycle of reincarnation.

Since they will not be able to liberate themselves from the cycle of reincarnation, of what benefit is such superficial practice? Even if they continue such practice, it will not solve the basic problem of life and death. In the end, such practice will not enable them to have control over their own birth and death and achieve eternal happiness. They will simply become bogged down in superficial practice and will not deeply penetrate the Buddha Dharma.

Obviously, such superficial practice is the most evil obstacle facing those practitioners who truly want to end the cycle of birth and death! In learning Buddhism, you need not fear if you are not naturally endowed or if you are dimwitted. You only need to fear not seriously practicing, not strictly complying with the Buddha Dharma, treating the solemn Buddha Dharma casually, as if it were a mundane matter, practicing superficially, viewing the liberating Buddha Dharma with a mundane mentality, and using a mundane perspective to conjecture about and assess the holiness of the Buddha Dharma. None of these can be of any use.

Therefore, when practitioners benefit others, it should be different from when ordinary people do good and help others in the worldly sense. Whether one is truly practicing Buddhism, whether one truly has a heart of great compassion, whether one benefits all living beings with a heart of great compassion can all be seen from the nature of one's beneficial conduct. One must raise this beneficial conduct to a higher level in order that it not be just superficial practice. Only then can one truly end the cycle of birth and death and reach the state of being in control of one's own life and death!

3. The Superficiality of Donating When One Is Miserly

The word *miserliness* refers to those who unceasingly covet money, those who excessively cherish money. They are overly parsimonious and do not wish to donate anything to others. This type of person will often stoop to anything in order to obtain money, even committing heinous acts of immorality. Their wealth and so-called happiness are built upon the suffering of others.

Such people, on the one hand, and other people who are diligent and frugal, on the other hand, are totally different! Those who are diligent and frugal value money and appreciate the wealth they have. They are, therefore, frugal and do not waste. They do not spend money frivolously. However, they donate to others prudently when they should. They always act with a heart concerned about the welfare of others. They definitely do not disregard the needs of others in order to satisfy themselves. This type of frugality is a virtue. It should be held in esteem.

Diligence and frugality are worthy of emulation. Those disciples who are diligent and frugal, who appreciate the wealth they have, are good disciples who are acting in conformity with the teachings of Sakyamuni Buddha. But stinginess should be disdained by people of the world. Those who are miserly are unconcerned about whether others live or die. They only care about their own enjoyment and will stoop to anything in order to accumulate wealth.

Those who are miserly generally do not engage in charitable activities. Even if they do engage in such activities, their donations are tainted. They will definitely not donate out of compassion and sympathy for others. If they did not have to, miserly people would never donate to others. When they donate to others, often it is because they have no alternative or because they are forced to do so. Then and only then will they make what is in their eyes such a "stupid move." The charitable contributions they do make are closely related to their own personal interests. They do not engage in charity unless it concerns their own interests or benefits them (at least in their own minds).

Generally speaking, those who are miserly will only donate to others under the following circumstances:

- Charitable donations made under demand or threat from others.
- Charitable donations made at a time when the donor's life is in danger.
- Charitable donations made indirectly as a result of being cheated by others.
- Charitable donations made in order to make more money.
- Charitable donations made in order to seek fame and social recognition.
- Charitable donations made in order to please the Master.

- Charitable donations reluctantly made in order to satisfy another person.
- Charitable donations made under threat to themselves or a few of their relatives.
- Charitable donations made because they want to be reincarnated as a human being in the next life.
- Charitable donations made out of fear of being judged in hell.
- Charitable donations made out of greed for future wealth and supernormal powers.

In summary, an obvious characteristic of miserly people is that their charitable donations are made very unwillingly. They do not willingly donate in order to benefit others and help living beings. Thus, as far as they are concerned, making charitable contributions is an extremely painful thing. Quite often, after they make a contribution, they feel that they have lost some money, that they engaged in a losing transaction. They will then devise all sorts of schemes to earn back such money so that they can make up for what they perceive to be a loss. They then intensify their efforts to accumulate money. They often do not care what methods they use to make money, whether such methods go against their conscience or morality, how much negative karma they may be producing, or how many people they entrap!

Therefore, when miserly people donate, it can only be considered as donating in form. Such donating is done out of ulterior motives. They do not understand at all the true reason and function of donating. They also do not understand at all what is correct donating. They do not understand the incomparably wonderful significance of donating and its merit. One can say that those miserly people who donate are pitiful people! Those miserly practitioners who do not understand the significance of donating are even extremely ignorant people!

They think that their stinginess is in accord with the teachings of the Buddha and is an expression of appreciating the wealth that they have. However, they do not truly understand the meaning of appreciating the wealth that they have. They are simply miserly and do not love others. Not engaging in charitable activities is not the conduct of a true practitioner. Those who engage in charitable activities prompted by a miserly mind are engaging in charitable activities in form only. Such charitable activities are not those of a true, pure Buddhist disciple! This is because being miserly is an extreme manifestation of a view of self, which appears in the form of selfishness.

There is also another type of extremely incorrect superficial charitable activity. Many miserly people (this even includes some people engaged in cultivation) have a misconception. They think that after they do something bad, if they donate some money to a Buddhist temple or to monks or nuns, or if they practice some charity, they will not receive karmic retribution. This is what is meant by the Chinese saying, "Spend money to eliminate calamities." Is this really the case? Actually, this is an evil view that is antithetical to the law of cause and effect.

Of course, such superficial charitable activities do in fact bring about merit. Even if the motive for donating is impure, there is still merit. However, merit is merit and wrongdoing is wrongdoing. The merit they have accumulated will bring about karmic rewards. The wrongdoing they have committed is likewise subject to the law of cause and effect. Thus, in the same way, there will be karmic retribution resulting from negative karma when the conditions for retribution are ripe. To believe that one can "spend money to eliminate calamities" is a wrong view. It is a view that is ignorant of the law of cause and effect!

The only way to truly avoid calamities and not receive any karmic retribution is to truly cultivate oneself, not commit any wrongdoing, and not produce any negative karma. Realizing the nature of emptiness would be even better. In this way, one will naturally not bring about karmic retribution.

Some people might think that since one will suffer karmic retribution even if one engages in charitable activities, then one might as well simply not engage even in such superficial charitable activities. This would avoid suffering a financial loss on top of being punished. Such thinking is even more flawed. This is because there is supreme merit connected with charitable contributions. If one does not engage in charity, then one cannot accumulate the Buddhist resources necessary to become a Buddha, and one cannot perfect one's merit. One cannot even attain good fortune in the future. One would only be adding to one's pain and negative karma.

The above described types of charity performed with a miserly mindset are all impure charity. Such charity should not be practiced by those practitioners who deeply understand the Buddha Dharma. This type of conduct merely touches the surface of the practice of Buddhism. Disciples who are truly practicing Buddhism and who truly engage in cultivation must repudiate this type of hypocritical practice. Only then can they realize wonderful accomplishment!

4. For Those Who Practice Vajrayana Buddhism, The Superficiality of Practicing While Not Abiding by the Samaya Precepts

Here I am referring to those practitioners who cultivate themselves according to Vajrayana Buddhism. What is meant by the term *Samaya* is a number of precepts particular to Vajrayana Buddhism. They are called the Samaya Precepts. They cover all precepts and principles of the Dharma.

What is specifically meant by the phrase *practitioners of Vajrayana Buddhism*? Practitioners of Vajrayana Buddhism means those practitioners within each major school of tantra who want to or who have already realized enlightenment by cultivating themselves. For example, of the ten major schools, there is one in which Bodhisattva Mahayana practitioners cultivate themselves. This school is often called the school for becoming a Buddha in this very lifetime. This is what is meant by Vajrayana Buddhism. Practitioners of Vajrayana Buddhism are those practitioners who cultivate themselves within Vajrayana Buddhism.

Such practitioners often say that they can become a Buddha or Great Bodhisattva in this lifetime. Such words are true. It is definitely possible for them to realize Buddhahood in this lifetime. This type of cultivation can surely lead one to such goal! Of course, they would only be able to realize the state of the Three Bodies. This is far lower than the high, perfect, magnificent, supreme state of enlightenment attained by Sakyamuni Buddha. That is, they might be able to practice and realize the Dharmakaya, Sambhogakaya, and Nirmanakaya. However, their state of realization would be far lower than the perfect Three Bodies state of Sakyamuni Buddha!

Although such a state can be realized, one must practice according to the Dharma methods particular to Vajrayana Buddhism and must abide by the precepts particular to Vajrayana Buddhism. Therefore, in such practice, the most important thing is to abide by the Samaya Precepts!

Simply put, any practitioner of Vajrayana Buddhism who does not abide by the Samaya Precepts will not be able to attain any accomplishment in his practice of any tantra. Such person's practice will merely be superficial and nothing will be gained!

What, then, are the Samaya Precepts of Vajrayana Buddhism? Where do they come from? The Samaya Precepts of Vajrayana Buddhism were laid down by the highest leader of tantra, Adharma Buddha. There are also those who say that they were laid down by Vajradhara. The ancient Buddhas knew all of these precepts. These precepts are Dharma rules that have existed since beginningless time within the practice of Vajrayana Buddhism. They must be adhered to by all practitioners of Vajrayana Buddhism. In order to help practitioners remember and practice them, the ancient Buddhas gave them the name "Samaya Precepts."

What is Samaya? Samaya is a Tathagata Brightness state of right concentration. Precepts that were created from this state of right concentration are called Samaya Precepts. Put simply, these precepts are pure, bright, and without any defects. If anyone violates these precepts, then such person will surely descend into the Vajra Hell!

Thus, all practitioners of Vajrayana Buddhism must understand the necessity of abiding by the Samaya Precepts. If one does not abide by the Samaya Precepts, no matter how vigorously one practices the Buddha Dharma and no matter how devoutly one learns all of the tantric teachings, one's efforts will all come to naught!

The practice of Vajrayana Buddhism is based upon the practice of exoteric Dharma. Any practitioner of Vajrayana Buddhism must first learn a few of the major commentaries. In short, such person must learn exoteric Dharma. Only after learning exoteric Dharma is one able to deeply penetrate Vajrayana Buddhism. Only then can one ring bells and beat drums,[27] practice visualization, chant mantras, practice in accordance with the rules and rituals described in Dharma books, practice the rules and rituals of one's own yidam, practice the supreme rules and rituals, or enter the state of solitary practice.

In summary, with respect to any practitioner of Vajrayana Buddhism, no matter how such person practices, if he does not abide by the Samaya Precepts, then his practice of any Dharma is superficial and in vain!

All practitioners of Vajrayana Buddhism must understand the following principle: The Samaya Precepts were distilled and carried out over many years by the Buddhas, Bodhisattvas, and ancient Masters, such as Master Padmasambhava and Master Marpa, and are the result of their experiences. There has never been any practitioner who, having violated the Samaya Precepts, was able to maintain a useful practice or attain any accomplishment!

Those practitioners who violate the Samaya Precepts must correct themselves. They must thoroughly repent. Then and only then will they be able to ultimately attain accomplishment. This has been proven by history. It is also something that I, Pamu, have personally seen and experienced and that I am now personally announcing.

Thus, practitioners of Vajrayana Buddhism should heed the admonition of the Masters who lived through the ages: If one does not abide by the Samaya Precepts in one's practice, especially if one is a practitioner of Vajrayana Buddhism, then one's practice will not be of any use. It will be an extremely superficial practice of the Buddha Dharma!

5. For Buddhist Monks and Nuns, The Superficiality of Practicing While Not Abiding by the Precepts

If monastics[28] do not abide by the Buddha Dharma precepts and tenets, there will be mistakes in their practice, and their practice will become superficial. Such practice will not produce any true accomplishment.

Sakyamuni Buddha spoke of those monks who do not abide by the precepts of Buddhism. He said that even if they do not covet the affection and love of others, they still covet personal gain and the offerings of disciples. This means that those monastics who do not abide by the precepts will covet worldly gain and will thus not have minds set upon cultivation. Naturally, it will not be possible for them to become accomplished.

Most contemporary practitioners who have gone forth from the household life do not abide by the precepts. These range from certain Dharma Teachers and Rinpoches all the way down to the myriad monastics.

Before monastics went forth from the household life, they were attached to worldly feelings of affection and love. They therefore had thoughts of worldly affection and desire. They were no different from the ordinary person. After they cut off their hair and went forth from the household life, if they did not renounce worldly desires, the defilements that obstruct enlightenment naturally would not vanish. They would not be able to cut off the defilements. At this time, even though they are not allowed to give rise to feelings of desire, it is difficult for them to stop coveting their own gain and the offerings of disciples. Thus, the longing they have at this time is longing for their own gain and the offerings of disciples. Therefore, their attachment to the five aggregates is still strong. As monastics, they are not able to abide by the Dharma and precepts. Their practice becomes false, and in the end they are not able to accomplish anything.

Many monks do not abide by Buddhism. They covet their own personal gain and the offerings of disciples. They pretend to be pure. They quietly sit in meditation, yet their thoughts run wild. They long for the objects of the five desires[29] and are deluded by sounds, smells, and tastes. They have hearts covered with ignorance and are bound by craving.

Such phenomena are described in writings on the Dharma and are manifested in the practice of a portion of those practitioners who have gone forth. Many monastics have the appearance of being pure. While practicing, they show refined and exquisite expressions. They lower their heads and are serious in speech. They often say "Amitabha!" They are frequently seen meditating in a remote, quiet place. They very much appear to be true cultivators, but in fact they are not.

Although these monastics give the impression of being very pure and scrupulous in their practice, they still have not understood the principle that all Dharmas and all things are empty. Why have they not understood this? Because their six bases are not yet pure. Their attachment to things of the world is not yet broken. Thus, they still crave forms, sounds, smells, tastes, touches, and thoughts. They still think that the five aggregates of form, feelings, perceptions, mental formations, and consciousness are not empty. They cannot cut off their infatuation with things of the world and thus engage in distorted, dreamlike thinking. They still allow themselves to be tossed about by the illusory things of the world. They cannot see clearly that such things, in essence, are empty. Thus, they are constantly obstructed from attaining enlightenment due to the defilements. Both day and night, they cannot avoid such confusion.

Hence, this type of monastic, although appearing to be at peace, in truth has not yet become aware. Although they meditate, their thoughts run wild and are manipulated by the outside environment. Their thoughts are confused due to both inner and outer devils. They are unable to give rise to right mindfulness. Their thoughts are affected by the external environment. Their negative karma, born of ignorance, covers their original bright nature. They are obstructed and disturbed by the defilements. Although their bodies are in one place, who knows where their minds have roamed! Other people meditate and enter into a state of concentration. Their thoughts, however, are scattered, and they think of other things. They sit in the meditative posture, but they allow their good and bad thoughts – the two types of obstructions in attaining concentration – to pour into their minds in waves. They cannot attain peace.

There are a number of those who have gone forth from the household life, including some Dharma Teachers, who covet personal gain and the offerings of disciples and who devise ways to obtain money. In the end, they ruin their reputation and destroy their moral integrity. Those who ruin the reputation of Buddhist disciples are numerous. One often hears about such things.

Since monastics of this type have not yet cut off their defilements and are not permitted to fulfill their desire for love and affection, they then turn to seeking improper gain. It is just as Sakyamuni Buddha said. They will definitely turn to coveting personal gain and the offerings of disciples. Many monastics, under the pretense of furthering Buddhist affairs, cheat good Buddhist followers out of their money and property. Every now and then, some of them secretly embezzle such money or property. Some of them openly incite others to do bad. Some even brazenly steal money and property that would have been used in the furtherance of Buddhism.

There are also those who use the Buddha Dharma in other ways in order to cheat people. For example, there are many people who stand in front of certain Buddhist temples in Tibet. Holding an alms bowl, they force others to contribute money to them. Additionally, some people prostrate themselves a few times on the ground before another person, get up, and then thrust their alms bowl before this person, forcing him to contribute something.

There are many who covertly accumulate wealth. It can be said that they are experts in making money. In the end, they ruin the reputation of true monastics, who are the majority of monastics. They cause people of the world to think that all Dharma Teachers and monks cheat people out of their money, that all of those who have gone forth, whether true or false monastics, are birds of the same feather who hoodwink devout men and women out of their money.

These monastics do not abide by the precepts of the Buddha Dharma. They not only destroy themselves since they ultimately cannot become accomplished and will descend into the hell realm, they also destroy the Buddha Dharma.

When their lowly, foul conduct is revealed to the world, it not only causes a great uproar in Buddhist circles, it also causes some practitioners to be unable to practice in peace. These practitioners fall into a state of improper desires. It further causes people of the world to be unable to distinguish between who is true and who is false, who is sincere and who is fake. It causes people to think of leaving the Buddha Dharma. It stirs up prejudice towards even those who are upright monastics. It causes those who have roots of kindness to stay away from the Buddha Dharma. It thus cuts off people's interest to learn Buddhism and realize liberation.

If this continues, it will be a huge disaster for the Buddha Dharma and a great misfortune for living beings. If these practitioners who have gone forth do not immediately cease such behavior and repent, they will harm themselves by descending into the hell realm. This might not matter to them. However, causing countless sentient beings to stay painfully trapped in the burning house of the six realms of samsara for eons and eons without attaining liberation is an offense that is extremely worrisome. The consequences of such an offense are too dreadful to contemplate!

I have thus vowed not to accept any offerings. This demonstrates that one can cultivate oneself, propagate the Dharma, and benefit living beings without accepting offerings. It is easy for living beings to give rise to prejudicial thoughts that will cut off their interest to learn Buddhism and realize liberation. This is caused by some monastics who neglect the Dharma and violate the precepts.

It can be said that these people cannot possibly become accomplished. Even if they meditate and recite sutras every day just like others, their cultivation will always be superficial. It will not produce any results.

There is the following old story. A monk went to a certain village on his alms round. He constantly reminded himself that he must carefully abide by the precepts and must not violate the Buddha Dharma or proper etiquette. When he arrived before the door of a certain house, the woman of the house invited him inside in order to test whether he strictly abides by the precepts. She said that she greatly respects those who cultivate themselves and that she wanted to offer him the best roasted barley flour and cheese.

Who would have known that as soon as he stepped into the house, this woman immediately jumped up and locked the door shut! She then said, "There are three things – if you do any one of them, I will give you the key and let you go. Otherwise, do not even think of leaving here." This monk, having no other choice, could only ask, "Tell me, what three things?" The woman cunningly smiled and replied, "First, I have here a jar of wine. Drink it all. Second, on the table there is high quality mutton. Eat it. Third, if you and I engage in sexual relations, I will let you go. Of these three, you must do one. You choose!"

After the monk heard this, he was greatly surprised, since all three things involved violating the precepts. He was at his wits' end and did not know what to do. He thought of grabbing the key away from her, opening the door, and escaping. However, she was a woman, and such conduct was not befitting of practitioners who have gone forth from the household life. On the other hand, he feared that if he did not leave, people would certainly become suspicious.

He reasoned that of those three things, sexual misconduct and eating meat were both serious violations of the precepts, whereas drinking wine was the lightest violation of the precepts. After thinking it over again and again, he decided to drink the wine. After he drank the entire jar of wine, he was completely drunk. He could not tell the difference between north, south, east, and west. Thus, he ate all of the mutton and engaged in sexual misconduct with that woman. He committed all three violations of the precepts. One can imagine the consequences of such conduct!

This story has been passed down and disseminated widely within Buddhist circles. Its meaning is self-evident. It tells all practitioners, especially monastics, of the seriousness of violating the precepts. Not one of the precepts may be violated. Even if it appears to be an insignificant precept, one must be very scrupulous and absolutely must not violate it. If one violates one precept, then there will inevitably be a second violation. After one violates a relatively minor precept, there is the possibility of violating a major precept. If monastics cannot scrupulously abide by the precepts, then they may violate all of the precepts. In the end, they can only blame themselves and will reap what they have sown.

Thus, the practice of monastics who do not abide by the precepts will certainly be superficial. For them, becoming accomplished will be like the reflection of flowers on water or the appearance of the moon on a mirror – something that, in the end, they will not obtain.

There is the following saying in Buddhism: "At the door of hell are many monastics." Its meaning is what I just described. Those practitioners who have gone forth must be vigilant. They must be careful in upholding the precepts! Violating the precepts is committing an offense. Committing offenses will not lead one to the land of the Buddhas. Rather, it will lead one to the three evil realms to spend time in endless suffering!

6. For Laypersons, The Superficiality of Practicing Yet Not Diligently Cultivating Oneself

If those who cultivate themselves and learn Buddhism do not diligently practice and uphold the precepts, then becoming accomplished is nigh impossible. It will naturally be difficult for them to end the cycle of birth and death. Why do I refer only to laypersons when speaking of not diligently cultivating oneself, thus falling into superficial practice?

One can cultivate oneself and penetrate the Dharma through learning exoteric Dharma. One can also follow esoteric Dharma to become accomplished. I am here referring to laypersons who do not diligently cultivate themselves, since they are more casual in their cultivation. They are not like Buddhist monastics who have morning and evening classes to recite the sutras, meditate, and practice the Dharma. These monastics are all subject to the same rules. They are not allowed to talk their way out of practicing. They are not allowed to be indolent in their practices or simply not practice at all. Each temple has its own rules. Thus, rarely does the situation arise when the monastics of the temple do not practice the Dharma or do not practice meditation.

However, since laypersons cultivate themselves at home, there is no one to control them or make arrangements for them. Thus, it is sometimes quite possible that they fail to practice the Dharma, that they occasionally do not do their daily meditation, and that they indulge themselves in laxness.

Furthermore, in their worldly life, lay practitioners are often bound by things of the world. They are entangled by matters involving their family, society, children, relatives, and work. They might indulge in the enjoyment of song and dance. They might be busy with making a living. They might engage in negotiations with others over business matters. They might dine out with others on a social basis. They might be government officials who need to make connections. They might have fun or travel with their family.

After falling into these worldly entanglements, they sometimes forget about cultivation. They only care about dealing with the external situation before them. Thus, they might allow themselves to be controlled by the turmoil within their own minds. In such a situation, how can one speak of cultivation?

This shortcoming of being casual in their practice has negatively influenced laypersons. I am therefore asking laypersons who cultivate themselves at home to be even more careful and conscientious than those practitioners who have gone forth from the household life. Even more than monastics in Buddhist temples, these laypersons should have a mind aware of impermanence, a mind determined to break away from samsara. They should constantly sound the alarm of impermanence for themselves. They should constantly remind and admonish themselves not to become confused by matters of this world. They should always remember to diligently cultivate themselves!

If a lay practitioner simply wastes his time in worldly matters, like ordinary people of the world who do not understand the principles of cause and effect and impermanence, if he acts foolishly, causing himself to be tossed about every day in the bitter sea of karma, if his practice does not have liberating qualities to it, then although he has a liberating Dharma treasure in his hands, it is as if he lacked such treasure. To know the Buddha Dharma yet not practice according to the Buddha Dharma is equivalent to not having anything to fall back upon to become accomplished. One would then lose one's support in the effort to end suffering. This would be most pitiful.

Furthermore, due to the different karmic destiny of lay practitioners, they have received and practice their own particular precepts. However, every day they are attached to things of the world, are moved by the Eight Winds, and are troubled by worldly matters. They do not diligently practice the Buddha Dharma. Thus, they will inevitably violate the Dharma, even though they know the Dharma, and will inevitably violate the precepts, even though they know the precepts. This will further increase their offenses and cause them to fall into deeper degeneration. Naturally, for them, liberation is pushed into the limitless future.

When lay practitioners who truly want to end the cycle of birth and death practice the Dharma, they do so diligently. They are not confused by worldly things. One must strive to be unmoved by the Eight Winds. One can then vigorously cultivate oneself. Only then does one have the capacity to become a Great Bodhisattva or Great Holy One.

Laypersons who are not conscientious and cautious will naturally be unable to practice according to the precepts and cultivate themselves according to the Dharma. They often lack perseverance, like the fisherman who fishes for three days and idles about for the next two days while his nets are drying. They might sometimes have thoughts of becoming accomplished and enlightened and will then practice the Dharma. When they do not have such thoughts, they spend the passing time by having fun, forgetting about practicing the Buddha Dharma.

Day after day passes. The time will come when they become old and their remaining days are few. At such time, to sigh with regret over wasting this very hard to obtain rebirth as a human being will be of no use. It will then be too late to repent!

The key to attaining accomplishment in one's cultivation lies in whether such cultivation is true. One must truly cultivate oneself, not falsely cultivate oneself. One must become truly enlightened, not falsely "enlightened." One must be truly scrupulous, not falsely scrupulous. With trueness, a beginning practitioner can live in a muddy world yet not be sullied by it. If lay practitioners who cultivate themselves at home diligently practice, then how could it not be possible for them to attain the fruits and stages[30] and realize great accomplishment?

Therefore, laypersons who do not diligently cultivate themselves have fallen into a superficial practice. This is of no benefit whatsoever!

7. The Superficiality of Only Studying Principles But Not Practicing the Dharma

It is not a bad thing for those who learn Buddhism and cultivate themselves to study principles intensively. What is bad is that certain laypersons who are old pedants or novice scholars, as well as certain monks, stubbornly adhere to a so called "rigorous and pragmatic style of study" and therefore harbor an attitude of doubt in learning Buddhism. According to a saying of Confucius, if one only believes in book learning, then one might as well not have any books at all.

These people treat the Buddha Dharma as theoretical learning to be researched and investigated. They regard the field of Buddhist studies as containing a vast amount of art and culture to be studied. One frequently hears people say, "So and so is very well-learned in the study of the Buddha Dharma," or "So and so is an expert in the study of the Buddha Dharma." The people spoken of are totally ordinary people! This is very absurd. How could the Buddha Dharma be that which can be studied by ordinary people?

For example, in the Buddhas Bestowing Nectar Initiation, the Buddhas bestow nectar from the sky. How could such a thing be studied?

People who speak like this have truly fallen into a state of misunderstanding. They think that learning the Buddha Dharma is a matter of studying principles or words written on the surface of paper. They think that it is a matter of deliberating over each sentence and each word they read concerning Dharma principles. They might simply enjoy the correctness of grammar or syntax in a writing. They might become wrapped up in considering whether the wording is lofty or whether the principles are meticulously presented. They might focus totally upon whether the reading experience itself is interesting or whether the logic and reasoning of what they read are sound.

There is another type of practitioner who, unlike the above mentioned practitioners, does not analyze words or weigh theories. On the contrary, they are extremely pious toward the Buddha Dharma and are extremely respectful toward Sakyamuni Buddha. They believe that the Buddha Dharma is truly the most precious treasure for liberating living beings. The principles of the Dharma have caused them to attain some realization of the truth. They attempt to practice according to the writings and principles of the Buddha Dharma.

However, the light of these temporary realizations does not continuously shine upon their path of learning the Buddha Dharma. In a short period of time, they abandon the practice and mindset of true cultivation. They might painstakingly study the principles of the Dharma and might know the precepts and sutras thoroughly. They might be able to speak of such things eloquently and endlessly.

However, there is one oversight in all of this meticulousness: they do not seek true realization. They can only win the empty title of a sutra teacher. They do not have the slightest state of true realization. To merely speak the words of the sutras and commentaries as a means of overcoming the demonic hindrance of death is no different than a praying mantis trying to stop a chariot. One will still be unable to extricate oneself from the cycle of birth and death. How sad that they learned only empty words and wasted an opportunity to learn the Buddha Dharma!

Presently, there are a great many practitioners who have fallen into this type of empty cultivation. It can be said that they are dedicated and that they exert great effort. However, their dedication and effort are not applied toward true realization and true cultivation. Rather, their dedication and effort are applied toward thoroughly memorizing the sutras and commentaries. They exert effort in studying principles and building up theoretical knowledge. When asked about the meaning of the Dharma and the doctrines, their answers indicate how much intimate knowledge they have. They speak voluminously without any effort at all.

However, they will have nothing to do with carrying out the practice of the Dharma. They do not practice any Dharma and do not adhere to any precepts. They do not do their daily morning and evening meditation. They are not diligent in their daily lives. What is the meaning of the word *cultivation* to them? They think that cultivation means acting as if nothing matters at all. They forget about the Dharma that was transmitted to them by the Master. Only their superficial work do they perform very well. When they speak of the various principles of the Buddha Dharma, it very much seems that what they say is correct. They know many Dharma principles. On the surface, it appears as if they understand the Buddha Dharma better than anyone else, that they are more awesome than anyone else, and that they can be called great scholars of Buddhism. However, of what use is this type of ability?

In learning Buddhism and cultivating oneself, one must strive for true realization. Without the skills of true realization, Dharma power will not manifest at the Buddhist altar. They can only be regarded as sutra teachers. They are not engaging in true cultivation.

Not applying in one's actual practice the principles that one learns is equivalent to saying one thing yet doing another. When principles and real practice do not match, then the principles become like a tree without roots. One would be assuming a dignified air, which is useless. One would lack the skills of true cultivation, which enable one to withstand tests. One would only be floating on the surface of cultivation. How could there be any usefulness in such ways? No matter how great one's innate faculties are or how great one's merit is, if one does not, in a down-to-earth manner, deeply engage in actual practice, then it will not be possible to attain any accomplishment.

For example, take someone who has a doctorate degree and extensive knowledge of the sutras and commentaries. Such person can be said to possess profound learning. If that person applies what he learns, then he could be molded into a great talent. He could bring to society immense benefits! He could do so many things to benefit people!

However, if he only holds on to his books, does not learn about matters happening outside the windows of his house, only knows how to mechanically study dead books all day long, is confined to his books and does not do any work, does not handle any real matters, does not deeply enter real life, does not apply the knowledge he has learned in society or in a job, then no matter how extensive his knowledge and talents may be, since he does not put such knowledge and talents into practice, in fact he is a totally useless person to society. Even if he has a doctorate degree and is a person of profound and vast knowledge, it is of no use at all to society and its people. No matter how much one learns, no matter how talented one may be, if one does not apply what one learns, of what use is it? What benefit can this type of person bring to himself and others?

Learning the Buddha Dharma is also like this. Although one may be able to memorize the sutras thoroughly, if one does not actually practice the Dharma, if one only understands the meaning of the Dharma and does not in real earnest strive for realization, then one is mistaken. This would be a case of producing flowers and being showy but in the end bearing no fruit and having no substance.

This type of cultivation is not in accordance with the teachings of Sakyamuni Buddha and could not possibly be of any real usefulness. If one maintains this attitude in one's cultivation, then one will ultimately fail to succeed and will obtain nothing.

In cultivating oneself, should one learn theories? Of course one should learn theories! In learning the Buddha Dharma, one should first read many books on Buddhism. One should begin with learning the meaning of the Dharma and its principles. One should understand why one undertakes the practice, what the goal of learning the Buddha Dharma is, how to start practicing, how to act in accordance with Buddhism, how to adhere to the precepts, what precepts must be adhered to, why one's three karmas must correspond with the teachings of the Master, how one's three karmas can correspond with the teachings of the Master, etc. One definitely must not acknowledge someone as one's Master or learn Buddhism in a muddle-headed way. One must not ignorantly follow others in one's practice! If one does not even know why one should cultivate oneself but only knows how to blindly follow the crowd and echo the views of others, then in the end one will not even be able to find one's direction.

Therefore, those disciples who have just taken up Buddhism should start with reading Buddhist books. They should first understand the principles, make clear their direction, and comprehend how to learn and practice. Then they will be able to gradually attain awakening, and their minds will give rise to awareness and right mindfulness. In this way, they can begin to practice according to the Dharma and its principles. They should begin with theories and later practice according to the discourses and Dharma teachings of the Master. This is the correct sequence.

On the other hand, if one does not learn theories, does not understand the doctrines of Buddhism, does not even understand the most basic principles of the Dharma, and in a muddle-headed way attempts to deepen one's practice of the Buddha Dharma, then one will fall into ignorance. One will not possess correct understanding or correct views.

Therefore, in learning and practicing Buddhism, not to learn theories is unacceptable. It is also unacceptable to only learn theories. If one only learns theories and does not practice the Dharma, one's practice will become empty and false. If one only practices the Dharma and does not learn theories, one's practice will fall into a state of ignorance.

Thus, theory and practice should coincide with each other. One must seriously study theories and must also actually practice. When one understands the close interdependent relationship between learning theories and practicing the Dharma and then perfectly engages in both, and when one strictly abides by the teachings of Buddhism in one's daily practice, then naturally this will be of great use. In such case, ending the cycle of birth and death will be as easy as turning over one's hand!

8. The Superficiality of Practicing the Dharma Without Knowing the Essentials of the Dharma

Those disciples who are already following a Master and who have taken refuge in Buddhism[31] should practice according to the Dharma. They should truly practice according to the teachings of their Master. They should diligently practice every day. Only then can they overcome the great problem of birth and death.

However, some practitioners engage in only a superficial practice. Although appearing to be just like others in their practice of the Dharma – others practice the Dharma and they, too, practice the Dharma – in the end, they do not know why they practice the Dharma. They also do not know how to practice the Dharma. Furthermore, they do not understand the meaning and essentials of practicing the Dharma.

The two types of Dharma practitioners mentioned above are absolutely poles apart. One type is soaring on heavenly clouds, coming and going as they please. The other type is digging up a mountain here on earth, with sweat pouring down their backs!

For example, the superficial type of practioner is unclear about how he should do his daily meditation, how he should visualize, what level of meditation he presently is on, how he should handle supernormal states that arise, how he should tackle the problem of drowsiness, and how he should deal with an unfocused mind when it arises. He may put the nonessentials before the essentials, confuse one thing with another, or become very drowsy or scattered. When he should strengthen his correct understanding and give rise to right mindfulness, he nevertheless fails to give rise to right mindfulness, lowers his vigilance, and becomes lazy. As a result, he does not know what happened to his object of concentration.[32] When his concentration becomes unsteady, he should not rigidly apply force to strengthen his concentration.[33] Nevertheless, he rigidly applies force in the hope of strengthening his concentration, which only results in another loss of a meditative state.

He does not know how to do his daily meditation. When demonic impediments arise, he does not know which method to use in order to overcome them. He is completely devoid of clear concepts. How could such practice of the Dharma be anything other than very empty, like a worthless check?

Another example is the practice of the mandala. He does not know the essentials concerning how one should visualize when chanting each sentence of the mantra, what posture one should assume, or what mudra one should use. After the Master transmits to him the Dharma, telling him the purpose and method of visualizing, he may completely forget such things. Perhaps he will later become like a blockhead, knowing that he should put his hands in a certain mudra and that he should chant a certain mantra, but completely ignorant of the meaning of the mudra and visualization!

While his fellow disciples are practicing the mandala offering Dharma and visualizing Mt. Sumeru and the four great continents around it, resulting in great benefits and increased blessings, he is practicing with double the effort and half the results. Although he practices more diligently than others, he does not know why he still experiences fewer beneficial effects than others do, and why the fruits of his practice are still less obvious than those of others! At this time, he does not look within for the answer, but consoles himself by saying, "My negative karma is so heavy!"

This type of situation is not rare. A large number of practitioners should ponder the following: Although you are cultivating yourself, how much of the meaning of the Dharma you are practicing do you truly understand? Although you know how to practice, do you also know why you are practicing? When you are practicing the Dharma, do you truly understand thoroughly the principles of the Dharma you are practicing?

A certain portion of practitioners do not understand the meaning of their ongoing practice. That is, in reality, they basically do not understand the principles of the Dharma. Of course, they will as usual continue to produce negative karma, violate the precepts, and commit offenses, just like ordinary people.

For example, take the most basic principle of the four limitless states of mind. Basically, everyone can state what they are. It also seems as if everyone practices them. However, why is it that some of the day-to-day speech and conduct of so many disciples run totally counter to and fall so short of the four limitless states of mind?

There are those who say that they know that a certain type of behavior is not in accordance with the principles of the four limitless states of mind, that it is not in accordance with the standards of immeasurable loving kindness, compassion, sympathetic joy, and equanimity. However, they say that they are unable to restrain themselves from acting in such manner. Therefore, they continue to scold, insult, and argue with people. They say that they are unable to control their emotions and behavior.

If you ask them whether they know why one should practice the four limitless states of mind, they will say that they know. They will say, "It is because one should accumulate good merit in one's practice. The Buddha Master taught us to love all living beings. Insulting and scolding people would be creating negative karma. One would then have to bear the negative results. One would have to receive karmic retribution."

Does this type of disciple truly understand the meaning of cultivation? They do not! They do not understand at all the principles of the Dharma. Of course, it sounds as if they understand all of the principles. However, unfortunately, their understanding is superficial. It is not that they truly have a correct understanding of cultivation. Why is this so?

Those who truly understand the meaning of cultivation will certainly fear descending into one of the three lower realms and will thus give rise to a mind determined to leave samsara. They will be extremely frightened of creating negative karma and receiving karmic retribution. They will understand that in this human life, everything is like a vanishing dream, like bubbles or shadows, like smoke or clouds passing before the eyes. It is all just a mirage. They will not continue to be attached to any of the manifold false appearances in this human world.

How could they then become angry over something someone said to them? How could they then become so upset over a trifling wrong done to them? Those who truly understand the four limitless states of mind, those who are determined in their practice, will laugh off such things, thinking that they are trifling matters not worthy of mentioning! They know that to become attached to such things would be causing oneself vexation, creating negative karma, and starting a fire that would only burn oneself!

Everything in the world is a test to see how well one has cultivated oneself; whether one truly loves all living beings in the six realms just as one loves one's own parents; whether one is truly able to treat all living beings as if they were one's own family members; whether one is truly able to give rise to loving kindness, compassion, sympathetic joy, and equanimity toward all living beings; and whether one is able to view worldly things in a way that avoids them from becoming true impediments.

Thus, disciples who truly understand the principles of the Dharma will not engage in superficial cultivation. They will attempt to thoroughly understand things and thoroughly cultivate themselves. After understanding the external appearance of worldly phenomena, they will then delve into the deep essence of such phenomena, going to the root of things. Out of the most trifling of matters, they will become aware of the principle of impermanence with respect to all worldly matters. They will practice the Buddha Dharma with profound devoutness. They will indeed deeply penetrate the principles of the Buddha Dharma. They will resolve to break away from samsara and will seek a path of true liberation. On the path they take in their practice of the Buddha Dharma, they will follow a true Vajra Master and will arrive at the other shore – nirvana.

Such practitioners practice the Buddha Dharma with a true understanding of its principles. They are different from those Buddhist disciples who merely superficially practice without understanding the principles of the Buddha Dharma.

Of course, in the end, those practitioners who superficially practice the Dharma without delving deeply into its principles will experience endless suffering, since they will not achieve liberation. This includes some Dharma Teachers and Rinpoches. However, those practitioners who engage in true cultivation and who thoroughly understand the principles of the Dharma will undoubtedly become amazing people of great accomplishment!

9. The Superficiality of Teaching People While Not Acting in Accordance With the Dharma

There is an ancient saying: "One who wants to edify others must first edify himself. How can one edify others if he himself has not been edified?" Its meaning is that if one wants to teach others, one's own speech and conduct must first be correct. Only then will others follow one's teachings. Those who are teachers or professors must first themselves act in accordance with the principles they teach. If they themselves cannot so act, they are not qualified to ask that others so act.

Practicing and learning the Buddha Dharma is the same thing. If someone who cannot practice in accordance with the Dharma proceeds to teach others, then this only proves that he is not serious about cultivation, that he is only cultivating himself in a perfunctory manner, that he has fallen into superficial cultivation, that the foundation of his cultivation is empty, that he is engaging in false cultivation, and that he is not conscientiously and truly cultivating himself!

There are a great many people like this within Buddhism. In both exoteric and esoteric Dharma circles, there are practitioners engaging in such conduct. These people place strict demands upon others (fellow disciples or their own disciples), but they themselves do not act in accordance with the Dharma.

For example, some Buddhist disciples who are Vajra Masters teach their own disciples to practice enduring insults, to walk on the Bodhisattva path, and to be magnanimous toward others in all matters. They themselves, however, do not act in such a manner in their own practice. The most trifling matter will cause them to become indignant. Their minds become filled with anger and hatred. They are unable to endure the slightest grievance.

When they are walking down the street, if others are not careful and get in their way, they will begin to shout abuses at them. They will utter all kinds of offensive and contemptuous language. They will despise and want to beat these other people in order to allay their hatred.

When staying in a hotel, if the attendant is a little bit lazy or is on one occasion negligent, they will immediately jump up and become furious. They will raise a colossal uproar and will be unwilling to end the matter peacefully. They will somewhat relent only when they have forced the attendant to kneel down or have had him fired. Even then, they still feel quite aggrieved. Afterwards, they even feel quite pleased with themselves, thinking that they have showed others who is boss. They then frequently say, "I am so awe-inspiring!"

They do not even know that their behavior is completely out of line with that of a cultivator. They do not even match up with ordinary people. Before doing such things, why did they not think of what they told their own disciples, namely, that one must practice enduring insults and mistreatment? This type of person is quite pitiful!

As another example, they ask their disciples not to speak falsely to the Master, not to cheat the Vajra Master. However, they themselves brazenly speak numerous falsehoods to their own Vajra Master, take their own Master's instructions very casually, and speak many untrue words. In front of their Master, they make up lies. Then, in front of their own disciples, they use the name of their Master to brazenly fabricate falsehoods and twist facts. They use the name of their Master to accumulate wealth. In so doing, they do great damage to the reputation of their Master and undermine the reputation of Buddhist disciples!

They then rejoice in secret, thinking that their Master does not know about such things. How could their Master not know? Their Master simply pities them, does not wish to embarrass them so that they can continue on, and does not want to cut off their roots of kindness. Thus, their Master does not expose to other people their lies and tricks. They do not stop to think that if their Master does not know anything, how is it that whenever they violate an important precept, their Master will sternly reproach them and point out their misconduct?

It can be said that these people do not practice in accordance with the Dharma. Nevertheless, they teach their disciples to abide by the Dharma and the precepts. Is this not extremely absurd? When they are speaking falsehoods in front of their Master or behind their Master's back, do they remember the admonitions they gave to their own disciples? Do they still remember the teachings of their Master that they should not speak falsely to the Master?

Perhaps under the lure of worldly status, fame, gain, money, and selfish desires, they cannot remember at all! Could it more often than not be a case of them cheating themselves? They have a cavalier attitude. They pretend that they do not remember, or they simply do not view themselves as cultivators. They forget that they have gone through untold hardships. They forget that they vowed to end the cycle of birth and death. They forget that they vowed to extricate themselves from the flaming wheel of rebirth into one or another of the six realms of existence! Perhaps they will be able to remember when their karmic retribution arrives!

There are also some people who repeatedly teach their disciples to cultivate themselves well and practice the four limitless states of mind – that is, limitless loving-kindness, compassion, sympathetic joy, and equanimity. Now then, do they actually practice this?

They occasionally help fellow disciples who practiced the Dharma together with them in the beginning or fellow disciples who joined them later. However, most of the time they are just like Shylock, the crafty and greedy Venetian businessman, in their pursuit of personal profit. They are calculating and unwilling to make the smallest sacrifice. They haggle over every little thing. They are like this even to their own fellow practitioners! Yet, they feel that they are smarter than Jewish people, that they are more careful than women from Chaozhou, that businessmen from Jiangxi Province are no match for them, that shrewd men from Kangba cannot beat them, that their thoughts are more organized than the thoughts of Germans, etc.

There are some occasions when they could provide minor assistance to their own fellow disciples without harming their own interests in any way, yet they are unwilling to provide such assistance. They fear that others will surpass them, that others will be wealthier than they are, and that others will be more famous than they are.

Some of these people not only do not help others, on the contrary, they add to the misfortunes of those who are already unfortunate. They maliciously slander others in front of their Master. Some even instigate others to sabotage a certain person's business so that his business will fail.

Many cultivators practice the four limitless states of mind in such a manner! This is how they accumulate merit through practicing the four limitless states of mind! These are the four limitless states of mind that they constantly tell their disciples to practice! When they are teaching their disciples, do they stop to consider what type of four limitless states of mind they themselves are practicing?

There are also Buddhist disciples who, with good intent, tell their relatives to be good people and treat others compassionately. They tell them that this will bring about good karma. Of course, there is nothing wrong with saying such things. By saying such things, they are walking on the Bodhisattva path and are helping people.

However, they themselves often cannot do these things. They themselves often cannot practice according to the Dharma! They themselves also, either intentionally or unintentionally, harm others through words or conduct. They insult others or even harm their own present-life relatives. It is clear that they are filled with erroneous views and bad habits.

This causes their own relatives to harbor certain incorrect, prejudicial views. These relatives will no longer believe in people who learn the Buddha Dharma, thinking that those who learn the Buddha Dharma are no better than this, that they harm others all the same, and that they are not even as good as those who do not learn the Buddha Dharma! How could those who teach others, but whose own practice violates the principles that they teach, instill belief in others and convince others to practice the original, correct principles?

This is like a teacher who says, "Remember, all of you must cultivate good habits and develop high moral character. You must return all money that you find!" All of the students remember what he said. However, when he himself finds a huge check on the street, he stuffs it into his wallet in front of the watchful eyes of all of the students. One need not say more. After this, the students will not only be unmoved by anything this teacher says, but they will even view him with great contempt. One can imagine the future behavior of these students!

This same principle also applies to the Buddha Dharma! Many practitioners feel sad that their own relatives do not hear Dharma discourses. This may be caused by the negative karma of ignorance, which has existed throughout the many lives of those relatives. But these practitioners should carefully consider whether they scrupulously abide by the principles of the Buddha Dharma in their own practice and whether they meet the standards of a Buddhist disciple. When they make demands on others, are they themselves acting correctly? If their own practice is not even in accord with the Dharma, how can they make demands on others?

This point should especially be borne in mind by Vajra Masters who are practicing and learning the Buddha Dharma! There are Vajra Masters who themselves cannot even practice according to the teachings of the Dharma yet who teach others the principles of the Buddha Dharma and demand of others that they practice according to these principles. Is it not sheer hypocrisy and utterly preposterous for them to ask their disciples to abide by the precepts, principles, and rules of the Buddha Dharma when they themselves do not do so?

Under the various enticements of worldly greed and desire, a number of Vajra Masters cannot maintain an open and aboveboard practice in which they themselves set an example for others. On the contrary, they themselves test the Dharma and in so doing continue to degenerate!

They teach their disciples not to be greedy, but their own hearts are filled with greed. They teach their disciples not to speak falsely to the Master or the Buddhas and Bodhisattvas, but they themselves often speak falsely to their Master. They teach their disciples not to engage in sexual misconduct, but they themselves give rise to lascivious, evil thoughts, abandon themselves to passion, and behave recklessly. They teach their disciples not to seek fame or profit, but they themselves yearn for and scramble after worldly fame and profit. They teach their disciples not to harm living beings, but they themselves brazenly harm and kill living beings. They teach their disciples not to break their vows, but they themselves do not fulfill their own vows. They break all of their vows and all of the precepts. They teach their disciples not to gamble, but they themselves go to casinos and gamble to their hearts' content. They even think that if they recite a mantra, they can win money. They totally forget the principle of cause and effect.

These are the same practitioners who teach their disciples to cultivate themselves well and abide by the Dharma and precepts, but who themselves do not practice according to the Dharma and precepts! They have totally failed to realize that being a Vajra Master in this life is the result of vigorous and diligent practice throughout many lives and eons during which they accumulated merit and good karma. If such marvelous underlying conditions did not exist, they would not be qualified to be Vajra Masters to serve living beings!

If a Vajra Master does not practice according to the principles and rules of the Dharma, but instead is deluded by karmic impediments, is attached to the illusions of this world, does not think of improving himself, only craves enjoyment, behaves degenerately, and produces much negative karma, then he will not only quickly destroy all of the merit he has accumulated throughout many lives, but he will also undoubtedly descend into the hell realm of uninterrupted suffering from having destroyed the interest of many people to learn Buddhism and realize liberation.

It can be said that the practice of those who do not themselves act according to the Dharma, yet who teach others, is merely superficial. They do not practice in order to accomplish ending the cycle of birth and death. Thus, this type of practice is unacceptable, and those practitioners are teaching erroneous views. Practitioners who truly seek to end the cycle of birth and death must not allow their practice to become like this type of superficial and erroneous practice!

Dharma King Yangwo Yisinubu said, "If one is to be a model of virtue for others, one's actions must match one's thoughts and one must do only what is good. Such person's subordinates will then emulate him. If the substance of what one teaches differs from what one thinks, then such person's students will leave him." These words truly deserve deep pondering by all practitioners!

10. The Superficiality of Instructing Others When One's Own Actions Do Not Match One's Words

One's own actions not matching with one's words means that one's deeds and one's words are contrary to each other or unrelated. The practice of those whose actions do not match their words, yet who instruct others, is superficial. Most of these people are shallow practitioners who do not have any real skills yet who like to instruct others wherever they go. In today's world, they are quite common.

A divergence between one's words and one's actions is a major malady among practitioners in today's world. If a practitioner does not combine theory with concrete practice and if his three karmas of body, speech, and mind do not totally correspond with the teachings of the Acarya Master, then his practice will be of no use.

These days, there are many practitioners who have the habit of using inflated speech but who take no action. They think that as long as their speech and mind correspond with the teachings of the Acarya Master, then that is enough. They are even quite proud of themselves and go around instructing others, telling them how they should do this and how they should do that. In fact, they themselves have already completely fallen into a state of ignorance. How are they able to instruct others? It can only be said that they cannot even save themselves!

There are a number of people who have become Buddhist disciples and who follow a Vajra Master. They are quite happy. At all occasions, they show great respect towards the Master. They also exhort others to follow Buddhism and the Master. They tell others how amazing the Master is and how one can have such good fortune by following the Master. They urge others to listen to the Master's words. They recount to others things that the Master said and did. They tell others how to do certain things in life, what things they should do, and what things they cannot do. All of this is done to show what devout, conscientious, and qualified practitioners they are.

However, perhaps because of ignorance, perhaps because of the evil influence of erroneous views, they themselves are unable to strictly abide by the rules of the Buddha Dharma. They occasionally violate the precepts and rules. They even sometimes half believe and half doubt the Buddha Dharma. In short, in various ways they manifest that their actions do not match their words. From this, one can discern whether their cultivation is true and sincere or superficial. It is obvious that this type of practice, where one's actions do not match one's words, yet one instructs others, is superficial and of no benefit.

Having summarized the ten types of superficial practice, each practitioner can compare them against his own practice. If one does not have any of these superficialities in one's practice, then one is a practitioner who is truly practicing the correct Dharma. If one's conduct includes any of these ten types of superficialities, then one should close this book and deeply introspect. Otherwise, one will experience the suffering of degeneracy from having cheated oneself and others!

Hence, we should deeply ponder why, after practicing my discourses entitled *The Dharma of Concentration and Visualization Essential for Enlightenment*, some people receive immense benefits by realizing great wisdom and great supernormal powers. However, some cannot even enter the fourth or fifth stages of meditation, let alone the ninth stage. The problem lies in one or more of the principles on which I just gave a discourse. After knowing what illness one has contracted, one should use medicine to cure it. I have already given you the prescription. Obtaining and using the medicine is up to you!

Chapter Four

SEEKING ENLIGHTENMENT AND WORLDLY AFFAIRS

MOST PRACTITIONERS HAVE a misguided conception. They feel that it is difficult to attain enlightenment while being immersed in worldly affairs. There is a common Chinese saying that one cannot have both fish and bear's paws.[34] They feel that holiness and worldliness are mutually exclusive and that one cannot consider both at the same time. It is as if the two are separated by a huge gap, that they are as different as a swallow and a swan, as different as towering green mountains and Erhai Lake.[35]

If this is the limited conception of practitioners of Hinayana Buddhism due to their limited capacity, then we will not reproach them. However, there are numerous followers of Mahayana Buddhism who are walking on the Bodhisattva path and who also make this clear distinction. They separate seeking enlightenment and handling worldly affairs. Such people have truly not attained enlightenment.

There are a great number of these people. Because of this one narrow viewpoint, this one misconception, they are far astray! I am afraid that by adhering to such a viewpoint, they will not realize any great accomplishment. Thus, I am truly quite worried! Hence, I will briefly discuss this subject.

There are many defects in the practice of a great number of practitioners of Mahayana Buddhism due to their lack of correct understanding and their unfamiliarity with the precise meaning of the Dharma. For example, ordinary practitioners do not understand that the defilements are the same as enlightenment.[36] Since they adhere to the viewpoint that worldly affairs and seeking enlightenment are poles apart, to them there is only worldly meaning to one's daily activities, such as walking, standing, sitting, and lying down. They do not view such activities as methods of cultivation. Rather, they give rise to various reckless thoughts. They think that Zen (Chan) Buddhism is dry, uninteresting, and as plain as water.

Although they participate in daily meditation with others, their minds wander somewhere else. They are just like the monk who perfunctorily tolls the bell every day. They simply muddle along.

They view making a living through their own efforts by opening up land for farming as being nothing other than a worldly matter that is not related to spiritual liberation. They reluctantly cook rice, carry water, and sweep inside and outside, since they have no other choice.

They are very eager to ascend to the inner or outer palace of the Tusita Heaven in one big leap. They view these types of daily matters as delaying their cultivation and their quest for enlightenment. Thus, these matters are quite a nuisance to them. But if they hear that a Great Virtuous One or eminent monk will be speaking on the sutras or Dharma or will be transmitting the Dharma, they become exuberant, thinking that only at such time would they be cultivating themselves.

Perhaps they only have the feeling of seeking enlightenment when they are meditating or contemplating the answers to koans.[37] To them, all of the rest of their time is spent engaging in ordinary activities about which they are indifferent. They feel that their quarreling with people and having reckless thoughts are not at all related to cultivation and seeking enlightenment!

Those who have attained great accomplishment instruct their disciples to cultivate themselves in ordinary worldly affairs. Yet, the disciples cannot figure out why they must do this. They think, "What do other people mean by, 'Eating is Zen, sleeping is Zen, the headboard of the bed is Zen, and wearing shoes is Zen'? How can this be? It obviously does not make sense and is groundless!" They then secretly speculate, "I think it must be that Master so-and-so does not want to transmit his own Buddha Dharma to me and so purposefully made these things up to trouble me."

They engage in such speculation concerning their Master and thereby become angry. They feel indignant but do not dare speak out. There are thus many instances of such people receiving the precepts and then breaking them. They do not realize the truth and are indeed ignorant.

These people of the Zen school who have not yet realized the truth engage in a type of practice that distinguishes between worldly affairs and seeking enlightenment. They do not know that the Buddha Dharma originated from worldly Dharma.[38] If one leaves behind worldly Dharma, then there is no

Buddha Dharma. Thus, there is no such thing as supra-mundane or non-worldly Dharma. This is a type of situation within the Zen school.

I have seen this type of Buddhist disciple myself. One day I ran across a Buddhist disciple who had violated 50 precepts in his practice. I decided to teach him. I sighed over the prospect that he would never amount to anything. In order to help him realize the truth, I ordered him to hold in his hands a bowl of water. The bowl was filled to the brim with water. If he was not careful, the water would spill over. I ordered him to carry this bowl of water while walking back and forth between the opposite walls of the room. He was not allowed to spill the water. I truly hoped that through a focused mind and in a state of non-attachment he would be able to understand his original nature.

Although he was very frightened, he dare not oppose my order. With utmost care, he carried the bowl back and forth a few times. His clothes were wet with sweat. Fortunately, the water did not spill over.

I ordered him to stop and asked, "With respect to what I have asked you to do, do you understand my intent?" Nodding his head several times, he answered, "I understand." I was secretly pleased and breathed a sigh of relief that the young man was worth teaching. I asked him, "What was my intent?" He replied, "I totally understand the Holy Mother Master's intent. It was to show me that I must do things carefully so as not to violate the precepts. Otherwise, I will certainly be punished. Having me carry this large bowl of water was a method used by the Mother to teach me." When he finished speaking, he respectfully kowtowed and thanked me for my teachings.

His response greatly disappointed me. I could only sigh with regret over his dimwittedness. I do not have any other method to save him. I can only educate him according to the circumstances that appear at the time.

On another day, a different disciple violated the Samaya Precepts for the first time. I used the same method as before and ordered him to carry water back and forth. He went back and forth three times. He then lifted the bowl of water to the top of his head and stood there motionlessly.

I asked him why he was standing there motionlessly. The disciple answered, "The Master ordered me to carry water. There is no truth in the water itself. At this time, there is also no water in my mind. Truth is in all places."

I then ordered him to show this truth for me to see. The disciple said, "This is where the truth is realized. My respected Master can see. However, if you have the thought of seeing the truth, then the truth has long since dissolved. If you cannot see the truth, then it is like carrying a bowl of water."

I then asked, "What about lifting the bowl to the top of your head?" The disciple answered, "That was to show non-attachment to being a monk." I said, "A monk has no hair on his head." The disciple replied, "According to my viewpoint, there is no head." I asked, "How could you lift the bowl to the top of your head without a head?" The disciple responded, "This is an illusory manifestation of causes and conditions." I said, "That which manifests may also be real." The disciple said, "It is the wonderful manifestation of true void, which is true bliss." I inquired, "Why did you obtain bliss?" The disciple answered, "I obtained bliss from not obtaining." When he finished speaking, he knelt on the ground and prostrated himself.

The realization of this disciple is truly worthy of my being happy. However, when the other disciple who carried water was talking to me about this incident, he shook his head and sighed over his own foolishness. When I heard him sigh, I laughed heartily!

This type of suspicion toward one's Master truly happens frequently and is not at all surprising. One cannot hold on to such views. This shows the low innate capacity of people in general. When one's negative karma manifests, one does not realize all of the care and thought that the Master has expended on his disciples. One even has biased views toward the Master, mistakenly believing that the Master is not kind and suspecting that the Master is narrow-minded. On the other hand, those who are able to attain enlightenment feel deep gratitude in their hearts toward the Master!

I just digressed. I was previously speaking about how there are followers of the Zen school who give rise to certain misconceptions concerning the seeking of enlightenment due to their Master's method of teaching. Thus, I expressed my feelings about this with examples applicable to many people. I will not go into any more details about this subject at this point. Of course, Zen practitioners are not the only ones who hold such misconceptions. There are also many lay practitioners with such misconceptions.

There are countless lay practitioners who cannot attain enlightenment. I will not speak about those false cultivators who use the pretense of cultivation to cheat people. I will only speak about those practitioners who have not yet attained enlightenment and who diligently practice, but who have fallen into misconceptions.

Type One:

This type of lay practitioner exerts a good deal of effort and treasures every spare moment he has to practice. Whenever he has an opportunity or free time, he will sit down and begin to meditate, naturally entering into a state of concentration. However, when he gets up from his sitting and enters the hubbub of worldly life, he roars out orders, is overbearing, and does whatever he pleases. After a while, he fully experiences the obstructions produced by his defilements and cannot help becoming irascible.

Thus, every time he sees the Master he says, "Master, I must go to a temple on a mountain to cultivate myself. There, I would not speak or think. This way I would not produce any negative karma. In handling worldly matters, each day I inevitably produce a great deal of negative karma. I totally wipe out all of my merit. If I continue in this manner, I will surely never become accomplished."

There are also lay practitioners who say, "Master, I must get a divorce and leave my family so that I can totally dedicate myself to cultivation. Only then will I be able to attain enlightenment." In fact, enlightenment itself has already become a hindrance to this type of disciple. He has taken on an erroneous view. In seeking the Buddha Dharma, if one leaves worldly Dharma, one will never be able to attain enlightenment.

Those who think in this way and those who engage in such practices are in fact dismissing the teachings of Sakyamuni Buddha that the laity can also engage in cultivation. These people have not yet attained enlightenment.

Type Two:

This type of lay practitioner exerts a good deal of effort, just like the previous type. He also seizes every moment to practice. He engages in a race with impermanence. He makes use of time to seek enlightenment and learn the Dharma, hoping that he will realize enlightenment in this very life, that he will at once become a Buddha. He seriously practices daily meditation and experiences numerous supernormal states.

He spares no effort in handling Buddhist matters that the Master orders him to handle. He has his own personal view that since he is handling Buddhist matters, he must handle them well by doing his level best. Although he feels that handling these worldly matters will unavoidably delay his cultivation, since it was the Master who assigned him such matters, he feels that he naturally must handle them well. He feels that even if it will delay his cultivation, he will handle them well.

As far as he is concerned, doing daily meditation is cultivation in the real sense, and listening to the lectures of the Master is seeking enlightenment. He feels that only by listening more and more to the teachings of the Master, only by focusing his time and efforts on listening to the Dharma and on meditating, can he realize enlightenment sooner.

This type of person is also a Buddhist disciple who is seeking enlightenment.

Type Three:

This type of practitioner seems to be different from the previous two types. They have heard a good deal about the teachings. Thus, they know that cultivation is not only composed of meditation and listening to the Dharma. They know that one's daily activities of walking, standing, sitting, and lying down are all part of cultivation. They know that only if one's three karmas of body, speech, and mind are good is one correctly seeking enlightenment. They know these things, but do not know why they are so. They hear these principles, but in the end do not know how to explain why they are so. Thus, although on the surface it appears that they do things very carefully, in their heart of hearts, they still sigh heavily over the rapid passage of time and how death is fast approaching. They wish that they could use all of their time to meditate and practice tantra, but they never pay attention to the effects of their daily conduct, speech, and thoughts.

Therefore, in their practice they often violate the Dharma precepts and rules. When conducting themselves in society, they do not scrupulously uphold the principle that helping others is fundamental. Rather, they harm others to benefit themselves. When harming others, they become quite pleased with themselves.

Thinking that those who learn Buddhism are better than others, they are extremely arrogant and complacent. Wherever they are, they act in an exceedingly proud, insolent, and overbearing manner. They swagger before others, thinking that they are inimitable and that people should hold them in awe. None of these practices should be engaged in by Buddhist disciples!

They constantly engage in unwholesome conduct, speech, and thoughts. They have a rather large number of bad attributes. They think that one or two instances of what they consider to be insignificant wrongdoing, such as pilferage or a small violation of a minor rule, is acceptable.

There are even more practitioners who have no regard for basic precepts and who violate the precept that prohibits sexual misconduct. Those who have a wife and children or those who are themselves somebody's wife, under the pretext of work or entertainment, promiscuously engage in sexual relations with various women and men in society. They do not have the concept of ethics or morality. They turn a blind eye to the precepts of the Buddha Dharma with which they are familiar. They take such a solemn thing as learning the Buddha Dharma to be a trifling matter.

They relegate to the back of their minds the fundamental requirement of Buddhist disciples to follow goodness in their conduct, speech, and thoughts. Because they crave momentary pleasure or certain unfair gains, they violate the precept prohibiting sexual misconduct and many other precepts. They have cavalier attitude. They forgive themselves. They would never dream that in fact they are engaging in conduct that debases themselves, that will cause them ongoing pain for many lives and eons, and that will cause them afflictions from which they will be unable to extricate themselves!

What is even more frightful is that the three lower, evil realms are waiting for them. Even if they sit down to practice meditation, they will not be able to enter into concentration. Their reckless thoughts will increase, nothing else!

These people consider their daily conduct, speech, and thoughts to be unrelated to cultivation and seeking enlightenment. With such a practice, they will not become accomplished and end the cycle of birth and death. Their search for enlightenment will naturally end unsuccessfully, without having benefited them at all.

If the fruits of one's practice do not match one's goals in seeking enlightenment, it is because the practitioner falls into one or more of the above-described three categories. Conduct falling into one or more of those three categories emanates from the practitioner's not yet understanding that seeking enlightenment and handling worldly affairs are one and the same and that the defilements are the same as enlightenment. Since they do not understand this, they engage in all kinds of reckless behavior. They clearly distinguish between seeking enlightenment and handling worldly affairs. They treat the two as if they were totally separate. They are unable to view them as one and the same. They are unable to conduct worldly affairs in a state of great enlightenment as a way of manifesting their realization of the truth.

With respect to lay practitioners, this truly is a major problem. It is something that they should view as a major taboo! When one thinks in such fashion, one cannot truly cultivate oneself and truly seek enlightenment. Even one's worldly life becomes a complete mess. One cannot carry out the practice of a cultivator, and one ultimately strays far from the correct path of the Buddha Dharma!

An ancient virtuous one said, "When eating peanuts, all people know that the taste is good. If one eats peanuts without knowing the taste, he might be called wooden. If one speaks of how good the taste is, then he would be attached to form, sound, smell, taste, bodily sensations, and mental objects. His six bases would be moved by external conditions, and he would be an ordinary person." Can you tell me why this is the case?

This saying about eating peanuts truly contains the principle of how to learn Buddhism and seek enlightenment. With respect to this trifling worldly matter of eating peanuts, those with great understanding will have a special appreciation of its meaning. Those with medium understanding will have a certain type of insight. Those who do not understand will have a viewpoint of non-understanding. How should one explain each of these levels of understanding?

Those who do not understand or who have only a slight understanding have fallen into the extreme viewpoint of eternalism.[39] Perhaps they are attached to the savory taste of peanuts and, through the five aggregates, their minds are moved. They thus manifest an ordinary person's state of mind. When one speaks of eating peanuts, their eighth consciousness[40] and their sense organs become all stirred up. Stored memories from their eighth consciousness arise, which recognize that the taste is good. When their ears hear how good the peanuts taste, when their eyes see the form of the peanuts and they know how good the taste will be, when their noses smell the fragrance of the peanuts, when their tongues taste the peanuts and it feels pleasant, their various kinds of consciousness are all moved, and they become attached to the objects of their sense organs. They do not have correct awareness. They only manifest the state of an ordinary person.

There are people who know that one who is attached to something is an ordinary person. Thus, although they are not attached to the savory taste, they are just like wood, not knowing at all that the taste is savory. It is as if they are drinking water or chewing wax. They are like dry rocks. They eat something without knowing its flavor and smell something without knowing its fragrance. This type of mindset is also that of an ignorant person. It is not the middle way. It is one of two extremes. Thus, it is not the correct way! They, too, are ordinary people.

These two types of mindsets are both unacceptable! Since ordinary people do not view their six bases as being empty, the external objects corresponding to their six bases[41] are also not viewed as being empty. They are thus attached to and moved by external conditions. They are attached to external objects and thereby contaminate their sense organs. They cannot purify their concepts concerning their sense organs and the corresponding external objects. Thus, obstructions that originate from mental impurity and that are experienced by ordinary people appear in their lives. They are unable to look within themselves and thoroughly realize the silent and still nature of their minds. They are unable to thoroughly realize the Dharma that nothingness and somethingness are not different.

Those with great understanding know that the flavor is savory, yet they are not attached to the savory flavor. They know that it is not a case of there being no flavor. They also know that it is not a case of there being flavor. That is to say, they know that the taste is not savory and also that it is not unsavory. Just like they perform their duties to save living beings, they know that the taste is savory but are not attached to it.[42] They know that all manifested things are true emptiness in essence. In a state of utter tranquility, they abide in emptiness but are not attached to emptiness. Thus, to them true emptiness or non-being is the same as wonderful existence or being! They do not cling to emptiness nor become attached to form. They thus avoid the two extreme viewpoints of total annihilation and perpetual existence. They realize reality but do not have the thought of realizing anything.

Thus, knowing how to eat peanuts is also a matter of seeking enlightenment. One speaks of eating peanuts in the mundane sense, which is also the holy sense. It is all one and the same. There is no distinction. If one sees the Dharma body, which is the nature of emptiness, then one can realize that the defilements are the same as enlightenment.

Therefore, seeking enlightenment is thus. Eating peanuts is also thus! As such, this is the meaning of the one, undivided truth of the Dharma!

It can be said that the principle for handling worldly affairs is also thus. It is all the same undivided truth. One must not fall into one or another of the two extreme viewpoints – total annihilation and perpetual existence. By maintaining the viewpoint of the middle way, one will truly see that there is no distinction between the mundane and the holy, between worldly Dharma and the Dharma that liberates one from this world. Additionally, one will not have the relative concepts or competing notions of handling worldly affairs and seeking enlightenment.

One who truly renounces this world can live within the hubbub and tumult of this world yet still maintain the state of mind of one who renounces this world. As for one who does not have the state of mind of one who has renounced this world, even if he flees to a wild forest or remote mountains, he will still be an ordinary person. It is a matter of whether one has attained enlightenment, whether one has understood the truth.

Those who do not yet understand the truth do not know that handling mundane matters and seeking enlightenment are one and the same. Such people are attached to the various mundane matters that they handle. Their sense organs become contaminated by external objects. They do not know how to attain purity. Thus, if they do not lean too much to the left, then they lean too much to the right.

Perhaps they think that they can live in the mundane world, but that if they abandon their families, give up their property, act in an extreme way, do not inquire into any matters, do not think about anything, do not say anything, and become like a knot on an elm tree, they will then be able to attain purity. This method of seeking enlightenment is truly an erroneous method.

Perhaps they practice within the mundane world but are deeply entrapped as a result of all of their karma producing deeds. They are attached to trifling details concerning what they do, say, and think. This attachment contaminates and obstructs them. Nevertheless, they expect to realize enlightenment by relying on short daily periods of meditation.

These types of people have yet to understand the truth. Naturally, they cannot be said to have realized enlightenment.

However, if one understands the truth but does not act according to the principles of the Dharma and does not follow the precepts, then one is still no different from one who has not yet realized enlightenment. This is exactly what is meant by the saying, "Those who understand do not necessarily see, and those who see do not necessarily realize enlightenment."

Thus, although they clearly understand principles, they are still unable to have control over their own life and death. One cannot attain true peace by simply understanding. One's speech and actions must be consistent and one must seek true realization. Only then will the enlightenment one has attained be real.

However, in today's world there are many people who have incorrect views and who steal fame by deceiving the public. They say things such as, "When one's thoughts have not yet reached the state of understanding, one is an ordinary person. After one's thoughts reach the state of understanding, one becomes a holy person." Or they will say, "As soon as one reaches the state of understanding, one has control over life and death." All of these are erroneous views. Such statements are nonsense spoken by those who have yet to realize enlightenment.

With respect to those who understand, in the final analysis, it is a matter of their understanding principles. They engage in empty talk and theorizing. They do not possess true skills. Even though they know that they should not be attached to anything, that they should not be attached to their continually flowing thoughts, they are not necessarily able to put into practice this true principle.

Thus, they must add to this knowledge of principles true realization. They must realize the state of reality. Only then will they be able to be liberated from the cycle of birth and death and attain complete freedom and control.

If a person believes that as soon as he understands principles he will then be able to end the cycle of birth and death, then such person will easily fall into dissipation, loss of the way to liberation, and a state of nihilism.[43] Such person will not practice any Dharma and will hold tightly to Dharma principles. He will consider himself to be a Buddha and will not feel the need to continue to diligently cultivate himself. He will thus easily violate the precept that prohibits one from telling others that one has attained true realization and true accomplishment when one has not. In the end, he will fall into degeneration and will lose more than he gains.

Thus, practitioners should know that understanding principles is the prerequisite for enlightenment. Only after a person understands principles is it possible for that person to attain enlightenment.

On the other hand, one who seeks the Dharma without understanding principles will easily fall into a state of ignorance. He will be like one who wants to enter into a room to find a treasure but does not know where the entrance is and does not know what the treasure looks like. Thus, he will linger about without being able to enter through the door. Even if he is able to enter the room, he will still be unable to discover the treasure. In the end, he will just bang his head against the walls and come out with a bleeding and bruised head, without accomplishing his goal. He will be unable to find the treasure.

But one who understands principles is like a person who has already found the door leading to this treasure and who knows what the treasure looks like. All that he needs to do is exert further effort, open the door, and walk inside. He will then be able to take away this treasure.

Thus, to realize enlightenment, it is absolutely necessary for one to have thoroughly understood principles. However, one must not be attached to mere understanding of principles. There are some practitioners who understand principles but who have fallen into a state of arrogance. They take the mere understanding of principles as something that they can rely upon to end the cycle of birth and death and do not practice true cultivation. Thus, in the end, they are unable to find the treasure and obtain control over life and death.

People of former times said, "Those who have great doubts (questions) will obtain great understanding. Those who have small doubts (questions) will obtain small understanding. Those who have no doubts (questions) will not obtain any understanding."

Only by awakening to the true meaning of the one undivided truth and by turning away from all external objects and looking within oneself, is one able to attain accomplishment. One is said to have attained something. In truth, there is no attainment. To speak of attaining something is an expedient method of communicating. It is the same with the three types of prajna. Prajna obtained through the written word and prajna obtained through contemplating reality are both cultivated in order to realize the prajna of ultimate reality. When practitioners seek the realization of prajna, they are really seeking the realization of the prajna of ultimate reality. They should not just seek prajna obtained through the written word and prajna obtained through contemplating reality.

Thus, one achieves prajna obtained through the written word and prajna obtained through contemplating reality in order to realize the prajna of ultimate reality. The first two types of prajna are the prerequisites for the last type of prajna. It is the same with understanding principles and true realization. Only when the prerequisite of understanding principles is met can one achieve true realization.

Why should one master prajna obtained through the written word and prajna obtained through contemplating reality? Knowing how essential these two types of prajna are, one will first master the principles contained within the written word prajna. One will know how to apply this prajna. One will know that one must realize the prajna of ultimate reality in order to end the cycle of birth and death. Mastery of principles will cause the practitioner to attain a certain understanding or awareness.

Having attained such understanding or awareness, one must begin to practice according to the prajna one has obtained through the written word. One must then cultivate prajna obtained through contemplating reality. Through such contemplation, one can then attain the state of realization of ultimate reality. I speak of attaining such state. In fact, there is no such state to attain. This is what is meant by the path of one undivided truth.

When one realizes ultimate reality, one totally understands the principle that true emptiness or non-being is the same as wonderful existence or being. In such a state, one can abide in total peace and freedom. One then knows that to abide in true emptiness is not a matter of abiding in a dull type of emptiness, like a piece of wood or a rock. It is also not total emptiness where there is absolutely nothing. Realizing ultimate reality, one does not ignore all form and only think of emptiness. Nor does one ignore emptiness and only think of form. Form and emptiness are one and the same. This is what is meant by the oneness or sameness of emptiness and somethingness.

When the practitioner realizes these principles, he will naturally and thoroughly perceive what is meant by prajna. In fact, there has never been prajna obtained through the written word. Also, there is no Dharma of prajna. Thus, there is no prajna that can be realized. These names were established simply as an expedient method to enable people to attain understanding or awareness.

Thus, what enlightenment is there to seek? How is there enlightenment that must be realized? The defilements are the same as enlightenment. Originally, there are no defilements and there is no enlightenment. When one realizes this, one does not hold the concept of a permanent self or individual soul that is separate from others. Also, unlike the Arhat, one is not attached to the Dharma of liberation. When one is not attached to the concept of self and the Dharma of liberation, then one has already become a person of great accomplishment.

Thus, those practitioners who have not attained enlightenment might want to seek out a forest in which they can leave all worldly matters. However, their conduct must be in accord with *Dharma That Every Buddhist Must Follow* on which I am now giving discourses. They must cultivate themselves according to the principles contained therein.

Attempting to seek enlightenment by not speaking or thinking at all and by not involving oneself in any way with worldly matters is unwise. Being attached to meditating as the only way to end the cycle of birth and death, being attached to practicing the Great and Perfect Empty Brightness Dharma or the Qie Jia Tuo Ga Dharma, solely desiring to transform oneself into the rainbow body through manipulation of energy channels and energy points, or being completely indifferent to violating the Dharma and precepts in one's daily conduct, speech, and thoughts, are all unenlightened actions. Those who engage in such actions have already fallen into practicing one of the two extreme viewpoints. They have not understood the oneness or sameness of emptiness and somethingness.

They should know that since the Buddha Dharma exists within this very world, full enlightenment must include awareness of the ultimate realities of this world. To speak of the Buddha Dharma without being concerned with worldly matters would be engaging in empty and incorrect talk. To handle only Buddhist matters while separating oneself from all worldly matters is also an empty and mistaken practice. To think of handling ordinary worldly matters and practicing the Buddha Dharma as being opposite to each other is totally against the teachings of Sakyamuni Buddha that householders or laypersons are also able to cultivate themselves. This is truly an erroneous viewpoint.

This is especially true in the practice of tantra, which is not like Zen Buddhism in which the practitioners leave the world to cultivate themselves. Much of the practice of tantra is carried out within the world. The practitioner seeks the Dharma and walks on the path of truth while remaining in the mundane world. There is no such thing as separating oneself from worldly matters in order to seek the Dharma by which one can liberate oneself from this world.

True practitioners who have attained total awareness can practice anywhere at all without being moved or influenced by external conditions. They will not change their practice based upon where they may be. They understand and are at ease. They abide in peace. Thus, to them, seeking enlightenment is not difficult!

Having said such things today, I am not instructing practitioners not to exert effort or not to be energetic in their future practice. I am not saying that seeking enlightenment means only caring about one's worldly conduct. I am not saying that one need not care about how many defilements one gives rise to or that one need not pay attention to how many attachments one has since, after all, the defilements are the same as enlightenment and worldly Dharma is the same as non-worldly Dharma! Any practitioner who has such an interpretation has truly fallen into ignorance and has an inferior innate capacity. There is no need for further commentary. The principles I have just spoken of will only be useful to those who, in the future, will attain either gradual or sudden awakening.

With respect to these matters, there is something that practitioners must always remember. Those who have not yet been able to attain the state where their thoughts are unmoved by any external conditions, those who are still unable to be both aware of and unattached to external conditions, and those who are still unable to treat external conditions lightly, must strengthen their meditation practice, their practice of the Mahamudra of Brightness, or their practice of the Mind Within the Mind. Through such practices, one can increase one's concentration or mental focus. Only then will one's consciousness not be easily moved and scattered due to external conditions, thereby losing correct awareness. Thus, such practices are truly indispensable to all such practitioners.

Those who have already attained the great concentration of a Tathagata already abide in a state of freedom and peace. They have realized the great accomplishment. Thus, to them, there is no such thing as practicing concentration. At such stage, concentration is concentration. Non-concentration is also concentration. Eating, sleeping, and wearing clothes are all part of concentration. The defilements are the same as enlightenment. Handling worldly matters is the same as walking on the spiritual path of truth. The Dharma relating to living in this world is the same as the Dharma that leads out of this world to liberation. The conditioned is the same as the unconditioned. While living in the mundane world and handling all kinds of matters, they have no worries or attachments at all. They live in the world yet are not in the least bit contaminated by it. At such stage, the discourse I just gave does not apply to them. Such discourse does not refer to them.

Chapter Five

UNDERSTANDING CAUSE AND EFFECT AND CLEARLY BELIEVING IN CAUSE AND EFFECT

IN LEARNING AND PRACTICING the Buddha Dharma, it is important to understand the principle and workings of cause and effect. This is because the Buddha Dharma can be condensed into the words *cause and effect*. All conditioned phenomena[44] are subject to the processes of cause and effect and the four stages of arising, subsisting, changing, and passing away. Those who realize the unconditioned[45] obtain enlightenment as a result of certain causes. Yet, they are not attached to the thought of obtaining enlightenment. Therefore, all Buddhist disciples must understand cause and effect.

One can see from this that, with respect to those who cultivate themselves, understanding cause and effect seems to be everything! Of course, generally speaking, people think that one who understands cause and effect should be regarded as a good Buddhist disciple. Under the same reasoning, they think that one who does not understand cause and effect cannot be called a good practitioner.

In our present time, when people are already accustomed to using this viewpoint to judge who is good and bad, one who understands cause and effect may even be regarded as a prophet of the Buddha Dharma or at least a person of great virtue. He will thereby become quite respected.

However, this type of viewpoint is one-sided and unclear. It is biased and inappropriate. If one maintains this viewpoint, one will be unable to make progress in and perfect one's cultivation. One will definitely be unable to raise one's state of realization.

This is not alarmist or unrealistic talk. In fact, when people maintain the concept that one who understands cause and effect is a good practitioner, they have the problem of not comprehending clearly what is the right view according to the Buddha Dharma. It is precisely this problem that is shared by thousands and thousands of practitioners! Of course, not every practitioner realizes the serious hindrances that this problem causes in one's cultivation and the urgent need to solve it!

Why do I say this? We should have seen by now that more and more people are taking "understanding cause and effect" to be a precise goal in their practice. In seeking to attain such goal, they have already fastened on themselves a set of heavy shackles. On their path of cultivation, they are unable to walk energetically. Rather, they remain at a standstill or even regress considerably. Ordinary practitioners are accustomed to having mere understanding as their goal. They do not realize that this is a serious hindrance in their cultivation. This problem stems from a blockage that has formed in their minds. The origin of this blockage is the concept that one who understands cause and effect is a good practitioner.

If this situation is not corrected, countless practitioners will become both pioneers and successors of erroneous and biased views! This would not only result in suffering for multitudinous followers of Buddhism, it would also be a great calamity experienced throughout all Buddhist circles!

Why do I say this? When practitioners sink into this type of viewpoint, they will lay undue stress on seeking the understanding of cause and effect. Mastering the principles of cause and effect will naturally become their primary goal.

They will go and listen to the discourses of the Buddhas, Bodhisattvas, and the Master. They will also seek out the teachings of those with foresight, such as eminent monks, Great Virtuous Ones, Rinpoches, and Dharma Teachers. Their spirits will be roused. They will be elated and inspired.

Admittedly, receiving teachings on the meaning of the Dharma is a good thing. However, after listening to the discourses, these practitioners often become attached only to "understanding." They think of themselves as being quite good for having understood the principles of cause and effect. At the very least, they consider themselves to be half-great, rather accomplished practitioners. When they walk around outside, they have a feeling that they are much more honorable than the multitude of other people walking around. Naturally, they assume the solemn airs of a Great Virtuous One and are extraordinarily smug.

They are proud inside, and their egotism swells. Having mastered these Dharma principles (that is, having a rudimentary understanding of the principles of cause and effect), they think that they do not have to exert any more effort since they are already quite accomplished.

Even if they do not consider themselves to have already solved the problem of ending the cycle of birth and death, at the very least, they think that they have accumulated merit from having listened to the Dharma, that they are highly learned scholars of Buddhism, that they naturally no longer need to worry about feeding and clothing themselves, that they will surely be able to stay far away from disasters, that they will, of course, not be disturbed by the defilements, and that becoming an Accomplished One will certainly not be difficult!

As time passes, signs of the danger of this type of thinking can be seen. Why is this? Since these practitioners are attached to the one aspect of having already understood the principles of cause and effect, they think that they need no longer fear cause and effect. They start to take their skills at theorizing as true realization. They take the understanding of these principles itself as a goal of their practice, which they have already met. Therefore, they no longer examine their own practice. They do not consider whether what they do is wrong, whether their practice is in accord with the Dharma, precepts, and rules, or whether their attitude toward living beings truly accords with the teachings of the Dharma.

That is, although they understand the principles of cause and effect and karmic retribution, they consider this to be something merely on the level of "principles." They understand these principles in their hearts but do not practice them. They understand the principles of cause and effect on the whole and are able to speak about them.

I will use a simple example. If a few of those people get together, they might discuss cultivation in a very solemn manner and might start to debate, or even study, the subject of cause and effect. Mr. A may say, "My mother does not engage in cultivation. She does not believe in the teachings of the Dharma. What do you say? Is this a matter of cause and effect?" The others will immediately break into loud laughter. With expressions of contempt on their faces (This fellow disciple Mr. A does not even understand this. How pitiful!) and without the slightest doubt in their voices, they will say, "Of course this is a matter of cause and effect. Speaking a sentence is a matter of cause and effect. Speaking a few words of abuse to someone is a matter of cause and effect. How could this not be a matter of cause and effect?"

After saying this, they feel quite pleased with themselves. They think that Mr. A is so lousy since he does not understand even this most simple principle. They think that Mr. A simply cannot be compared with them. Hence, they increasingly view themselves as being dazzling. In fact, what is the case? Actually, Mr. A may weigh one half pound, but they themselves only weigh eight ounces each. They are the same!

Among people like these who discuss cause and effect, perhaps there are good people in the real sense of the term who not only understand the principles of cause and effect, but who are also able to abide by such principles and practice according to the meaning of the Dharma. They are able to conscientiously practice according to the principles of cause and effect. However, there are, after all, only a small number of such people. Most people have only one more positive attribute than the practitioner Mr. A, who asked the original question about cause and effect. Their one more skill is merely that they understand the principles of cause and effect! Other than this, they are no more better off than Mr. A, the person who asked the original question!

This is an extremely interesting phenomenon that calls for deep thought! The underlying reason why people who understand the principles of cause and effect act sanctimoniously is this understanding itself! They actually go so far as to ridicule and look down upon people who ask questions like the one posed by Mr. A, even though their disdain for such people may only be in their hearts and not expressed openly!

How should such people, who consider themselves to be wise, be evaluated? Candidly speaking, they lack a clear estimation of themselves!

This situation is similar to the following. In a certain village, there is a Mr. C, who understands why people must plant crops and all of the benefits of planting crops. Even though he is gluttonous and lazy, does nothing, and would not condescend to plant crops, nevertheless, in his heart, he still looks down upon those like Mr. D who do not even understand why people must plant crops! Even though those like Mr. D may be ignorant in this respect, it is possible that after they understand the principles of planting crops, they will go into the fields and diligently engage in tillage, resulting in an abundant harvest.

The only advantage Mr. C has over Mr. D is that Mr. C understands these principles. Mr. C surely does not have any other advantage.

Another example is as follows. There is a person who knows the benefits and principles of planting trees. Although he himself would never plant a single sapling, he feels that he still has the qualifications to ridicule those who do not understand why trees must be planted!

Likewise, there are those who understand the principles of cause and effect but who totally neglect using these principles to help themselves attain liberation and end the cycle of birth and death. Yet, these people feel sorry for those who do not understand the principles of cause and effect! They feel extremely proud of themselves for having understood such Dharma. To them, it is as if ending the cycle of birth and death is now totally under their control. They think that they have the right to look down upon others!

These people certainly do not understand why they are so pitiable! More importantly, this type of person will receive karmic retribution for having said they attained realization when in fact they had not. This is why I am repeatedly emphasizing this point today.

Master Milarepa said, "After hearing the Dharma on cause and effect, any observant and conscientious person will believe in it and will also energetically cultivate himself to live in accord with it." If one is unable to deeply believe in the Buddha Dharma, then mere understanding of some principles of cause and effect is of no use. With such mere understanding, it will be difficult not to be moved by the Eight Winds. Therefore, in following Buddhism, the most important thing is to believe in cause and effect. Those who do not believe in karmic retribution may discuss the principles of emptiness, or they may discuss the actual realization of emptiness. However, in truth, this is merely idle talk without any real value.

Those practitioners who only want to cursorily read about the principles of cause and effect or who only "understand" the principles of cause and effect must carefully look within themselves. Practitioners who are confined to merely "understanding" cause and effect are unwilling to use the principles of cause and effect in their real practice to solve their worldly problems. They are unwilling to deepen their belief in cause and effect. They are unwilling to clearly and devoutly believe in cause and effect. They are unwilling to do good according to the principles of karmic rewards for doing good. They are unwilling to rid themselves of evil according to the principles of karmic retribution for doing evil. They are unwilling to do these things in order to bring true happiness and good fortune to themselves and others. These are the under-lying reasons why those practitioners who have attained so-called "understanding" of cause and effect often commit offenses.

Since those who "understand" cause and effect understand its principles, how could they not know the relationship of cause and effect, whereby rewards result from good karma and punishments result from bad karma?

Of course those practitioners know! But knowing seems not to have much effect. As far as they are concerned, karmic retribution seems to mani-fest its power only when it is experienced by others. Only when others experience karmic punishment do those practitioners realize that they should do good things in order to increase their merit and attain great blessings.

However, in their treatment of other people, they frequently place their own interests first. They are number one, and all others are behind them. In seeking their immediate interests, they do not perform any of the good deeds that they are able to perform.

They know that to do evil will cause their own suffering and will bring about karmic retribution. Yet, when they compete with others, they will use all kinds of foul language, engage in all kinds of base actions, and maintain lowly mor-als, causing harm to others despite all of the consequences. Although they understand many principles of cause and effect, they have a cavalier attitude. They do not think that they have committed any mistakes or that they have betrayed others. They also do not think that this type of conduct will in fact bring upon themselves fruits of punishment or result in their own suffering.

Those who "understand" cause and effect understand that there is a karmic debt that must be paid back from having reviled people. However, they still rebuke and humiliate people. They even describe such conduct euphemisti-cally, saying, "I am just venting my fury, just venting my resentment. I simply cannot hold this anger in any longer!"

Those who "understand" cause and effect know that making offerings to the Buddhas and Bodhisattvas and the Three Jewels will bring about limitless merit and blessings and will be of great use to them. Yet, when they are actu-ally performing Buddhist matters, they still will be calculating and unwilling to make the smallest sacrifice, fighting over every little thing. They may not even perform any Buddhist matters at all. Based upon their conduct, their "understanding" is simply rote or mechanical understanding. Whether they practice according to the principles they "understand" is an entirely different matter.

Those who "understand" cause and effect know that they should not utter lies to cheat the Master, the Buddhas, and the Bodhisattvas. However, in order to attain certain benefits, they will still proceed without hesitation to lie to the Master, having no qualms at all.

From all of these types of conduct, we are able to realize why "understanding" cause and effect is not necessarily worthy of people's great admiration. In a certain sense, those who "understand" cause and effect are even more pitiable than the countless number of worldly people who do not understand cause and effect.

Worldly people commit offenses through ignorance. However, those practitioners who "understand" cause and effect commit offenses knowingly. Thus, their offenses are more serious. The karmic punishment they will receive will be more painful and heavier than that of worldly people. The disasters they will experience will be much greater!

Therefore, "understanding" cause and effect is definitely not the same as being able to help oneself according to the principles of cause and effect. Those who merely "understand" cause and effect are definitely not those who clearly believe in cause and effect.

Understanding cause and effect and clearly believing in cause and effect are two entirely different things! Why is this? Master Milarepa previously said, "The root of all Dharma is believing in cause and effect. The most important thing in following Buddhism is to diligently do good and diligently eschew evil." Those who cultivate themselves should be even more cautious than ordinary people in their decisions to do good and eschew evil according to the principles of cause and effect.

Hence, those who clearly believe in cause and effect are, due to their clear belief, terrified and disgusted at the prospect of doing evil in the world! Since they clearly believe in karmic retribution, they are cautious in their daily conduct, fear making mistakes, and fear that harming other living beings will result in their own karmic punishment.

Those who clearly believe in cause and effect are able to conscientiously and earnestly perform good deeds and earn merit. They do not constantly fuss over worldly so-called benefits or blessings.

Those who clearly believe in cause and effect feel great pain and contrition over their past and present evil conduct. They deeply understand that if they do not diligently cultivate themselves and realize the state in which the cycle of birth and death is ended, they will descend into the lower realms to experience all kinds of suffering and torment. Thus, they are able to exert a vast amount of energy in the hope of attaining liberation and leaving the six realms of reincarnation.

Those who clearly believe in cause and effect are able to energetically practice enduring insults.[46] They do this through tolerating that which ordinary people are unable to tolerate, bearing that which ordinary people are unable to bear, and suffering wrongs that ordinary people are unable to suffer. They will use any adverse circumstance to practice enduring insults. They will not fly into a rage or do something inappropriate when someone speaks abusively toward them or blames them. They deeply understand the merit earned through the practice of enduring insults. They also deeply understand that slight negligence may lead to great disaster, that the slightest frivolity and imprudence may destroy overnight all of one's accumulated merit.

Those who clearly believe in cause and effect will be devoutly respectful toward the Three Jewels. They will be extremely loyal and pious toward the Master and the Buddhas and Bodhisattvas, since they know that the Master is the foundation for their attainment of liberation, and the Buddhas and Bodhisattvas function as their strong protective shield during their pursuit of liberation. They know that as long as one's three karmas perfectly correspond with the teachings of the Buddhas, Bodhisattvas, and the Master, and one relies on the Three Jewels, one will naturally attain liberation without meeting hindrances.

Since they clearly believe in cause and effect, they are very rigorous in their practice. In their treatment of other people, they are polite, modest, and gentle. They offer to others their compassion, love, and friendship and do not have the slightest bit of fierceness or malice.

Since they clearly believe in cause and effect, they strictly abide by the rules and precepts. They are quite circumspect. They are able to completely abide by the precepts. They deeply understand that if a practitioner does not strictly abide by the precepts, after death he will descend into one of the three evil realms, and his karmic punishment will be endless.

Since they clearly believe in cause and effect, they carry out what they say. Their conduct is upright and is in total accord with the Dharma rules. They never break their oral vows. They never make empty promises. They do not have a high opinion of themselves and are not proud and arrogant. They also do not improperly belittle themselves. They are not like those whose minds do not contain upright thoughts.

Those who clearly believe in cause and effect are able to freely proceed into or freely step back from favorable or adverse circumstances that they may face. They will not become delirious with joy over their favorable circumstances. They will also not sob with sadness over their adverse circumstances. They know that everything is a matter of cause and effect. Thus, they have no attachments, joy, anger, or sadness. Obtaining something, they are not glad. Losing something, they are not sorrowful. Thus, they have crossed over into the state of non-attachment.

Those who clearly believe in cause and effect deeply understand that everything in the world is just like passing clouds or passing smoke. Nothing can be held on to and nothing can be kept forever. In fact, there is nothing. There is nothing to obtain, seek, lose, or take. In the final analysis, everything in the world comes into being through the occurrence of certain causes and conditions and passes away with the cessation of such causes and conditions.

Through the above described comparisons, one can see that "understanding" cause and effect and clearly believing in cause and effect are two entirely different matters. They cannot be mentioned in the same breath.

Those who "understand" cause and effect know that principles of cause and effect exist but feel that they can ignore them. They overstep such principles without fear. They feel they can be completely indifferent to these principles. These principles have no restraining power over them. Thus, it can be said that those who "understand" cause and effect are not as good as those who clearly believe in cause and effect. This "understanding" of cause and effect has no effect on them whatsoever and is of no use at all. At the very most, it simply provides them with the knowledge that in this world such principles exist.

Those who clearly believe in cause and effect know that correct principles of cause and effect exist and that the true essence of everything in the universe lies therein. Thus, they firmly believe in such principles. As a result, they give rise to fear, determination to leave the cycle of reincarnation, strict abidance, and sincere belief, as described below.

They fear that through their good and bad karma, they will continue in the cycle of reincarnation. They fear that through the bad and good karma they produce, they will ultimately descend into one of the lower realms and be unable to attain liberation. Thus, they feel fear about what they do.

After they clearly believe in cause and effect, they are determined to leave the cycle of reincarnation. They are not attached anymore to the six realms of reincarnation, which are all like an illusion or a dream. They give rise to a heart that is disenchanted with the cycle of reincarnation. They then resolve to leave the six realms of reincarnation.

Strict abidance is practiced after they resolve to leave the cycle of reincarnation. They strictly abide by the correct Dharma. Whatever they do is in accordance with goodness, and they do not do anything bad. They absolutely do not degenerate as a result of being moved by the Eight Winds. They no longer are confused by greed, hatred, ignorance, craving, joy, anger, sorrow, or pleasure. They engage in upright conduct and steadfastly abide by the Dharma.

They have sincere belief; that is, they have profound faith in the correct principles of cause and effect. Thus, they do not have the slightest erroneous view or engage in the slightest incorrect behavior. They sincerely believe that through learning Buddhism, practicing the Dharma, and acting correctly they will ultimately leave the six realms of reincarnation. They sincerely believe in promoting good and avoiding evil. They sincerely believe that if they devoutly cultivate themselves, they will ultimately attain a state of realization that is no different from that realized by the Buddhas and Bodhisattvas.

Thus, "understanding" cause and effect is definitely not the same as clearly believing in cause and effect! "Understanding" cause and effect is like a plastic flower, which cannot emit any true fragrance. Those who "understand" cause and effect are merely pedants who engage in researching cause and effect or Buddhism just for the fun of it. These so-called researchers or scholars are worthless people without any real use. We respect those who truly cultivate themselves, not those who merely "understand." Of course, those who both understand and truly cultivate themselves can be called teachers.

For the foregoing reasons, practitioners absolutely must not fall into the category of those who merely "understand" cause and effect, allowing this "understanding" to obstruct their vision and practice. One must not take "understanding" to be the goal in one's practice and the basis for becoming pleased with oneself. One should be a person who clearly believes in cause and effect. As Master Milarepa said, only by clearly believing in cause and effect can one energetically cultivate oneself, realize the end of the cycle of birth and death, and attain the supreme state of a Buddha. This is the only correct path for practitioners to take to attain liberation!

⇜ Chapter Six ⇝

A RESPECTFUL HEART AND CORRESPONDENCE OF THE THREE KARMAS

BUDDHIST MONKS AND NUNS, as well as male and female lay adherents, are all able to venerate Sakyamuni Buddha and all of the other Buddhas. Furthermore, they prostrate themselves in worship in order to show the level of their respect. Supposedly, it should not be difficult for these four types of practitioners to end the cycle of birth and death and attain liberation, since they have such respect and strictly adhere to the teachings of the Master. This strict adherence emanates from their respectful hearts.

However, in reality this is not the case. There are so many Buddhist disciples who practice the Dharma, yet there are quite few who attain liberation. Additionally, there are countless Buddhist disciples who practiced the Dharma yet who reincarnated into the hell realm or one of the other two evil paths after they died.

These facts easily cause people to be surprised and baffled. As a result, there are many who feel discouraged, who remain puzzled after thinking about these facts repeatedly, who want to cease all of their efforts, and who totally lose heart. Could it be said that the result of learning the Buddha Dharma and venerating the Buddhas is to experience all kinds of suffering? When deeply pondering this question, practitioners must carefully consider how much respect they have in their own hearts.

All people who learn Buddhism and who cultivate themselves should have a respectful heart. However, the degree of respect may be deep or shallow, and the respect itself may be true or false!

Take, for example, a practitioner who learns the Dharma at the place of his Master. The respect he has in his heart toward the Master in whom he has taken refuge and from whom he learns the Dharma is nowhere near the respect he has in his heart toward Sakyamuni Buddha and Master Padmasambhava. Thus, he follows all of the words of Sakyamuni Buddha and Master Padmasambhava. However, he does not altogether approve of the Dharma teachings of his own Master. Yet, he still has a certain basic level of respect in his heart toward the Master.

There is another type of respect. This is the respect one has in one's heart when the Master manifests miraculous powers. When, due to the maturing of certain causes and conditions, the Master manifests his limitless supernormal skills in front of people, one will then, from the bottom of one's heart, give rise to the greatest respect. One will be extraordinarily respectful and obedient. The respect one has in one's heart at this time is extremely strong. Because of this respect, this disciple is able to receive limitless empowerment from the Master. But this type of respect is only temporary. It does not have the strength to continue for long. Influenced by worldly thoughts, it quickly loses its great strength, just like a small stream becomes a minute, weak, trickling flow of water.

Another type of respect is extremely complex. Within it are contained the various elements of respect, devotion, doubt, and indifference. Practitioners with this type of respect can at times be very respectful, manifesting an extremely devout attitude toward the Buddha Dharma. However, when it comes to the discourses of the Buddhas and Bodhisattvas and the actions of the Master, such practitioners constantly give rise to doubt and repeatedly engage in speculation and comparison. One moment they are at ease. The next moment they are respectful. One moment later they express indifference toward the Buddha Dharma, thinking that the Master is rather ordinary and no better than common people, since he gets sick, becomes angry, sad, happy, etc. Thus, their respectful heart gradually becomes an "ordinary heart." This is a type of "respect."

The types of respect just described are representative of the types of respect that Buddhist disciples have today. One cannot use the simple terms of *right* or *wrong* to categorize them. This is because these types of respect are closely related to the innate faculties and karmic destiny of the person who gives rise to the respect. This is what is meant by the principle, "Those who are deep, see deeply. Those who are shallow, see shallowly." Therefore, rather than saying that these types of respect are not right, it would be more appropriate to say that they all contain a certain one-sidedness to them!

Let us leave aside for the moment why these types of respect are inappropriate. All practitioners should deeply reflect upon what benefits or other things a respectful heart can bring to one's cultivation.

The great Master Milarepa attained liberation by cultivating himself according to the Tibetan tantra of undergoing difficulties and hardships. His disciple Gampopa asked him the question of when he, Gampopa, could expound the Dharma to living beings. The Master answered, "When the respect in your heart enables you to consider the person before you as being no different from Sakyamuni Buddha, then you can expound the Dharma to living beings."[47]

Such is how wonderful a respectful heart is! In a few words, Master Milarepa explained the function of a respectful heart. Even if a practitioner has attained the state of bodhi, he still must perfectly fuse this state with a heart of respect. Only then will he be able to walk the Bodhisattva path and save living beings. This is all the more true to attain ending the cycle of birth and death, which is an ordinary attainment compared to the state of enlightenment of Bodhisattvas.

Of course, the Master does not need the compliments of disciples! True Vajra Masters are born into this world as a result of the arrangements of the Buddhas and Bodhisattvas and their own Mahayana vows. Now then, what type of person can be called a true Vajra Master?

Of course, such a person must have mastered both exoteric and esoteric Dharma, plus the Five Sciences. More importantly, when such person performs an Inner-Tantric Initiation, there must be a manifestation of supernormal Dharma power at the Buddhist altar area. If the specific Dharma powers relating to the five divisions of Inner-Tantric Initiations are manifested and if one meets the standards I just spoke of, then such person is one of great accomplishment and is a Great Mahasattva!

Such a person is extremely humble and maintains a heart of humility in his practice. He does not need his disciples to praise him all day long as a Buddha in order to be happy. Whether or not they praise him, he is still one of great accomplishment. This is beyond all doubt. Words of praise from disciples only serve to aid these disciples in perfectly corresponding their three karmas of body, speech, and mind with the teachings of their Master.

The stronger the respect one has in one's heart toward the Master, the more one's three karmas are able to correspond with the teachings of the Master, and the more one is able to receive great empowerment from the

Master, the Buddhas, and the Bodhisattvas, whose abilities to empower are boundless. This is the lesson of my Buddha Master. Of course, the beneficial effects of one's practice will increase with more empowerment.

The respect one has in one's heart may reach the level where one is able to treat the Master as Sakyamuni Buddha or as being no different from Kuan Yin Bodhisattva. One thinks and truly acts in such a manner. One unreservedly offers all of one's actions, thoughts, and possessions to the Master, who is like a Buddha. As such, at all times and in all places, one is able to view the actions of the Master as the actions of the Buddhas.

When such person hears the words of the Master, he thinks that each sentence is spoken in the voice of Sakyamuni Buddha. He feels that the thoughts and views of the Master are the thoughts and views of Sakyamuni Buddha. No matter whether the Master's appearance, according to worldly standards, is dignified or ugly, whether the Master's words are pleasant to the ear or grating on the ear, whether the Master's practice appears to be beautiful or odious, his view of the Master does not change one bit. From beginning to end, he considers the Master to be Sakyamuni Buddha and does not make the slightest distinction between the Master and all of the Buddhas!

He does not compare his Master with other Great Virtuous Ones, thinking that his Master is inferior to these other masters. He does not compare his Master with worldly people. He has only one simple, holy, and pure mindset. He thinks that there is no distinction between the Buddhas and Bodhisattvas, who are as myriad as the sands of the Ganges River, and the Master. He thinks that there is no difference between Sakyamuni Buddha and the Master! After such disciple attains this level, the Buddhas and Bodhisattvas will personally lift up their Dharma Treasure Staff of unlimited power to empower him.

Precisely because of this simple and pure mindset, the level of his respect is raised to perfection, and he thus reaches an incomparably pure state! Because of such supreme respect, his three karmas are able to perfectly correspond with the teachings of the Master, and the empowerment he receives from the Master and the Buddhas reaches the greatest level.

Under the Master's radiant empowerment, like 10,000 rays of light shining down, this disciple's whole body and mind are totally purified. Under this immense and limitless empowerment, negative karma and impurities carried over from many previous lives disappear without a trace. They are replaced by holiness and purity, by that which is totally devoid of any defilement or obstruction.

The respect that other people offer the Master is mixed with doubt and lacks sincere belief. Thus, they are unable to extricate themselves from the obscurations caused by their present knowledge.[48] They are painfully caught up in things of this world and are unable to attain liberation. On the other hand, the disciple with supreme respect, unlike these others, has already totally obtained the empowerment of the Master. He has totally absorbed the wisdom, supernormal powers, blessings, accomplishments, and realization of the Master and the Buddhas and Bodhisattvas. Not one of these has he failed to absorb. Availing himself of the empowerment of the Buddhas and the Master, his negative karma carried over from many previous lives melts away, just like the melting snow. In other people's eyes, he is already one who, in a wondrous way, raises high the banner of the correct Dharma. They view him as a magnificent one of great accomplishment, a true Vajra Master, a true Great Rinpoche. Thus, he is not one of those who undeservedly hold the title of Great Rinpoche.

These are the immense benefits that are brought about by a most wonderful heart of respect! Many people should now understand why they do not obtain any benefits out of their practice and why, although they appear to be just as respectful as others, there is, nevertheless, such a great disparity between them and others.

Some practitioners do not contentedly learn Buddhism at the side of their Master, even though their Master is heir to a true spiritual legacy. They think that others are more awesome than their Master and that they should learn the Dharma from other Masters. Only then, they think, will they be able to attain liberation.

As such, they are physically in one place, yet their hearts are in another place. They are not eager to make progress. Naturally, they are unable to give rise to absolute confidence in the Master. Giving rise to a respectful heart is even more problematic. Day after day passes until finally they regard the Master as being no different from ordinary people, such as themselves. They even hold a slight amount of contempt for the Master. With such a mindset toward and opinion of the Master, it is ridiculous to even discuss the possibility of their three karmas corresponding with the teachings of the Master.

They are thus unable to give rise to the slightest respect toward the Master. Given such a circumstance, if they were still able to receive the Master's empowerment, would that not be incongruous with the precepts and the Dharma? Furthermore, they say that they themselves are better than the

Master in some areas, that their insight is on a higher level than that of the Master, and that they have traveled to many more places than the Master. While not saying that they are several times better than the Master, they do say that, comparatively speaking, it could not be that they are too much worse than the Master! With respect to receiving empowerment from the Master, they say, "I do not care. As long as I am able to receive empowerment from Sakyamuni Buddha or the Buddhas and Bodhisattvas, I am happy." They think that receiving empowerment from a certain Dharma King or a certain Great Rinpoche is almost the same as receiving empowerment from the Buddhas and Bodhisattvas.

Why do I not receive ordinary practitioners, ordinary Rinpoches, and ordinary Dharma Teachers as my disciples? Because they possess the mental hindrance of comparing one master favorably to another master. As soon as they would become my disciples, they would look down upon the master they previously followed. Then, because of me, they would produce negative karma by maligning their previous master. Thus, rather than receiving ordinary practitioners as disciples, it would be better if such people studied my books and discourses.

Of course, the selection of a master by a practitioner is truly of particular importance. If one's master is not truly proficient in both exoteric and esoteric Dharma, if one's master does not understand the teachings contained in the sutras, if one's master does not have any Dharma power when conducting initiations, if one's master clings to the erroneous view that the self or ego is real, if one's master has karmic hindrances closely following him wherever he goes, like demons closely attached to his body, if great practitioners sigh at the mere sight of one's master and try to avoid one's master, then how can one possibly receive empowerment from such a master? Of course, one cannot receive even the slightest empowerment from such a master. On the contrary, one might become diabolically possessed.

This is how wonderful it is to have a respectful heart! When you respect the Master as if he were Sakyamuni Buddha, then the empowerment you receive from the Master is equivalent to that which you would receive from Sakyamuni Buddha. When you treat the Master as if he were an ordinary person, then what you will receive as "empowerment" will only be the karma of an ordinary person. When you treat the Master as someone lesser than yourself, as someone more foolish than yourself, this will not only result in your not receiving any empowerment at all, it will instead reduce your merit and blessings. This is what is called paying a double penalty!

When a practitioner continuously maintains a respectful heart, this enables him to attain enlightenment more easily and quickly. With the aid of this respectful heart, he is able to better absorb the teachings of the Master. The teachings of the Master may cause him, in any completely accidental situation, to look within himself, give rise to bright awareness, and understand the principles of the Dharma. At such time, he will experience a feeling of light peace or even great peace. He will sincerely believe in the Buddha Dharma. Hence, he will have an even deeper level of understanding of the Master and the Buddha Dharma.

This instantaneous introspection is mostly due to a heart of respect. This introspection also strengthens one's heart of respect. Thus, there is a relationship of close interdependence between the two, which can cause the practitioner to become perfectly accomplished, give rise to bright awareness, realize the empty nature of things, attain control over his own life and death, and be in total control as he wishes.

One can thus see the relationship between a respectful heart and correspondence of the disciple's three karmas with the teachings of the Master. The more respectful the practitioner is toward the Master, the deeper is his reliance upon and belief in the Master. He will then naturally be able to treat the Master with the purest of actions and thoughts and abide by the teachings of the Buddhas and the Master.

Thus, his three karmas truly correspond with the teachings of the Master. He does not violate the principles of the Master's teachings. All that he does is in accordance with the teachings of the Master. It can be said that his three karmas are pure and undefiled. He cultivates himself in any given situation. Since his three karmas correspond with the teachings of the Buddhas, the Bodhisattvas, and the Master, he is able to receive empowerment bestowed by the Master and clearly understand the true meaning of the Buddha Dharma.

In their attitude toward the Buddha Dharma and their treatment of the Master, the other kind of practitioners, however, are often half believing and half doubting, half serious and half indifferent. They think that it is impossible for their three karmas to perfectly correspond with the teachings of the Master. They feel that giving rise to an immaculate heart of respect is a difficult thing. Thus, they treat the Master with the same attitude with which they treat worldly people. They treat the Buddha Dharma in the same way that they treat worldly matters.

They do not treat the Buddha Dharma with a true and sincere heart. They also are unwilling to tell the Master their true thoughts and feelings. Hence, they constantly have a guarded mindset toward the Master. They are wary when with the Master. They treat the Master as if he were someone with whom they do business. They are extremely cautious in front of the Master. They fear that the Master will discover what offenses they previously committed, what impure karma they have accumulated, and how much property they have. They fear that in the course of the Master's saving living beings, such as themselves, the Master will add to their troubles. They fear that the Master will tell them to take care of certain Buddhist matters. They fear that the Master will discover that they are telling lies. Unable to face their erroneous conduct, they engage in more lies to cover up their previous lies. They become nervous and worried. They thus selfishly apply their methods for handling worldly matters and their methods for dealing with worldly people in their treatment of the Buddha Dharma and the Master.

These people will not open up their hearts to the Master, the Buddhas, and the Bodhisattvas. When they plan something, when they consider something, when they weigh the pros and cons of something, at all times and in all places, they never forget to think of themselves. They do not know that they have already separated themselves from the Master, that their three karmas already do not correspond with the Buddhas, the Bodhisattvas and the Master.

At such time, when someone tells them that their three karmas are already awry, they become quite irritated. They will then look within themselves. After they reflect on this, the conclusion they reach is that their three karmas do correspond with the teachings of the Master, and the other person is being intentionally hypercritical.

There is another type of disciple who is hoodwinked by a hidden devil. They have lost their correct view of the Buddha Dharma. They think that their three karmas correspond with the teachings of the Master and that they obey all of the words of the Master. Normally, they enthusiastically and wholeheartedly make offerings to and work in the service of places related to the Master, such as the Master's main temple, as well as subsidiary temples, centers, monasteries, group cultivation places, and foundations.

In places where fellow disciples get together, there will be differences in each person's habitual tendencies and viewpoints. Thus, there may be some differences of opinion or verbal conflicts. When these occur, this type of disciple I now speak of will suddenly give rise to a diabolical obstruction born of ignorance. They will immediately separate themselves from these organizations that are related to the Master. From that point on, they will no longer do all they can to further the Master's undertaking of spreading the Dharma and benefiting living beings.

Perhaps the Master has appointed a disciple to take care of a certain organization. Since it is not being taken care of by the Master himself, they have many complaints about how this fellow disciple operates the organization. They then euphemistically describe what they will do as follows: "I will be infinitely loyal to the Master himself and will practice according to the Dharma. However, I will not go to that organization, which is so full of gossip and quarrels! " Not only do they themselves not go, they even incite fellow disciples with whom they are close friends and who have viewpoints similar to their own not to go. They incite these people to leave the organization. Nonetheless, they actually think that they are truly respectful toward the Master himself!

In fact, they have entered into a diabolical state wherein their practice is futile. Having entered such state, their situation is infinitely frightening. Not only will they be unable to attain liberation, on the contrary, they will descend into one of the three evil paths.

The major reason why they commit such offenses is that they do not understand a certain truth. That is, all of the sites established by the Master to benefit living beings are sites that spread the Dharma for living beings. They are temples for seeking the enlightened mind. All of the Buddhas and Bodhisattvas of the infinite past very much respect, praise, and support such temples! The type of disciple I just described and their fellow disciples should try their best to walk the Bodhisattva path for the betterment of all the sites the Master has selected to spread the Dharma. They should be practicing for the betterment of all living beings. Given such a wonderful opportunity, they should not be influenced by personal disputes or contradictory viewpoints!

Yet, there are ignorant disciples who hold demonic viewpoints. They exploit conflicts, quarrels, and grievances among fellow disciples in order to domineer over their fellow disciples at the very site that is used to spread the Dharma and benefit living beings. In fact, this is equivalent to concentrating their anger on the Master himself. Why do I say this? Because the Master, the sites he established, and the spreading of the Dharma are a trinity. Each person has the responsibility to do all that he can to support this trinity. Nobody is the least bit qualified to undermine a site used to spread the Dharma and benefit living beings! To do so would be committing a terrible offense that is just as grave as the offense of directly maligning the Master!

In Tibet and internationally, this type of odious conduct born of ignorance occurs quite a bit. Buddhist disciples who have committed the above described offenses should immediately repent and reform themselves. From this point on, they must not commit such offenses.

They should understand that all of the sites established by the Vajra Master where disciples congregate, such as temples, secret locations, meeting places, enclosed meditation centers, monasteries, etc., represent places for spreading the correct Dharma of the Tathagata. Thus, no matter who violates such sites, such person is engaging in demonic conduct. This person is doing damage to the cause of spreading the correct Dharma of the Tathagata and will undoubtedly experience heavy and terrible karmic retribution!

However, they themselves think that they are respectful toward the Buddhas, the Bodhisattvas, and the Master. At times, this respect appears to be great. I say that it appears to be great since occasionally they are so moved by the Master's great toils in furthering the Buddha Dharma and benefiting living beings that they break into streams of tears. However, such occasions are extremely rare!

The time that they spend in this lifetime learning the Dharma and the time that they spend rolling about in worldly matters greatly exceeds these very "occasional" moments. Their thoughts on worldly matters and on the ways of the world are many times more numerous than their thoughts on the Buddha Dharma. Their reverence for those in the world who are adept at making money is much stronger than the respect they have toward the Master. Their admiration for those in the world who are in high positions of power and who possess enormous wealth is much greater than the respect they have toward the Master.

Thus, in their treatment of the Buddha Dharma, sometimes they test certain worldly ways with which they are most familiar. They become disrespectful toward their Master. They are even secretly happy that their methods seem to be quite effective. However, they fail to realize that the Buddha Dharma Master revered by thousands of people is completely unperturbed by any such testing of worldly ways. The Master, smiling, easily sees through all of the "awesome" worldly methods they use to manage and control other people – methods that have been handed down through the generations.

This being the case, they figure that they might as well guard against the Master and protect themselves. They think that there will thus be no danger of anything going wrong. Hence, they again fall into their old habits. They even feel at peace about this, thinking that no matter whether it has to do with their worldly life or with their learning the Buddha Dharma under the Master, they will not be disadvantaged in the least!

These people think that the Master has the ability to be sharp-sighted about details but that he is unable to see the big picture. They thus feel free to boldly play tricks to fool the Master! Actually, the Master has long since known that their karmic obstructions are great and that they cannot be saved.

Thus, the "respect" they have in their hearts is extremely complicated. They feel that they will not suffer any "loss." In fact, the situation is that they will never again receive any "gain."

When one's respect contains impurities, it is like dust in the air. Although not easy for ordinary people to see, it is clear and distinct to the Holy One.

Using this type of "respect" to deceive the Buddhas and the Master is like pouring tiny particles of sand into a glass of water and then stirring the water so that others will be unable to distinguish the water from the sand. However, there is a certain point that they fail to see or that they pretend not to see: The tiny particles of sand will ultimately sink to the bottom. The water will still be water and that which will sink to the bottom of the water will be those small particles of sand! Yet, ordinary people think that the small particles of sand can be successfully mixed with the water! In the virtuous Master's penetrating vision, water is water and sand is sand. Water and sand are mixed together, but the virtuous Master is not confused, since he knows that water and sand have nothing to do with each other.

Hidden within this type of "respect" is conjecture, comparison, doubt of the Master, doubt of the Dharma, etc. Practitioners who have this type of "respect" know in their hearts that the name for this type of "respect" is "false respect"! If they truly do not understand this, then they are deceiving themselves and others. Perhaps they are pretending that they do not know this. I am afraid that even true cultivators cannot distinguish true respect from false respect.

Those with true respect engage in good conduct. Through their genuine cultivation, they have understood and verified the truths regarding correspondence of the three karmas. Naturally, they will receive abundant karmic rewards.

Because of their false respect, what is experienced by those false and superficially clever practitioners is not the happiness and accomplishment that they were expecting, but rather an unlimited amount of suffering and disaster. Such are the inevitable results brought about by the law of cause and effect!

≈ Chapter Seven ≈

TWENTY TYPES OF FUTILITY

ALL THOSE WHO CULTIVATE THEMSELVES hope that they will obtain perfect good fortune and wisdom and that they will accumulate enough Buddhist resources in order to realize supreme enlightenment. Thus, they use various methods in their cultivation. However, if in their practice they slightly deviate from what is correct or fail to deeply grasp the essential points, then their good fortune and roots of kindness can easily be destroyed, and their striving for perfect enlightenment can easily be obstructed.

Thus, I will now briefly explain the 20 types of futility that were expounded by Master Padmasambhava. This Dharma is venerated by the Buddhas and Bodhisattvas in the ten directions. Hence, I hope that each of you will devoutly receive this Dharma!

The 20 types of futile Dharma practices are as follows:

1. The futility of arousing bodhicitta when one does not give up harming sentient beings.
2. The futility of being initiated when one does not abide by the Samaya Precepts.
3. The futility of listening extensively to teachings on the Dharma when it does not benefit one's heart.
4. The futility of performing meritorious deeds when one also commits evil deeds.
5. The futility of following the Master when one engages in wrongdoing.
6. The futility of being a teacher when one does not practice the Dharma and one also does evil.
7. The futility of one's cultivation when one is moved by the Eight Winds.
8. The futility of following a teacher when one treats sentient beings, who are like one's mother, in a malevolent manner.

9. The futility of saying that one fears hell when one often engages in wrong-doing.
10. The futility of practicing charity when one does not act through an enlightened state of mind and does not have devout faith.
11. The futility of receiving the precepts when one has not resolved to strictly abide by them.
12. The futility of cultivating peacefulness and forbearance when one does not control one's anger.
13. The futility of practicing meditation when one often becomes drowsy or unfocused.
14. The futility of vigorously practicing when one does not yearn for enlightenment.
15. The futility of cultivating prajna if one does not eliminate jealousy and the five poisons.
16. The futility of practicing the Mahayana Dharma when one does not have a heart of great compassion.
17. The futility of cultivating concentration if one does not know one's original nature.
18. The futility of receiving mantras if one does not apply them.
19. The futility of doing things that benefit sentient beings when one does not act out of bodhicitta.
20. The futility of reading books and listening to the Dharma when one does not understand the meaning and principles or cannot put them into practice.

I will now describe each of these.

1. *The Futility of Arousing Bodhicitta When One Does Not Give Up Harming Sentient Beings*

Many practitioners have gone through untold hardships and have trudged over wilderness, deserts, rough hills, and remote mountains in order to seek the path of liberation from the cycle of birth and death. Some practitioners have not hesitated to leave their native place, spend their entire fortune, and give up their wife and children in order to seek the correct Dharma. Their respect and devotion toward the Buddha Dharma comes quite close to that of some Great Virtuous Ones and eminent monks who have already realized great accomplishment in the Buddha Dharma. Ordinarily, with this level of determination to leave the six realms of reincarnation, they should be quite achieved in their practice of the Buddha Dharma. However, due to various karmic obstructions, what they have accomplished in their practice is ordinary. They have not attained any wonderful state of realization. Their situation is pitiable!

The primary reason for this is the view they hold regarding how to treat living beings. How one treats living beings is the most fundamental factor influencing one's ability to attain liberation. One's practice of the Mahayana Dharma must be based upon bodhicitta and the aspiration to lead living beings to liberation. With this bodhicitta, there is something to fall back upon when saving living beings.

However, it is not enough for those who practice Mahayana Buddhism to merely arouse bodhicitta. They must also engage in real practice in order to attain true realization of the enlightened mind. Otherwise, arousing bodhicitta in order to save living beings would be like a tree without roots. This would not be the way of a Mahayana Bodhisattva. Their vows to realize the enlightened mind and save living beings would be empty words. Those vows would be empty vows.

Thus, arousing bodhicitta must be closely combined with cultivation. The most important aspect of this cultivation is how to truly love all living beings in the three spheres and the six realms as if they were one's own family members and how to truly maintain a Mahayana awakened heart of compassion in treating other living beings. This is of utmost importance!

Anyone can arouse bodhicitta. However, whether one carries out one's bodhicitta vows is a whole other matter. Out of a heart of compassion, many practitioners arouse bodhicitta and vow to save living beings. Yet, in their actual practice, they are unable to treat all living beings as their own family members. Therefore, after they arouse bodhicitta, they continue to consciously or unconsciously engage in conduct that harms sentient beings. Of course, this is not the practice of a true Mahayana practitioner.

If one gives rise to a consciousness that is harmful to living beings, or if one even goes so far as to engage in action that is harmful to living beings, it can be said that one has already gone against the bodhicitta one has aroused. Such a person has broken the bodhicitta vows he made. He has already lost his bodhicitta. As far as cultivators are concerned, this is extremely frightening and distressing. It means that their cultivation has been in vain and that they will be unable to realize liberation. Moreover, they will experience heavy karmic retribution for having broken their vows.

Harming sentient beings after one has aroused bodhicitta happens easily. The reason for this is that one cannot constantly maintain the heart of compassion that existed at that moment one aroused bodhicitta. Thus, one breaks one's promise made to the Buddhas and Bodhisattvas and to living beings.

The following is a very typical example. An extremely small number of disciples who aroused bodhicitta feel that they have no other choice than to kill living beings when they treat their superiors or other business connections to meals. They specially order the type of fish or meat that their superiors like to eat and also have live fish killed on the spot.

Afterwards, these disciples are quite sorry. They feel that they committed the offense of killing living beings, that they did something which is totally opposed to their cultivation, that they broke the precepts and violated their vows. As a result, they go to the Master to repent, hoping that their negative karma can be cleansed. Yet, the next time when a certain superior arrives in town, they will still do as before. Even though in their hearts they are very much unwilling, they will still do as before in order to win the favor of these superiors. To put it more frankly, they will still do as before in order to maintain their job and protect their own worldly interests!

Of course, I am not saying here that lay practitioners should not consider worldly blessings and benefits in their learning of Buddhism and in their cultivation. Just the opposite! If one who learns Buddhism and engages in cultivation does not receive any worldly blessings or benefits, then would the saying, "Learning the Buddha Dharma will bring wisdom and increase one's blessings," not be an empty saying that deceives people?

Actually, in learning Buddhism and cultivating oneself, not only should one consider worldly blessings and benefits, one should also, through cultivation, be happier, more blessed, and receive more wonderful benefits than other people in the world. This shows the advantage of learning the Buddha Dharma. However, the prerequisite for experiencing these results is that the practitioner must act according to the Dharma.

If one does not act according to the Dharma, it will be of no use. One of the founders of the Vajrayana, Master Padmasambhava, once said that he never saw a disciple who learned Buddhism and cultivated himself starve to death. This means that those disciples who truly learn Buddhism and truly cultivate themselves will definitely receive true empowerment!

This relates to increasing one's worldly blessings. However, one who learns Buddhism and cultivates himself must consider carefully the following question: When worldly interests, on the one hand, and the principles of the Buddha Dharma and the demands of one's practice, on the other hand, are contradictory, how does one properly resolve this conflict?

Actually, this question has already been clearly answered at the time each practitioner began to follow Buddhism. Having become a Buddhist, one must act according to the Dharma and must not violate the Dharma for any particular person. The true Buddha Dharma helps living beings end the cycle of birth and death and attain liberation. That is, if one does not act according to the meaning of the Buddha Dharma, it will be impossible to end the cycle of birth and death.

Having aroused bodhicitta, one should carry out one's bodhicitta vows to save the countless living beings and to cut off the limitless defilements. If Buddhist disciples who are learning the correct Dharma do not even place the Buddha Dharma in the first and foremost position, then it is clear that the vows they made when taking refuge and arousing bodhicitta were empty and unreal. Those who made such vows were deceiving themselves and others.

Those Buddhist disciples who truly vow to become accomplished should be willing to give up their lives rather than give up the Dharma. The Dharma is even more important than their own lives!

Of course, some practitioners have not yet reached this state of realization. I will, therefore, not make excessive demands upon them for the time being. This is a matter of one's state of realization. They need to gradually reach awareness and gradually raise their state of realization.

After they truly understand how precious and hard to come by the principles of the Buddha Dharma are and after they deeply understand that all phenomena in this world are empty and unreal, they will attain thorough awareness and will not become attached to anything at all. At such time, they will naturally be able to give up their lives rather than give up the Dharma.

There are those Buddhist disciples who not only fail to carry out the principle of giving up one's life rather than giving up the Dharma, they even fail to carry out the following principle: One must act according to the Dharma and not violate the Dharma for any particular person. When there is a conflict between their worldly ways of doing things and the Buddha Dharma, they definitely will be totally attached to their worldly interests. To them, their worldly ways are higher than the Buddha Dharma. They even disregard the precepts and principles of the Buddha Dharma in order to seek worldly power, position, or gain. Their learning of Buddhism is in vain. They know the precepts yet break the precepts. They will definitely descend into the lower realms since they are hypocritical, fake disciples. The only result waiting for them is again entering the cycle of reincarnation to experience all kinds of suffering.

The Buddha Dharma does not urge lay practitioners to forsake worldly gains or blessings, to be indifferent toward everything, and to give up all of one's worldly fortune under the reasoning that as long as one wholeheartedly seeks the Dharma, that will be enough. This viewpoint is not correct! The Buddha Dharma advocates that one should have good fortune and Buddhist resources. If one does not have any good fortune and Buddhist resources, then this indicates that one is still unable to practice one's preliminary practices well, not to mention, of course, one's main practices.

Therefore, those who learn Buddhism and cultivate themselves should clearly understand this point. Under no circumstances can they have a hazy or confused understanding of this point whereby they lose their correct understanding. Either they are too much to the left or too much to the right. Their state of understanding is muddled. Since they are unable to raise high the banner of correct Dharma and correct understanding, they are unable to cultivate themselves well! Remember that in learning Buddhism, one practices to obtain the two types of Buddhist resources: good fortune and wisdom.

The harming (killing) of sentient beings after one has aroused bodhicitta often happens at any given place and at any given time. Afterwards, these disciples feel both distressed and wronged. They think that they did not originally have the intent to kill living beings but that the situation forced them to do it. They think that they truly had no alternative.

It is indeed painful to hear this type of meaningless excuse. I feel that those people are ignorant and pitiable. They still have not yet thoroughly understood the meaning of the word *cultivation* and the meaning of the phrase *arousing bodhicitta*. Actually, arousing bodhicitta is not only for the sake of others. It is primarily for themselves. This is because when one arouses bodhicitta, it is like building a bridge between oneself and the Buddhas and

Bodhisattvas. There is a means through which communication can take place. Only then will the Dharma Protectors, such as the Dakinis, based on one's desire to benefit and make happy all sentient beings, come to protect and uphold one's practice, wipe out one's demonic obstructions, and assist one in becoming accomplished. One's road to accomplishment is thereby further safeguarded.

Those who provide excuses for themselves for having killed or harmed living beings do not know that all types of excuses and reasons for such conduct are totally meaningless. Such excuses and reasons cannot change the fact that they directly or indirectly killed living beings! When someone finds excuses for and defends his own heinous offenses, there is nothing left of his heart of great compassion and bodhicitta. Their motivation for finding excuses is their hope that the Buddhas, the Bodhisattvas, and the Master will "understand" their acts of killing. If so, they think they can luckily avoid experiencing karmic retribution, as if they never violated their vows.

They regard their bodhicitta vows as matters that the Master and the Buddhas and Bodhisattvas want them to do. They think that if the Master speaks one certain sentence, then their offenses will be wiped out, as if the law of cause and effect did not exist. They are ignorant to such a degree! They cannot give rise to awareness from deep within their own hearts. They do not understand that treating living beings as if they were members of one's own family is truly necessary, of immediate concern, and part of one's natural abilities.

This is a problem that relates to the quality of a person and his level of awareness. Of course, their level of awareness is also shared by countless living beings. If a person does not even understand this point about treating living beings as members of one's own family, then one can imagine how such a person carries out his bodhicitta vows and how he engages in cultivation.

When they aroused bodhicitta, they vowed to treat all living beings as members of their own family. In the end, just the opposite happens. Not only do they not carry out this vow, they feel only the slightest compunction and engage in only the slightest self-reproach when killing living beings. More often than not, they feel at ease and justified when killing living beings. They try to shirk their responsibilities and find excuses for their conduct. This is truly too pitiful!

If they personally saw their own parents or children stabbed to death by their superior, lying in a pool of blood, I am afraid they would immediately become enraged and would quickly pounce on that superior. They would not care whether the killer was their superior. They would tackle the butcher to the ground and vengefully stab him to death. After doing this, would they still be able to say in a dignified manner, "I did not want to do it. I was forced to do it. Do not blame me. I had no alternative. I did not make him my superior. If I do not obey him, I will lose my job!"? If there really were such strange people in this world, people who have lost all reason, then I am afraid the world would have long since not tolerated them. Wherever they go, they would be treated like mice crossing the street – people would scream at them and beat them.

One can see from this that it is not just a problem of putting worldly matters or worldly gain before the Buddha Dharma. Such conduct reflects more important concepts held by these ignorant practitioners. These concepts are as follows: "Not all living beings are equal! The lives of other species of sentient beings are of no great importance. The lives of human beings are true lives. Furthermore, the lives of my own family members in this lifetime are the most important and precious of all human lives."

Therefore, when their family members are killed, they wail and are so overwhelmed with grief that they hardly wish to live. They vow to find the true culprit. Bursting with rage, they wish they could cut off the head of the true culprit. Yet, if a chicken or fish is killed, they do not care. At the very most, they feel a tiny bit of compassion and ask the Master to transfer its consciousness to a higher realm.[49] To them, there is no need to make a fuss over such a trifling matter.

Yet, when they originally aroused bodhicitta, they vowed to view all living beings in the three spheres as equal and as one's own family members. What happened to such thoughts? It is extremely difficult to imagine how one can possibly give rise to great compassion and Mahayana bodhicitta if one is unable to treat all sentient beings as one's own family members. Their "bodhicitta" is truly absurd!

Those who attempt to make excuses for their acts of killing do not try to deeply understand the essential meaning underlying the principle of not killing or harming living beings. They understand this principle simply as a teaching of the Master. They may, for a time, feel frightened over what they have done, fearing that such acts will negatively influence their cultivation and ability to become accomplished. However, this is only a superficial fright over the sufferings involved in future rebirths. Their fear of having to repay their karmic debt by descending into hell is superficial. They do not truly experience an acute pain in the deepest part of their spirit for the offenses they themselves have committed. They do not experience a type of extremely sharp and strong pain, like being burned by raging flames or pierced by steel needles, that is accompanied by feelings of remorse and fear!

Anyone in this world who understands and experiences this type of acute pain will immediately let go of the knife that either directly or indirectly kills or harms living beings. He will use the sword of wisdom – that is, an understanding which is in accordance with the correct Dharma – to resolutely cut off all possibilities of killing or harming living beings. He will never commit the same offenses again. A Buddhist disciple who truly has deep roots of goodness should act in such a manner.

As for those people who only ostensibly arouse bodhicitta, who only feel superficial fear, who repeatedly kill living beings and then repeatedly repent, the day when they truly feel acute pain will be when their negative karma ripens and their karmic retribution befalls them. Only when they themselves are in the raging flames hell being burned by raging flames, or are in the mountains of swords hell being lacerated by swords, will they thoroughly understand the reason for and the need to arouse bodhicitta and save living beings. Only then will they thoroughly understand the reason for and the need to abstain from harming or killing living beings. However, by then it will already be too late!

Therefore, when those with deep roots of kindness who truly arouse Mahayana bodhicitta and who truly vow to save living beings see a fish or a chicken being killed, they think that perhaps this is the fate they will suffer in the future if they harm sentient beings. Yet, those who casually arouse bodhicitta, who do not act in accordance with the Mahayana Dharma, and who pretend to save living beings see nothing more than a fish or a chicken being killed!

Since they kill and harm living beings, their path of cultivation has become one that submits to evil views and evil conduct. Thus, it is a path leading to hell. As a result, they will not realize enlightenment. On the contrary, such conduct causes them to degenerate. It directly contravenes their bodhicitta vows. It is of no benefit at all!

All practitioners should know that it is futile to arouse bodhicitta when one does not give up harming sentient beings!

2. The Futility of Being Initiated When One Does Not Abide by the Samaya Precepts

First of all, everyone must understand what is meant by initiation. In the section on initiation, I explained what is meant by initiation. I will now only briefly explain its meaning.

Initiation is a type of ceremonial procedure performed within Vajrayana Buddhism whereby Dharma is transmitted. Simply put, it is a type of ceremony wherein Dharma is transmitted according to tantra by means of the Master's limitless merit and power. During the ceremony, the Master visualizes that he becomes one with a Buddha or Bodhisattva.

Initiation is divided into Outer-Tantric Initiation and Inner-Tantric Initiation. What is Outer-Tantric Initiation? In substance, Outer-Tantric Initiation is a type of theoretical initiation. What is Inner-Tantric Initiation? In principle, during Inner-Tantric Initiation, the Master must communicate with the Buddhas and Bodhisattvas based upon his own Dharma power. The Master personally introduces the initiate to a Buddha or Bodhisattva, who accepts the initiate as a trusted disciple. Therefore, during the Inner-Tantric Initiation, miraculous Dharma power is manifested.

Inner-Tantric Initiation is divided into five divisions. Actually, only these five divisions of Inner-Tantric Initiation can be considered as true tantric initiations. The thousands of other types of initiations besides these five divisions can only be called ordinary tantric initiations. I will not say anything more about this here. If one would like to know more details, consult the chapter on initiations in the book *Entering the Door of the Dharma*, which I wrote.

These five divisions of initiations are as follows:

- The first division is Vajra Samadhi Initiation.
- The second division is Auspicious Selection Initiation.
- The third division is Dharma Wheel Communicates With the Holy Ones Initiation.
- The fourth division is Buddhas Bestowing Nectar Initiation.
- The fifth division is Picking Slips From a Golden Vase Initiation.

During the initiations listed in these five divisions, unlimited supernormal Dharma powers will be manifested. Miraculous powers will be exhibited in front of disciples who are being initiated, and there will be communication with the Buddhas and Bodhisattvas.

Precisely because there is a manifestation of such great merit and awesome supernormal powers, some Buddhist disciples who have been initiated begin to allow their fancy to run wild. They think, "Since today I received an Inner-Tantric Initiation by the Master, I do not have to abide by the Samaya Precepts. I can become accomplished without meeting any hindrances." This is how proud and self-satisfied they are! However, will they be able to become accomplished by acting in such manner? Even though a practitioner was able to receive an Inner-Tantric Initiation, if such person does not abide by the Samaya Precepts, that is, if such person violates these precepts, then that person will surely not be able to become accomplished!

All practitioners should understand that although such disciples have received an Inner-Tantric Initiation and have established communication with those such as Buddhas, yidams, Dharma Protectors, Dakinis, male and female sect leaders, deputy sect leaders, and the Vidya-Rajas,[50] this does not mean, however, that they will easily become accomplished without any hindrances. This is the same as the principle of correspondence of the three karmas.

These people have overlooked one point. Having established communication with the Buddhas and Bodhisattvas is one thing; the necessity to abide by the rules is yet another thing.

For example, you receive a pass that enables you to travel between two countries. However, this does not mean that after you receive the pass, you have no worries whatsoever when entering and leaving the two countries. It does not mean that even if you commit the offenses of murder, arson, robbery or poisoning, it all does not matter. It does not mean that from the time you receive the pass, you will no longer undergo inspection by customs officers, you can swagger right into the other country unchecked, and you can freely travel between the two countries.

Even if you obtain such a pass, you still must undergo inspection by customs, follow the procedures for entering and leaving the countries, and not commit offenses. Only then will you be able to legally travel between the two countries. This is the meaning of having such a travel pass! It does not mean that as long as one has a travel pass in one's pocket, one can treat customs as if it were an organization which did not exist, one need not undergo routine inspection, and one can commit offenses and still be forgiven.

This issue relates to Dharma rules and discipline. The Samaya Precepts lay out the principles governing how one should act. These precepts tell practitioners what they should not do, what they should do, what they should practice, and what they should not practice. As such, these precepts tell practitioners how to correctly cultivate themselves.

Only if practitioners act according to such Dharma rules and discipline will they be able to ultimately obtain benefits from the Dharma they received when being initiated. This is the theory and the function of the Samaya Precepts.

What are the Samaya Precepts? They are the precepts and discipline specially laid down by the Buddhas and Bodhisattvas. They are not the same as the precepts and discipline of sects or sub-sects outside Vajrayana Buddhism. They are not the same as the precepts and discipline of exoteric Dharma. In brief, there is quite a large difference between the Samaya Precepts and the Eight Precepts, the Five Precepts, the Precepts for Monks,[51] the Bodhisattva Precepts, and the Three Comprehensive Precepts!

The Samaya Precepts must be followed by all practitioners of tantra. They are supreme, bright, and magnificent precepts. These precepts restrain us during the process of cultivation so that we avoid taking an evil path, a diabolical path, or a path that leads us into misconceptions, resulting in non-correspondence of the three karmas!

To abide by these precepts is like being in control of the helm so that the boat will be steered in the right direction. Abiding by these precepts, practitioners will be able to push forward without resistance in their quest for enlightenment, directly reach the state of enlightenment, and realize perfect accomplishment.

Therefore, it is not the case that after receiving an Inner-Tantric Initiation, one can act recklessly and without fear, get away with things scot-free, and do whatever one wants, having flung the precepts to the four winds. All practitioners must bear this in mind!

In learning the Buddha Dharma, remember that there are reasons why one must follow each and every precept and rule of discipline. The precepts and rules of discipline are perfect. There are not too many of them, nor are there too few of them. None of them are superfluous or useless! Simply put, the Samaya Precepts govern all of the acts of every practitioner in the three spheres of existence. Thus, practically speaking, there are a great deal of rules contained within such precepts. They are very detailed. However, each rule is extremely penetrating. One absolutely may not violate them in the slightest way.

For example, one often hears others say that they have attained realization or accomplishment when they have not. That one must not do this is a very important rule within the Samaya Precepts!

There are some disciples within Tibetan Tantric Buddhism who, after receiving an Inner-Tantric Initiation and after their learning reaches a certain level, feel that they are amazing. This especially happens after they receive the Vajra Acarya Initiation during which the Master tells them, "You are now a Vajra Acarya."

At this time, these practitioners begin to easily violate the precepts. Because of various worldly causes exercising their evil influence over them, as each day passes they gradually inflate their own reputation. Not having attained realization, they say that they have attained realization. Not having attained accomplishment, they say that they have attained accomplishment. They then call themselves Great Acaryas. Next, they call themselves Great Rinpoches. In the end, they are small Rinpoches who falsely claim to be Great Dharma Kings. It goes on and on. This is violating the rule that one must not declare that one has attained realization or accomplishment when one has not.

In today's earthly realm, there are great number of Rinpoches who violate this Samaya Precept, especially small Rinpoches. Within only a few days, they shake their bodies and suddenly change into a great founder of a particular sect! They even have others carry a great yellow umbrella over them wherever they walk or go so far as to have others lay out a carpet for them to walk upon. They have numerous believers who are ignorant of the facts kneel upon the ground to welcome them. At such time, they think they are Great Jewel Dharma Kings. They get carried away with their own importance and do not know the goal of practicing the Dharma. In truth, they cannot even perform an Inner-Tantric Initiation. It is obvious what kind of Rinpoche they are and what the state of their practice is.

What is a true Rinpoche? All practitioners must understand that a true Rinpoche must possess the Five Sciences. They must have mastered both exoteric and esoteric Dharma. They must have mastered the Sutras, the Vinaya, and the Abhidharma,[52] which are part of exoteric Dharma. They must have mastered all of the esoteric Dharma. For example, they must understand initiation ceremonies and their procedures. They must understand the teachings of the tantric texts. They must be able to exhibit Dharma powers at the Buddhist altar. Although they may not be thoroughly conversant in the Five Sciences, at least they must possess them.

However, the books written by some of today's so-called Rinpoches are full of mistakes. Despite this, they still call themselves Rinpoches or Dharma Kings. They are truly quite pitiable! Even books written by some Great Rinpoches with high reputations and positions contain page after page of mistakes. After careful examination, one finds that these so-called Great Rinpoches do not possess the Five Sciences and have not mastered either exoteric or esoteric Dharma.

There are so many of these types of things that I will no longer speak of such people. With respect to being a Dharma King, it is easier said than done. In order to be rightly called a Dharma King, one must be a future "successor" of the Buddhas, a future Buddha, or a Buddha who has come again to this world! How could a person on the level of an ordinary Rinpoche hold a candle to a Dharma King? To be a Dharma King is not as simple as the common person thinks.

To be a Dharma King, one must completely possess the Five Sciences, have unsurpassed mastery of exoteric and esoteric Dharma, and have perfect command of the Tripitaka. Such a one must completely comprehend the ten sets of scriptures of Vajrayana Buddhism. Additionally, his abidance by the precepts and rules must be incomparably strict. More importantly, a Dharma King must possess a Dharma King Dharma Wheel. This is indispensable! This Dharma Wheel has unlimited Dharma powers, miraculous powers, and powers to transform itself. Such a person must also be able to successfully invoke nectar in front of his disciples. Only one who possesses such qualities can be called a Dharma King!

As a Dharma King, one must be thoroughly familiar with the Samaya Precepts. Therefore, oftentimes when a Dharma King announces certain tantric proprieties, he will admonish Rinpoches not to say that they have attained realization or accomplishment when they have not.

However, nowadays, those who are called ordinary Rinpoches go so far as to falsely claim that they are Great Rinpoches or even boast that they are Dharma Kings! Actually, if practitioners would take a moment to think about this, they would easily discover the real facts about these people.

Have these people attained the Samaya state of concentration? How many commentaries and books have they written? Are they thoroughly conversant in the Five Sciences? While not demanding that they attain perfect mastery of exoteric and esoteric Dharma, are they at least capable in the Five Sciences? The true situation is that they frequently are incapable in all of these areas! They have not even attained one fifth of Great Dharma King Yangwo Yisinubu's state of realization and virtue. Yet, they actually have the audacity to call themselves Dharma Kings! They are truly charlatans!

Thus, those small Rinpoches and other practitioners who pretend to be Great Rinpoches or Great Dharma Kings must face themselves squarely. The lives of human beings are so short. One must not bring upon oneself the fate of not only failing to attain liberation, but instead, descending into hell! If one only cares about eating, drinking, and merrymaking, if one only cares about enjoyment and being greedy, then one is taken in by mere momentary pleasures. I am afraid that they will not escape from hell. After descending there, they will never be able to leave, since the Samaya Precepts are unforgiving!

Having set out to attain accomplishment, one must cultivate oneself with a heart of humility. If one violates the Samaya Precepts, one must sincerely and deeply repent. Otherwise, one will degenerate. One must devoutly seek the Dharma from a great Vajra Master who has Dharma power and who is heir to a true spiritual legacy. At all times, one's three karmas must correspond with the teachings of the Master. Only in this manner will one be able to save oneself and other sentient beings.

Thus, all practitioners must be sure not to think that once they have been initiated, they can violate the Samaya Precepts and still attain accomplishment without any hindrance! Such precepts absolutely cannot be violated. Once violated, it will be impossible to attain any accomplishment! Whoever violates such precepts must bear karmic responsibility. One will descend into the Vajra Hell. There is no room for the slightest leniency!

If one does not carry out the Samaya Precepts after being initiated and instead often violates them, one must correct oneself to become very careful and attentive. One must repent and sincerely correct one's errors. Otherwise, no matter how energetically one practices, one's practice will be futile. It will never be of any use.

Practitioners must keep this point firmly in mind. Otherwise, there is not much time left!

3. The Futility of Listening Extensively to Teachings on the Dharma When It Does Not Benefit One's Heart

Often hearing teachings on the Dharma benefits cultivators in attaining understanding, raising their level of realization, and reaching a penetrating vision into the meaning of the Dharma. Thus, it will not be easy for them to fall into ignorance and erroneous views. After hearing, one thinks. After thinking, one cultivates. Extensively listening to teachings on the Dharma is a very good way to learn.

Only if Buddhist disciples often hear the Dharma teachings of the Master, understand the Buddhist principles taught, and then follow the Master's teachings by acting in accordance with the principles he expounds, will their practice not fall into a state of confusion. Only then will they not be at a loss to understand the rules and discipline of the Dharma. Only then can they find correct standards and principles for their cultivation.

Thus, hearing the Dharma is like having a compass on a long journey. It can guide the traveler in the correct direction. It is also like a lighthouse on the vast ocean, warning ocean navigators about their path.

Listening to teachings on the Dharma is quite wonderful. If one is able to practice according to the Dharma taught by the Master, then one will naturally receive much benefit and will become accomplished quite easily.

However, if one is only interested in hearing the Dharma but does not act according to the Dharma principles one hears – that is, if one only wishes to hear Dharma teachings but does not make any use of such teachings, and such teachings do not improve or benefit one's thoughts and actions at all – then hearing Dharma teachings is futile. Why is this so?

Indeed, it cannot be denied that one earns merit from hearing the Dharma. Additionally, only through the maturing of countless wonderful causes and conditions that can be traced back through beginningless time, is one able to have the good fortune to hear the Buddha Dharma. One will especially be able to vastly increase one's merit by hearing the discourses and Dharma teachings of true Vajra Masters who are like Buddhas, equal to Buddhas, or more wonderful than Buddhas.[53] The same is true with respect to hearing the discourses and Dharma teachings of Great Bodhisattvas who have attained quite a high state of realization. However, if one only listens to the Dharma but does not practice according to the meaning of the Dharma, then listening to the Dharma is of no use.

It is like a student who sits in a classroom and listens to the lessons. He attends class every day. He listens to the explanations of the teacher. However, he does not absorb the teachings. He does not incorporate the teachings into his mind. The teacher could be describing something so colorfully that it seems as if flowers are cascading from the sky, yet it still is of no use. The student does not transform the principles of the teachings transmitted to him into that which he himself masters. He does not assimilate these principles, which can help him become a useful person and which he must understand. No matter how good his innate qualities may be, no matter how gifted he may be, no matter how clever or smart he may be, it is of no help to the matter. He will all the same still not receive any benefit from the teacher's lessons.

Perhaps he knows that what the teacher says is correct and that he should act according to the principles taught. Yet, when he encounters situations in his life in which he must act according to these principles, he does not do so. Thus, the result will be just the opposite of what he wants.

For example, when a child is very small, the teacher will tell him not to steal other people's things, explaining that stealing is improper conduct, against the law, and a crime that will result in imprisonment. The child heard others speak of these principles, and he understands them. However, under the lure and influence of certain negative factors, he does not obey the words of his teacher and ultimately commits theft. As a result, he is arrested and sent to jail. From that point on, suffering accompanies him throughout his life.

This type of conduct can be said to be a knowing violation of the law. Everybody knows that this type of thing often occurs in society. This is a worldly example of the principles I am expounding. From the perspective of the Buddha Dharma, one cannot, in a simple manner, clearly announce the basic relationship between causes and effects relating to such conduct. You cultivators must attempt to realize this basic relationship yourselves.

If one who cultivates himself and learns the Buddha Dharma knowingly violates the precepts, such person will not only suffer during this lifetime, he will further experience extremely grave consequences in many future lives. Moreover, there are those who have heard the Dharma and who therefore understand to a certain extent some of the principles of cause and effect and karmic retribution. They thus know the suffering that they will experience if they degenerate. Yet, they provide rationalizations for their conduct to set their minds at rest, such as, "I am not seeking to end the cycle of birth and death. I am only seeking a peaceful mind." They utter such diabolical words. With open eyes, they see themselves degenerating, yet they do not make any effort to save themselves. They do not experience any distress from fear of the consequences of their actions. They will suffer a very pitiful and sad fate.

Knowing violation of the precepts or Dharma is not the same as knowing violation of ordinary worldly law! If someone who does not know the Dharma commits several impure offenses, he would be creating negative karma out of ignorance. But one who knows the Buddha Dharma, the precepts, the discipline, and the rules and yet still violates them is, according to the meaning of the Buddha Dharma, knowingly violating the Dharma. His offenses are, therefore, on a greater level. The karmic retribution he will receive will be millions of times greater than the karmic retribution he would receive from having violated worldly laws.

Furthermore, there are those practitioners who have received certain precepts. For example, some have received the Yan Shen part of the Samaya Precepts, some have received the precepts for monks, some have received the precepts for nuns, some have received the Bodhisattva Precepts, etc. They have not fully abided by the precepts they received and have violated many of them. These practitioners have not only knowingly committed such violations, they have also destroyed their vows. They have desecrated the precepts they received. Of course, they must undergo unending suffering as their karmic retribution. It is often the case that those practitioners who have violated multiple precepts must descend into hell.

In summary, there are practitioners who often hear the Dharma yet do not assimilate its meaning into the deepest part of their spirits. That is to say, they hear the Dharma but do not use it as the standards to discipline themselves and as the principles of their practice. As such, although there is the Dharma, they do not follow it. Although there are principles, they do not follow them. To them, it is as if there were no Dharma, although there is the Dharma. To them, it is as if there were no principles, although principles exist. That this Dharma and these principles assist one in ending the cycle of birth and death is, to them, nothing other than empty talk. How they cultivate themselves to attain enlightenment is worth pondering deeply.

If hearing the Dharma is of no benefit to one's heart, then this is a false hearing of the Dharma. What one hears goes into the left ear and comes out of the right ear. The Dharma that they hear is of no importance to them. To put it in worldly terms, they are unable to cultivate their minds and improve their character. To put it in Buddha Dharma terms, this is not the type of practice in which cultivators should engage. One must definitely not act in such manner. Thus, one's cultivation is futile if hearing the Dharma is of no benefit to how one thinks and acts!

4. *The Futility of Performing Meritorious Deeds When One Also Commits Evil Deeds*

Ordinary people of the world sometimes perform a few meritorious deeds. Of course, those who cultivate themselves perform more meritorious deeds.

Basically, those who cultivate themselves will perform some meritorious deeds. Whether many or few, all such deeds are meritorious. By no means is it the case that since the merit from a deed is small, such deed cannot be called meritorious. This is exactly what is meant by the saying, "One unit of merit means one unit of accomplishment." Thus, offering an incense stick at a temple or Buddhist altar has its merit and has its accomplishment. There is contributing money for Buddhist causes, such as building stupas, etc. To contribute one dollar is meritorious. Of course, this contribution also has its accomplishment.

Either unintentionally or intentionally, worldly people occasionally perform some meritorious deeds. They do this out of ignorance, yet they are establishing good karma.

Those who cultivate themselves and learn Buddhism should perform more and more meritorious deeds. The more, the better. The meaning of the phrase *the more, the better* in this context is quite deep. One should perform more meritorious deeds but should not be attached to such deeds. Only when one performs meritorious deeds with the mindset that doing so is simply part of one's original nature, is one truly performing more meritorious deeds!

All people who cultivate themselves know that one should perform meritorious deeds. This is because learning Buddhism and cultivating oneself entails establishing merit and accumulating Buddhist resources. Only after one has perfected one's preliminary practices can one speak of being qualified to engage in one's main practices. Only then can one speak of attaining great accomplishment.

However, this is just like worldly people making money. They make money, and they also spend money. Someone can make a large amount of money in a short period of time. It is also possible for such person to become penniless in an instant.

Performing meritorious deeds may also be like this. Performing meritorious deeds is good. However, there is no guaranty that the performer will not damage his merit.

Some Buddhist disciples are like this. They may devoutly perform great meritorious deeds. Yet, at the same time they are performing these great meritorious deeds, they are also completely canceling out all of their merit. This is due to performing evil deeds during the same time they are performing meritorious deeds.

Take the example of pouring water into a cup. Of course, it should not be difficult to fill the cup with water. If water is poured into the cup, it will quite easily become full. However, if one drills a hole into the cup, there will arise the following vicious circle: Water is poured into the cup, and the water immediately flows out through the hole. While pouring, the amount of water in the cup may stay the same or it may diminish. The water may even totally flow out. Therefore, it seems that this cup can never be filled up. It may not even be able to retain any water.

The principle of both performing meritorious deeds and committing evil deeds is also like this. Performing meritorious deeds is like pouring water into the cup. Committing evil deeds is like drilling a hole into this cup of merit. If one performs meritorious deeds, on the one hand, and commits evil deeds, on the other hand, in the end, it is as if one never established any merit. They cancel each other out. Sometimes, the evil karma totally wipes out all of one's merit. It is somewhat similar to a fierce wind that blows away all of the remaining clouds. Thus, it is as if one never accumulated any merit at all. This often causes those who cultivate themselves to become dispirited!

Could it be said that this is the hoped for end result of cultivation and performing meritorious deeds? I am afraid every practitioner must sincerely ask himself this question! It is worth repeatedly pondering whether you yourself are also performing meritorious deeds in such manner. You must look within yourselves!

There are cultivators who have accumulated a rather large amount of merit by performing many good deeds. Yet, in the end, they often fall into a state of suffering. Some of them experience mental suffering. Some of them experience physical suffering. Some of them experience suffering in their livelihoods. Some of them learn Buddhism but do not experience any supernormal states and do not make any progress in their cultivation.

They cannot figure out exactly what it is that is causing them such suffering. They ask themselves how it is they have fallen into such a state, having handled so many Buddhist affairs and having accumulated merit as large as Mt. Sumeru. The most important reason is that at the same time they were building their mountain of merit, they were also continually committing evil deeds. The facts prove that cultivation composed of accumulating merit, on the one hand, and committing evil deeds, on the other hand, is totally futile.

For example, some Buddhist disciples are very devout toward the Master and the Buddhas and Bodhisattvas. They satisfactorily complete all of the tasks that the Master tells them to do. As a consequence, they accumulate a limitless amount of merit. However, in their homes or at their work places, they hit or scold their family members or their colleagues. They often threaten to abandon their own family members. They may dislike such family members for being incapable, for not being good-looking, or for being too stupid. They feel that such family members are burdensome and will drag them down. They quarrel with people, engage in verbal abuse, and give rise to hatred and jealousy in their hearts. Their words and behavior are odious. They frequently harm others. Their speech is bitterly sarcastic. They continually engage in evil conduct. In so doing, at the same time they are building their mountain of merit, they are also digging away at their mountain of merit.

Hearing the teachings of the Master is building good karma. One can thereby accumulate Buddhist resources of good fortune and wisdom. When one does not practice the four limitless states of mind in one's treatment of others and instead commits evil deeds, then one is creating impure karma. One thereby sets up obstacles on one's path of cultivation. When one commits evil deeds at the same time one is performing deeds in furtherance of Buddhism, then naturally one is performing such meritorious deeds in vain. This type of cultivation is futile.

I am most distressed about certain Rinpoches, Dharma Teachers, and others who have accumulated great merit. They faithfully and conscientiously perform deeds in furtherance of Buddhism. Based upon their level of understanding and their particular circumstances, they clearly believe in a limited form of cause and effect (except for that which they themselves have not been able to realize). On the whole, they know about cause and effect and karmic retribution. In the end, they can be considered as cultivators who, to a small extent, understand the Buddha Dharma. These Rinpoches and Dharma Teachers uphold and spread the Buddha Dharma, teach their disciples, propagate the truth, and clarify people's confusion. They do all of these things that a teacher is supposed to do. When performing deeds in furtherance of Buddhism, they almost always do so with great vigor.

However, it is a pity that after they become masters, they think that since they have accumulated so much merit, they can relax the demands they place upon themselves. They thus do not strive to make progress. They do not think about improving themselves. Gradually, they change into worldly people. They seek worldly things, such as enjoyment, power, empty titles, etc. Their desires continuously increase. They become no different from common worldlings.

There is another aspect to this. The precepts and discipline of tantra provide in strict terms that the Vajra Master is the embodiment of the Three Jewels. Disciples of a Master must view their Master as being no different from a Buddha. However, when disciples call their Master a Holy Master, certain masters become puffed up with pride. These masters think that their state of virtue and state of realization are on the same level as a Buddha or Kuan Yin Bodhisattva! They boast without shame that they are Buddhas or Great Jewel Dharma Kings. Everywhere they go, they brag and deceive people.

What is even more absurd is that since they view themselves as Buddhas, it seems to them that as a matter of course they are entitled to figure out how many "Dakinis" they should marry and bring home.[54] They then become openly promiscuous. They bring some worldly women home without going through any ceremony or Dharma verification and without considering the underlying karmic connection between them. They cannot possibly still be Rinpoches. Clearly, they are devils who are degenerating!

To them, it is as if they were Sakyamuni Buddha living in the world. Each of them says, "I am a Dharma King" or "I am the leading contemporary Master." They are simply ordinary people who are charlatans. Nevertheless, they think of themselves as being no different from Sakyamuni Buddha. They do not maintain a heart of humility and do not truly cultivate themselves. They do not examine themselves well. They do not look at themselves squarely and ask, "What type of person actually am I? What level of merit have I attained? What is the level of my state of realization and state of virtue? What meritorious deeds have I performed? What qualifications do I have to be mentioned in the same breath with Sakyamuni Buddha? Am I qualified to be on the same level of Kuan Yin Bodhisattva?"

Yet, they think that they are amazing for having attained a slight amount of accomplishment. They think that they no longer need the Master, that they need not continue to obey the Master's words, and that the Master's words no longer have any value! When instructed by the Master to perform deeds in furtherance of Buddhism, they think that they can bargain with the Master over the terms of performance. Hence, they treat the Master in a casual fashion, as if he were just a worldly businessman. The earnest teachings and admonitions of the Master are of no use whatsoever to them. When, on occasion, they realize that they can make some use of the Master or that they need the Master, they will reluctantly obey a bit of his teachings and admonitions.

Anyway, it all depends on how they feel. If obeying will bring them power and profit, then they will obey some of his teachings and admonitions. They will perform deeds in furtherance of Buddhism if in so doing there is benefit to themselves. If they think performing any such deeds would harm their interests in the slightest way, they will run far away. Their own matters come first. The demands of the Master come last. They do not view the Buddha Dharma, precepts, discipline, ceremonies, and rules as being of any importance. Thus, it goes without saying that they are unable to energetically cultivate themselves!

Of course, when I speak of the Master, everybody must bear in mind the following: One must clearly determine whether such person is a true Master with virtue. Only then can one follow such person!

Now then, have these disciples always been this way? Not at all! When they first became Buddhists and took refuge in the Master, they were not like this. At that time, they took up the learning of Buddhism with the resolve to end the cycle of birth and death. At that time, they made great efforts to learn the Dharma under the Master. They also obeyed the words of the Master. They viewed the Master as Sakyamuni Buddha and thus treated the Master with the same respect and love with which they would treat a Buddha. They accumulated a great deal of merit.

However, later, they viewed this merit and accomplishment as capital that they could use to seek worldly good fortune. They gradually got into the habit of accumulating merit, on the one hand, and committing evil deeds, on the other hand. They thus totally tore down their towering mountain of merit.

All of the merit they accumulated was totally canceled out. In the end, their negligence led to great disaster and they failed to succeed.

It can be said that these people gradually changed from the devout Buddhist disciples they were in the very beginning to sham cultivators. In so doing, their cultivation became futile. Their cultivation became totally useless in ending the cycle of birth and death and attaining liberation! Actually, if they would have continued learning Buddhism as they were doing in the very beginning, they all could have realized great accomplishment!

Various circumstances clearly show that performing meritorious deeds is futile if one is also continually committing evil deeds!

5. The Futility of Following the Master When One Engages in Wrongdoing

Engaging in wrongdoing refers to what one does. That is, one produces impure karma through actions, speech, and thoughts. It is not conduct that is truly for the good of oneself and others.

All cultivators should know that the karmic effects of engaging in wrongdoing are inevitably painful. Such conduct is of no benefit to oneself. One unit of cause produces one unit of effect. You yourself will receive back as punishment the exact same amount of pain that you give to others. The average follower of Buddhism understands this principle. However, those who truly give rise to fear due to this principle and thereby engage in conduct that only produces pure karma are very few. We will not speak at great length about this here.

However, there is a point that is related to this topic. There is a wrong viewpoint maintained by the average cultivator that must be corrected. It is the following viewpoint maintained by very many cultivators: "No matter how many mistakes I commit, no matter how much negative karma I produce, it is all unimportant. As long as I follow the Master, everything will be all right. The Master will bear all of my offenses. With the protection and empowerment of the Master and with the kind care of the Buddhas and Bodhisattvas, it will be no problem at all to become accomplished. Engaging in wrongdoing is not of importance. I can all the same become accomplished and end the cycle of birth and death!"

These people think that as long as they follow the Master, they can successfully hide the truth. They think that having the Master, they have everything. It does not matter to them if they engage in all kinds of wrongdoing and produce enormous horrible karma. As far as they are concerned, why care?

It is truly distressing to see this. I am afraid that if cultivators with this level of ignorance do not go to hell, then they will descend into the animal realm! I am not trying to frighten you. Although many of you present here are Rinpoches, you still must be careful!

Buddhists who want to realize enlightenment through cultivation, especially those who learn tantra, should cultivate themselves by following a Vajra Master! The Master is the embodiment of the Three Jewels and is the foundation for accomplishment. Thus, those who cultivate themselves must follow a Vajra Master with a true spiritual lineage, a Rinpoche who has mastered both exoteric and esoteric Dharma and who is thoroughly proficient in the Five Sciences. Only then will they have the foundation for achieving the goal of ending the cycle of birth and death.

Since following a Master has such significant ramifications, all cultivators who set their minds on leaving the cycle of reincarnation have gone through untold hardships and passed through many places in order to seek out a genuine Vajra Master with a true spiritual lineage, an Acarya who possesses the true Dharma of the Tathagata. However, after cultivators follow a Master, they often place all of their hopes on to the Master. They do not place strict demands upon themselves. They do not act in accordance with the principles of the Dharma. They do not act in accordance with Buddhist proprieties. They do not cultivate themselves by following the words and imitating the actions of the Master. They do not make their three karmas correspond with the teachings of the Master.

Instead, they think that the Master will help them take care of everything. They think that they can sleep in peace, without any worry, and that they will still be able to end the cycle of birth and death. They thus engage in much wrongdoing yet are still cheerful, confident, and at ease. In fact, this type of cultivation is extremely wrong. It undoubtedly is a futile type of cultivation.

No matter how great the abilities of the Master whom one follows may be, if one's three karmas do not correspond with the teachings of the Master, then one will not be able to solve the basic problem of ending the cycle of birth and death! Those who cultivate themselves should understand this principle. The abilities of the Master belong to the Master. Such abilities do not belong to others. The Master cannot, after all, substitute himself for others. However, as long as one's three karmas correspond with the teachings of the Master, it should be no problem at all for the Master to easily lead such person to attain liberation. It could be said that this is a small matter to the Master!

The Master transmits to practitioners the method by which to cultivate oneself and become accomplished. But it is the practitioner himself who practices the Dharma. There is no way for the Master to substitute for the practitioner when it comes to cultivation! This is because the Buddha Dharma calls for clearly believing in cause and effect, not denying cause and effect.

There is a common saying: "When one plants melons, one gets melons. When one plants beans, one gets beans." This describes the principle of cause and effect. It is absolutely impossible to gather in crops if one has not planted anything. The type of thinking that holds that the Master can bear everything in place of the practitioner goes against the principle of cause and effect. It is an incorrect viewpoint! If the Master were able to substitute for the practitioner when it comes to cultivation, if, with the empowerment and protection of the Master, the practitioner need not cultivate himself yet would still be able to end the cycle of birth and death, then all living beings on earth, even all living beings in the three spheres, would not need to learn the Buddha Dharma. Why?

Sakyamuni Buddha has unlimited Dharma power, unlimited brightness, unlimited miraculous powers, and wonderful, unhindered Buddha wisdom. Kuan Yin Bodhisattva's heart of great compassion is incomparable. She will respond to every request. There is also the limitless compassion of the Buddhas and Bodhisattvas, who number in the billions, like the sands of the Ganges River. According to the thinking of these misguided practitioners, as long as these Holy Ones continually empower living beings, everything will be all right. Living beings will be able to avoid suffering and the defilements.

This way of thinking on the part of these people is quite ignorant. They do not understand cause and effect at all. Of course, there is empowerment with unlimited Dharma power. However, only when one's three karmas correspond with the teachings of the Master is empowerment of any use!

If cultivators blindly rely upon the Master, look to the Master to solve all of their problems, and do not make any efforts themselves, then even if Sakyamuni Buddha were in the world today as their Master, it would still be of no use. He would not be able to help them. In the end, they will have come to this human world in vain and will not have gained or accomplished anything. If they ought to descend into the one of the three lower realms, then they will still have to descend. Even Sakyamuni Buddha would not be able to save them.

This can be compared to eating. The Buddhas and Bodhisattvas, as well as all of the Great Accomplished Ones who aroused bodhicitta and vowed to save living beings, have already eaten to their satisfaction. When they see that you are so hungry you are about to faint and that you are in great pain, due to their compassionate hearts, they pity you and transmit to you the method by which you can eat to your satisfaction.

For example, they tell you that you should take hold of chopsticks or a fork and knife or just use your hands. They tell you to make use of these things. They tell you that you should then open your mouth, use your teeth to chew, and swallow. If you do these things, they say, you will be able to eat savory food and will be able to eat to your satisfaction, just like them.

If you act in accordance with the method taught by these Great Accomplished Ones, then you will be able to be the same as the Buddhas and Bodhisattvas. You will be able to eat to your full satisfaction and will not suffer pain. You will be very comfortable. You will experience a type of transcendent feeling.

However, if you insist on not acting in accordance with the method taught by the Buddhas and Bodhisattvas, do not use your hands, chopsticks, or a fork and knife, and do not even open your mouth, then no matter how great the method transmitted by the Buddhas and Bodhisattvas may be and no matter how delicious the delicacies placed before you may be, you will just continue to be hungry and will continue to suffer. You will be unable to enjoy the food.

When other people are, one after the other, eating to their full satisfaction from having followed the method taught by the Great Accomplished Ones, your belly, however, is still rumbling with hunger. You are so starved that your chest is stuck to your back, and you are on the verge of death. Can you blame others? You can only blame yourself! You do not do anything. You are not even willing to open your mouth. Whom can you blame? That the Buddhas and Bodhisattvas eat to their full satisfaction has to do with them. What does it have to do with you? No matter how full they fill themselves with food, in the final analysis, it is they themselves who are eating, not you who are eating. The food is entering their stomachs, not your stomach. They therefore are able to satisfy their hunger. They no longer fear hunger. Yet you are still struggling while in hunger. You are still writhing in pain. You are unable to be comfortable and at ease.

The Accomplished Ones who told you the way to eat are equivalent to the true Vajra Master who guides you into Buddhism, who shows you how to practice the Dharma, whom you found after going through untold hardships, and whom you decided to follow. The method of eating is equivalent to the method of cultivation the Master transmitted to you. Using chopsticks, a knife and a fork, or your hands to eat is equivalent to truly carrying out one's cultivation. The utensils or your hands are equivalent to the Buddha Dharma that you use to become accomplished. Correspondence of your three karmas with the teachings of the Master is equivalent to your movements made in correct sequence whereby you place the food inside your mouth according to the instructions of others. Opening your mouth is equivalent to your truly wanting to cultivate yourself. Eating to your satisfaction and feeling comfortable is equivalent to the permanent happiness you receive from having realized enlightenment as a result of cultivation.

Therefore, following a Master is essential. Without a Master transmitting to you the Buddha Dharma, you will have no way to begin to learn. You would thus be in the dark about how to become accomplished. But, when you follow a Master, you must obey the Master's teachings and not commit evil deeds. Your actions must not harm other people. You cannot engage in any wrongdoing at all. Only with this type of pure karma can you cause your cultivation to become impeccable. Otherwise, if you engage in wrongdoing, then your following a Master will be futile and of no benefit.

6. *The Futility of Being a Teacher When One Does Not Practice the Dharma and One Also Does Evil*

This futility has to do with those who are masters. Those people in the world who guide others, yet who are actually just engaging in high-sounding but meaningless talk, are not in the category of teachers I am referring to here. Being a teacher, one must possess qualities that surpass others, and one must be heir to a true Dharma legacy. This would include genuine eminent monks, Great Virtuous Ones, Dharma Teachers, Rinpoches, Great Lamas, etc. This would also include Great Bodhisattvas and Buddhas who voluntarily came to this world again in response to its needs and who are Great Mahasattva Masters or Dharma Kings.

In today's world, there are true teachers and there are also false teachers. Practitioners must open their eyes to carefully and clearly distinguish between the two. You must not follow those false teachers who cheat people out of money and property. Otherwise, you will be sorry when it is too late!

Actually, there are those who truly have a wonderful karmic destiny. They indeed have deep roots of kindness and the natural capacity to be a teacher. Yet, due to certain karmic obscurations, they also engage in some futile practices. These teachers are rather pitiable. The accomplishment of these teachers, of course, cannot even be mentioned in the same breath with the accomplishment of Great Mahasattvas or Great Dharma Kings. The state of realization of these teachers is far inferior to that of Great Mahasattvas or Great Dharma Kings!

However, using the Dharma to distinguish the genuine from the false, one concludes that they, in fact, are not "false great practitioners." This includes some Rinpoches and Dharma Teachers, etc. Actually, this is a very natural circumstance. Those on the first Bodhisattva stage do not know about what takes place on the second Bodhisattva stage. How can those on the fifth Bodhisattva stage know about what those on the tenth Bodhisattva stage do? Those on the second Bodhisattva stage see those on the first Bodhisattva stage as having impurities. Even those on the tenth Bodhisattva stage see those on the ninth Bodhisattva stage as having certain impurities. How much more so would they see the impurities of some small Rinpoches or small masters! Of course, the impurities and obscurations of these small Rinpoches and small masters would be greater than those of ninth stage Bodhisattvas! Nevertheless, those who are kind and benefit others can, after all, guide and transform living beings.

However, this does not mean that these Rinpoches, Dharma Teachers, etc., can do whatever they please, that they can casually violate the precepts, commit offenses, and then provide all kinds of excuses for their conduct. They cannot just say that such conduct is caused by fixed karmic obscurations produced in previous lives and be through with it!

Cultivators might allow their karmic retribution, the causes of which were produced in previous lives, to command how they carry out their three karmas of body, speech, and mind in this life. They might allow this karmic retribution to dominate all of their thinking and behavior in this life. If so, it will result in their turning a deaf ear to the precepts, discipline, and rules of the Buddha Dharma. Then, even if they realize the state of a Bodhisattva due to having accumulated great merit throughout many lives and eons, it will still be of no use. They will descend into lower realms all the same.

Furthermore, Mara, the Evil One, who is the lord of the sixth heaven,[55] along with his horde of demons, are making every attempt to hinder those with deep roots of kindness and those sincere cultivators who have already realized or are about to realize some wonderful accomplishment. Therefore, one who is a teacher cannot be indulgent toward his own mistakes and bad habits. This is especially true of practices that violate the precepts or the principles of the Dharma. Otherwise, one careless step will cause one to fall into the abyss of unlimited suffering!

For example, certain teachers, such as some Rinpoches, Dharma Teachers, etc., do not practice the Dharma and instead commit some evil deeds. As a master, if you yourself do not practice the Dharma, how could you teach disciples? Among teachers in today's world, there is truly no shortage of the following type of people. They do not practice according to the meaning of the Dharma. They do not meditate and do not read the sutras. They do not recite mantras or engage in visualization. They do not learn any Dharma principles. They do not practice the Dharma transmitted to them by the Master.

Instead, what they often do is engage in activities to protect their own personal interests, reputation, and power. They engage in activities to increase their wealth. They seek enjoyment. They are attached to things of the world. They engage in distorted, vain dreams. They do not think about leaving the cycle of birth and death. The alarm bell of the Buddha Dharma does not constantly ring in their ears. Their vigilance, of course, gradually vanishes. Their arrogant, wasteful, and licentious mode of life worsens as each day passes. Of course, their evil conduct grows due to greed, hatred, and ignorance.[56]

These Rinpoches even dream of receiving the supreme initiation from a Buddha so that they can immediately manifest supernormal powers and conquer other people. They do not understand that even if the Master agreed to perform such initiation, the Exalted Ones in the Dharma realms would not approve.

The 500 Arhats assembled three times after the demise of Sakyamuni Buddha. They feared that cultivators would not have anything to rely upon in their practice and that the Buddha Dharma would thus fall into a state of chaos. Ananda, who was Sakyamuni Buddha's close attendant and who never forgot anything he heard, recited by memory all of the teachings and discourses of Sakyamuni Buddha while he was alive. Those Great Accomplished Ones deeply entered into a supernormal Dharma state to verify the accuracy of Ananda's memory. After experiencing many hardships, they finally compiled the Sutras, Vinaya, and Abhidharma, which together compose the Hundred Dragon Tripitaka. So that Buddhism would not fall into chaos and so that Buddhist disciples of later generations would have something to rely upon in their practice, Master Padmasambhava and Master Marpa transmitted the four divisions of yoga.

Cultivators in today's world all use the precepts and disciplinary rules of the Buddha Dharma as principles by which they govern their practice. All practices that go against these precepts and disciplinary rules are seen as violations. All practices that do not accord with the Dharma principles expounded in the Sutras and Abhidharma are, of course, incorrect practices. They are practices that go against the correct Dharma. They are practices that cultivators should abandon.

There are very strict rules governing how cultivators should practice the Dharma, when they should practice, and where they should practice! These rules must be meticulously followed.

Take, for example, the summer retreat for monks and nuns. When the summer retreat begins and ends, where to spend the summer retreat, how many members of the sangha should spend the summer retreat together, etc., are all strictly governed by Dharma rules. One must not treat such rules casually and recklessly!

Another example would be masters who want to establish a new sect. This must be approved by the most esteemed Great Virtuous Ones. The master himself must have already realized the state of having ended the cycle of birth and death and must be thoroughly conversant with the Tripitaka. Otherwise, a master may not establish a new sect.

Thus, if cultivators do not practice in accordance with the Dharma, then they have completely lost their basic qualifications to be a Buddhist disciple. They are acting in a way that runs counter to the rules of the Buddha Dharma. Of course, they will undoubtedly descend into one of the lower realms. I need not even mention how serious it is when a Vajra Master who guides others in learning Buddhism and cultivation does not act in accordance with the Dharma.

The state of virtue and realization of a Rinpoche or Dharma Teacher is vastly inferior to the supreme state of virtue and realization of a Buddha! All cultivators must go through many lives and eons of vigorous practice, must attain true realization through personal effort, must follow the Dharma, the precepts, and the disciplinary rules, and must abide by the teachings of the Master in order to attain, step by step, the limitless accomplishment of a Buddha and reach the same state as a Buddha.

Even if one unrelentingly and tirelessly practices, it is still not easy to attain the realization of a Buddha. This is all the more true for one who is still unable to act in accordance with the Dharma and who does not devoutly practice the Dharma. It is obvious that these teachers who do not practice the Dharma will only distance themselves more and more from attaining accomplishment. It will definitely not be possible for them to become accomplished. By acting in such manner, they are unable to save themselves. How could they guide and save others?

Actually, the interrelationship between not practicing the Dharma and committing evil deeds is like the interrelationship of parasites who rely on each other to multiply. The interrelationship between the two is inevitably one of mutual continuation and mutual dependence!

Not practicing the Dharma will weaken their correct thoughts regarding the Dharma and will lead them far astray from the essentials of the Dharma. Gradually, they will separate themselves from the practices of those who cultivate themselves, and they will violate the teachings of the Master. This will develop into an indifference toward the Dharma, precepts, and rules. They will then totally disregard the Buddha Dharma, precepts, and discipline, violate the precepts they received, break the vows they made, follow their own course despite the advice of others, and stray in the opposite direction of the correct path. They will inevitably do as they please and thereby commit evil deeds, such as speaking words that sow discord, speaking harshly, lying to the Master, and harming other living beings. They will easily give rise to hatred. Their desires will multiply. They will not think of leaving the cycle of reincarnation. They will use every means at their disposal to seek their own greedy ends. Their attachment to the concept of self will be strong. Defilements born of ignorance will grow by the day.

In the more serious cases, there are those who even violate the Eight Precepts. In the end, they dare to commit even the worst offenses. They have no misgivings about violating any precept. They are no different from worldly people. They are even worse than some people who have never learned the Buddha Dharma. Their odious conduct is a horrible influence upon Buddhism, causing Buddhist circles to be in utter chaos! Moreover, those who act in such manner include those who are in the category of masters. This is all the more reason why their conduct causes people not to take refuge in the Three Jewels and not to learn the Buddha Dharma.

Even if there are still people who follow them, these followers will increasingly tend toward evil and increasingly descend into ignorance! These followers cannot possibly become accomplished!

How could these people still be Vajra Masters? How could they be Bodhisattvas who aroused bodhicitta in order to guide living beings toward cultivation and accomplishment? They do not uphold or spread the Buddha Dharma at all. Rather, they destroy the Buddha Dharma! Of course, they completely destroy themselves as well. Step by step they degenerate and finally descend into hell!

Thus, not practicing the Dharma and committing evil deeds are two bad factors that play on each other. They can only negatively influence those who cultivate themselves. Those masters (Rinpoches, Dharma Teachers, etc.) who guide others in practicing the Buddha Dharma must especially understand this point. One must not become dizzy with success or delirious with joy due to being a master! One must not think that just because one has a small amount of accomplishment, one is therefore amazing, can therefore seek pleasure, and need not vigorously expend effort in one's cultivation.

If one maintains this way of thinking, one can only degenerate. The vast merit one accumulated will be canceled out. One's cultivation will become a futile practice.

Thus, it is futile to be a teacher when one does not practice the Dharma and one also does evil!

7. *The Futility of One's Cultivation When One Is Moved by the Eight Winds*

The Eights Winds are also known as the Eight Worldly Dharmas. They are gain, loss, disgrace, honor, praise, ridicule, suffering, and pleasure.[57] In the Visesacinta-brahma-pariprccha-sutra, the following is written: "Gain and loss; disgrace and honor; praise and ridicule; suffering and pleasure – these eight Dharmas commonly lead people around."

Because of the Eight Winds, people give rise to craving and hatred. The Eight Winds cause people to fall into confusion. They stir up people's hearts. They are like hurricanes that wreak havoc. People get lost in them. That is why they are called the Eight Winds. As stated in the Xin Zhong Ji Yi Shang, "The Mahaprajnaparamita-sastra provides, 'Loss, gain, disgrace, honor, praise, ridicule, suffering, and pleasure; four are agreeable and four are disagreeable. They can stir people's emotions and are called the Eight Winds.'"

Because of their nature, greed, hatred, ignorance, craving, joy, anger, sorrow, and pleasure correspond to the Eight Winds. The following can be said:

Because of gain, greed is aroused.
Because of greed, one seeks gain.
Because of loss, hatred is aroused.
Because of hatred, one loses.
Ignorance brings about disgrace.
Disgrace abets ignorance.
Because of craving, one seeks honor.
Because of honor, craving is aroused.
Because of praise, joy is aroused.
Because of joy, one wants to be praised.
Anger causes ridicule.
Because of ridicule, one becomes angry.
Because of sorrow, one suffers.
Because of suffering, sorrow is aroused.
Pleasure brings about the desire for more pleasure.
Pleasure causes attachment.

One can thus see that the relationship between the two factors contained in each pair mentioned above is truly close. Each factor affects the other. Each factor neatly corresponds with the other. As such, karmic causes and effects continue on and on, and the seeds of reincarnation are never extinguished.

Thus, it can be said that the Eight Winds compose the main component of the fire-wheel known as the six realms of reincarnation. The Eight Winds are pretty much equivalent to the axle that controls the turning of this fire-wheel. If one day these Eight Winds lose their effect, then this fire-wheel will crumble apart. It will no longer have any power.

The most important thing that cultivators must work on is not being bound by these Eight Winds. If one is truly able to separate oneself from and be completely unmoved by these Eight Winds, then one has already almost totally liberated oneself from the fire-wheel known as the six realms of reincarnation.

When speaking of gain, one must also speak of greed. Without gain, greed would not arise. With gain, people seek things out of greed. Greed refers to attachment born of greed. It includes greed aimed at obtaining, seeking, or taking things for oneself. There is also greed for sex, wealth, power, profit, glory, and high positions. Because of gain, there arises the attachment of greed. Because of greed, one desires to receive gain or even more and more gain.

Gain and greed act on each other. Gain cannot be separated from greed. With greed, one desires more gain. The relationship between greed and gain is like the relationship between the senses and the corresponding objects of the senses. They are inseparable.

From ancient times until the present, the lives of countless worldly people have revolved around the word *greed*. Because of gain, greed is aroused.

In ancient times, there was the saying, "Books contain beautiful women and houses of gold."[58] This way of thinking has continued for generations. It tells worldly people why they should diligently read books. The answer is nothing other than one thing: greed! The reason is nothing other than one thing: gain!

This way of thinking holds that by reading books, one can stand out among others. Thus, one can have beautiful women to hold, become a government official, have power, and be an influential person. For the sake of gain, people have tried all possible ways, even to the extent of suffering physical pain, in order to concentrate their minds on reading. There is the story of a student in a poor family who cut holes in his wall so that he could have a little bit of light from his neighbor's room in order to be able to read books. There is also the saying, "After ten years of hard study noticed by none, his fame fills the land once he becomes the top successful candidate in the imperial examination!"

Even those people full of learning and talent who were content to be immersed in the pages of books and who did not seek honors or fame also desired certain types of "gains." They desired "gain" from their literary skills. They desired "gain" from reading or writing flowery or profane words. When reciting and composing poetry with others, they could receive certain oratory "gains." They received "gain" from expressing their gloomy feelings through the written word, thereby receiving consolation.

There have been those who were far away from the imperial court but whose hearts were constantly tied to it. They were banished from the court to outlying areas and became recluses. Although they said that they did not care about honor or fame, they often sighed deeply over having unrecognized talent. Thus, there were those who took to drinking in order to relieve their grief, only to produce more grief. There were those so unbearably depressed that they took their own lives. There were those who wrote poetry to express their thoughts and feelings. There were those who wandered about ostensibly to enjoy the beauties of nature but who had ulterior motives. There were those who leisurely appreciated scenery and seemed to feel content but who were actually not content.

Can it be said that these people were truly unattached to things of the world, that they did not desire worldly gains or benefits? Not at all! With respect to most of them, they were in one place, yet their hearts were in another! What they wrote and spoke did not reflect their true thoughts.

Some of them thought that they had already transcended worldliness. However, unbeknownst to them, hidden in their hearts were desire and attachment born of greed, which were stronger than the desire and attachment harbored by worldly people. Some of them actually cared more about honor and riches than even worldly people, yet they comported themselves in a untrammeled and easy manner, as if they were totally carefree. They vowed to die for the benefit of others, since they claimed to view death as merely returning home.

If they actually were as they made themselves out to be, then why did they write so energetically in an attempt to express themselves, taking pleasure in mocking themselves and in issuing so-called lofty "warnings" to the world? If they really did not care about anything, if they really considered fame and gain to be utterly without value, then why did they toss and turn in their beds, unable to sleep at night?

In reality, these false recluses had more pain in their hearts, more extravagant hopes, and more greedy desires than worldly people. They were not any less attached to "gain" than worldly people, yet they purposefully covered up this attachment. Although the attachment of worldly people has always been openly manifested, the attachment and greedy pursuits of these people were kept secret and hidden.

Their secret pursuit of gain was in fact no different from worldly people's pursuit of gain. Their pursuit of gain tormented them even more intensely and painfully than the pursuit of gain torments worldly people. This pursuit of theirs slowly gnawed away their spirit, just like a silkworm gnaws away a mulberry leaf, causing them to often fall into a state of dejection, hesitation, and worry. Yet, many of these people are extolled by the world, and their fame continues through the ages. They are praised as being people of ideals who possessed literary and military skills, accomplished thinkers and writers, etc.

If one were truly able to let go of attachment to worldly gain, one would follow the principles of the Buddha Dharma and engage in meditation in order to perceive the truth. One would proceed to deeply understand the falseness of life's superficial beauty. One would proceed to seek out the root of impermanence and suffering by overcoming dreamlike or illusory thinking that only looks at the surface of things. One would proceed to clearly understand the essence of the six realms of reincarnation. Then, one would proceed to thoroughly understand the nature of the mind and clearly comprehend the law of cause and effect. This would be truly seeing the world as it is, truly desiring to leave the world, truly seeking to renounce the world.

I am not trying to belittle people similar to those mentioned above. Worldly people know about such people but do not comprehend why they were the way they were. This lack of comprehension is quite pervasive! This is due to the collective karma of worldly people and should not be considered strange.

I would now like to explain a fact. From ancient times until the present, gain and greed have truly played a decisive role in the thinking of human beings. Gain and greed can be said to be deeply ingrained in the thinking of human beings. Gain and greed are unfathomably deep. Even certain people who are quite famous and who have been venerated throughout generations could not extricate themselves from the entanglement and perplexity caused by gain and greed. One can see how broad and deep the influence of gain and greed is!

From ancient times until the present, from the highest levels of society to the lowest, worldly men have coveted beautiful women. A major example of this would be losing the empire for having attempted to please a certain woman. Examples of lesser importance would be lavishly spending money on beautiful women and leading a dissipated life. In the end, many of these people wound up all alone, with their heads held low. It was as if they were drawing water with a sieve – they achieved nothing at all.

Because of coveting the "gain" of money and wealth, people have done things that have caused them to be thrown into prison, expelled from their families, and forsaken by their friends and allies. People like this have included emperors, monarchs, members of royal families, marquis, generals, social elites, ministers, and officials. Of course, there is no shortage of people like this among the common people in different walks of life. All of these different people soon degenerate due to their various greedy desires.

In short, where there is greed for gain, there is killing and the smoke of gunpowder. There is contention and fighting among people. There is open robbery. There is secret plundering. This greed for gain has resulted in scenes of suffering and devastation wherever one looks. It has resulted in the masses becoming destitute. It has caused people to commit very foolish acts. It has caused fights among brothers.

Generally speaking, people seeking gain based upon greed leave everything in their path beaten, scattered, and routed. This is what is left behind for people due to greed for gain. Absolutely nothing else is left behind.

This is only a brief description of principles from a micro point of view. From a macro point of view, all living beings in the three spheres are born into one of the six realms due to thoughts of greed. In the end, what they actually "gain" is all kinds of frustration and dissatisfaction and much suffering. Because of thoughts of "greed for gain," one plants evil causes, and life after life one is tossed to and fro within the six realms of reincarnation, never being able to achieve liberation.

People of the world do not understand these principles. They steep themselves in bitter water and never get tired of it. They drift along, continuing to be greedy. They see worldly gains and do not know of enlightenment. They do not have any real estimation of who they are. Thus, they recommit the same errors. If a reasonable person who learns Buddhism, cultivates himself, and tries to understand Buddhist principles still thinks in such manner up to the time of his death, then this would truly be pitiable!

The above is a brief explanation of one of the Eight Winds – gain – and its counterpart of attachment born of greed. As mentioned, there is greed, hatred, ignorance, craving, joy, anger, sorrow and pleasure; gain, loss, disgrace, honor, praise, ridicule, suffering, and pleasure. As for these others not yet described, they are all like this.

The countless sentient beings are bound by hatred. Thus, there are those who make pillows of their spears, waiting eagerly for daybreak to engage in battle. There are those who seek revenge for the smallest grievance. The words, thoughts, and actions of these people who are bound by hatred cause the descent of other people. The evil karma so produced will bring about retribution due to hatred. This retribution will cause them to decline much more than others.

Because of ignorance, one is confused. One is lost in erroneous ways. One might be attached to the ways of the world and not believe in cause and effect, resulting in self-destruction, disgracing oneself and others, and being unable to attain liberation. This in turn brings about the karmic retribution of ignorance. Thus, ignorance and disgrace alternate as causes and effects in an unending vicious circle, which results in unlimited suffering.

Because of being bound by craving,[59] one gives rise to the desire to grasp things. One grasps for honor. One is attached to things due to craving. One grasps for that which one craves. One separates oneself from that which one does not crave. Because one is bewitched by the false phenomenon of honor, one gives rise to craving for honor. Thus, honor and craving affect each other without end. One thereby falls into distorted dream-thinking. One wallows in illusions and worldly desires. One considers the illusions to be real. All of this causes one's negative karma to increase further. Craving and honor rely on each other and give rise to many attachments.

Joy causes one to jump up and down when one obtains something. Yet, when one loses something, one is very sad. If one comes into contact with something good, one becomes joyful. If one finds oneself in a bad environment, one becomes dejected. If others are pleased with someone, they praise that person. The cause of joy brings about praise. Joy is manifested by praise. All of this is the result of one's mind being influenced by external circumstances and one's holding on to the concept of self. One is thus continually receiving the results of negative karma, which in turn produce more karmic action related to joy and praise. One repeatedly engages in negative karma due to joy and praise. One's mind is repeatedly influenced by external circumstances. One is thus unable to attain purity.

People usually allow those who are agreeable to them to prosper. However, due to anger, people destroy those who go against them. People become angry when they are ridiculed. They bristle with anger. They become out-raged. They cannot help responding with their own ridicule and derision. This evil behavior results in others being ridiculed and further infuriated. These others will then come back with even more ridicule. This results in still more anger. The pattern of producing evil karma and receiving its nega-tive consequences continues without end. People are influenced by external circumstances. Karmic retribution comes from evil karma. All of this is due to attachment to what is seemingly real but truly empty and the karmic obscurations thereby produced. Thus, one cannot receive pure and good karmic fruits.

When one is separated from what one craves, or when one is too troubled, one becomes sorrowful. One is confused by the external circumstances. One is unable to distinguish between the false and the real. Thus, one suffers due to the external environment, which seems to be real but is actually false. Because of suffering, one becomes sorrowful. One knits one's brows and does not smile. The more sorrowful one is, the more suffering one experiences. Suffering again causes sorrow. They are like two sisters or a married couple. They disturb the mind, and one is thus unable to attain correct understand-ing.

People are always motivated by pleasure. If one is benefited, one becomes pleased. However, if one is harmed, one becomes worried and sad. One feels quite pleased when there is pleasure. However, without pleasure, one becomes sad. Being pleased creates the greed for more pleasure. Because of the cause of pleasure, one desires even more pleasure. One's mind is influenced by and follows the external circumstances. One therefore is unable to accumulate pure karma. One cannot attain right mindfulness and clear awareness. Being attached to pleasure, one creates negative karma, which results in returning to the cycle of reincarnation.

In summary, being attached to these Eight Winds will give rise to greed, hatred, ignorance, craving, joy, anger, sorrow, and pleasure. The two sets of eight correspond to each other like the sense organs of the physical body correspond to their respective external sense objects. They affect each other. The cause brings about the effect, and living beings place themselves on the wheel of karma, which carries them into the six realms of reincarnation.

The fundamental reason for this is attachment to the five aggregates, thinking that they truly exist when they only illusorily exist. One takes the false to be true. One is contaminated by visible objects, sounds, odors, tastes, body-impressions (tactile objects), and mind-objects (thoughts or ideas). One's mind is influenced by external circumstances. One is blown about by the Eight Winds. As such, one definitely does not have the foundation to realize enlightenment!

If those who cultivate themselves desire to become accomplished, they must not be confused by these Eight Winds. They must give rise to correct understanding. As the Buddhas said, one must not be moved when the Eight Winds blow. One's cultivation will then not be futile!

8. The Futility of Following a Teacher When One Treats Sentient Beings, Who Are Like One's Mother, in a Malevolent Manner

This futility is practiced by a great number of Buddhist disciples. It is the result of bad karma from previous lives. One's practice thus strays onto the wrong path and becomes futile.

Dharma King Yangwo Yisinubu said, "All practitioners should constantly reflect upon the following: The things that you are presently using were all made by living beings. They came from living beings. If it were not for the acts of living beings, how could you be what you are right now? You would long ago have ceased to exist!"

Hence, cultivators must understand that they must practice loving-kindness, compassion, sympathetic joy and equanimity toward all living beings in the six realms of existence. They must cultivate themselves and become accomplished for the sake of their dear relatives, that is, for the sake of all living beings in the six realms. They must arouse Mahayana bodhicitta and vow to save all sentient beings, since all sentient beings are in fact their closest relatives. This is how cultivators save others and themselves. This is the path of saving oneself and benefiting others.

Furthermore, Sakyamuni Buddha said that living beings in the six realms of existence have been our closest relatives (our fathers, mothers, brothers, and sisters) throughout many lives and eons. However, many disciples forget this important fact. They think that cultivation is simply cultivation, that following a Master is simply following a Master, and that arousing bodhicitta is simply arousing bodhicitta. To these disciples, treating all living beings as if they were one's own children is something totally different from and unrelated to cultivation, following a Master, and arousing bodhicitta.

These disciples, like others, follow a Master and learn Buddhism. Like others, they cultivate themselves. They want to become accomplished. They want to end the cycle of birth and death. Each of them wants to become a Bodhisattva. They do not want to be a practitioner of Hinayana Buddhism who does not hear about any matters taking place outside the walls of his own abode.

These aspirations are praiseworthy. However, their mentality leads their actions off course. Although they learn Buddhism under a Master, due to their mentality, they do not know why one must treat all sentient beings kindly, nor do they know how one should love and be compassionate toward all living beings.

Therefore, although they learn Buddhism, in the end, they have perverse dispositions, treat living beings malevolently and rudely, and are arrogant and overbearing. This malignant tumor can cause cultivators to accomplish nothing in their practice. It can cause all of their efforts to be in vain. This situation must be dealt with immediately. Taking out this tumor is imperative.

The source of this malignant tumor is a problem in one's mentality. The problem lies in thinking that being kind to living beings and one's cultivation are two totally different matters unrelated to each other. It also lies in thinking that being kind to living beings and arousing bodhicitta are two totally different matters unrelated to each other. Because of such mentality, many cultivators have broken their vows to become great Bodhisattvas and save living beings. They do not know the purpose behind making such vows, nor do they investigate such purpose. They do not look into why it is that they broke their vows.

The result of breaking such vows is that they will descend into hell. Is it possible that they do not know this? Of course they know this. It is just that they never thought that there is a connection between how they treat living beings and breaking their bodhicitta vows! In short, one makes bodhicitta vows for the sake of living beings. Breaking such vows is also connected with living beings. Cultivating the four limitless states of mind – limitless loving-kindness, compassion, sympathetic joy, and equanimity – toward all living beings is likewise for the sake of living beings. Moreover, treating living beings kindly is for the sake of living beings. However, treating living beings kindly and breaking one's vows by treating living beings badly will bring about different results!

Treating living beings kindly is a true manifestation of arousing bodhicitta. Cultivating oneself according to the words of the Master is also an extension of arousing bodhicitta. Treating living beings kindly and cultivating oneself according to the words of the Master are in fact one and the same. There is no difference at all between them!

Cultivation is not just meditating, visualizing, reciting mantras, or studying sutras. The word *cultivation* is richer and includes more than just these things. It includes the tiniest details of our actions, speech, and thoughts.

Whenever one engages in any action, speech, or thought that is not in accordance with the Buddha Dharma, is not in accordance with the principles of one's vows, and is not in accordance with the criteria necessary to become accomplished, then one is not engaging in true cultivation, and one is not truly saving living beings. This is because one's thinking with respect to the treatment of living beings is still numb, and one has not given rise to awareness. One does not understand what the relationship is between oneself and other living beings. This causes such people to neglect to conduct themselves correctly by treating all living beings kindly! Not seeing deeply and in a real way the type of karmic relationship they have with other living beings, these people are unable to give rise to awareness!

This karmic relationship is that living beings in the six realms of reincarnation have been, throughout many lives and over many eons, our mothers, fathers, brothers, and sisters. Additionally, what we eat, what we wear, our places of residence, and our vehicles for transportation have all been provided to us by other living beings!

Even with respect to the book you are now reading, the pages were made by other living beings, and the words were printed and typeset by other living beings. Furthermore, the binding, design, and transportation of this book were handled by other living beings for us. Without these other living beings, we would not have this book to read. Everything else that we use in life is also provided to us by other living beings.

Therefore, only because there are other living beings can we exist. Without other living beings, we would not exist. The cultivation undertaken by every cultivator and any accomplishment achieved are dependent upon and made possible by other living beings.

This close family relationship we have had with other living beings has resulted in countless living beings having provided each and every cultivator with unlimited kindness since beginningless time. Additionally, such kindness has its meaning according to the law of cause and effect! Other living beings have provided us with an unlimited number of existences. Cultivators exist today and are able to have all that they have as a result of this. Thus, from the perspective of cause and effect, we must repay the kindness of the countless living beings in the six realms of existence. Otherwise, we will violate the law of cause and effect.

Based upon this, cultivators should be grateful toward living beings, should give rise to an enlightened mind of great compassion, and should treat living beings kindly. They should not treat sentient beings malevolently!

Some people say that they truly treat living beings as their own closest family members, as their own father or mother, according to the teachings of Sakyamuni Buddha and the Master. However, in fact, they do not act in such way. They might totally ignore those they dislike. They might utter sarcastic, disparaging, or abusive remarks to those they dislike. Some might even beat up those they dislike. If they truly treated other living beings as their closest family members, as their own father or mother, then they would surely use every possible means to protect other living beings and show them compassionate love. In such case, how could they still be so malevolent and cruel?

Some practitioners will say, "Pamu, Master Marpa was also that tough and merciless." I will tell you something! Such were the skillful means used by a Vajra Bodhisattva to save another living being. You must not imitate him. You are not qualified to imitate him in such a manner!

We can thus see that practitioners who mistreat other living beings regard the teachings of Sakyamuni Buddha and the Master simply as obligations or responsibilities that must be met. They do not have a true understanding of such teachings. They have not given rise to complete awareness. That is why they treat sentient beings, who are like their own mother, in such a manner!

No matter how wise their Master may be and no matter how much merit their Master may have accumulated, no one can violate the law of cause and effect by malevolently treating sentient beings in such a manner. No one can avoid the fact that this type of cultivation will definitely result in descending into the lower realms. They have utterly failed to understand the law of cause and effect! Hence, their cultivation will, of course, be futile!

If one wants to truly help these pitiable cultivators, one must fundamentally change their perspective and attitude to align with the meaning of the Dharma. One must make these cultivators, who treat other living beings rudely, look within themselves so that they can give rise to true understanding and realization. They will then understand and realize why they must cultivate compassionate thoughts toward living beings; why they must, out of great compassion, arouse bodhicitta; why they must vow to save living beings; why they must practice Mahayana Buddhism and save living beings, even if it means that they must break any inappropriate vows they made that go against practicing Mahayana Buddhism; and why it is that treating the teachings of the teacher in a half-hearted manner, without real care or interest, is committing an offense against oneself and is acting irresponsibly toward oneself.

It never occurred to these cultivators that treating living beings malevolently due to ignorant thinking, unawareness, and not strictly abiding by the teachings of the Master is in fact treating themselves in the most fierce and cruel way. Such treatment of living beings will cause these cultivators to proceed in the direction of suffering, and they will ultimately descend into hell. This is an indisputable fact!

Thus, it is futile to follow a teacher when one treats sentient beings, who are like one's mother, in a malevolent manner.

9. *The Futility of Saying That One Fears Hell When One Often Engages in Wrongdoing*

This futility is commonly practiced by many cultivators. Those who practice this futility are not just ordinary cultivators. Generally, they are people who have a definite foundation in Buddhism and who somewhat understand the principles of the Buddha Dharma. At the very least, they can explain a bit about cause and effect, karmic retribution, and the circumstances of living beings in each of the six realms of existence.

In most cases, these disciples have a bit of a foundation in learning the Buddha Dharma. Perhaps they have been following a Master for a relatively long period of time, or perhaps they have attained a small degree of true realization. It is extremely easy for them to fall into this type of futile practice.

These disciples are often very energetic and diligent in learning the Dharma. They practice the Dharma in the morning and in the evening. They recite sutras and read commentaries on the Dharma. They inevitably speak of how important it is to end the cycle of life and death, how death comes so quickly, and how we must diligently cultivate ourselves to attain great liberation and quickly realize enlightenment! At every opportunity, they advise others to learn the Dharma under the Master, to seize all opportunities to learn the Dharma, to recite in earnest Amitabha Buddha's name, to perform good deeds, and to abstain from any wrongdoing.

When they hear the Master expound the Dharma, each of them deeply senses how painful the process of reincarnation is. They deeply feel that living beings in the three lower realms are truly pitiable. They feel compassion for these sentient beings in the three lower realms. In their hearts, there is a small amount of fear that they, too, may descend into one of the three lower realms. However, they do not have this fear every day. Basically, it only exists during the moments they look within themselves. It does not exist continuously. Often, within a few days, this fear gradually fades from their memory. This being the case, it is quite seldom that they have a feeling of fear over becoming one of the living beings within the three lower realms of existence, especially becoming one of the living beings in the hell realm.

At various times and in various settings, they may say, "Living beings in hell have committed too many evils. They are so pitiful. The hell realm is so frightening. I am very much afraid that I will descend into hell when my karmic retribution ripens. When I think about this, I tremble with fear!" Nevertheless, this state of fear they speak of has already changed. It is not truly as they describe it.

Why is this so? When they speak such words, they appear to be sincerely frightened. They say they are afraid. They say they are frightened. They say they fear receiving karmic retribution and descending into hell. However, what they actually do is different from what they say. Through their practices, they produce much impure karma. They are continually doing, saying, and thinking evil things.

One moment they are sulking over somebody's inappropriate statement. The next moment they are complaining a little bit about their living conditions. The next moment they immediately show their contempt and impatience when somebody's handling of a matter is not to their satisfaction. The next moment they pour out a stream of complaints over somebody's having betrayed them.

They sometimes do some things in furtherance of Buddhism and feel that what they have done is quite meritorious. They become arrogant and conceited. In front of others, they assume great airs, thinking that they are higher than others and that they have made great contributions in furtherance of the Buddha Dharma. They think that even the Master should be somewhat awestruck by them.

Sometimes they incite some of their fellow students who do not have correct understanding to join them in ostracizing a certain other fellow student. Sometimes they keep a lookout over the Master's movements, spying on the Master. They use extremely contemptible means to test the Master. They secretly listen to the Master's words. They invent stories. They issue orders to others based on fraudulent authority.

In order to cheat people out of money or accomplish some other hidden goal, they will wantonly fabricate lies, falsely claiming that they have a certain relationship with the Master that nobody else ever imagined. In order to seek some benefit or make others respect them, they sometimes will recklessly boast about how they are on the same level as certain eminent Masters. Sometimes they will groundlessly slander the Master or other Great Accomplished Ones in front of other people. They sometimes engage in erroneous thinking in which they use an absurd worldly mentality to measure and conjecture about Holy Ones and Great Virtuous Ones.

Even though they engage in such practices, they do not feel that their conduct is in any way inappropriate. If asked whether they fear descending into hell, they will immediately appear frightened, responding, "I do fear. How could I not fear? I have always cultivated myself very energetically. I constantly bear in mind the teachings and lectures of the Master. Descending into hell is just what I fear. The hell realm is truly so frightening, so painful. Therefore, I have always placed strict demands upon myself." Their words resonate throughout the room like the sound of a bronze coin falling on the ground. Their faces do not in the slightest way blush out of shame. On the contrary, their words are sonorous and forceful. Yet, they do not reflect upon their wrongdoing. It seems as if they never heard anything about the Buddha Dharma at all!

It is truly hard to imagine such strange things. Do they knowingly violate the Dharma or do they have no understanding whatsoever of the Dharma? Are they truly confused or are their minds like a clear mirror? Do they have no knowledge whatsoever of their mistakes or are they unable to control themselves? Actually, the tricks they are up to are only too evident!

I am afraid it is in fact the case that they, in essence, openly treat the Buddha Dharma with contempt, that they take a dim view of the law of cause and effect, and that they are totally unconcerned about descending into hell.

Can this method of cultivation, where people commit a wrongdoing at every turn, be considered cultivation based on fear of hell?

Thus, it is not just a matter of their treating the Buddha Dharma with an insincere and impure heart. More importantly, these practitioners treat themselves with an insincere, deceitful attitude. They say that they fear hell. Through their actions, however, it is as if they are happily running toward hell without any letup and that they cannot wait to get there. It is as if they are very eager to jump right into a burning oil cauldron in the hell of the volcanoes and painfully roll about therein. It is as if they wish they could provide other practitioners who also do not cultivate themselves in accordance with the Dharma with a model of suffering to see whether these other practitioners will use this model of suffering as a lesson and thereby not continue to repeat the same mistakes.

In fact, they do not wish to undergo such suffering. However, the consequences of their behavior cannot be changed, since the law of cause and effect never errs.

In Buddhist circles today, there are quite a number of people who are like these cultivators. The facts show that these people do not truly fear descending into hell. Rather, they are people who admire hell. Harboring beliefs that cause them to disregard their own personal danger, feeling that they have a compelling obligation to do what they do, acting like they are heroes, either quickly or slowly, they run toward the terrifying gate of hell. Their steps are so hurried, yet they are so unconcerned. They are truly people who traverse the path toward hell! The realm of hell will definitely provide them with a totally new way of thinking and a totally new way of life.

Presumably, when they enter this state of hell, words will not be enough to express their regret. They will then discover that their self-deceiving way of learning Buddhism and cultivating themselves was futile. In all likelihood, they will then understand what evil fruits are produced from often engaging in wrongdoing, how one should treat other living beings, and that it is truly important and necessary to treat sentient beings kindly!

Thus, when a cultivator often engages in wrongdoing, yet says that he fears hell, his cultivation is futile!

10. The Futility of Practicing Charity When One Does Not Act Through an Enlightened State of Mind and Does Not Have Devout Faith

Before addressing other aspects of practicing charity, there is the aspect of practicing charity as a preliminary practice whereby one accumulates the Buddhist resources of good fortune and merit. Practicing charity is a very good way for cultivators to increase their good fortune.

Practicing charity can be divided into different types, depending upon the nature of the charity practiced. There is impure charity and pure charity. That is, there is charity practiced with worldly and selfish motives and without worldly and selfish motives. The most important thing to consider is whether the person practicing charity does so with an unconditional, unlimited state of mind or does so due to worldly and selfish motives, such as greed for worldly benefits.

In short, it is not what worldly people presume. That is, it is not that the amount of money or the value of a thing actually given as charity will result in the exact same amount of corresponding karmic reward. To a large extent, the amount of karmic reward from charity depends upon the mentality of the person who is giving.

Take the case of two people who at the same time contribute the same amount of money or contribute property with the same value. They do so in furtherance of a Buddhist undertaking. Nevertheless, they each receive a different amount of empowerment and, as a result, they each reach different levels of good fortune and wisdom. Many people will be very confused about this, not understanding why this is the case. Thus, I will now explain the reasons why, one by one.

In today's society, there frequently are activities to help the victims of disasters or other philanthropic activities. Some philanthropic activities advance a certain cause and, through the dissemination of written material, people are urged to contribute. In some philanthropic activities, people walk the streets asking others to contribute on the spot. In others, there is a box set up for contributions.

It cannot be denied that these activities all benefit living beings. They are real acts that help sentient beings. These acts of charity are all very good. However, due to various causes and conditions that are different for each person, the quality of the charity performed and its karmic rewards will likewise be different for each person.

First Type – The Situation is the Same But the Motivation is Different

For example, there are two people on the street who at the same time contribute money toward helping mountain children who are deprived of education. These two people are both poor college students. Economically speaking, they are in very straitened circumstances. They rely upon their families to mail to them $100 each month in order to cover all of their expenses at school.

When they are walking on the street and see that there is an activity to aid impoverished children who are deprived of education, one of them becomes quite moved. He becomes very sad, since he is also from the mountains and previously experienced many setbacks and difficulties before managing to enter college. There were many times when he was almost unable to continue his studies due to lack of money. He decides to contribute all of the $15 he saved up by pinching and scraping, which he was going to use to buy books. Although he is poor, he feels that he ought to do everything he can to help the mountain children who do not have money to attend school.

At this time, the other college student, who is likewise very poor, sees this situation and feels embarrassed. He feels that if he does not contribute money in front of everybody, he will lose face. Thus, he pretends to be impassioned and, in a determined manner, he contributes the $15 he carefully saved, which was to be used for living expenses.

After he contributes this money, this student feels quite uncomfortable. He thinks, "I no longer have living expenses. I should not have contributed beyond my means in order to look impressive. Why did I try to save face? Why did I join in the excitement? Contributing money is something done by rich people. I really would not have done anything wrong had I not contributed. Now I do not have any money for food." He therefore feels dejected, regretful, and very upset.

This is an example where the external circumstances of the contributors are the same, and the contributions are the same. The only thing different is the state of mind of the contributors. One of them feels for others and sincerely desires to help others. The other reluctantly contributes out of the desire to save face.

Of course, as two students who are very poor and who themselves need the assistance of others, their having contributed all of their living expenses in order to help others is extremely rare. Their giving over all that they had was a great act of charity. As a result, they will bring about for themselves tremendous blessings. Their charity is respected by all.

However, it is very obvious that the first student will receive greater blessings than the second student. This is because the first student contributed out of a heart of great compassion and with sincere thoughts. Thus, he engaged in incomparably pure charity.

He acted out of a boundless state of great compassion in accordance with his innate Buddha-nature. He acted out of a heart of great compassion whereby he was perfectly willing to suffer for the well-being of others. In this state of great compassion, he truly loved others more than himself.

His heart of great compassion was boundless. Therefore, he will receive boundless blessings and the compassionate empowerment of the Buddhas. His contribution was magnanimous and natural. He did not have the slightest selfish thought. When he made his contribution, he did not give the least thought to what type of difficult living conditions he would have to face. He did not consider himself at all. He just wholeheartedly desired to help children who were deprived of education.

Thus, there were no defilements mixed into his act of charity. His contribution was incomparably pure. The merit earned from this donation is even loftier than towering Mt. Sumeru. As a result, the blessings he will receive will naturally be limitless.

Although the other student is also extremely poor and likewise contributed all of his living expenses, his act of charity was, nevertheless, impure charity. He deeply regretted having contributed the money, thinking that such an act of charity was a stupid thing to do. He donated only for the sake of his own self-respect, only because he did not want others to look down upon him. When contributing, he did not consider how those pitiable children who are deprived of education need assistance. That is, his contribution did not emanate from a heart of great compassion.

Of course, this type of charity was not performed out of a boundless, unconditioned state of mind. It was performed with the state of mind of an ordinary person. Therefore, his donation was made with worldly and selfish motives. It was not a contribution that emanated from the great compassion of an enlightened state of mind.

Hence, even though he contributed the same amount of money as the first student and even though his contribution will earn him a rather large amount of merit, nevertheless, his merit cannot be compared with the merit earned by the first student. His type of contribution cannot be placed in the same category as the pure type of contribution made by the first student.

Thus, charity that emanates from an enlightened state of mind and charity that is not based upon an enlightened state of mind are not the same.

Second Type – The Situation is Different and the Amount Contributed is Different

Most cultivators who learn Buddhism have a very superficial understanding of charity. They think that the more one contributes, the more merit one earns. Thus, there is a pervasive mentality among them which holds that it is the Buddhist disciple who contributes the most money or property who earns the most merit! This understanding is very one-sided. It is a mistaken understanding. It is a narrow concept, and those who hold it lack deep and correct understanding.

However, in Buddhist circles today, practitioners on the whole, including even some Great Virtuous Ones, have this misconception. It can be said that this is very unfortunate. Practitioners with this way of thinking must strengthen their understanding and raise their state of realization. They must extricate themselves from this erroneous view. Otherwise, they will violate the law of cause and effect.

In fact, throughout history, most Great Virtuous Ones did not establish a clear, definite, and strict Dharma system relating to charity. They only spoke of charity in general terms. Practitioners are therefore required to delve deeply into the Buddha Dharma in order to attain correct understanding of this subject. Only then will they not be misled by misconceptions.

According to the Dharma, the correct assessment of charity is not merely a matter of one's mentality or attitude. There is also the issue of how to measure the charity. This cannot be done in a single-faceted manner based upon how much one has contributed. Measurement of charity is more closely related to the causes and conditions surrounding the person performing the act of charity.

For example, there are two disciples who learn the Dharma from the same Master. They are equally devout. On one occasion, they heard the Dharma and were moved to benefit living beings. Hence, they concurrently contributed different amounts of money.

One of the two disciples has a net worth of $100,000,000. The net worth of all of the property of the other disciple amounts to $2,000.

When the multimillionaire disciple made his offering, he contributed $5,000,000 to be used in the furtherance of Buddhist affairs. The other disciple only contributed $1,000. Of these two disciples, which one performed more charity? Which has a purer heart?

Of course, many people will think that the merit obtained by the disciple who made the $5,000,000 offering is tremendous and that the charity he performed is much greater than that of the disciple who offered $1,000. They will think, "How can one compare $1,000 with $5,000,000? Naturally, the merit obtained by the multimillionaire disciple is much greater. His heart is also much purer. He is, of course, furthering many more Buddhist affairs!" In fact, this type of thinking is very erroneous!

Looked at superficially, it would seem that the merit obtained by the multimillionaire from performing this charity is great. Of course, there is truly a great gap between $1,000 dollars and $5,000,000! However, people only see what is on the surface, that is, the amount of money contributed. They then measure how much merit each of these two disciples obtained from furthering Buddhist affairs according to the amount of money each contributed. However, these people do not carefully compare what percentage of the total savings or total net worth of each of these two disciples was contributed in order to further Buddhist affairs! When compared in this manner, certain things can be seen.

With respect to the multimillionaire disciple, $5,000,000 is equal to one-twentieth of $100,000,000. That is, the multimillionaire contributed 5 percent of the total worth of his property.

The total worth of the property of the other disciple is $2,000. He contributed $1,000. One thousand dollars is equal to one-half of two thousand dollars. That is, this disciple contributed 50 percent of the total worth of his property.

It may well be asked, can 5 percent and 50 percent be mentioned in the same breath? Can they be placed in the same category?

I will make another comparison. The multimillionaire who contributed 5 percent of his total worth of property can still live very comfortably and leisurely. Just as before, he is a rich man who does not have to worry about the necessities of life. Yet, the disciple who contributed 50 percent of his total worth of property only has $1,000 left. He only has $1,000 to live on!

One can imagine the great pressure he will experience to meet his material needs and how difficult and poverty stricken his life will be! One can imagine how hard it will be for him to get by! Perhaps after a period of time, even feeding himself will be a problem. Perhaps he will fall into a state of hardship where even the basic necessities of life cannot be ensured! Could it be that the Dharma Protectors looking down from space would not know about this?

Can these two types of charity be compared? After comparing in this manner, what type of impression and understanding should those who thought that the multimillionaire disciple obtained greater merit now have?

One should be able to see that the charity performed by the multimillionaire disciple and the charity performed by the poorer disciple are not in the same category. The difference between the two types of charity is not just an ordinary difference. In fact, the difference is very great!

However, disciples who cultivate themselves often cannot see this point. They think that they are great just from having made a small contribution. They even compare the amount of the contributions they make with the contributions of poorer fellow disciples.

When they see that the contributions of other people are not as much as their own, they regard their contributions as being greatly meritorious. They think that the merit they obtained is greater than that of others. They then become pleased with themselves and do not diligently strive forward. They even say, "I have contributed enough. I will leave a little room for other people to establish merit!" Yet, they never deeply think about whether the charity they performed can truly match up with the charity performed by other disciples. It also never occurred to them that the money that they keep cannot be taken into hell in order to bribe for better treatment. At such time, of what use is money?

If disciples whose economic conditions are not good lack correct understanding, they will always think that the meritorious deeds they performed are never enough. They will then sometimes become obsessed and will contribute all of their property. In the end, they contribute everything they have. They wind up lacking even the minimal personal resources to support themselves so that they can continue their cultivation. As such, their good fortune from having cultivated themselves is no longer ensured.

These disciples do not know that the merit they obtain from contributing $10 is sometimes much more than the merit some people obtain from contributing $10,000. Because of this obstruction in their understanding, they measure contributions simply based upon the superficial amount of the contribution. If other people contributed $10,000, they also, no matter what, must contribute $10,000! After they have contributed all of their property, they still think that the meritorious deeds they performed do not match up with those of other people. They think that the charity they performed is not as great as that of others.

As a result, they cause themselves anguish. They become desperately poor. All day long they busily run around trying to obtain the necessities of life and earn a living. They have no thoughts of seriously cultivating themselves. In the end, they wind up delaying themselves. These people never heard of the following true story.

A long time ago, there was a poverty-stricken old lady. Every day, she begged for food on the streets in order to stay alive. When she saw many rich people go to the temple to make offerings to the Buddhas and Bodhisattvas and contribute butter lamps that shine a long time, a strong desire arose in her mind. She thought of how good it would be if she could offer to the Buddhas and Bodhisattvas a butter lamp that shines a long time! She then resolved that this desire become reality. From that point on, when she begged, she always beseeched others to only give her butter. She told others that it would be all right if they did not give her food.

After doing this for a very long period of time, this poverty-stricken old lady finally had enough butter to light up a butter lamp! With a joyful heart, she entered the temple and devoutly lit up a butter lamp filled with her butter. She was finally able to make an offering to the Buddhas and Bodhisattvas! The butter lamp she offered emitted bright rays of light.

The next day, the monks in the temple were surprised to discover that all of the butter in all of the butter lamps had already burned away, and all of the lights had died out – except for the butter lamp offered by this poverty-stricken old lady, which was still shining. Its bright flames did not die out even after such a long time! It provided the temple with unlimited brightness!

At such time, the countless ancient Buddhas predicted that this old lady would definitely become a Buddha in the future! This poverty-stricken old lady became the magnificent Kindler of Lamps Buddha, Dipamkara!

Thus, cultivators should understand that one cannot simply look at the amount contributed in order to measure the amount of merit from the contribution. To one who is short of money, a ten dollar contribution is not a small amount. To one who is worth $100,000,000, a $10,000,000 contribution is not necessarily much! A poverty-stricken old lady underwent a great deal of hardship and contributed everything she had. She was still only able to offer one butter lamp. Nevertheless, due to this cause, the ancient Buddhas prophesied that she would be the Kindler of Lamps Buddha.

The contribution of a millionaire who casually gives away $100,000 is far behind in matching up to one butter lamp contributed by a poverty-stricken old lady! A $100,000 contribution can buy countless butter lamps. Why is it, then, that a $100,000 contribution cannot match up to this one butter lamp? Why, after all, is this the case? Could it be said that there is no value to the $100,000? It is not that there is no value to the $100,000. It is simply that within this lamp was all of the merit derived from the boundless heart of a person who was in the most straitened circumstances. The most important lesson from this story is having devout faith with all one's heart!

Therefore, when cultivators speak of charity, they should not measure merit just from the superficial amount or worth of the contribution. More important is the trueness of the thought underlying the contribution, having a truly enlightened state of mind suffused with great compassion and bent on benefiting others, and having a mind of unlimited devotion that is intent on performing charity, making offerings, and furthering Buddhist affairs. This type of mind is extremely pure. It does not have the slightest impurity or ulterior motive!

A $1,000,000 contribution from a rich man who is worth $10,000,000, who weighs the pros and cons, calculates, and thinks back and forth before contributing is not a large contribution, and the merit obtained is not great. A one dollar contribution from a Buddhist disciple in unusually straitened circumstances made with a totally uncontaminated, pure, unconditioned, enlightened state of mind suffused with great compassion cannot be considered a small contribution, and the merit obtained is not small!

To sum up, in learning Buddhism and cultivating oneself, one must have a most devout mind, a totally pure mind, and a mind bent on doing one's utmost. One must likewise have such a mind when performing charity and doing meritorious deeds. Without a pure and enlightened state of mind, without the most devout and wholehearted faith in the Buddhas and Bodhisattvas, the merit obtained from performing charity will not be boundlessly wonderful, and one's cultivation will lose its meaning. As a consequence, the benefits of cultivation will not be seen!

Therefore, it is futile to practice charity when one does not act through an enlightened state of mind and does not have devout faith!

11. The Futility of Receiving the Precepts When One Has Not Resolved to Strictly Abide by Them

In order for practitioners to realize enlightenment, they must have sincere faith, energetically strive forward, truly cultivate themselves, and clearly believe in the law of cause and effect. Additionally, on their path of cultivation, they must possess a powerful sword to conquer evil spirits and demons and eliminate all hindrances. This powerful sword is something that is indispensable to all practitioners. This sword is the precepts of the Buddha Dharma! Only with this sword can one overcome all evil obstructions, smoothly arrive at the other shore, and become accomplished.

Yet, if one who possesses this powerful sword places it in some corner and forgets about it, then it cannot manifest its unlimited awesome power! One must carry this sword with oneself at all times and in all places. This sword must never leave one's body, hands, and mind. If one does not carry this sword, it is as if one does not have this sword. In such case, no matter how much this sword is able to conquer demons and evil spirits, and no matter how great its power is, it will never be put to good use.

The obstructive demons are like a flood. They are like wild animals. They harbor evil intent. They are always secretly casting their greedy eyes upon practitioners. As soon as there is an opportunity, they immediately seize upon it to mercilessly and furiously attack. If one does not carry this powerful sword, it is as if one were physically weak. One would then allow oneself to be trampled upon, ordered about, and manipulated. One would become a delicious meal for the demons. One's right mindfulness would completely vanish.

One can thus see that the harm resulting from this is extraordinary and truly cannot be underestimated! This is why one must carry this powerful sword. Practitioners should regard the precepts as being of utmost importance for eradicating erroneous views and evil hindrances. Practitioners must not only know that they must abide by the precepts, they must also abide by them with extreme strictness!

Only with such abidance can the practitioner be considered to be carrying this powerful sword. With it, one is protected. The benefits from such scrupulous abidance are naturally tremendous. One will certainly advance rapidly on one's path of cultivation and become greatly accomplished. The defiling obstructions will have no way to draw near to oneself.

It is easy to abide by the precepts for a short while. Continuous abidance, however, is difficult!

When speaking about the requirement to abide by the precepts, cultivators will nod their heads and utter words of approval. They deeply feel the need for this requirement. However, generally, they are able to abide by the precepts for only a day or so. There are very few who are able to continuously abide by the precepts over a long period of time. They are as few as the stars at dawn!

Ordinarily, disciples are especially unable to strictly abide by precepts transmitted to them by the Master. They commit many violations. Some of them even violate most of the transmitted precepts. Once in a while they will not violate a certain transmitted precept. Such precept often is the precept prohibiting killing. Yet, without scruples, they will completely violate the other transmitted precepts. Nevertheless, this cannot be thought of as the worst case.

Those who violate all of the transmitted precepts are the worst. Not one precept is left unviolated. They even use a disguised form of violating the precept prohibiting killing. They say, "You say that one cannot kill living beings. This matter can be easily solved. I myself will not directly do the killing. Through dropping hints, I will instigate another person to do so. Isn't the problem solved by using that person? Since I was not the one who personally did the killing, I did not violate any precept, right?"

In short, due to various excuses and reasons, one disciple is unable to abide by the precepts, and his fellow disciple is also unable to abide by the precepts. They are at the same level. Each does not mock or have misgivings about the other. Each one lets the other do as he likes!

This is a true description of how many cultivators abide by precepts. I am not exaggerating a bit or being evasive about the facts! These two disciples understand each other's failure to abide by the precepts but do not express this understanding in words. They are unable to continuously abide by most of the precepts they received. This being the case, no matter how important the precepts that the Master transmitted to them are, such transmission is futile. It is of no benefit. On the contrary, transmitting precepts to them will only exacerbate their degeneration.

Why is it such a serious matter when one does not abide by the precepts? Because in so doing, one increases one's negative karma. Also, the Dharma Protectors looking down from space will not lend their assistance to empower such a person!

In most cases, the Master transmits precepts to a certain disciple because that disciple's innate faculties are good. The transmission is the result of good karma planted over many lives. The Master will transmit different precepts to his disciples based upon the karmic destiny of each disciple. The Master may transmit the Shramanera Precepts.[60] He may transmit the Precepts for Monks. He may transmit the Bodhisattva Precepts. He may transmit the Three Comprehensive Precepts, and so on.

If one has already received the precepts, this indicates that the seeds of enlightenment have already been planted. Such a disciple need only strictly abide by the precepts he received and follow the teachings of the Master. If he can do this, he will surely win the respect of both people and celestial beings. He will be protected by the Dharma Protectors. With his sword of the precepts, he will conquer evil hindrances, achieve liberation, and realize unlimited accomplishment.

Otherwise, if practitioners receive precepts and do not abide by them, the Dharma protecting Bodhisattvas will certainly become angry and will justly uphold the Dharma by severely punishing such people. Some of them will be beaten black and blue. Some of them will be disturbed by ferocious ghosts. Some of them will be seriously injured. Some of them will experience a great loss of property. Some of them will die prematurely. All such scenarios are very tragic. The karmic retribution experienced is different for each person. There are too many types of retribution to enumerate.

Perhaps the Dharma Protectors will become indignant and leave. They will no longer protect such people. In such case, the multitude of demons will become joyful and will harm and disturb such people. These demons will think of all kinds of ways to gnaw away at the correct views of these people, causing their bodies and minds to become uneasy. These people will be hindered and bewitched by erroneous views. Their practice will become more and more perverse and disordered. They will be unable to return to correct behavior. The negative karma they produce will surely increase with each day, and they will fall into derangement and ignorance. They will undoubtedly degenerate.

From this we can see that receiving precepts is indeed a good thing for the practitioner. The practitioner must rely on and abide by these precepts in order to become accomplished. However, there are those who receive precepts because they are just curious, because they are following what others are doing, or because of a momentary desire to leave the cycle of reincarnation. Afterwards, they ignore the precepts transmitted to them, casting them aside. They do not abide by the precepts they received. Perhaps they frequently violate them. Perhaps they seldom violate them. In so doing, they break the precepts and destroy the discipline. Failure to observe the precepts they received will cause them to degenerate.

For example, those who violate the precept that prohibits defaming the Master will certainly descend into the hell realm. Those who violate the precept that prohibits practicing erroneous and evil ways will descend into the animal realm. Those who violate the precept that prohibits lying to and deceiving the Master will not receive any benefits from their practice, will not receive good fortune in life, and will die poverty-stricken. Therefore, receiving precepts is a Dharma treasure for those practitioners who are able to adhere to the precepts they receive. This Dharma treasure can be used on the path leading to accomplishment in order to remove all hindrances and conquer all evil spirits and demons. However, for those disciples who cannot even observe a portion of the precepts, receiving precepts is not necessarily a good thing.

Yet, it is not only the disciple who must, before receiving precepts, carefully consider whether he is, after all, able to abide by the precepts received. The Buddhist Master who is transmitting the precepts to the disciple should also act with utmost caution. A certain disciple's karmic destiny to receive precepts may not be mature, and he may not possess the qualifications required to receive precepts. In this case, the Master cannot be overly lenient, act carelessly, and misjudge the disciple based on affection, resulting in the premature transmission of precepts. If this happens, then this Master also must bear responsibility. Further, this Master will likewise experience karmic retribution.

This is because a Buddhist Vajra Master who transmits the Dharma must also strictly adhere to the precepts and rules. Before transmitting the Dharma or precepts to a disciple, the Master must deeply enter into a meditative state in order to examine and clearly see the innate faculties of that disciple. In this way, the Master can determine whether the Dharma or precepts really can be transmitted.

For example, a certain disciple asks the Master to transmit to him a certain Dharma. If this disciple does not meet the rules for transmission of this Dharma, yet the Master still transmits the Dharma to him for fear of hurting his feelings, not only will the Dharma protecting Bodhisattvas not arrive at the transmission ceremony, the ceremony site will also lack any supernormal states. Furthermore, this Master cannot be regarded as a Vajra Master. He himself has violated the precepts of the Buddha Dharma! As such, while this disciple is continuously degenerating, this Master is also degenerating along with him.

Transmitting precepts is also like this. When the Master transmits precepts to a disciple who is not qualified, and the disciple fails to abide by the precepts received, this disciple will fall into degeneration. This Master who acted in violation of the Dharma will also fall into degeneration!

Thus, it is required that the disciple possess the necessary conditions and qualifications to receive precepts. The Master must also perform a careful and strict examination. He must realistically, cautiously, and penetratingly view the disciple from every angle. If the underlying conditions of the disciple are truly not yet mature, and the disciple does not meet the standards of the Dharma, then the Master absolutely cannot be overly lenient. In such case, precepts cannot be transmitted until the Dharma conditions are mature. Those practitioners who have met the standards of receiving precepts and who have the opportunity to receive precepts must continuously abide by them. If they do not continuously abide by them, they will delay their accomplishment and will experience unavoidable suffering.

Thus, it is futile for practitioners to receive precepts when they have not resolved to continuously abide by them!

12. The Futility of Cultivating Peacefulness and Forbearance When One Does Not Control One's Anger

Greed, anger (hatred), and ignorance are the three great obstacles of cultivators. If one does not eliminate these three obstacles, it will be impossible for one's cultivation to result in accomplishment. Thus, in order for cultivators to leave the cycle of reincarnation, they must separate themselves from these three obstacles. Only then will their three karmas be immaculate, will there be no impure hindrances left, and will they be able to directly reach the other shore.

Of these three obstacles, anger is the great enemy of peacefulness and forbearance. Thus, if one wants to moderate and subdue one's actions and thoughts, if one wants to cultivate placidness and patience, then one must control this anger. Only then can one succeed.

Being peaceful and forbearing, simply put, means enduring insults[61] and being composed. In all situations, one does not become angry and hateful, since one is able to remain unmoved and unconfused. If cultivators are not peaceful and forbearing, then the negative karma they produce will certainly multiply, and they will be unable to attain purity and utter tranquility.

It is exactly this anger that leads one's actions awry and disturbs one's cultivation. Therefore, cultivating calmness and tolerance is imperative. Yet, why do I say that it is futile to cultivate placidness and patience if one does not control one's anger?

Anger refers to a mentality of attachment whereby one gives rise to resentment, hatred, or animosity toward other people or other living beings. As a result, it is extremely easy for the mind to give rise to various kinds of thought, speech, and action that are filled with aggression, vengeance, disgust, and hate.

Thus, as soon as this type of mentality appears, impure karmic causes in the areas of thought and action are immediately planted. This leads to the cancellation of all of the good karma that has been accumulated. At this time, the calmness and tolerance that one has been cultivating in order to become accomplished loses all of its meaning and value. This is one of the important reasons why many cultivators who practice diligently do not receive any benefits from their practice.

We often see cultivators who are very active and enthusiastic when it comes to furthering Buddhist affairs. They are extremely devout. They always want to keep in mind the teachings of the Buddhas and Bodhisattvas by practicing peacefulness and forbearance. They are very energetic and strive for accomplishment. Therefore, most of the time they are able to cultivate themselves in accordance with the Dharma.

However, at a certain time, their latent bad tendencies come to the fore and flourish, causing them to be unable to control their emotions. Thoughts of anger and hatred instantly cover up their positive state of realization. The placidness and patience they had been diligently practicing totally disappear in an instant. Many impure karmic hindrances are again produced. One cannot deny that this is extremely regrettable.

There are many cultivators like this. They treat the Buddha Dharma with caution and meticulous attention. They are very respectful toward the Buddhas, the Bodhisattvas, and the Master. They truly want to cultivate themselves. They did not become Buddhists just to follow the popular trend or pretend that they are refined and religious. Nevertheless, they still are unable to restrain themselves from violating certain Dharma principles that they have incorporated into their practice.

Their actions are reflected in the popular saying, "One is fully aware that one should not do something, yet one still perversely does it." During the time one is cultivating calmness and tolerance, these perverse actions can be seen quite clearly.

If a practitioner sees in a state of meditation the merit in practicing peacefulness and forbearance, then he certainly will immediately cultivate peacefulness and forbearance. After he sees this, when he meets others, he will have a pleasant, benign face. He will be extremely cordial. He will love people as if they were all Buddhas. This is because he will still remember all that he saw in his state of meditation.

However, after a short period of time when such right mindfulness has almost vanished, he will become impatient. He will begin to be restless, and his angry state of mind will arise spontaneously. Certain qualities of others that he previously thought of as lovable immediately become countless detestable shortcomings. Even their faces seem to be a bit disgusting and more and more unpleasant to his eyes. When he was cultivating enduring insults, he still managed to tolerate the unlovable qualities of others. Now, these qualities appear more and more unbearably ugly.

At this time, it cannot be said that he is cultivating enduring insults. He is not even capable of the minimal tolerance of others that one shows in everyday life! Because of thoughts of anger, he speaks words that are biased, cruel, malicious, resentful, and slanderous. He performs acts that are filthy and base. Such thoughts and acts erupt from him like a volcano. That which had been boiling within him for a long time, that which he had repeatedly repressed but which had nevertheless built up within him for a long time, explodes out of him, causing him to almost burst a blood vessel.

At such time, through the forces of ignorance, negative karma, and negative habitual tendencies, the great door of placidness and patience that had locked up bad karma finally is struck open. The lava of anger and hatred gushes out, like water when the floodgate is opened. It surges forward over an expansive area, covering the snow mountain of merit accumulated from practicing calmness and tolerance. It instantly melts this mountain of merit to the ground! In an instant, the merit from practicing peacefulness and forbearance has totally vanished. Nothing is left!

From this, one can see how frightening anger is! It can, with the greatest of ease, totally shatter one's practice of placidness and patience. At the same time, it causes countless cultivators who make painstaking efforts in their practice to become like shoots that fail to flower, never attaining accomplishment. In cultivating peacefulness and forbearance, all practitioners must totally avoid anger. Otherwise, in the end, one will fail.

Nevertheless, cultivating placidness and patience is not something one can totally master in just a short period of time. It not only requires persistent and arduous practice, it also requires constant self-examination and self-encouragement. One must thoroughly understand the nature of one's mind. It is not a matter of simply acting in accordance with the teachings of the Buddhas and Bodhisattvas.

Practitioners must become active in cultivating calmness and tolerance, not passive. They must regard peacefulness and forbearance as the first thing they must cultivate. They must understand that becoming accomplished is dependent upon mastering placidness and patience. They must understand that this mastery will guarantee that they will attain wonderful states of realization.

It is just as Sakyamuni Buddha said. He said that there is nothing that surpasses prajna and that enduring insults is the highest method of cultivation!

Thus, if cultivators do not eliminate anger, cultivating peacefulness and forbearance is futile!

13. The Futility of Practicing Meditation When One Often Becomes Drowsy or Unfocused

What is meant by meditation? I will not go into this subject in detail here. Working on one's concentration and meditation is a necessary and very important aspect of cultivation.

During meditation, being drowsy and unfocused are not correct states of mind. They are the results of negative karma produced by delusion. Thus, they are labeled erroneous. These two erroneous states are the great enemies of meditation. If one is able to leave these two enemies behind, then it will be very easy to attain concentration!

If the practitioner falls into a state of drowsiness when meditating, then he will not give rise to a correct state of mind. He will not hold in his mind the object of meditation upon which he should be exclusively concentrating. He will feel that his eyelids are heavy and will become sleepy. These are the signs that he has fallen into a state of drowsiness. The demon of sleep is about to arrive.

If, while meditating, the practitioner finds it difficult to maintain a correct state of mind, is often easily confused and moved by states of attachment, and finds his consciousness easily drifting away, then these are obvious signs that he has fallen into a state of being unfocused. These signs often appear at the third and fourth level of the practitioner's meditation practice.

The subtle signs of being unfocused mostly appear at the fifth and sixth levels of meditation practice. At these levels, the practitioner is able to peacefully focus upon the object of meditation. However, there is also the phenomenon of thinking about external matters. Although the practitioner will not be easily distracted from the object of meditation, it is still possible for him to regress to lower levels.

Because these subtle signs of being unfocused are extremely attenuated, they are often difficult for the practitioner to discover. Thus, due to inattentiveness and numbness, the practitioner loses the object of meditation and regresses to a lower level of meditation. Hence, at the fifth and six levels of meditation practice, one must all the more apply the power of correct understanding and be vigilant and careful. One must all the more maintain a correct state of mind.

Since the two erroneous states of being drowsy and unfocused hinder the practitioner's cultivation of concentration, they are the great enemies of enlightenment. In order to overcome these two erroneous states, the practitioner must constantly give rise to a state of mind bent on leaving the cycle of reincarnation. He must constantly bear in mind the impermanence of all conditioned things. He must constantly ponder the suffering involved in descending into one of the three lower realms of existence, the merit in attaining an enlightened mind, and the need for his three karmas to correspond with the teachings of the Master. In so doing, he will naturally be able to eliminate these two hindrances.

If practitioners want to investigate in detail these two erroneous states and correctly engage in meditation, then they must read and rely upon *The Dharma of Concentration and Visualization Essential for Enlightenment*, which is a collection of my discourses. They will then be able to cultivate themselves without worry. I will not say anything more about this here!

14. The Futility of Vigorously Practicing When One Does Not Yearn for Enlightenment

Those who learn Buddhism and cultivate themselves must first clearly understand what the goal of their cultivation is. They absolutely must not be like those who shoot arrows randomly, without any target at all. They absolutely must not take up Buddhism in a muddle-headed manner. They absolutely must not blindly follow others in acknowledging someone as their master and blindly follow others in learning the Dharma. Of course, I am not referring here to those Buddhists whose understanding of the Buddha Dharma is limited only to occasionally lighting incense and worshipping statues of the Buddha.

In Buddhist circles, there is a rather large number of people who do not know why they are practicing. They diligently practice and arduously study. They get up early and go to bed late. They quite successfully stick to their routine practices in the morning and evening during which they recite the sutras and worship the Buddha. They vigorously practice day after day in this manner. Yet, despite this, in the end, they can at most be regarded as "half-cultivators"!

Why? The reason is that they are unclear about their goal in learning Buddhism. This goal is very obscure to them. In their learning of Buddhism, they are basically indifferent about whether they will realize enlightenment, become accomplished, and end the cycle of birth and death.

Yet, they understand one thing very clearly: There is something advantageous in learning the Buddha Dharma and having the Master transmit the Dharma to them. That is, they think that the Buddhas, the Bodhisattvas, and the Master will not abandon them. If by chance they experience some disaster, the Master will help them. They have something to depend upon after all. They practice every day the Dharma that the Master transmitted to them. Occasionally, they perform some good deeds. In so doing, they think that they are ensuring that, at the very least, they will be able to pass through this lifetime peacefully and worry-free.

They think that with such Buddhist resources, their next life will naturally not be too bad. They think that things such as the Master's safety and whether other people develop their roots of kindness, receive blessings, become accomplished, or realize happiness all do not have much to do with them. They are indifferent to such things and feel that such things have nothing to do with their own personal interests.

Thus, they have this attitude of indifference and do not yearn for enlightenment. Yet, they very vigorously and diligently cultivate themselves. This type of cultivation is astonishing! They have quite obviously given careful consideration to their cultivation. It is not as if they have no goals whatsoever. One goal of particular importance in their vigorous cultivation is to leave the cycle of reincarnation. However, due to their actual practice, they will be unable to leave the cycle of reincarnation. Practitioners in this category might also have goals such as seeking for themselves a life of peace, realizing worldly so-called "happiness," and building a foundation to obtain blessings in this lifetime and the next.

From this we can see that these people are not the same as the common people of the world who believe in Buddhism yet who lack any understanding of the Buddha Dharma. It can be said that such worldly people lack any understanding of the principles and truth of the Buddha Dharma. But the type of practitioners just described do understand some principles of cause and effect. At the very least, they have heard a little about these principles.

We can say that the practitioners just described are very blessed since, due to good karma, they have the opportunity to come into contact with correct Dharma principles. However, when viewed from another angle, they are no different from those worldly people. Both those worldly people, on the one hand, and these practitioners who have a little understanding of Buddhist principles, on the other hand, each have the same goals underlying their belief in Buddhism.

Both types prostrate themselves and worship in front of the Buddhas and Bodhisattvas in order to obtain worldly blessings and benefits and in order to beseech the Buddhas and Bodhisattvas to bestow peace and happiness upon their family members. They do not care whether sentient beings realize enlightenment and ignore the many sufferings of sentient beings.

Thus, both types seek only their own peace and happiness. They do not care about the life or death of others. Whether other living beings are doing well or poorly is not relevant to them. Even if they benefit others, most of the time it is somehow related to their own self-interest.

Therefore, the selfish nature of these two types of people and their motivation for worshipping the Buddha are totally the same! This being the case, both types are very pitiful living beings. Both use an extremely narrow viewpoint to understand and treat the Buddha Dharma.

They regard learning and practicing the Buddha Dharma as capital by which they can earn worldly material benefits. They worship the Buddha and learn the Dharma in order to seek worldly so-called "happiness," which is illusory. They do not know that this type of happiness is essentially like clouds or smoke that passes before one's eyes. Such happiness is just a colorful, enchanting, flowery, and insubstantial illusion that easily vanishes!

These soap bubbles of worldly happiness, which delude ordinary people and have so much allure when viewed superficially, will suddenly burst. They are illusory and will not stay with these people forever. Seeking them will only exacerbate the evil tendency of these people to be greedy. These bubbles have nothing to do with real happiness. People with this type of thinking are, as the Chinese saying goes, "like mice who can only see an inch of light." They are extremely shortsighted and shallow.

However, comparatively speaking, those practitioners who have a little understanding of Buddhist principles are even more ignorant than those worldly people who believe in Buddhism yet who lack any understanding of the Buddha Dharma! Why? Those worldly people do not understand the principles of Buddhism. They do not know that through learning and practicing the Buddha Dharma, one can abide in eternal bliss, leave the bitter sea of the six realms of reincarnation, truly leave suffering behind, and realize liberation! They do not know what the goal of learning Buddhism and cultivation is! Thus, every day they live ordinary lives. Based upon the power of karma that is already set, they experience suffering as their retribution. They know and experience suffering yet find themselves helpless. They are in a passive position of being beaten, yet they simply sit still waiting for death. Hence, this type of ignorance is truly pitiful, yet it is understandable.

However, the other type of Buddhist adherents, on the other hand, do clearly understand certain principles of the correct Dharma. Nevertheless, they do not follow those principles to attain eternal bliss and enlightenment.

Thus, they do not cause themselves, their close family members in this life, and their close family members in many previous lives to realize true happiness.

On the whole, they know the principle that any cause will produce a result of the exact same magnitude. They understand that helping other people is in fact benefiting themselves. They understand that liberation can only be found through following the teachings of the Buddhas and the Master, becoming accomplished, and ending the cycle of birth and death. They understand that liberation is the result of vigorous cultivation, walking the Bodhisattva path, and realizing the state of enlightenment. They understand that this is the only way one can truly save oneself and one's close family members!

Yet, despite this, they are constrained by their negative habitual tendencies of greed and selfishness concerning worldly things. They are attached to trifling profits of the moment. They are attracted to and bewitched by these illusions, which are false, which easily vanish, and which cause them to lose understanding of the correct Dharma. They are blocked by their greed for things of the world. Their view of the important is overshadowed by the trivial!

Although they understand certain Buddhist principles, they do not seek enlightenment. Rather, they just think of having their existing state of affairs continue in this life and future lives. They think that if in this life and future lives they can lead peaceful, happy existences, then there is nothing to worry about. They plan on holding on to this mentality until they pass away; yet, how is the attainment of such peace and happiness possible?

With this mentality, no matter how vigorously they cultivate themselves, it is of no use. It is not possible that the Buddhas and Bodhisattvas will bestow empowerment upon such people. They will be unable to obtain true happiness. On the contrary, because of their own ignorance and because they do not compassionately save other living beings – who have been their closest family members throughout many lives and eons and who have been suffering in the sea of misery throughout many lives and eons – they will bring upon themselves negative karmic retribution.

If they continue in this manner, they will ultimately descend into one of the three lower realms of existence! This is exactly like the man from Zheng in an old Chinese story, who showed great lack of judgment. Their losses will outweigh their gains and they will, in the end, pass away with regrets. As such, although these people have a Master, it is as if they did not have a Master. Although they learn the Dharma, it is truly as if there were no Dharma. One can easily see their ignorance!

Yet, these people take delight in worldly things and never get tired of them. On the one hand, they are complacent. They are satisfied with enjoying the pleasures of the world, which are actually "bitter pleasures." They are carefree and leisurely and are at peace with their present circumstances. On the other hand, they learn Buddhism under the Master and diligently cultivate themselves. Nonetheless, they do not think of leaving the cycle of reincarnation. They do not give rise to a mind bent on transcending the cycle of birth and death. They do not yearn for enlightenment. They are not aware of the suffering inherent in pursuing worldly things.

To put it more directly, they are already in a state of numbness. They are unmoved by the Dharma. Nevertheless, they hope that by vigorously practicing they can both avoid descending into one of the three lower realms after they die and still enjoy the "blessings" of this world in this lifetime.

This can only result in their getting the opposite of what they want. It is like one who has fallen into a pool of mud. There is a good person nearby who extends his hand in order to assist the fallen person. This good person also tells the fallen person how to extricate himself. However, the fallen person says, "I feel that this pool of mud is quite good. It feels very good to be inside of it. I will not come out! What you say may be right. I do not deny it. I can try to do as you say, but I am more faithful to my own feelings. I do not want to leave this mud. If I were to do as you say, my goal would not be to leave this place, which is full of enticement. Rather, it would be to stay in this mud pool for a longer period of time. Although it is not incredibly comfortable here, and although occasionally there is suffering and misery, yet it is still quite enjoyable!"

Such words and feelings truly make one sit up and take notice! Yet, when their circumstances change and they are pulled deeper and deeper into the pool of mud, there will ultimately be a day when the mud comes up to their mouth and nose and then covers the top of their head. After they experience this calamity of drowning, their previous misconceptions will be mentioned with great sorrow when others offer condolences over their death.

Nothing more need be said. Practitioners should look within themselves and be cautious. Following a Master and diligently practicing, yet not yearn-ing for enlightenment, will bring about endless troubles. One's practice of the Dharma will be futile!

15. *The Futility of Cultivating Prajna if One Does Not Eliminate Jealousy and the Five Poisons*

The Dharma of prajna is the highest Buddha Dharma. It expounds the original nature of all the Tathagatas and all living beings. It is the truth of the universe. Any practitioner who wants to liberate himself from the cycle of birth and death must realize prajna!

The explanation of the Dharma of prajna by the Buddhas and Bodhisattvas can be as lengthy as the 600 volumes of the prajna sutras or as simple as the wordless manifestation of Dharma by Manjushri Bodhisattva. All of these show the supreme, unsurpassed essence of the Dharma of prajna.

The Dharma of prajna is deep, lofty, and wonderful. The ordinary person, of course, cannot realize it. Nonetheless, one who does not realize the meaning of prajna cannot become accomplished. Therefore, it is truly indispensable for the practitioner.

If the practitioner wants to realize the ultimate state of prajna, he must first use prajna obtained through the written word in order to understand the overall meaning of prajna. He must understand this overall meaning according to the words he reads. Next, he must use the prajna obtained through contemplating reality in his practice of contemplation. He will then realize the prajna of ultimate reality. These are the three steps in realizing the Dharma of prajna.

In order to realize the prajna of ultimate reality, one must penetratingly comprehend the principle that the nature of all things is originally empty. One must know the impermanent nature of all things. One must know that all worldly phenomena are illusory, empty, and false. Such phenomena are like dreams, illusions, bubbles, and shadows. All such phenomena have no true substance.

Thus, if the practitioner wants to realize prajna, he must understand the truth of emptiness. He must eradicate his greed, craving, and attachment concerning things of the world. Jealousy and the five poisons[62] must all be eliminated. They cannot remain.

All worldly phenomena exist in a false manner. In fact, they arise due to the convergence of causes and conditions. They vanish when these causes and conditions break up. If one is not able to comprehend this principle, one cannot realize the nature of emptiness. Thus, one will not be able to realize the truth underlying the cycle of birth and death.

Hence, practitioners must eliminate jealousy and the five poisons, which are all illusory. People who are jealous have a tendency to compare themselves with others. This tendency aggravates their jealous disposition and makes them hate other people. As a result, they might secretly play dirty tricks on people. They might openly attack others. They might abuse others verbally. They might ridicule and deride others. They might create all kinds of difficulties for the people of whom they are jealous.

They might not care that their conduct violates the law and morality. Because of thoughts of jealousy, they might think of taking revenge upon someone. They might use various lowly and despicable means, such as those used by bums, to strike out at others, to malign them, etc. All of this is odious conduct.

With respect to the five poisons, the situation is even worse! The *five poisons* is an overall name for all different types of evil conduct. It is a metaphor for karma that is defiled and based on delusion. Thus, the erroneous things that people do in the world can all be classified into one or more of the five poisons. These five poisons arise through the convergence of certain causes and conditions and are truly antithetical to the Dharma of prajna. Holding on to them will prevent one from realizing the prajna of ultimate reality.

One who gives rise to these five poisons will commit acts that will produce extremely bad karma. Because of jealousy and the five poisons, some practitioners cannot stand it when other fellow Buddhist disciples have any qualities that are superior to their own. If the Master even slightly praises a certain other disciple, they become jealous and resentful. They earnestly wish they could immediately step all over that fellow disciple in order to vent their poisonous flames of rage.

Because of poisonous thoughts, they even give rise to feelings of dissatisfaction toward the Master. They malign the Master wherever they go, saying that the Master does not treat people equally. If there were a female disciple of this sort, she might even go so far as to slander the Master by saying that she had an affair with him and by explaining how unusual their relationship is. She might tell others how excellent and special their relationship was in the last life and is in this life.

A disciple is committing the most heinous offense when he or she spreads rumors within Buddhist circles that cause people who do not know the truth to think of quitting Buddhism, thereby destroying their foundation to attain enlightenment. This type of practitioner is acting out of jealousy and the five poisons and will definitely receive karmic retribution, perhaps even in this very lifetime. If this person does not repent thoroughly of his offenses, he will surely descend directly into the hell of uninterrupted suffering! One can thus see the evil inherent in jealousy and the five poisons!

Worldly people, even more than Buddhist disciples, commit all kinds of evil due to jealousy and the five poisons. Some people see their colleagues receiving promotions at work and cannot contain their thoughts of jealousy. They wish they could immediately pull these colleagues down so that they themselves could forcibly occupy the positions of these colleagues. With this goal in mind, they make unfounded accusations against these colleagues. They stir up enmity toward these co-workers and destroy the reputations of these co-workers. They even invent out of thin air incriminating stories about these fellow workers, causing these innocent people to suffer wrongs and perhaps imprisonment.

Some people, incited by jealousy and the five poisons, will hire a criminal to kill someone whose business is more successful than theirs or who they fear constitutes a threat to them. They might set fire to such person's house, resulting in that person not having even a place in which to live. The end result may be that lives are lost and property is destroyed.

There are some people who, due to the five poisons, cannot stand seeing other people getting along amicably. They then instigate fights and killing. They engage in unjust military ventures. They stir up discord. They find pleasure in other people's pain. They do not care if they are universally condemned. As long as they are enjoying themselves, everything is all right! It can be said that this type of person is no different from a demon!

Since these people have produced negative karma, they must eventually receive retribution. None of them will be able to escape this! This is the ultimate result of jealousy and the five poisons. There will not be the least bit of leniency. There are no exceptions for any worldly person or for any cultivator, no matter how eminent the cultivator may be.

Thus, you should understand that, be it jealousy or the five poisons, they all are causes that result in living beings remaining in the stream of samsara and continuing to suffer. If the practitioner engages in jealousy and the five poisons, yet at the same time cultivates prajna – that is, the Dharma to end the stream of samsara – then he will surely experience many hindrances in such cultivation, and the merit from such cultivation will be destroyed.

Defiled acts that spring from a jealous heart and poisonous mind cover up one's original bright nature. A person performing such acts does not harbor correct views. Rather, he follows erroneous views. He is not able to comprehend his original nature according to the principles of prajna obtained through the written word. Naturally, he is not able to end the cycle of birth and death, realize the prajna of ultimate reality, or attain the wisdom that penetrates into the empty nature of all phenomena.

This type of practice is also futile!

16. The Futility of Practicing the Mahayana Dharma When One Does Not Have a Heart of Great Compassion

In Buddhism, the Master should teach disciples in accordance with their aptitudes. Disciples who learn the Dharma should practice and study according to the Dharma. This is how learning the Dharma should fundamentally be carried out.

Thus, the Mahayana Dharma cannot be transmitted to everyone. Not everyone will be able to practice the Mahayana Dharma. The Master must discern the particular karmic destiny of the disciple in order to decide whether or not to transmit the Mahayana Dharma. The Master absolutely cannot recklessly teach the Dharma wherever he goes and to whomever he meets. This is not permitted by the Dharma.

The Arhat realizes Arhatship in order to end his own cycle of birth and death. The Mahayana practitioner is able to become a Bodhisattva since he gives rise to a heart of great compassion and wants to save all sentient beings. Thus, practice of the Mahayana Dharma is predicated upon the great compassion of bodhicitta. In other words, without a heart of great compassion, one cannot practice the Mahayana Dharma. If one forcibly practices without this heart of great compassion, one will not attain the goal.

Why is this? The Mahayana Dharma is not something that ordinary people can receive. Moreover, in order to save living beings, one must first seek one's own salvation. During the process of seeking one's own salvation, one must open up one's awareness and give rise to thoughts of compassion.

Only then will one be able to carry out one's vow to save sentient beings from the danger they are in.

Even though one may have such compassionate thoughts, the Buddhas, the Bodhisattvas, and the Master must still test such person. Only when the Buddhas, the Bodhisattvas, and the Master firmly believe that such person's vow is steadfast will they empower him and transmit the Dharma to him. Only then will such person be able to practice the Mahayana Dharma and receive, in accordance with the Dharma, the unlimited empowerment of the Buddhas and Bodhisattvas.

If one does not have a heart of great compassion, then one's study and practice of Mahayana Dharma principles will be like a tree without roots. One will not have a strong foundation, and one's practice will be lacking. This type of practice will definitely fail, as the tree without roots will surely decay.

For example, due to the continuation of negative habitual tendencies carried over from previous lives, most Mahayana practitioners will still tend to engage in some negative karma during the time they are practicing the Mahayana Dharma. Occasionally, they will do harm to or take away the lives of living beings. This is truly hard to avoid.

Since they have not been able to attain the level of virtuous conduct of the Buddhas, Bodhisattvas, and Holy Ones, since they are still in the stage of cultivation and study, it is thus difficult for their conduct to be perfect. Because of these causes, they will engage in negative karma. As the Chinese saying goes, "People are not sages. Who can be without fault?"

This type of negative karma is caused by demons. These demons exert immense effort and use all kinds of schemes in order to hinder and disturb the cultivation of Mahayana Buddhists. Thus, such practitioners are influenced to commit serious evils. They are beguiled by these demonic hindrances. When they become hotheaded, there is nothing they will not do. Angry thoughts swell up within them and engulf them. Their temperament then becomes haughty, arrogant, and domineering. They become wrathful over the tiniest things and are not able to control themselves. In such state, it is possible that they will commit any kind of cruelty, such as even killing people or other living things. This type of evil conduct will truly cause them to descend into hell.

Furthermore, since such practitioners do not have a heart of great compassion as their foundation, they would misapply any supernormal powers they had. They would take advantage of their abilities and skills in the Buddha Dharma to do everything they are capable of doing. They would plunge people into misery, suffering, and tragedy. The color of the sky and the earth would change and the mountains and rivers would become dark. Even if they came to their senses, it would be too late to repent! Therefore, with respect to the Vajra Dharma, especially with respect to nectar initiations, the recipient of the Dharma must be qualified according to the Dharma. Only then will the Dharma Protectors arrive at the site of the initiation. Otherwise, nectar will not be bestowed.

Being qualified according to the Dharma does not mean being qualified for a short period of time. One has the qualifications to receive the nectar initiation only when all of one's conduct and thoughts are always in accord with the Dharma. This is because once such initiation is successful, the recipient becomes a Holy One. If such a disciple still had bad tendencies, then this would be tragic for living beings in the world. A disciple with bad tendencies is not permitted to receive the great Dharma of nectar.

How could a disciple with bad tendencies increase the well-being of living beings? His practice of the Mahayana Buddha Dharma would inevitably bring calamities and pain upon sentient beings. He would not benefit or bring happiness to sentient beings. Furthermore, it goes without saying that his learning the Mahayana Dharma should be a blessing for living beings in the six realms of reincarnation within the three spheres of existence. In fact, due to his bad tendencies, just the opposite occurs. Practitioners who bring about such tragedies cause themselves to be reborn in hell due to their mental confusion. They completely destroy people's foundation to attain enlightenment. Thus, their troubles will continue on without end!

Bringing about such tragedies is not coincidental. It is the manifestation of causes planted over many lives. The practice of the Mahayana Dharma by such disciples not only does not bring about the abiding happiness of sentient beings, on the contrary, it brings disasters upon sentient beings. Therefore, the Master must carefully examine the faculties and qualities of the disciple and must teach the disciple according to his aptitudes. Only then can the Master avoid a careless move that would plant the roots of disaster and bring calamity upon the pitiable multitudinous living beings!

Practitioners who practice and study the Mahayana Dharma must think carefully before they act. They must have the great compassion of bodhicitta. They must study and practice the Mahayana Dharma with a heart of great compassion. Only then will it be possible for them to truly bring blessings and wisdom to all sentient beings.

When the practitioner who learns the Mahayana Dharma has a heart of great compassion, he is able to quickly realize the nature of his mind, understand thoroughly the principles of the Dharma, and know his original nature. Therefore, he can eliminate the karmic hindrances of greed, hatred, ignorance, craving, joy, anger, sorrow, and pleasure, which disturb the practitioner. This is like a rainfall that extinguishes the poisonous flames of ignorance, anger, and hatred, allowing the Mahayana practitioner to peacefully engage in correct cultivation without making mistakes.

It is very difficult to imagine how a cultivator who does not have a heart of great compassion could truly seek the welfare of sentient beings and save living beings. One can only say that this type of person would not truly work for the benefit of living beings. Since he has not attained thorough awareness, of course he will not have a heart of great compassion. That is to say, since his level of realization has not yet reached that stage, he will definitely not love all sentient beings. Why?

When a person does not understand that other living beings have all been, at one time or another, his closest family members throughout past lives and eons, he will not give rise to a heart of great compassion and will not take the bodhicitta vows. Of course, such a person will not walk the Bodhisattva path. This is inevitable.

Even if he occasionally performs some acts that benefit and bring happiness to other people, such acts are the result of momentary introspection. Such acts were not performed in a very natural manner after he penetratingly viewed his original nature. These are two different concepts. Practitioners must distinguish between the two.

For example, there is a common worldly person who as a child had to beg for food in order to fill his stomach and maintain his life. Later, he becomes wealthier and no longer begs for food. When he then sees a beggar on the street, painful emotions will be evoked. He will recollect the time of his childhood. At such moments, he will be quite magnanimous and as a result will contribute more frequently and in greater amounts than other ordinary people of the world.

His decision to contribute is the result of reflecting upon how he himself was in the same circumstance at one time. Such decision was made because of certain conditions in his past that triggered his present heart of compassion. Still, this is not the manifestation of the Mahayana enlightened mind and compassionate heart.

Sometimes people such as that man seem to exhibit more compassion than those Mahayana practitioners who truly arouse bodhicitta of great compassion! However, the compassion of people such as that man can at most only match that of a Hinayana practitioner whose level of compassion is at the beginning stage. The compassion of people such as that man sometimes may not even be commensurate with one-tenth of this beginning stage compassion.

This is because their compassion is temporary. It is the result of momentary reflection. It cannot last long. Furthermore, it is often the case that even though these people give rise to this type of compassionate heart, they continue to live according to their old way of life and continue to treat other living beings according to their old principles.

That is, if they kill other living beings as a livelihood, after they contribute to this beggar, they will still kill other living beings as a livelihood, just as before. Every day, in the same manner, they will kill living beings. If they maintained their livelihood by treating others unscrupulously and by doing ruthless, wrong things, then they will likewise not turn over a new leaf. They will not discontinue such evil actions simply because of a moment of compassion wherein they contributed to a beggar.

Therefore, one cannot simply consider the superficial acts of people when determining whether someone is good or bad, kind or evil. Also, one cannot simply consider certain momentary conduct when judging and analyzing other people. One may see a certain person occasionally performing a good deed and, therefore, consider such person to be a Great Bodhisattva who saves others from suffering and disaster, a Mahayana practitioner who aroused the great compassion of bodhicitta. Perhaps such person is actually a brutal killer whose hands are filled with blood – an evil demon who has committed innumerable murders!

Thus, with respect to a heart of great compassion, there is the distinction between true compassion and false compassion. A heart of great compassion that is true is not necessarily expressed very openly. However, a false heart of compassion is sometimes easily exhibited in front of other people. Therefore, it is difficult to distinguish between the true and the false. One needs a standard by which to judge.

One with true compassion views all sentient beings as if they were one's own children. He puts other living beings first and himself second. He puts the teachings of the Buddhas, the Bodhisattvas, and the Master first. He considers his own gains and losses second.

However, those with a false heart of great compassion are always emphasizing themselves. Perhaps they ordinarily appear to be concerned about others, yet at the critical moment they will not extend a helping hand to assist others. In order to protect their own interests, they will not hesitate to violate the teachings of the Buddhas, disregard the Buddha Dharma, disregard other living beings who have been their close family members throughout many previous lives, and disregard their close family members in this life. Their mentality is extremely selfish. There are those who go further and mercilessly abandon their own close family members simply based upon an arbitrary assumption. These are the actions that are performed by those practitioners who maintain a false heart of great compassion.

Thus, those people who only momentarily give rise to a heart of compassion might actually not even be as good as an ordinary Hinayana practitioner. Of course, they cannot even be mentioned in the same breath with a Bodhisattva who maintains bodhicitta of great compassion.

One certainly cannot say that people such as these truly have an enlightened and compassionate mind. This is the reason why their level of realization and understanding is not the same as that of Bodhisattvas. Those who do not have a heart of great compassion cannot be considered to be Mahayana practitioners. It is impossible for them to do things that are done by Mahayana Bodhisattvas. This is closely related to their state of realization!

If one's true state of realization has not yet reached the level of having a heart of great compassion, yet one still manages with effort to practice the Mahayana Dharma, then one will naturally not receive any benefits from this practice. Moreover, one will lead others astray, harm others, and harm oneself. One must definitely not engage in this type of cultivation. It is a way of doing things that goes against the Buddha Dharma. Of course, such a person will not be able to truly increase the good fortune of other living beings and bring them happiness.

Yet, reaching the state of having a heart of great compassion is not so easy. It requires the practitioner to deeply penetrate his original nature. He must analyze himself and gradually attain thorough understanding based upon the principles of the Buddha Dharma. Only when one truly understands certain principles can one reach the state wherein one gives rise to a heart of great compassion.

The future Lion's Roar Buddha personally told me the following: "I feel great gratitude toward other living beings. All living beings in the past have, and all living beings in the future will, rely upon each other in order to exist. Without living beings, I would not exist!"

This same principle was expounded by Sakyamuni Buddha as follows: Since beginningless time, living beings in the six realms within the three spheres have been our fathers, mothers, brothers, and sisters.

Actually, most practitioners have heard of this principle. However, not all practitioners who have heard of this principle are able to personally apply it. Although perhaps they understand this principle, they nevertheless do not wish to practice it. They maintain their worldly biases, just as before. They regard their own close family members in this life as precious. They are unmoved by this principle that was taught to them by the Master. They think that their parents in this life are their only true parents whom they must love and respect. They are completely indifferent to their parents in previous lives. They therefore do not inquire about or pay attention to other people. Some of them even act in the same manner as ignorant worldlings and go about killing and harming living beings. These things have become quite common. Of course, they are relatively undisturbed about all of this. Otherwise, when they see others raise a butcher knife at living beings, they would not be indifferent, calm, or joyous!

When all is said, it boils down to a few sentences. Those who are able to carry out the Dharma principle of Sakyamuni Buddha just mentioned are Mahayana Bodhisattvas who possess true compassion. Those who are not able to carry out this principle – that is, those who have not yet perfected their state of realization to this level – cannot be considered as people of great compassion. Of course, they are not qualified to practice the Mahayana Dharma!

Thus, it is futile to practice the Mahayana Dharma teachings when one does not have a heart of great compassion!

17. The Futility of Cultivating Concentration⁶³ If One Does Not Know One's Original Nature

What is one's original nature? What is concentration? No matter whether the practitioner is a monk or nun who has gone forth from the home, or a layperson who lives at home, they all practice the Dharma by following the teachings of Sakyamuni Buddha. All of them must practice according to the meaning of the correct Dharma. There is no other way to attain liberation from the cycle of birth and death.

This practice of the Dharma to end the cycle of birth and death will take on different forms according to the particular karmic destiny of each person. There are 84,000 different Dharma methods for realizing the end of the cycle of birth and death. Yet, only one method is most basic. That is, one must attain prajna and understand one's original nature. Based upon this understanding of one's original nature, one undertakes the practice of meditation and concentration. Through the practice of concentration, one can also thoroughly understand the original nature of the mind, realize the truth of emptiness, and comprehend the nonexistence of a real self in human beings. Only then is one able to leave the cycle of reincarnation.

That is, if one wants to leave the cycle of reincarnation, one must realize the truth concerning one's original nature. In order to realize this truth, one must truly practice meditation, the Mind Within the Mind Dharma, the Mahamudra Dharma, or the Great Perfection Dharma. It is futile to practice meditation in order to realize the truth of emptiness if one does not know one's original nature. Why is this?

To realize the truth concerning one's original nature, one must go from understanding to vision, from vision to penetration, from penetration to realization. This is the sequence leading to attainment. If one only seeks realization and does not practice according to the Dharma, then ultimately one will not even know what it is one is supposed to realize. In one's practice of meditation, one will simply enter into a state of mental confusion. Even if, upon reflection and introspection, one's original nature suddenly manifests before oneself, one will still not recognize it.

To give an example, it is like someone who was separated from his real parents when he was a small child. Other people raised him, and he does not know any of the circumstances surrounding his true parents. Even if one day he ran across his true parents on the street, he would still view them as strangers. He would not know anything about them. Therefore, he would pass by his real parents and would not come to know them.

In order to be able to meet his real parents, someone must tell him the secrets of his background and reveal to him where his true parents live, the special features of their appearance, their age, the sound of their voices, etc. Only after telling him these details about his true parents will he have enough clues to go and find them. He will then ultimately be able to meet them, the family will be reunited, and they will together enjoy their natural bonds.

Cultivation and seeking enlightenment are also like this. One must know why one is engaging in cultivation. When one understands that one must realize enlightenment in order to end the cycle of birth and death, one must then know how to seek enlightenment. Only by finding the Dharma leading to realization and by practicing according to such Dharma can one attain enlightenment.

The Masters and Accomplished Ones elucidated the Dharma that one must practice. They said that if one seeks enlightenment to end the cycle of birth and death, one must first realize prajna. If one does not realize prajna, one cannot attain liberation. In order to realize the prajna of the ultimate nature of reality, one must first understand what this reality is by way of the meaning of the Dharma. Through written words, one can first understand the meaning of this reality as it is described. In order to master prajna obtained through the written word, one must understand what one's original nature is.

If one does not know one's original nature, then one does not know anything about attaining enlightenment. This is truly like one who travels without a compass. He does not know which road to travel. Even if he traverses mountains and streams all day long, thereby exhausting himself, he will still accomplish nothing. Even if his destination is right before him, he will still not know how to locate it. He will continue to run around all over the place and ultimately accomplish nothing.

The importance to cultivators of knowing the principles concerning one's original nature and realizing one's original nature is quite obvious. In other words, if cultivators do not know their original nature, in the end, they will not become accomplished. Their cultivation will be futile.

What, after all, is one's original nature? One's original nature is the pure Dharma body of all sentient beings within the three spheres of existence. It is united with the universe. It has no form or shape, no physical body or appearance. It is the original nature of living beings. All people possess this original nature of living beings. This original nature is without any bias toward one person or another. It is not more in one person and less in another. It is not bigger in one person and smaller in another.

The original nature of each sentient being is the same as the Dharma body of the Tathagata. It does not come and does not go. It is not too much nor is it lacking. It is immaculate. It is just that the Dharma body realized by living beings has not reached the level of perfect realization attained by the Buddhas.

In the Dharma, there are many terms for the concept "one's original nature." It may be called original nature, the Dharma body of the Tathagata, wonderful prajna wisdom, Buddha-nature, etc. Yet, no matter what term is used, its meaning is the same.

I said that it is futile to practice meditation and concentration if one does not know one's original nature. Here the phrase "know one's original nature" should not be taken to mean "directly realize one's original nature." The phrase "know one's original nature" is really referring to hearing or reading about the principles or theories pertaining to one's original nature. It is referring to knowing about the concept "one's original nature."

In other words, if the cultivator practices meditation and concentration so as to end the cycle of birth and death, yet has not even heard of the term "one's original nature," does not even know what, after all, the original nature of living beings is, has never come into contact with the concept of "one's original nature," and does not know even a few Dharma principles about "one's original nature," then such practice of concentration is in fact tantamount to no practice at all.

When Great Master Padmasambhava spoke of "knowing one's original nature," he was referring to hearing and thereby knowing the principles pertaining to one's original nature. He was referring to understanding the theories pertaining to one's original nature. He was not speaking of direct realization of one's original nature.

Here I am saying that the cultivator should carefully investigate and thoroughly understand these principles and theories. Why do I say this? Because cultivators know that in order to attain concentration, one must follow the sequence of morality, concentration, and wisdom.[64] Simply put, if one does not behave morally by following the precepts, one will not attain concentration. Without concentration, one will not attain wisdom.

The wisdom I am referring to here is wonderful prajna wisdom. If one wants to realize this wonderful prajna wisdom, one must practice and attain concentration. Only then can one realize this wonderful wisdom.

It can be said that no matter how eminent the practitioner may be, if such person does not practice meditation and concentration, if such person does not attain true realization by way of his skills in meditation and concentration, then it will be impossible for such person to directly reach his original nature and attain wonderful prajna wisdom. Only by practicing concentration and attaining correct and great concentration can one give rise to wonderful prajna wisdom. Only then can one deeply enter the great concentration of a Tathagata and end the cycle of birth and death.

This wonderful prajna wisdom is referring to the Tathagata Dharma body of living beings, which is originally pure. This Dharma body is no different from the original nature of the Buddhas.

Therefore, it can be said that without concentration, one will be unable to realize one's original nature and abide in the Tathagata Dharma body. If living beings were able to calmly abide in the great concentration of a Tathagata and attain the supreme and wonderful prajna wisdom, then they could have control over life and death and leave the six realms of reincarnation.

Hence, in this context, "knowing one's original nature" does not mean directly realizing one's original nature. It means hearing or reading about the principles and theories pertaining to one's original nature and thereby knowing what one's original nature is.

Knowing these concepts, one will not be at a loss when one practices meditation and concentration. One will avoid the situation of not recognizing one's original nature when it clearly appears during a moment of reflection. One will thus not lose such opportunity due to lack of knowledge. It is like the example explained above where the person sees his true parents yet does not recognize them.

Thus, in one's cultivation, it is futile to practice concentration if one does not know one's original nature.

If you good practitioners wish to further understand principles regarding the emptiness of one's original nature and what wonderful prajna wisdom is, then you should study the 600 volumes of the Great Prajna Sutras, *The Mahamudra of Liberation* written by Great Dharma King Yangwo Yisinubu, or *The Prajna of Ultimate Reality*, which I wrote. In so doing, you will certainly receive enormous benefits!

18. The Futility of Receiving Mantras[65] If One Does Not Apply Them

According to the meaning of the Buddha Dharma of Vajrayana Buddhism, practitioners must go through a Master who is heir to a true spiritual legacy to receive oral transmissions and must learn from the Master's own example. Furthermore, they must go through several ceremonies wherein Dharma is practiced by the Master and is orally transmitted to the practitioner. Only then can the practitioner practice what he has learned. Practicing the Dharma on one's own without going through the Master is futile.

However, there are many practitioners who, after formally acknowledging a certain Master, and after the Master formally transmits the Dharma to them in the form of certain mantras, do not apply such mantras. That is, after they receive such mantras, they do not in fact put them into practice. Thus, in the end, their efforts are fruitless. This is truly a very lamentable thing within Buddhism. Because of this, it will be impossible for them to obtain the fruit of happiness.

There are many practitioners of this kind within Buddhism. There are not just a small number of them. They devoutly beseech the Master to transmit the Dharma to them. After the Dharma is transmitted to them, they are very enthusiastic for a short period of time. Some of them can diligently practice all through the night without sleeping. Although others are not enthusiastic to this degree, they nevertheless are very excited and make it a point to practice every day. Yet, this delightful scene cannot last long. After a few days or a certain period of time, they do not recite the mantras transmitted by the Master. With respect to some, the situation is even worse. Because of indulgence in worldly pleasures, they even totally forget the mantras.

With such lack of practice, of what use is it to teach them mantras? The basis of any type of cultivation is practice. No matter how high and wonderful a certain Dharma may be in its ability to cause living beings to become greatly accomplished and end the cycle of birth and death, without practice it would still be ineffective. Without practice, it is impossible for any Dharma to cause sentient beings to become liberated.

This is because the prerequisite for liberation is absent. It is like a tree without roots or a housewife who has run out of rice. No matter how skillful the gardener may be, he is helpless, for a tree without roots cannot grow into useful timber. No matter how skillful the housewife may be, she is helpless, for how can a meal without rice satisfy her family's hunger?

The path of cultivation is also like this! The Master's transmission of a mantra is just like the giving of a golden key that opens the gate to ending the cycle of birth and death. One should be well versed in the way to use this key and should correctly use it by following the instructions of the Buddhas and the Master. One can then, with great facility, open the gate leading out of the cycle of birth and death.

If one receives this key yet pays no attention to it, if one does not correctly use it by putting it into the keyhole and opening the gate leading out of the cycle of birth and death, then it would be better if one did not even have such a golden key. What is the difference between such people and those who, because they do not have the opportunity to obtain such a key, are strenuously wandering back and forth in front of this gate, experiencing difficulties and hardships?

If for just one day one does not practice the mantra, one's Dharma power will diminish greatly, and the Dharma Protectors will move far away. Not practicing even one day is no different from not practicing for ten days or one hundred days, since one has already quietly planted the seeds of calamity in one's life. I need not mention here the consequences of not practicing at all the mantra that was transmitted according to the Dharma.

There are practitioners who do not think in this manner and who disagree with this. They think that they have cultivated themselves for years and that they have attained great merit through strenuous efforts. Therefore, they treat the matter of reciting mantras casually and do not take these words I am speaking as a serious warning. Hence, as each day passes, they become more and more undisciplined. Their disrespect toward the Buddhas, attachment to things, dissipation, and arrogance quietly grow. It is like a neglected garden with weeds. If one does not diligently hoe up weeds, then weeds will soon grow up, ready to flourish. These people lose the concentration necessary for calm patience and serenity. Naturally, their moral integrity will be lacking.

It is the same principle with respect to the rise and fall of a country. If the people are not diligent in their labor, if they do not work with determination to make their country strong, if they do not vigorously strive to benefit their country, then their country will fall behind. It is like a boat sailing against the current; the country's people must keep forging ahead or the country will fall behind!

Certain leaders of countries are dissipated and do not think of making progress. There are also leaders who calmly draw up plans behind closed doors without reference to what is happening in the world. They are lost in their pipe dreams all night long. Unfortunately, their country may already be in a precarious situation. The situation outside their doors may be utterly different than before.

In the end, these leaders wind up being beaten, insulted, and abused by people. They bring upon themselves pain and are at a loss concerning what to do. They then blame themselves and feel remorseful and sad. This is like mending the fold after the sheep have been stolen. As the saying goes, "A man who loses position and influence may be subjected to much indignity." If they only knew what they would experience, why would they act as they did?

This was a brief discussion of worldly matters. The Buddha Dharma is even more like this. Countless living beings in the three spheres of existence hope for, but do not have, the opportunity to learn the Buddha Dharma that ends the cycle of birth and death. They hope for, but do not have, the opportunity to receive the Master's teachings and mantras. Such an opportunity is a blessing resulting from merit accumulated over many previous existences!

Yet, these practitioners do not cherish this extremely rare opportunity. On the contrary, they are attached to momentary greedy desires and do not practice the Dharma at all. They forget about the mantras transmitted by the Buddhas and the Master. They abandon their practice of the Buddha Dharma. They do not attempt to attain true realization by energetically applying the mantras. Such cultivation will amount to nothing.

Practitioners must not become confused. They should not care only about seeking the Buddha Dharma, without truly practicing it. Even if the Master transmits a mantra, if one does not apply it, then the transmission is futile. In the end, one will not attain liberation.

19. The Futility of Doing Things That Benefit Sentient Beings When One Does Not Act Out of Bodhicitta

When cultivators benefit sentient beings, generally they do so out of one of two mindsets. One type of mindset is the four limitless states of mind: limitless loving-kindness, compassion, sympathetic joy, and equanimity. The other type of mindset is bodhicitta.

The four limitless states of mind are the foundation of bodhicitta. Thus, the relationship between these states and bodhicitta is one of succession; that is, one comes before the other. It seems as if there is no absolute demarcation line between them. However, there is the following difference between them: In the first, one holds on to the notion of self, while in the second, one cuts off the notion of self. From the perspective of benefiting others, on the whole, it can be said that the two types are the same.

Benefiting sentient beings can be further divided into two types: acts done with an awakened mind and acts done with a mind that is not awakened.

Acts done with an awakened mind refers to doing things spontaneously and from one's innermost being. A person with such a mind does not need to draw support from anything in order to be motivated to perform acts that benefit sentient beings. To such person, performing acts that benefit others is something that is extremely natural and does not require considering any reward.

Acts done with a mind that is not awakened refers to benefiting sentient beings only because doing so is somehow related to one's own vital interests or because one is coerced into doing so by others, by law, by established rules, etc. The motivation for such beneficial acts is neither natural nor pure.

For example, there are certain public morals that society demands, such as being polite and courteous to others, not mistreating others by beating or scolding them, etc. This is a form of benefiting sentient beings. If everyone had misgivings over violating these moral principles, if everyone feared being a target of public censure as a result of violating these moral principles and, therefore, thought that they had no other choice than to follow these moral demands, then in fact they would be acting in a way that benefits others. This type of benefiting sentient beings does not arise from an awakened mind. Rather, such beneficial acts emanate from the restraints imposed upon people by societal morals and laws. Hence, such acts fall within the category of acts done with a mind that is not awakened.

With respect to acts done with an awakened mind, it is like what worldly people often say: "It is natural to do such beneficial things." This mindset is brought about through good karma accumulated over many lives and eons. When one with an awakened mind does things that benefit others, he gives no consideration at all to his own interests. He thinks that it is his duty to help others. He does not have any other motivation or thoughts. This is his impetus for performing acts that benefit sentient beings.

There is, on the other hand, a concept that should not be maintained by cultivators. This concept is benefiting sentient beings because one is compelled by circumstances. I have already discussed this problem. I will not repeat myself in detail here. Simply put, since the mentality of this type of cultivator is extremely impure, they regard the Buddha Dharma as a type of fetter and the law of cause and effect as something that they have no alternative but to follow, as they promised to do. Because of the Dharma, the rules, and the discipline, they will reluctantly practice benefiting others in an attempt to carry out the four limitless states of mind. However, their beneficial acts are often extremely limited. Sometimes they benefit sentient beings solely out of the desire to further their own interests. There are also those who benefit others in a most unwilling, discontented manner. I will not give any examples to illustrate this type of thinking.

In summary, one who truly pursues ending the cycle of birth and death will practice the Dharma and the rules with an awakened mind. He will help other living beings with an extremely pure heart. He will extricate other sentient beings from pain and difficulty. His commitment to bodhicitta will impel him to benefit sentient beings. He will not have any ill feeling or unpleasantness whatsoever in his heart when benefiting others. He will not try to find reasons or excuses to avoid benefiting others. He will not have an unhealthy mentality or an impure motivation when helping sentient beings.

Benefiting sentient beings out of bodhicitta is an unconditional state. When the beneficial acts are done, one lets go of them. One is not moved in any way by having benefited others. One acts to benefit others simply because one feels that it is what one ought to do and that it is what is natural to do. This is the aspect that is different from the four limitless states of mind.

Thus, it is futile to benefit sentient beings when one does not act out of bodhicitta.

20. The Futility of Reading Books and Listening to the Dharma When One Does Not Understand the Meaning and Principles or Cannot Put Them Into Practice

There are many practitioners today who are attached to and satisfied with reading Buddhist books or who consider listening to the Dharma as meritorious. Yet, these people do not put into actual practice what they read and hear. Thus, they are often unable to progress in their cultivation. They remain stagnant. This type of practice is truly futile. As a result, they will not become accomplished. Their efforts will be all for naught.

One often sees practitioners who, in response to questions, say that they have read this sutra book or that Buddhist book. There are some people who, as soon as they open their mouths, say, "I know such and such a Dharma. I read such and such a book. I also heard such and such a lecture." After they speak, they feel quite proud of themselves. To them, it is as if the essence of cultivation is simply reading certain Buddhist books or listening to certain Dharma, without any need whatsoever to engage in any further cultivation or practice! Therefore, based upon their perspective, they are totally satisfied with listening to a certain Dharma lecture. As far as they are concerned, there is nothing more to cultivation, and they should naturally be able to attain liberation without any hindrance.

In fact, after listening once or twice to a Dharma lecture, it can be said that they have not even understood its basic meaning and principles. When asked about what they heard, they do not know how to respond. How could it be that these people are cultivating themselves? They are experiencing a demonic hindrance and have fallen into error, yet they are unaware of this. Why is this?

These people are attached to the notion of reading or hearing something. They do not know that in cultivation, it is not enough to merely hear or read something. Cultivation requires practice. This is what is most crucial. No matter what sutra book or Dharma and no matter what type of practitioner, having read or listened simply indicates the existence of the fact that one has read or listened. It does not indicate that the person has digested and understood the information. What is meant by digestion is truly and clearly understanding the meaning of the Dharma read or heard and then applying such Dharma in one's actual practice of cultivation. Digestion means that the cultivator carries out the Dharma read or heard in all of his actions, speech, and thoughts – the three karmas. This is the real meaning of reading Buddhist books and learning the Dharma. How could attachment to the temporary experience of hearing something, seeing something, or reading something substitute for true and meaningful cultivation?

If cultivation were only a matter of being attached to reading books and listening to the Dharma, then Buddhists would not need to cultivate themselves, would not need to attain true realization, and would not need to practice according to the meaning of the Dharma. In such case, in the process of reading, one would naturally be able to lightly cast aside worldly cares and live aloof from the world, or leave this world to become a celestial being, or, without expending any effort at all, realize the ultimate truth and directly enter the holy state of enlightenment. This is simply too ridiculous!

Extrapolating from their viewpoint, the end result of cultivation would be that every cultivator would become a scholar of language and words, a scholar of empty theory, and a great listener of the Dharma. One would not need to pursue true realization. One would not need to do the solid work of cultivation! I will grant that they may truly know many theories or principles. However, no matter how many theories or principles they may know, how could reliance upon empty theories lead to truly ending the cycle of birth and death? I am afraid that this is just a beautiful pipe dream of theirs!

Thus, how could those people who are constantly saying that they heard such and such a Dharma or that they read such and such a Buddhist book be truly cultivating themselves? I am afraid that in truth they are not thinking clearly! Cultivators must be clear about something. When it comes to cultivation, it is not enough to just listen to a lecture or read a book. Cultivation requires true realization. It requires actually applying principles in one's cultivation. One must carry out the principles in one's practice of the three karmas, that is, in all that one does, says, and thinks.

Even if one has listened to a lecture or read a book, so what? Listening is not tantamount to understanding. Understanding is not tantamount to practicing. Even if one listens 10 times or 100 times, this itself is not true cultivation. One must understand, digest, and put into real practice the contents of the lecture one has heard. Only this can be called cultivation.

Reading Buddhist books is also like this. The more one reads, the better. The goal is to understand the principles contained therein and then use such principles to correct one's conduct. Thus, in learning Buddhism, it is absolutely not the case that reading or hearing is equivalent to understanding. You must remember this! Reading a book several times or listening to a lecture several times is not enough. It is like what Sister Yu Fei demanded of all students. She told them, "You must read Pamu's books more than 100 times and must act in accordance with their contents. Actually, the goal is that after you understand the books, you will put them into practice in whatever you are doing at the moment. This is what is meant by cultivation. Only in this way can one become accomplished."

All practitioners should act in accordance with this demand in learning Buddhism and cultivating themselves. It is not acceptable to merely look at others who are acting in accordance with this demand. If you yourself have not yet acted in accordance with this demand, then you are not on the path of cultivation.

It is just as the ancients said: "It is better to go back and make a net than to stand by the pond and long for fish." Cultivation is like this. When practitioners read books, they should reflect upon them. They should compare and contrast each and every principle in the book with their own conduct. They should seriously introspect, asking themselves whether they have successfully handled their practice and whether they are truly cultivating themselves in accordance with the Dharma.

I will give a very simple example. Numerous disciples have studied *Fifty Dharma Precepts Relating to the Master*. Each of them has made the determination to act in accordance with the contents of those precepts. However, in actual practice, the conduct of many disciples is not in accordance with the demands of those precepts. They violate one or another of those precepts. They are unable to smoothly put into practice those 50 Dharma precepts.

Perhaps they speak or act disrespectfully toward a Master who is heir to a true Dharma legacy. Perhaps they are unable to treat their fellow disciples with brotherly or sisterly love. Perhaps because of some other shortcoming or bad habit, they violate those precepts. Yet, as soon as these violations occur and they are asked whether they have read *Fifty Dharma Precepts Relating to the Master*, they all respond, "I have. I have read it many times!" When they are told to study it again, they will say, "I am continually studying it. I study it every day...."

Are they really studying it? One can say that they are not seriously reading it and that they study it inattentively. In fact, they do not put into practice its contents at all. They do not act in accordance with those precepts. What benefit can this type of reading bring about?

Furthermore, many Buddhist disciples study my books. Everywhere in the world, Rinpoches are studying my books and using them as teaching material. Some disciples have even read them a few dozen times. When you ask them whether they understand the books, they will say, "I understand them. I understand everything that I read." However, what is their real practice like after they read the books?

Some Rinpoches cannot understand why they still, even as a Rinpoche, occasionally experience hot and cold spells and headaches. Ordinary practitioners do not understand why they are still in dire poverty and why they cannot make a huge fortune even though they have studied Buddhism and practiced the Dharma for quite a number of years.

Some Great Rinpoches study my books every day. They cultivate themselves every day. Yet, the result is that they are attached to things of the world. All day long they give rise to greedy and erroneous thoughts. They yearn to become the National Teacher of a certain country or a high official. When they sit at the same table with a country's President, they become ecstatic and cannot sleep for days. They feel that this is such an incomparable honor.

Can it be said that these people have practiced cultivation well? They have not. Moreover, they are still very ignorant! When you tell them to go back and carefully read my books, understand them, and digest them, they will not accept this advice as being right. They will not take such advice seriously. They will even act as if they have been wronged. They will repeatedly say, "I understand all of the books. I read them so many times. Every day I act in accordance with them. Every day I cultivate myself in accordance with the teachings in those books!" If they truly practiced according to the contents of those books, then how could their cultivation be at such a low state?

These people are truly so pitiful and so ignorant. Why do they still not understand that reading is not the same as remembering, that remembering is not the same as practicing, and that only by practicing can one experience beneficial effects? If one reads my books but does not act in accordance with them, then even if one reads them 1,000 or 10,000 times, it will still be of no use. It will still be of no benefit to one's cultivation. One may have the opportunity to hear or read the correct Dharma yet not practice in accordance with its meaning. In such case, no matter how much Dharma one hears or reads, and no matter how wonderful the Dharma one hears or reads may be, it will still not aid in attaining liberation. This is the principle that the practice must be in accordance with the theories.

After one has read books or heard lectures on the Dharma, one may still not understand the true meaning of the principles read or heard. In such case, how is one justified in being pleased with oneself simply because one has read a certain book several dozen times or has heard the lectures of such and such a person several times? How is one justified in relying upon this to claim credit for oneself and become proud?

Among cultivators, there are quite a number of people who maintain this type of mentality. Each time I speak of such matters, they are unable to become clear-headed. In response to this situation, I have elucidated these matters here. I specially admonish practitioners not to fall into this type of absurdity so that they will not adversely affect the great task of ending the cycle of birth and death and becoming accomplished. One should understand that after reading books and listening to lectures on the Dharma, there is still the need to practice according to the meaning. Otherwise, such reading and listening are futile!

⌐ *Chapter Eight* ⌐

DHARMA TALK GIVEN ACCORDING TO THE SITUATION

WHAT IS MEANT BY THE BUDDHA DHARMA? Cause and effect is what is meant by the Buddha Dharma.

How does one end causes and effects? Through cultivation.

How should one cultivate oneself? According to the correct Dharma.

What is meant by the correct Dharma? The Tripitaka based upon the words of the Tathagata.

Is the Vajrayana true? Tibetan Buddhism is the deepest.

How does one select the correct Dharma? Inner-Tantric Initiation is the most brilliant.

Which Dharma is simply reciting mantras? Simply reciting mantras is practiced by a "mantra teacher"[66] who stubbornly adheres to this Dharma.

How does one examine a person's practice of the Vajrayana? See if he has mastered both exoteric and esoteric Dharma.

Initiations are divided into which sections? The three divisions concerning turning of the wheel of the Dharma.

Into which divisions is the wheel of the Dharma divided? The three divisions of Outer-Tantric Initiations, Inner-Tantric Initiations, and Secret-Tantric Initiations.

What is the highest vehicle on which one can rely? The Inner-Tantric and Secret-Tantric Initiations in which miraculous states appear.

What should one read for a detailed description of this? *Know the True Doctrines* contains a full description.

How does one find an enlightened teacher? One finds a teacher who is thoroughly proficient in exoteric and esoteric Dharma and who has mastered the Five Sciences.

Can one decide on a teacher based upon his spiritual lineage? The most important thing is whether the teacher has the power to perform true Inner-Tantric Initiations.

How can one tell whether a teacher has learned the highest Dharma? Such a teacher will be able to successfully invoke the Buddhas to bestow true nectar.

Besides this, are there any other practices? Transmitting the greatest Dharma requires initiations with true nectar.

Why is this the case? In order to prevent false teachers from deceiving people.

How should beginners pursue learning Vajrayana Buddhism? They should practice the preliminaries and should become familiar with the Tripitaka.

How should disciples penetrate deeply into the Dharma? Through Inner-Tantric Initiations.

How can one tell whether an initiation is true? There will be supernormal states that appear at the scene.

How many divisions of initiations are there? There are all together five divisions.

Can one find precise commentary on this? One should read the book *Entering the Door of the Dharma.*

Is it too deep to be explained in detail? I will not provide further explanation at this point.

Is it a great offense to violate the precepts? After one has produced certain causes by violating the precepts, it can be seen whether one will rise or fall.

Can those who have just begun to learn Buddhism save others? Those who are not enlightened themselves will misguide others.

Why must one be cautious? To guard against those who falsely claim to be sacred.

What about those who falsely claim to be a master and who accept disciples? They have entered into a diabolical state and will die early.

What about those who speak false Buddha Dharma? They will descend into the hell realm.

What state of realization must one have to accept disciples? Those who have realized the enlightenment of a Holy One.

What about those who have not realized enlightenment yet who attempt to save others? Death will take them away in iron chains.

Can they stop and thereby escape this? They will experience the cauldron of boiling oil and the mountain of swords.

What about those who destroy the opportunity for people to realize their original nature and wisdom? Such offense will result in their descending into the hell realm of uninterrupted suffering.

What is the most important aspect of cultivation? One's three karmas corresponding with the teachings of the Master and Buddhas.

What if one does not practice in such manner? One will definitely move in the opposite direction of realizing enlightenment.

How should fellow disciples treat each other? What should be avoided most of all is gossiping about each other.

What if one does not build moral character? He will confine himself to the state of an ordinary person.

What is a great obstacle on the path of cultivation? Secretly slandering the Master or the Master's wife.

What punishment will those who secretly slander the Master receive? They will die young and will then reside in one of the evil realms.

What about those who secretly criticize the Master's wife? They will die a tragic death.

What if such people do not show great remorse? Death will take them away in chains.

What about small matters and big matters? One cannot hide either type of matter from the Master.

What if one violates this principle? One will not be able to attain liberation.

What about those who have committed offenses and who rebel against the Master? Their ignorance will cause them to descend into the hell of uninterrupted suffering.

What if one speaks falsely to the Master? One will naturally not have any supernormal powers.

Will one receive empowerment and good fortune when one speaks falsely to the Master? One will not receive empowerment and good fortune in one's worldly matters.

Can recitation of a certain mantra transfer the consciousness of the dead to a higher realm? The ordinary person does not possess such power.

What if one practices evil ways? After one dies, one will then become an animal or ghost.

What if one spreads the correct Dharma? One will thereby increase one's blessings and wisdom.

How can one perfect one's merit? The most important thing is to select the right Master.

Can one measure a Master by his spiritual lineage alone? One must look to his qualifications as a Master.

How does one learn great Dharma? By acknowledging a true Dharma King as one's Master.

How does one determine who is a Dharma King? One should carefully read the book *Know the True Doctrines*.

Should the practitioner carefully select a Master? In so doing, the practitioner must thoroughly understand what is meant by true Vajrayana Buddhism.

All of you should carefully listen. I will give a brief explanation!

The innate faculties of living beings have been defiled throughout many lives. It is difficult for them to understand the deep meaning of the Dharma. I will now again give a discourse to them!

What is meant by the Buddha Dharma? Within the two words *Buddha Dharma* are contained the truth and the original nature of all conditioned and unconditioned phenomena in the universe. Simply put, the Buddha Dharma is all causes and effects in the universe. To understand all causes and effects, yet not be controlled by cause and effect, is to realize liberation and the Buddha Dharma.

One must penetrate and realize the Buddha Dharma in order to end the cycle of birth and death, attain supernormal powers, attain the power to assume different forms, and lack nothing at all! There is only one method to penetrate and realize the Buddha Dharma: taking refuge in the Three Jewels or the Four Jewels and cultivating oneself deeply. The cultivation one engages in must be in accordance with the Tripitaka of the Buddha or the scriptures of the Vajrayana.

Within the Buddha Dharma, the highest Dharma is that of the Vajrayana. The highest, greatest, and brightest Dharma of the Vajrayana is Tibetan tantra. Within Tibetan tantra, Inner-Tantric Initiations and Secret-Tantric Initiations can be considered as true initiations with manifestations. Simply put, such initiations reflect actual Dharma powers. True states of communing with the Buddhas and Bodhisattvas are manifested! This means that each disciple who receives such initiations is able to see with his own ordinary eyes supernormal phenomena.

Within the three spheres of existence, there are many Buddhists who recite mantras as their method of cultivation. Among them are so-called "followers of Vajrayana Buddhism" who only know how to recite mantras. This type of person is called a mantra teacher. They are not practitioners of the Vajrayana. Frankly speaking, they are not followers of Vajrayana Buddhism! A true follower of Vajrayana Buddhism should be thoroughly proficient in all of the doctrines and Dharma methods of Vajrayana Buddhism, plus the five divisions of tantra. Only then can such person be called a follower of Vajrayana Buddhism.

Before followers of Vajrayana Buddhism practice the Dharma, they must request initiation. All initiations come from Vajrasattva's turning of the Dharma Wheel, which is divided into three periods of time. The Dharma Wheel that is turned is divided into three classes of initiations: Outer-Tantric Initiations, Inner-Tantric Initiations, and Secret-Tantric Initiations. Each of these three classes is further divided into various Dharma methods.

However, the highest and greatest initiations are Inner-Tantric Initiations and Secret-Tantric Initiations. During any Inner-Tantric and Secret-Tantric Initiation, there must be supernormal states that are manifested in front of the disciples at the Buddhist altar area. These miraculous states must be in accordance with the Tibetan tantra laid down by the Buddhas. Actually, these initiations turn the disciples over to the Buddhas and Bodhisattvas right in front of the Buddhas and Bodhisattvas. Therefore, supernormal states are manifested! You can read the book *Know the True Doctrines*, which explains these things most fully.

In cultivating oneself, one must first select a Master. That is, one must select a Vajra Master who truly understands the Buddha Dharma and on whom one can rely. This Vajra Acarya cannot use his spiritual lineage in attempting to prove his state of realization! One must determine whether he is an authentic Vajra Master, a Holy One who has the merit and capacity to save living beings. One must determine whether he has mastered both exoteric and esoteric Dharma, as well as the Five Sciences. Emphasis must be put on whether he has the ability to conduct Inner-Tantric Initiations. Only after evaluating such criteria can one conclude whether someone is the best Vajra Master!

If one wants to learn the highest tantra, the Vajra Dharma King Master whom one selects must be able to successfully invoke the Buddhas to bestow true nectar. In front of the disciples, this nectar will fall from the sky into the bowl. No matter how great a person's abilities may be and no matter how great a Dharma King he may be, if he is unable to perform this nectar Dharma, then he does not represent the highest and deepest tantra, and he has not attained the highest position. This is because the greatest type of Dharma, such as the Great Perfection, Kalachakra Vajra, Shang Le Vajra, Lion Vajra, Dufamu, etc., as well as great Vajra Division Dharma, such as Zangyan and Fuzang, all require the Buddhas to bestow true nectar in order to perform the initiation. Without true nectar, all such initiations would not be in conformity with the Dharma. To put it more concretely, it would be difficult for one to receive any beneficial effects from such initiations that lack true nectar. Of course, if one cultivates oneself well in many aspects, then one will be able to receive some beneficial effects.

Why did the Buddhas lay down such a difficult requirement for great Dharma initiations? Because there are too many false Rinpoches in this earthly realm. Basically, out of 1,000 Rinpoches, more than 990 are false, or the Dharma they have learned is not perfect or complete. (This includes practitioners who hold the status of Dharma King.) In order to prevent these people from using their spiritual lineages as signboards to attract disciples when they in fact do not have any of the qualifications nor the state of realization of a true Dharma King, but rather deceive people into entering side paths, the Buddhas therefore laid down this requirement that one must have a deep state of realization with true Dharma power in order to perform great Dharma initiations. This requirement relates mainly to Great Dharma Kings. Great Rinpoches of various branches generally do not possess such state of realization and virtue.

Because of this requirement, only Great Dharma Kings who are genuine Holy Ones have the true state of realization to successfully invoke the Buddhas to bestow nectar. This requirement makes those Dharma Kings who do not have the qualifications to transmit great Dharma, as well as false Rinpoches and false Dharma Kings, feel quite helpless.

My Buddha Master, Great Dharma King Zun Sheng, said that there are basically two viewpoints from which one can distinguish a true Great Dharma King from a false one. The first viewpoint is based upon man-made conditions. The second viewpoint is based upon conditions that are not man-made.

With respect to man-made conditions, one can fabricate one's Dharma lineage. Organizations and their hierarchy are man-made conditions. People with no virtue at all can easily establish such things in a day. On the other hand, the Buddhas bestowing nectar from the sky in front of disciples who personally see this true scene is something that is not man-made. Those without virtue will always be helpless in this respect! Thus, it is said that when using both viewpoints to decide who is real and who is false, the false ones will not be accepted!

How should disciples who have recently taken up Buddhism learn tantra? They should first learn the Tripitaka and at the same time practice the preliminary practices. After they have satisfactorily mastered exoteric and esoteric Dharma, as well as the preliminary practices, they can then enter deeply into the Inner-Tantric Initiations. Inner-Tantric Initiations are divided into five major divisions. Each division is associated with supernormal states, which are manifestations of the Dharma. If you want to understand this in detail, you can read the book *Entering the Door of the Dharma*. I will not give a detailed explanation of this here.

Those who cultivate themselves and learn Buddhism cannot violate the precepts. If one violates major precepts, one will descend into hell. If one violates minor precepts, one will receive negative karmic retribution. One must also specially bear in mind that there are many charlatans in society who falsely claim to be Rinpoches. They have learned the Buddha Dharma for less than a few years. They do not have the slightest Dharma power or true realization. They have not even mastered the teachings contained in the sutras. They have not received the Acarya Initiation. Nevertheless, they claim to be Masters and fraudulently accept disciples. Since these false masters speak false Buddha Dharma, they have definitely entered into a diabolical state. They will die an early death and ultimately descend into the Vajra hell!

What type of practitioner has the qualifications to be a Master and save living beings? One who wants to be a Master and save living beings must himself already understand the Dharma teachings of the Tathagatas and must possess the depth of realization of an accomplished Holy One. At the very least, he must have received the Acarya Initiation. Only one who has enlightened himself can enlighten others.

What awaits one who has not yet realized the state of enlightenment, yet who falsely claims to be a Master so as to save living beings, is a death that will surely come as quickly as sudden thunder to carry him away in iron chains. The Holy Spirits who uphold the Dharma will carry out indescribably brutal punishment on him and will carry him away to undergo the hard labor he should undergo! Those who violate the precept against falsely claiming to be a Master and the precept against teaching false Dharma will be forcibly taken to the boiling oil cauldrons and the mountains of swords in the hell realm. Anyone who teaches false Dharma and who destroys people's foundation for realizing their own original nature and enlightenment is committing an offense that will definitely result in descending into the hell of uninterrupted suffering.

Why do so many cultivators not receive any beneficial effects from their practice? It is because they superficially cultivate themselves but in reality perform deeds that go against cultivation. They often do not even know that this is the case. Simply put, their three karmas of body, speech, and mind do not correspond with the rules of the Buddha Dharma. To use an analogy, they are told to eat something sweet, like candy. However, they do not listen. They feel that they must eat something bitter, like an animal's gallbladder. They are told to open their eyes while they walk. Nevertheless, they close their eyes while they walk. By walking in the opposite direction, one will naturally not make one's way to the correct path of liberation. By walking in the opposite direction, one will certainly walk toward the opposite door – the door that leads to the cycle of reincarnation.

With respect to how fellow disciples should treat each other, the most important things that must be avoided are maligning others, gossiping about others behind their backs, and making a fuss over things. This is not the moral behavior of a cultivator. Rather, it is the lowly behavior of an ordinary person.

There is a great obstacle on the path of cultivation. This obstacle arises as a result of criticizing or gossiping about the Master (this refers to a Master who has mastered the Inner-Tantric Initiations), the Master's wife, or their family members behind their backs. People who secretly malign a Master who holds the correct Dharma of the Tathagata will, in general, have their good fortune, wisdom, and life span come to a premature end. After they die, they will enter one of the evil realms, such as hell, where they will experience suffering! People who criticize or gossip about the Master's wife behind her back will certainly undergo immense suffering at the moment of death, after which they will enter the realm of the hungry ghosts or the animal realm! If people who commit such offenses do not immediately give rise to great repentance, turn over a new leaf, and cultivate themselves in accordance with the Dharma, then death will certainly come to take them away with chains around their necks. They will not be able to escape the sufferings of the cycle of reincarnation.

There is something that cultivators should bear in mind and be especially careful about. The Master is the basis for one to become accomplished. He is the person who is most reliable. Therefore, no large or small matter should be concealed from the Master. If one is considering whether a certain matter should or should not be reported to the Master, then one should immediately report this matter to the Master. This would be acting in accordance with the Dharma of the three karmas. Anyone who intends to conceal even a very trivial matter by not reporting it to the Master will have no hope of becoming accomplished and attaining liberation in this lifetime.

There are certain disciples who become very frightened as soon as they realize that they have committed many offenses. They then enter into an extreme point of view. They think that since they are offenders anyway, they might as well betray the teachings of the Master and enter into common, vulgar ways. Those ignorant people who adopt such behavior will undoubtedly descend into the hell of uninterrupted suffering without any possibility of being raised to higher realms. If one truly repents after committing an offense, with the empowerment of the Master, one will then naturally be able to practice correctly and attain liberation.

Every disciple who has received initiation has the potential to quickly obtain supernormal Dharma powers through practice. He has the potential to easily assume an infinite variety of forms. With respect to good fortune, he has the potential to quickly amass great wealth, no matter what his business may be. However, if he violates the precept of lying to his Master of great virtue whom he follows, even if it is a minor lie, then he will not be able to obtain any supernormal powers or good fortune. This is a Dharma rule contained in the Samaya Precepts. If he immediately repents after violating this precept and resolves never to violate it again, then his offense can be forgiven. Having corrected his behavior, he can then naturally receive benefits from practicing.

An ordinary person will be unable to deliver the dead to higher realms no matter what mantra he recites.[67] Those who have the state of realization of an Accomplished One are able to successfully practice the Dharma to raise the consciousness of the dead to higher realms. Think about it. If you cannot even save yourself, how can you save others? When those who do not have the state of realization of an Accomplished One practice the Dharma to transfer the consciousness of the dead to higher realms, it can only be said that they increase the merit of the dead by reciting the transference-of-consciousness mantra! If one practices erroneous and evil Dharma in attempting to raise the consciousness of the dead to higher realms, then one will definitely become an animal or hungry ghost after death. Such a one will undergo great suffering without any possibility of being raised to higher realms.

There is only one way to increase one's good fortune and wisdom and end the cycle of birth and death. That way is propagating the correct Dharma of the Tathagata, creating various conditions that make it easy for others to often hear the correct Dharma, and engaging in true and sincere cultivation!

How can one perfect one's merit? The most important thing for perfecting one's merit is selecting a Master. In selecting a Master, one should not simply consider his ostensible position. Even if he is called a Dharma King or Great Rinpoche, one must still look into his true skills. Actually, both real and false Rinpoches have spiritual lineages. Thus, one's main focus should not be on his particular lineage. The most important things to consider are whether he has mastered both exoteric and esoteric Dharma, whether he is thoroughly proficient in the Five Sciences, and whether he has the Dharma power to perform Inner-Tantric Initiations. It would be best if he met all of these tests! To put it more directly, one must determine whether he is a Holy One with true Dharma power. After one has properly selected a Master, one has a beacon that lights up one's path. One's merit will naturally increase.

Ordinary Rinpoches are not capable of transmitting the supreme, great Dharma. Only real Great Dharma Kings have the qualifications to transmit such Dharma and perform for others true nectar initiations. With respect to the matter of how to distinguish a true Dharma King, there is a book within Tibetan Buddhism called *Know the True Doctrines*. It explains this matter very clearly.

In short, cultivators should be careful in selecting a Master. If one wants to learn the true tantra, then one must understand what it means to have fully mastered both exoteric and esoteric Dharma, what it means to be thoroughly proficient in the Five Sciences, what the specific supernormal states are that must be exhibited during Inner-Tantric Initiations, etc. One must consider the person's true skills. One should not accept someone just because of his empty talk concerning his spiritual lineage. This is because a spiritual lineage can be fabricated. Furthermore, one's spiritual lineage cannot represent one's state of realization, Dharma powers, or qualifications to be a Master. Therefore, we often see masters who have a real spiritual lineage yet who have not attained the corresponding level of accomplishment. Some of these masters even die a premature death.

This shows that the Buddha Dharma is the Buddha Dharma. Being accomplished requires having true Dharma powers. One's knowledge of theories and one's spiritual lineage do not indicate whether one is accomplished. Being accomplished requires realization of the truth. Therefore, a person's spiritual lineage can be used for reference only, since it is a source for receiving empowerment. The true Buddha Dharma state of realization of the Master is what should be relied upon to attain liberation.

Chapter Nine

THE MIST OF THE MORNING DEW

EARLY MORNING DEW IS SOMETHING THAT is sweet and pure. How rare is such a thing! Yet, even sparkling and crystal clear dew is not fully beautiful, just like worldly affairs do not turn out as exactly as one wishes. For example, perhaps there is a drop of dew that has been contaminated by an impure, dirty branch. Yet, this drop of dew does not know from what place the contamination arose. Thus, out of ignorance, it became contaminated and can no longer manifest its purity and translucence. It has become sullied and has lost its beauty. This is due to the contaminated branch.

Every sentence of those who truly learn Buddhism will relate to cultivation, and every word they speak will relate to walking the path to liberation. I just now mentioned the example of the drop of dew because practitioners are also like this!

There are people who have just begun to learn Buddhism. Many of them have followed the Master and practiced for a brief period of time, perhaps only three or five months. Quite often, they do not experience any beneficial effects from their practice. When they sit down and meditate, there are no supernormal states. A good deal of their worldly affairs do not turn out as they wish. Perhaps they lose one or more family members. Perhaps their financial situation becomes more and more difficult. Perhaps their business does not go smoothly, their stock investments go down drastically, or their real estate investments fail. It becomes extremely difficult for them to maintain a livelihood. They often suffer from open or latent diseases and ailments. Perhaps in their dealings with others they often engage in quarrels and cannot maintain good relations with people.

In short, their wishes are not fulfilled, and it seems as if troubling matters arrive in quick succession. Every cultivator has extremely high aspirations, yet the results are often barely satisfactory. Thus, they become tired from rushing around. Their minds become fatigued. They are not as proud or satisfied as they were at the beginning.

As a result, many cultivators give rise to doubts about the Dharma and the Master. They want to give up and return to the worldly path, which leads to further reincarnation. They engage in ephemeral worldly affairs. They are tossed about by their own karma, like a small boat on the ocean. They allow their negative ways to go unchecked. The circumstances of this type of cultivator are like the circumstances of the drop of morning dew in the mist, which I just mentioned. I sigh over them with pity!

Actually, this type of disciple is committing an extremely grave mistake! They have just begun to follow Buddhism. It can be said that they do not know anything. They know nothing about discipline, procedures, and rules relating to the Dharma and about the three karmas of body, speech, and mind! If you ask them what the Buddha Dharma is, why one should learn the Buddha Dharma, what the true meaning of learning Buddhism is, what kind of effect ending the cycle of birth and death has on cultivators, why cultivators must end the cycle of birth and death for the sake of all living beings, what the three karmas are, how one can make one's state of realization perfectly correspond with the Dharma, etc., they will not know how to respond!

These things can only be gradually understood during the process of following and learning from the Master. Understanding these things cannot take place in one day. One cannot completely understand the principles of the Dharma in a brief period of time.

They are even more unable to comprehend the real meaning of extremely profound Buddha Dharma principles, such as the three prajnas,[68] the holiness of bodhicitta, the way of a Bodhisattva, transforming the four limitless states of mind into the state of enlightenment, the significance of Hinayana Buddhism, the six paramitas, the law of cause and effect, karma, etc. Furthermore, even if they understand the essential meaning of such Dharma, they still do not know how to put such meaning into practice, how to carry out such meaning in a concrete fashion.

To give further examples, those people who have just begun to learn Buddhism do not understand the main practices and the preliminary practices related to cultivation, what is meant by practice without mistakes, what is meant by practice with mistakes, what types of practice must be avoided, etc.

I am not saying that their innate faculties are dull or that they are of shallow intelligence. Because of underlying causes and conditions that resulted in their having taken up Buddhism for only a short period of time, they do not understand the meaning of a great deal of Dharma and how to undertake various practices. They should not be blamed too much for this. They cannot be criticized for the shortcoming of not knowing the Dharma.

However, there are certain offenses for which they cannot shirk responsibility. Since these practitioners do not understand the essence of the Dharma, they are far from entering the true practice of the Dharma. They are people who merely close their eyes and meditate, recite mantras, and visualize. They therefore do not experience any beneficial effects from their practice. They commit the offense of giving rise to doubt. Perhaps they doubt the truth of the Dharma. Perhaps they doubt the authenticity of the Master. Perhaps they doubt the usefulness of learning Buddhism.

This type of doubting the Dharma causes these practitioners to be even more unable to experience beneficial effects from their practice. Additionally, they will receive karmic retribution. Furthermore, it will not be possible for them to attain great liberation!

These practitioners have just begun to learn the Buddha Dharma. They have not yet succeeded in learning the Dharma, yet they are so eager to see the fruits of accomplishment. Therefore, they become annoyed and impatient. They have not engaged in true cultivation, yet they yearn for the fruits of true cultivation. Thus, they neglect true cultivation. They want to attain the highest level in one step. They want to immediately have the great powers of Kuan Yin Bodhisattva. They want to become accomplished, feel at ease, and not experience any hindrances. They want all of their negative karma to completely disappear. They want to receive great wealth and blessings, have great supernormal powers, and attain complete wisdom. They want to be in full control of all of their worldly and spiritual affairs. They want to be able to assume an infinite variety of forms simply by shaking their body. They want to be able to go through walls without any hindrance. They want to be able to suddenly appear in another location and suddenly disappear without leaving any trace whatsoever. This is violating the great taboo against being too eager for quick success!

I tell all of you here that I myself do not yet have such great skills! On the third day of March of this year, my elderly attendant's body disappeared and turned into light. In this form, she arrived at the Buddhist altar area of

Great Dharma King Yangwo Yisinubu to deliver a letter of authorization to my dear holy sister. The dozen or so people who were there saw the letter wrapped in light floating down to the ground. They did not see what my attendant looked like. They were moved to tears. The Great Dharma King took advantage of this opportunity to conduct a very unusual type of teaching session for the benefit of future generations of living beings.

However, these dozen or so disciples have just begun to learn Buddhism. What do they know? They should transform their crying into cultivation. In so doing, there will be a day when no matter what light this elderly attendant transforms herself into when appearing before them, she will be unable to escape their spiritual eyes, which catch everything. To these disciples, I say strive forward together so that you may, as soon as possible, catch up with this elderly attendant, who is your fellow disciple! You are practitioners who have very deep roots of kindness. It is because of this that you were able to become disciples of the greatest Dharma King of the present day and that you were able to witness the manifestation of several different types of supernormal states in just a few days' time. Those disciples who did not have the opportunity to see such things do not have such good fortune at this present time. Of course, if they maintain steadfast sincerity, they will have such good fortune in the future and will enjoy even greater blessings.

I was just explaining how the ordinary Buddhist disciple who has just begun to learn Buddhism is unable to experience any beneficial effects from his brief practice and, therefore, starts to adopt worldly viewpoints. This is a common mistake committed by cultivators! Because after a brief period of time they do not see any fruits of accomplishment, they give rise to doubts about the Master and the Dharma. A great many of them then violate the principal precepts!

Accomplishment from cultivation is easier said than done! Sakyamuni Buddha was able to attain enlightenment under the bodhi tree and realize the supreme state of Buddhahood due to wonderful causes and conditions planted over many lives and eons during which he diligently cultivated himself. Only then did he attain such a state of realization and enlightenment.

I am sure you have heard the Dharma saying, "My Master was able to see Dipamkara Buddha. It took many eons for my Master to become a saint who perfected the practice of enduring insults." Of course, this is referring to what Sakyamuni Buddha went through before realizing the supreme position of a Buddha.

Ordinary people who want to become accomplished must exert even more energy in practicing the Buddha Dharma. One must go through the sequence of hearing Dharma principles, understanding Dharma principles, gradually acting in accordance with these principles, gradually walking the correct path, and so on. It is a process in which one advances step by step. Accomplishment is not something that can be attained in one day. If one cannot face this, then one's practice will surely go awry.

Practitioners who have just begun to learn Buddhism are unable to understand in detail the vast amount of Dharma principles contained within Buddhism. It is all the more impossible for them to practice in accordance with such Dharma principles. Therefore, they do not experience beneficial effects from their practice. Not seeing any useful states resulting from their practice, these practitioners not only do not examine their practice to see whether it conforms to the rules and procedures, on the contrary, they give rise to confused and foolish thoughts. They give rise to different types of conjecture and speculation concerning the Master: "Perhaps the Master in whom I took refuge lacks true spiritual skills. Perhaps he does not possess the correct Dharma. Perhaps the Master does truly possess the Buddha Dharma and is heir to a true spiritual legacy, yet he does not teach us true Buddha Dharma. He only casually teaches us some things that are useless." (Of course, one must clearly determine beforehand whether the Master is qualified in the Dharma.)

They engage in such doubt over the Dharma and the Master. Their thoughts are changeable and unsteady. The correct Dharma is available to them, yet they do not learn it. A beneficent Master teaches them, yet they do not practice. They engage in conjecture and doubt all day long and thereby commit many offenses. They will descend into one of the three lower realms of existence.

In addition, they do not understand right mindfulness. They do not understand Dharma principles. They are undisciplined in their practice. They have no understanding of the principle of cause and effect. Thus, they frequently engage in wrong conduct. The planting of such negative causes will naturally bring about continual negative consequences.

Furthermore, they are unable to purify their negative karma accumulated over many lives. They add to this negative karma by the above described conduct, which makes matters even worse. This prevents them from experiencing good fortune. On the contrary, they frequently suffer karmic retribution and misfortune!

There are those who do not understand the principle of cause and effect. They say that learning Buddhism and cultivating oneself is of no use whatsoever. They say that learning Buddhism and cultivating oneself will instead bring about karmic retribution. They tell practitioners that it seems as if their circumstances are now even worse than when they were not cultivating themselves. Giving rise to such absurd thoughts is tantamount to committing many offenses against the Buddha Dharma and the Master, yet they are unable to understand even this! They are truly pitiable people.

The Buddha Dharma is nothing more than cause and effect! Those who do not clearly believe in the principle of cause and effect, who do not act in accordance with the correct Dharma, will definitely be unable to attain great accomplishment and experience great beneficial effects from their practice. Those who have just begun to learn Buddhism do not even understand these principles. How, then, could they act in accordance with the meaning of the correct Dharma? They do not understand or act in accordance with the correct Dharma. They do not cultivate themselves. They contravene the Dharma. It is no wonder they do not experience any beneficial effects from their practice. This is a matter of cause and effect!

Furthermore, how could their negative karmic obstructions that have formed over many past lives be purified in just one day? Those who engage in such fanciful thinking are ignorant people who do not understand the law of cause and effect! Even the Buddhas and Bodhisattvas do not ignore the law of cause and effect and do not deny karmic retribution. They, too, must reap the fruits of the causes they plant. How could those practitioners who have just begun to learn Buddhism repudiate the karmic consequences of their deeds performed over many past lives?

Knowing this, these practitioners should give rise to clear understanding. They should immediately understand that they have just begun to practice the Buddha Dharma and that nobody can avoid the law of cause and effect and karmic retribution. The frequent manifestation of negative karmic retribution at this point in time in their lives is because the conditions for such retribution have matured. Karmic retribution should take place at this point in time. The manifestation of such negative consequences is not due to their learning Buddhism and cultivating themselves!

There are those who suffer karmic retribution during the period when they have just begun to learn Buddhism and cultivate themselves. They place the responsibility for these negative consequences upon the Master. They attribute these consequences to the Buddha Dharma that they practice as not being authentic and to the Master as not being good. This truly is extremely ignorant!

Have these practitioners never heard of the ancient saying, "In order to untie the bell on the tiger, the person who tied it is required"?[69] If practitioners understood this saying and carefully investigated their own faults, they would inevitably come to a sudden awakening. They would then devoutly take refuge in the Buddha Dharma. They would follow the Master and act cautiously. Their three karmas would correspond with the teachings of the Master. In such case, their becoming accomplished would, of course, not be difficult!

When they become accomplished, they will be like the morning dew – sparkling and crystal-clear. How could they then commit mistakes and become sullied? If you practitioners do not wake up now, when will you stop your wrong conduct?

☞ *Chapter Ten* ☜

How One Should Forever Love One's Dearest Family Members

No matter whether the cultivator is a layperson or one who has gone forth from the household life to become a monk or nun, it is not necessarily the case that their original motivation to cultivate themselves and learn Buddhism arose from having deeply understood the suffering related to worldly things and the cycle of reincarnation. Many practitioners hide themselves in Buddhism in order to escape from various worldly entanglements and disturbances. There are also those who take up Buddhism because they have become disillusioned with the world, disheartened, or are unable to recover from a setback. Later, they slowly understand through their cultivation that the Buddha Dharma is a treasure that is hard to come by in even millions of eons. Hence, they give rise to a mindset that is intent on leaving the cycle of reincarnation.

There are those who learn the Buddha Dharma in order to seek wealth, blessings, and a peaceful life. There are those who have no choice but to seek a livelihood through cultivation because their living conditions are so grim or because of other causes and conditions. There are those who want to escape from the world due to family discord. Additionally, some practitioners believe in the Buddha Dharma since they come from families who have been Buddhists for generations, and they have been influenced by what they constantly see and hear. To a certain extent, they have thus become learners of Buddhism.

Of course, there indeed are some practitioners who have given rise to awareness. They have given rise to a mind that is disenchanted with worldly things. They strive for accomplishment and ending of the cycle of birth and death. There are also those Holy Ones who have voluntarily come to this world again. Such Holy Ones do not necessarily learn Buddhism soon after they come to this human realm. However, as soon as their karmic destiny matures, they will immediately follow a Great Virtuous One, and their three karmas will correspond with the teachings of this Great Virtuous One.

In short, although these various types of cultivators do not use the same method of cultivation, nevertheless, they still have one point in common: They are all cultivating themselves and learning Buddhism!

Let us put aside the question of whether they are engaged in true cultivation or pursue Buddhism in a half-true and half-false manner. Let us also put aside the question of whether they learn the Buddha Dharma in a scientific manner or a superstitious manner. (The word *superstitious* here refers to those people who do not understand what the true Buddha Dharma is. They worship and revere worldly fortune tellers who pretend to communicate with ghosts and spirits and who fabricate wild stories. They worship and revere witches and spirit mediums. They consider spirits to be holy figures in the Buddha Dharma. They consider sorcery to be the Buddha Dharma. They do not truly understand the principle of cause and effect. Their practice is not guided by a clear belief in cause and effect. Thus, they are called superstitious.) These different types of cultivators who are learning Buddhism have a certain predestined connection with the Buddha Dharma. Therefore, although their ways of cultivation are all different, this does not prevent them from being called Buddhists.

Other than those Holy Ones who have come to this world voluntarily, all Buddhists – no matter what the reason was for their having taken up the Buddha Dharma and no matter what method they use to cultivate themselves – cannot cut off the connections, ties, links, and affection they have with their family members in this life. This causes them to be deeply perplexed.

On the one hand, they deeply understand that one must rid oneself of all disturbances caused by the Eight Winds, that one must refrain from missing or worrying about one's family members, and that one must wholeheartedly learn the Buddha Dharma to reach enlightenment. They deeply understand that after reaching enlightenment, they can then help their family members to learn the Dharma, thus enabling their family members to end the cycle of birth and death and leave the six realms of reincarnation. Only this is benefiting one's family members in the true sense.

Being sentimentally attached to one's family members will truly become a hindrance in one's cultivation. Being constantly worried about one's family members prevents cultivators from thoroughly understanding that human beings do not have any real or permanent self. Since they do not thoroughly understand that the six great elements are empty, and since they cannot eliminate their attachment to the concept of self, they cannot end the cycle of birth and death.

They truly find it difficult to cut off their worldly affection for their family members. Therefore, they are unable to help their family members to become accomplished in the Buddha Dharma. In order to satisfy the requests of their family members, they allow their emotions to sway their judgment. In satisfying the various desires of their family members, they increase the negative habitual tendency of their family members toward greed. They increase self-based seeking, self-based grasping, self-based desires, self-based thoughts, self-based feelings of love and hate, etc., in which their family members engage.

As a result, when the heavy karmic retribution resulting from these acts comes to fruition, since they helped their family members in the wrong way, not only will they have caused their family members to descend into lower realms, they themselves will no longer have the opportunity to become accomplished in the Dharma. In the end, they will be unable to liberate their family members, as well as themselves.

There are many cultivators who very much understand this principle. Nevertheless, they often do not handle such matters very appropriately. As a result, they cultivate themselves their whole lives, yet accomplishment for them remains distant and indistinct. Of course, ending the cycle of birth and death is out of the question.

How to correctly treat one's family members in this life is a matter that causes cultivators great headaches. It is a matter that most cultivators cannot resolve very well. This may appear to be a trite subject; however, for the vast majority of cultivators, it is not within the category of common, easy to solve Buddha Dharma obstructions.

Milarepa was willing to give up his life for the Dharma. He treated his family members based upon correct understanding of the supreme Buddha Dharma. He treated this matter as a practitioner who truly wanted to end the cycle of birth and death and who thoroughly understood that the four great elements are all empty would treat this matter.[70] It is difficult to find even one practitioner out of ten million who is like Milarepa, including even some present day practitioners who have cultivated themselves quite well.

How to treat one's own family members has become a matter for great regret within Buddhism. For thousands and thousands of Buddhist disciples, it is also a very worrisome matter that is a great obstacle on their path toward accomplishment. How to appropriately handle this matter has already become a problem that Buddhist disciples must immediately face.

Master Milarepa was a man of great accomplishment within Tibetan Buddhism. His correct understanding should be deeply revered by all of the millions of Buddhists. Complying with the instructions given to him by Vajrayogini, Master Milarepa traveled from the Himalayan mountains to the interior of Tibet in order to save living beings. On the way, he met a husband and wife who were unable to conceive a male offspring. This couple heard that Master Milarepa was a Great Accomplished One who had learned tantra. They thus showed him great respect and had great confidence in him.

They invited the Venerable One, Master Milarepa, to their home. They asked the Venerable One not to continue his life of wandering in all directions, a life in which the basic necessities could not even be guaranteed. They asked him to stay with them and be their son. They said that they would provide him with a vast amount of wealth for his use and enjoyment. They said that they would find him a beautiful, virtuous, wise, warm, and tender woman to marry. He and this wife would then have a son or daughter and form a family. This family would then live in the most opulent and beautiful house, which would be tall and large. They would have much fertile land, which they could never use up. This couple hoped that Master Milarepa would, together with his future close family members, share in the joys of family life. They hoped that he would lead a harmonious, stable, and happy life.

Hearing the promises of this extremely kind couple, Master Milarepa remained totally unmoved. He told them that he could not renounce all of those things soon enough, let alone embrace them. The Venerable One imparted his teachings to them by way of songs. Master Milarepa taught them the truly disadvantageous effects one's worldly family members have on one's cultivation and worldly life. He taught them the suffering involved with worldly things, how worldly things are impermanent, and how they are like dreamy illusions and empty bubbles. He taught them how all conditioned phenomena are empty and how such phenomena are ultimately subject to the law of cause and effect.

After hearing these teachings, this husband and wife each gave rise to a resolute mind. They became disenchanted with impermanent things and worldly life. They understood that all of the different kinds of worldly emotions and love must ultimately vanish into emptiness, like smoke or clouds that pass before one's eyes. They therefore gave up all of their worldly possessions and wealth. They cut off their attachment to the concept of self and diligently cultivated themselves. In the end, they realized the state of enlightenment.

The average practitioner cannot attain the state of realization that Master Milarepa attained. Of course, practitioners who are laypersons, as opposed to those who go forth from the home to become monks and nuns, do not really need to give up their family members in order to seek enlightenment and learn the Dharma, as Master Milarepa did. Moreover, cultivation nowadays does not have the same type of demanding requirements as that which existed in the past. Practitioners who live at home and who get along with their family members harmoniously can just the same cultivate themselves. The problem is that in their practice and quest for enlightenment, practitioners who live at home will have to withstand even more trials and tests. Only after successfully withstanding such trials and tests will they be able to save themselves and their family members.

It would be quite lamentable if cultivators could not properly handle their relationships with their family members, if they clung tightly to their family members in this life and were unwilling to let go of them. This would result in their family members actually becoming stumbling blocks on their path of cultivation, demonic hindrances on their path to learn the Buddha Dharma, or obstacles on their road to accomplishment. This situation requires cultivators to make a very stern decision. In this decision, one should take the path of enlightenment to be most important. After one has liberated oneself, one can then make arrangements for one's family members!

Not just a small number of practitioners – rather, a great deal of practitioners – handle conflicts between the Buddha Dharma and their family members with extreme lack of seriousness. Because of their ties with their family members, these practitioners often ignore the principles of the Buddha Dharma, which results in their committing offenses.

For example, due to certain underlying causes and conditions, some cultivators have taken a vow related to a certain Buddhist matter. They are prohibited from telling others – including even their own closest family members in this life – the content of such vow or what Buddhist matter they performed. Otherwise, they will suffer karmic retribution or even descend into the hell of uninterrupted suffering.

Some people are able to stick to this holy and solemn Buddha Dharma vow. Their compliance with the Buddha Dharma brings about great blessings and benefits for them. However, a number of practitioners are influenced by family members who use all kinds of tactics, both gentle and severe. Perhaps such family members resort to threats. For example, there are husbands and wives who tell their spouse that if one spouse is not candid and frank with the other, then it is best that they divorce. Some family members will say, "We are relatives. How could there be anything that we cannot straightforwardly and openly discuss?"

Thinking that there is no alternative but to act against their own better judgment, and in order to please and save the face of their family members, these practitioners discontinue regarding the Buddha Dharma and the precepts as paramount. With a strange expression on their faces, these practitioners then secretly whisper words into the ears of their family members and tell them the entire story. They relate certain Buddhist matters and Buddha Dharma arrangements that they should not disclose. They perform certain acts that are contrary to the principles of the Dharma and contrary to their connection with Buddhism.

Of course, the result of such action is that they please their family members. On the surface, it seems that they have maintained good feelings among family members (which feelings are in fact as thin as paper). However, they have acted against the Buddha Dharma and the precepts. They have acted against their own connection with Buddhism. Their violation of a great precept has life and death consequences!

They will undoubtedly pay a heavy price for such ignorant conduct. They will descend into the hell of uninterrupted suffering or will suffer other severe consequences. Not only will they themselves taste the bitterness of karmic retribution, their so-called worldly family members who instigated them to violate a precept will likewise suffer severe karmic retribution. These cultivators who have no regard for Buddha Dharma precepts, who pay no heed to underlying circumstances relating to the Buddha Dharma, originally thought that they could maintain their relationship with their so-called family members. Little did they know that these wonderful acts of "love" for their family members harmed themselves and others. In the end, no benefit will come of such acts.

All of this comes about because there are people who learn the Buddha Dharma but who do not regard the Dharma as being most important. They regard the Dharma lightly and emphasize other people's wishes. When there is a conflict between the Buddha Dharma and the wishes of their family members, they act according to the wishes of these other people and not according to the Dharma. In the end, they receive karmic retribution! The underlying conditions of the Buddha Dharma require that the cultivator must instead **act according to the Dharma and not the wishes of others!**

If a cultivator cannot carry out this basic Buddha Dharma principle of acting according to the Dharma rather than the wishes of others, or if a cultivator's actions are diametrically opposed to this principle, then his regrets will not just be for one lifetime. The negative karmic retribution sometimes will continue for a few lives or even a few dozen lives without being totally expiated. Sometimes negative karma will accumulate to the extent that the karmic retribution it produces becomes inexhaustible. In the future, wherever he goes, this negative karma follows, like a rolling snowball. In such case, the suffering will be inexhaustible.

Acting according to the Dharma rather than the wishes of others is a principle that all Buddhist disciples must follow. If one does not select the Dharma as being most important, but rather considers the hindering influences of one's worldly family members as being even more important than the Dharma laid down by the Buddhas, then one is engaging in wrongdoing that violates the precepts.

To give another example, some cultivators clearly see that one or more family members, or one or more fellow disciples with whom they together practice the Buddha Dharma, engage in conduct that is not in accordance with the Dharma and the precepts. Such conduct violates the demands of the Master. Yet, these cultivators fear that by reporting this to the Master, they would cause the violators to be reproached and punished for having violated the precepts. They fear that if these people one day find out who reported them to the Master, these people would retaliate against and hate them. They fear that this would break the bond between them and the violators. They fear that there would no longer be peace and harmony between them and the family members they report. Therefore, they conceal such erroneous conduct and do not report it to the Master. In so doing, they practice deception on behalf of others (such as family members). In attempting to please themselves and others, they leave things to chance.

Nevertheless, the exact opposite of what they want actually occurs. In the end, these cultivators not only do not truly help their own family members, instead, they destroy themselves together with their family members. Not only have they violated the precepts and rules of the Buddha Dharma, they have also engaged in false speech and deception toward the Master. Their three karmas do not correspond with the teachings of the Master. This type of practice will certainly prevent them from attaining the fruit of accomplishment. More importantly, they will suffer various types of karmic retribution.

Actually, these people are rather foolish. Why? They fear that the Master will take their family members to task. Thus, they act in a way that is diametrically opposed to the meaning of the Buddha Dharma and Buddhist principles. They do not understand that although the Master's taking their family members to task may involve reproach or other forms of education, all of these methods are Bodhisattva actions performed in order to cause such family members to attain enlightenment and realize the fruits of the practice. Such actions are kind actions.

These actions of the Master are performed in order to cause such family members to truly attain accomplishment and from that point onward move in the direction of leaving the six realms of reincarnation. Any living being who wants to attain true accomplishment must totally eliminate his poisonous qualities so that he is not tainted in the least. Not even the slightest sediment of poison can remain within him. Having any sediment of poison within him will prevent him from ending the cycle of birth and death.

Therefore, the Master uses all kinds of methods to teach living beings, including hitting, scolding, reproaching, having them to do work, and having them perform arduous tasks. In some cases, this even causes disciples to perspire, bleed, or become exhausted. Yet, there is only one goal underlying the use of these various methods: to teach disciples according to the underlying circumstances of each disciple, thereby causing them to attain accomplishment.

Thus, when Master Milarepa was following Master Marpa in learning the Buddha Dharma, Master Marpa made him build nine houses so that he would be deeply and genuinely repentant and would truly resolve to leave the cycle of reincarnation. Additionally, Master Marpa used this method to expiate Master Milarepa's prior wrongdoings. Master Milarepa carried stones from the foot of the mountains to the top of the mountains. He built one house and then was told to dismantle it. After he dismantled it, he was told to build another house. Marpa hit him and scolded him. He used his fists to hit Milarepa and his feet to kick him.

This continued day after day, year after year. This conduct on the part of Marpa was incomprehensible to others, including his wife, Buddha Mother Dagmema, who was infuriated over this. She felt that Master Marpa purposely made it difficult for Master Milarepa and that he purposely tormented Master Milarepa. Other disciples all learned the Dharma without a hitch. They received mantras and initiations. Actually, this is a case of first stage Bodhisattvas not understanding matters relating to second stage Bodhisattvas and fifth stage Bodhisattvas not understanding the conduct of tenth stage Bodhisattvas!

On the surface, it appeared that Master Marpa was treating Milarepa in almost a cruel fashion. Yet, the great Master Marpa was secretly shedding tears, which sprang from the great compassion of an enlightened mind. Finally, when the conditions were truly mature, Milarepa not only learned the Dharma, he also discovered that Master Marpa transmitted to him the most mantras and the best mantras. In the end, Master Marpa enabled Milarepa to become a person within Vajrayana Buddhism who attained enlightenment by truly undergoing hardship and suffering. Milarepa's negative karma was expiated, and he became a most magnificent Great Accomplished One.

His merit, reputation, and accomplishment were as great as the resounding sound of the bell Master Marpa struck on the day he first met Milarepa. Throughout Buddhist history, Master Milarepa has been venerated by myriad cultivators. He will forever be revered by Buddhist cultivators. He is a magnificent forerunner for all cultivators to follow in their aspiration for the realization of enlightenment and true cultivation!

From beginningless time spanning over eons and eons, living beings have been living under delusion and have therefore been tainted by countless ingrained negative tendencies. This is analogous to having many poisonous sediments. These poisons are spread all over the bodies of living beings, preventing them from giving rise to enlightened understanding and preventing them from extricating themselves from the bondage of reincarnation.

The various methods of teaching used by the Buddha Dharma Master are like different sharp knives that are used to cut away, bit by bit, the poisonous sediments that exist in each cultivator. These different methods of teaching are very useful. It is similar to a traditional Chinese doctor prescribing the correct medicine for the particular disease after he has performed the four methods of diagnosis – looking, listening, questioning, and feeling the pulse.

Hence, the Master teaches disciples in accordance with their aptitudes. He does not teach the Dharma in a uniform manner applicable to all disciples. More important, unless these poisonous sediments are fully removed through the teachings of the Master, they will become more and more potent. Their poison will spread more and more. In the end, the cultivator will become like a lifeless vegetable and will not even have the opportunity to seek enlightenment.

The speech of the Master is tantamount to the gem of the Dharma. The body of the Master is tantamount to the gem of the sangha. The thoughts of the Master represent the gem of the Buddha. According to tantra, the Vajra Master is the total embodiment of the seven jewels.[71] Thus, how foolish these cultivators are! They do not understand that their family members should accept the various teaching techniques used by the Master. Instead, these cultivators try to avoid having their family members be taught by the Master. Yet, they still maintain that they are acting compassionately toward their family members. On the contrary, their acts actually harm themselves and their family members.

This type of "love" toward family members is based upon incorrect understanding. It is quite similar to parents who, due to lack of understanding, spoil their children. Is spoiling one's children considered as loving one's children? Perhaps it can be called love, but it is a type of perverted love. It is a type of incorrect love. Frankly speaking, such parents are damaging their own children. They are not considering the true good of their children.

Some people in the world have caused their children to be inclined toward degenerate ways as a result of spoiling their children. There are so many examples of this type of tragedy. However, there are more and more parents who are rejecting this narrow method of so-called "loving their children." Parents are more and more using correct methods to guide their children toward proper development. They are more and more using correct love to scold their children in order to protect them and cause them to grow in a healthy manner. This is a good thing!

Buddha Dharma principles are also like this. One must act according to the Dharma and not the wishes of others! No matter how close the family member may be – including even one's mother, father, son, or daughter – one must unhesitatingly engage in any action that is truly good for them, will lead to their accomplishment, and will aid in their leaving the cycle of reincarnation.

The teachings of the Master are like the teachings of the Buddhas. Such teachings only benefit living beings. They absolutely do not harm living beings. The love the Master has toward living beings is truly vast and selfless. This love is completely devoid of even the slightest bit of selfish thoughts. It is the holiest and purest love. It is impeccable love that flows from his Dharma nature. This love, which arises from an enlightened mind, is extensive. It is the most superlative love. It is a love based upon supreme rationality. It is incomparably wonderful.

No type of worldly love can even be mentioned in the same breath with the Master's love. Why do I say this? I will give a simple comparison. The greatest love in the world is that of parents toward their sons and daughters. Nevertheless, can the love of parents toward their sons and daughters cause their sons and daughters to end the cycle of birth and death and become free from reincarnation? How great is the power of parents to eliminate the various types of difficulty and pain that their sons and daughters experience in life?

The love of parents is a type of love that is powerless to render real assistance. When their sons and daughters in the course of life experience great pain, great blows, great pressure, and other forms of distress, the parents are unable to bear such distress in their stead. The parents also cannot totally prevent their sons and daughters from experiencing distress. At most, the parents can lose sleep over the distress of their sons and daughters. Their love is a type of love that is powerless to render real assistance.

More important, due to faults in their understanding and their different levels of imperfection, parents in the world either directly or indirectly lead their sons and daughters into experiencing suffering. Therefore, no worldly love can be mentioned in the same breath with the love of the Buddhas, Great Mahasattvas, and Great Bodhisattvas.

Thus, due to incorrect understanding, these cultivators regard the precepts and discipline of the Buddhas as rope that constrains them. They regard the teaching methods the Master applies, the Master's assistance, and the Master's guidance as that which causes them embarrassment, discomfort, and suffering. They overestimate their own so-called worldly love and the level of its rationality and completeness. They also overestimate how correct their own understanding is.

They think that their way of treating their family members is higher than that which is prescribed by the Buddha Dharma. They think that their acting according to the wishes of others and not the Buddha Dharma is reasonable and moral. This type of love towards family members is an extremely erroneous love. In order to temporarily avoid having their family members scolded by the Master, they lead themselves and the people they dearly love into degeneration. Furthermore, because of this, they and their family members will suffer pain and torment for a few dozen lives or even forever. They are so foolish!

It can be said that these people do not understand the Buddha Dharma at all. They cannot clearly distinguish right from wrong. They cannot differentiate the correct from the erroneous. They handle matters in an unthinking manner, as if their minds were wooden. We must wait for them to deeply enter the practice of the Buddha Dharma and attain understanding. We must wait for them to gradually attain realization.

There is another type of conduct that is also along the lines of acting according to the wishes of others and not the Buddha Dharma. This conduct is even more serious than the above described conduct and is extremely odious. That is, when their own family members have become demonic obstacles, when their own family members, without any restraint, proceed to do great damage to the Buddha Dharma and defame the Master and the Buddha Dharma, these cultivators do not urge them to stop and do not take heed of such actions. On the contrary, these cultivators purposefully conceal such actions from others. They cover up these evil, demonic actions. Additionally, there are even those who join in the evildoings of their family members and cooperate with these demonic obstacles. They collude with their family members who harm the Dharma, and together they perform deeds that harm the Dharma.

This is a typical type of acting according to the wishes of others and not the Buddha Dharma. Those who engage in such acts will undoubtedly descend into hell. The Samaya Precepts of Vajrayana Buddhism provide that one will definitely descend into the Vajra Hell realm if one drinks one cup of water together with a demon.

The wives, husbands, sons, daughters, or other relatives of certain cultivators are unable to thoroughly see the magnificence of the Buddha Dharma, since they do not understand the Buddha Dharma and since their karmic obstructions are so deep and heavy. It may be that although such family members deeply believe in the Buddha Dharma, they nevertheless do not have the slightest understanding of Buddha Dharma principles. They are unable to understand Buddha Dharma conditions that underlie certain matters. Thus, they are instigated by their own ignorance. They speak recklessly. They defame the Buddha Dharma. They slander the Vajra Master and verbally attack certain Great Accomplished Ones. Everywhere they go, they malign the Buddha Dharma and the Great Accomplished Ones. It does not matter whether these people do not believe in the Buddha Dharma or whether they consider themselves to be Buddhists – in short, they are all pitiful!

They have only a limited amount of social experience, going back perhaps a couple dozen years or a dozen years. Yet, they think that they are highly qualified individuals with a vast amount of experience. They limit themselves by thinking that what they already know is enough and is correct. Not only do they not seek the truth of the Buddha Dharma, they think that they are amazing, that they have seen a great deal, and that they have deep and extensive knowledge. They use limited and pitiful worldly knowledge to measure the Buddha Dharma, which is immeasurably broad, profound, noble, and mysterious. It can truly be said that these people are unaware of their own limitations and have an exaggerated opinion of their abilities and understanding!

Before the Buddha Dharma and the Great Accomplished Ones in the Buddha Dharma, these people are nothing more than a frog at the bottom of a well. The totality of what they know is merely a tiny piece of sky. Yet, they presumptuously compare themselves with the Great Accomplished Ones in the Buddha Dharma. They even think that they themselves are more awesome than these Great Accomplished Ones.

When they are moaning and screaming after they descend into hell or one of the other lower realms of existence, when they discover that these Great Accomplished Ones have control over their own life and death, and when these Great Accomplished Ones, together with some devout and enlightened beings whose three karmas correspond with the Buddha Dharma, come to save them, perhaps they will then realize the limitations of their own abilities and understanding. Perhaps they will then realize that they harbored foolish and exaggerated notions of their abilities and understanding, which cannot even be compared with the abilities and understanding of these Great Accomplished Ones.

Why are they so foolish? It is primarily because their educational level is too low! Generally, their level of education is between high school and college. It is not that I, Pamu, am belittling them. If you give them *The Prajna*

Treatise or *The Hetu-Vidya Treatise*, they will not understand its contents. Such low level of education is truly quite pitiful!

There are some people who, although they have read only a few books or even have not read any writings, nevertheless do not close themselves off from new knowledge by thinking that what they already know is enough and is correct. They are like a blank piece of paper when they read a new book. As soon as you teach them something, they will immediately grasp it. Their negative karma is quite light. Therefore, it can be said that it is not important whether one has had an education. What is important is being humble and knowing the limitations of one's abilities and understanding. There is a vast amount of sky that one cannot see from the bottom of a well. One will not be able to attain true happiness if one is confined within the boundaries of one's own so-called "knowledge"!

Either these people do not understand the Buddha Dharma and true Buddha Dharma practice or, although they understand, they nevertheless do not want to practice according to the Dharma, since their innate faculties are dull. They therefore spread rumors to confuse people. They sow discord. Out of ignorance and incorrect understanding, they fan the flames of trouble. They entice cultivators through desire for worldly things. They do damage to the great undertaking of spreading the Buddha Dharma. They destroy the roots of kindness of living beings. They prevent other people from sincerely believing in the Buddha Dharma and from practicing according to the Buddha Dharma.

Some of these people go further. They prevent their own wives from learning the Buddha Dharma by threatening them, tempting them with money or material gain, hitting them, scolding them, or insulting them. Some wives use the worldly tactic of first crying, then making a fuss, then threatening to commit suicide, as well as all kinds of other means, to prevent their husbands from engaging in cultivation. Some of these people entice their close friends with small worldly gains so that their friends will no longer sincerely pursue the Buddha Dharma, engage in cultivation, and seek enlightenment. Some of them use the method of completely ignoring their sons and daughters, coupled with beating them, in an attempt to prevent them from learning the correct Dharma.

All such types of conduct are demonic. Some people think that their family members who engage in such ways do so simply because they are muddle-headed and ignorant. They think that it would be overly serious to call such family members demons.

What are demons? Those humans and non-humans who damage the Buddha Dharma and the great undertaking of spreading the Buddha Dharma, who do not practice according to the correct Dharma, who obstruct the cultivation of living beings, or who obstruct living beings from seeking the Dharma, ending the cycle of birth and death, realizing enlightenment, and attaining the fruits and stages of the practice are all called demons. The practice of these humans and non-humans is called evil practice. Their views are evil views. The Dharma that they abide by is called evil Dharma. Their clamorous words show them to be in the camp of evil views. The conduct of these demons are diametrically opposed to the Buddha Dharma.

Therefore, their destination after death is different from the destination of those who are accomplished through cultivation of the correct Dharma. Those who are accomplished as a result of practicing according to the Buddha Dharma will be reborn in the Western Paradise or the Land of the Buddhas in the ten directions. However, demons will be reborn in one of the three lower realms. Most of them will receive karmic retribution by being reborn in the hell of uninterrupted suffering.

There is no absolute dividing line between demons and people who walk the correct path. Sometimes, with just one correct thought, a demon can become a person who practices the correct Dharma! Also, one mistaken thought can cause a person who is walking on the correct path to become a demonic obstacle!

When some people hear about demons, they become very frightened. However, in actuality, demonic obstacles are always by your side. Sometimes, the thoughts, words, and conduct of the cultivator himself totally reflect the thoughts, words, and conduct of a demon. Therefore, sometimes an upright cultivator will become a demon. On the other hand, one who is very bad and engages in erroneous ways can attain great understanding through a sudden change in his thoughts. He can thereby become a very good Buddhist disciple.

The key point in all of this is whether one practices according to the correct Dharma, whether one makes decisions about problems and handles matters according to the standards laid out in the Buddha Dharma.

Precisely because the understanding and views of a great many practitioners are flawed, precisely because they do not use the content of the

Buddha Dharma to evaluate problems, therefore, sometimes when the words and conduct of their family members have already become the words and conduct of demons and such family members have actually already become demons, they themselves are still totally unaware of this. These practitioners even help their family members in their evil ways. Together with their family members, they produce negative karma out of ignorance and damage the Buddha Dharma. They therefore bring endless trouble to themselves and their family members. Such matters occur often. To quote a Chinese worldly saying: "He who handles vermilion will be reddened, and he who touches ink will be blackened."[72]

For example, due to karmic effects brought about by causes planted over many previous lives, some cultivators learn the Buddha Dharma for a long period of time yet still experience great hardships. They are burdened with karmic hindrances. They wear a worried frown all day long. They do not understand why they still live a difficult life after having learned the Buddha Dharma for so long.

A family member who is not learning the Buddha Dharma, such as a husband, may say to one of these cultivators, "Why learn the Buddha Dharma? I do not learn the Buddha Dharma, yet every day my business is still so good. I can eat and drink whatever I want and have whatever fun I want to have. But look at you. You have learned the Dharma for so long yet have nothing to show for it. Instead, you wear a sad face. Nothing goes well for you. Forget it. What's the use in learning the Buddha Dharma. One should not believe in it. You and I should do business together. We should expand our business together. I guarantee that you will obtain more from this than from learning the Buddha Dharma...."

The belief of the cultivator who hears these words, which was originally firm, now begins to gradually waver and crumble. As a consequence, he or she follows this family member in pursuing worldly desires. Not seeing and not knowing, the world seems so beautiful to such people. From this point on, they completely forget about practicing the Buddha Dharma. They originally thought that the Master was incomparably magnificent. Now they feel that he is no different from an average person.

They then give rise to doubt about the Master. Everywhere they go, they spread rumors and malign the Master and the Buddha Dharma. Furthermore, they urge others not to learn the Buddha Dharma. They use their own experience as a model for others not to learn the Buddha Dharma. They serve as a visible, cheerful, and self-satisfied model to convince others not to learn the Buddha Dharma. Influenced by the evil views of this family member who became a demonic obstacle, these people not only do not think of extricating themselves from the six realms of reincarnation, they themselves have even become a demonic obstacle due to their ignorant conduct. In the end, they themselves, as well as this family member, will descend into the hell of uninterrupted suffering.

They were bewitched by the evil understanding, evil views, and evil conduct of a close family member who became a demonic obstacle. That is, they acted according to the wishes of others and not according to the Dharma. They caused themselves to degenerate into servants of demons. Examples of this kind among cultivators are truly quite numerous — too numerous to recount.

All of this is brought about because these cultivators lack correct understanding, because they do not solve problems according to the Buddha Dharma, because they do not judge right from wrong according to the principles of the Dharma, because they do not evaluate things of the world according to the correct Dharma, and because they do not regard all conditioned phenomena according to the Buddha Dharma truth of cause and effect and karmic retribution.

At the critical moment, they do not act according to the Buddha Dharma; instead, they act according to the wishes of another person. They believe the slanderous talk of a person who is a demonic obstacle. They believe the sermons of a demon. In the end, this causes those family members who are like demons to descend. At the same time, these cultivators themselves are also destroyed. Together, they are reborn in hell where they will experience suffering and torment! This is unfortunate for cultivators and for the Buddha Dharma. It is truly a disaster for living beings. It is something that is hard to explain in just a few words!

Thus, cultivators must act according to the Dharma and not the wishes of others. When handling any matter, one should ponder it, weigh it, and come to a conclusion about it based upon the meaning of the Buddha Dharma. Be sure not to allow your present limited knowledge to become an obstacle in learning new things. Be sure not to judge the broad and profound Buddha Dharma according to what you have learned from your experiences in worldly life. To do this would be extremely foolish. Using the worldly concept of who is a family member in weighing the feelings of family members is also not acceptable.

At this point, I would also like to state that one's family members in this life are merely one's family members in one life out of countless lives spanning over eons of time. If one only loves one's family members in this life, isn't one ignoring other living beings who have been one's family members throughout many previous lives? Isn't this type of conduct hypocritical, unethical, and odious? Can this be called love?

Some people will say, "I only care about my family members in this life. I do not have the ability to care about family members in other lives. Furthermore, I have no idea who such previous family members are. I do not even know what I did in my last life! Since I do not know anything about my prior existences, they cannot blame me!"

Although this is an excuse, these people truly cannot be blamed. Because of karmic obscurations, the causes of which were planted over many previous lives, they have already totally forgotten about their original nature. They do not even know what they themselves are. In such case, how could they possibly accept any demands placed upon them to be responsible for family members in previous lives? Nevertheless, sentient beings in the three spheres and the six realms of existence have all been one's family members in previous lives spanning over eons of time. This is an objective and irrefutable fact.

I will give an example. Suppose you are someone's son or daughter. An auto accident occurred that affected your brain. As a consequence, you suffer from amnesia. After the doctors and nurses save you through emergency treatment and you become conscious, you suddenly realize that everything around you is totally new. All prior events stored in your brain are expunged. Your entire memory is as blank as a piece of paper. You do not even remember who your father and mother are, what their names are, and what they look like.

Even if your father and mother stood before you and swore that you were their dearest family member, you would still harbor doubts in your mind. You would half believe and half doubt them. Perhaps you would have a lukewarm attitude toward them or be polite but somewhat aloof. Your entire state of consciousness would be completely governed by your then existing abilities to analyze and judge. Using this state of consciousness, you would determine whether they were, after all, your parents. Even if you, in fact, were born by them, and even if the two of them went through all kinds of toil to rear you into adulthood, you still would not remember any of this at all. You would know nothing at all about their situation.

Of course, you would not want to bear any responsibility for them. Although they are your parents, you would not be very willing to admit this. You would first want to conduct an investigation and gather evidence!

Worldly people are also like this! Because of negative karmic effects from causes planted over many previous lives and because of their being enveloped in ignorance, their original nature has been covered up. This has caused them to completely forget who they are. They do not even know that their present body is a result of karma.

From one life to another, they are driven by the currents of karma. They are led along by their karma. They do not know where they will be led. Because of good karmic causes and conditions and after much difficulty, they were able to have the opportunity to be reborn into the human realm. Yet, due to the obstruction of ignorance, they have completely forgotten what took place in their last life, not to mention all that occurred in many previous lives. (Of course, due to the particular underlying causes and conditions of certain sentient beings, they are able to remember things relating to their last life or previous lives. There is quite a large number of real examples of this in today's world. Nowadays, people regard such things as so-called "miracles" and research this subject. Basically, such phenomena exist in every country. There are many written accounts of such things in some history books and various documents.)

Thus, if a sage told them where their parents in their last life have now been reborn and other pertinent detailed information, they would react exactly like the patient just described, who suffered from amnesia. They would not be able to accept this information for a temporary period of time or even for a long period of time. Perhaps they would not believe this information altogether, thinking that the sage had certain ulterior motives or that he devised a certain plot. They absolutely would not be willing to believe the words of the sage.

I will give another example. One day a certain person suddenly asks you what you did when you were one year and two days old. This person asks you to recount each thing you did that day, one by one. If you cannot recount them, he will cut off your head! You will think of excuses and argue strongly on the basis of reason. You will state that you do not remember such things, since you were too small. You will tell him that this is only human and that even he cannot recount such things! You will ask him what person in this entire world could remember the things they did when they were one year and two days old. (Of course, this does not include Great Holy Ones.)

Honestly speaking, I am afraid that there are few people in the entire world who can answer this question. However, it should be of no consolation even if there were nobody in the entire world who could answer this question. If that were the case, it would only show the common misfortune of everyone in the world. It would mean that everyone in the world is enveloped in ignorance and delusion, which has resulted in a common lack of awareness and lack of enlightenment! This is definitely not a good thing. A cultivator cannot use this as an excuse to absolve himself and feel complacent or proud. Could it be said that it is a matter worth celebrating if everyone in the world has the same negative habitual conduct? Not at all!

For example, a great fire occurs in a mountain and forest region, which causes tens of thousands of people to lose their homes and wander about. So many people at the same time experience this common disaster. Could it be said that this is a matter worth celebrating? This is also a case where, due to common karma[73] and common negative habitual conduct, everyone suffers karmic retribution!

Another example is when an extremely strong earthquake causes a medium-sized country to become rubble overnight. Everywhere, a scene of devastation meets the eye. Blood flows over the ground like water, and corpses are everywhere. There is nothing left of that country's prosperity, wealth, and strength. It is a terrible tragedy in this human world.

This is the common karmic retribution of the sentient beings who live in that country, which was also brought about by their common karma and common negative habitual conduct. It is not the common misfortune of just one or two people. Could it be said that we should be indifferent to the common situation shared by all of these people? Just the opposite. This situation should prompt all people to face and ponder the question of why it happened. The question of why it happened should not be asked by cultivators only.

People generally just accept such hardships. They regard such things that occur before their very eyes as natural happenings. They do not ponder what, after all, are the basic reasons that caused such occurrences and what is the nature of such occurrences. Some scholars simply research subjects such as the movement of the earth's crust, the core of the earth, the earth's mantle being disturbed and influenced by certain materials and elements, etc. They then say that as a consequence, there are so-called structural changes, volcanic eruptions, and ground collapsing earthquakes. They say that certain high or low atmospheric pressure changes cause tornadoes or typhoons.

I will give another example. A fairyland of mountains and palaces often appears in the sky or on the surface of the ocean. This scene is more beautiful than any scenery that ever existed on earth. Occasionally, one can see birds, flowers, and a stream of people walking slowly about. One may even see hordes of soldiers and horses or a garden of phoenixes. These sights truly appear live before one's eyes. Scientists give this phenomenon a beautiful name: mirage. They say that it is caused by the weather.

These scientists are truly ignorant. They do not stop and think whether there is another dimension or another world. Those live people who vividly appear are even dressed in the popular clothing worn in ancient times. It could not possibly be caused by the weather as those ignorant people claim!

The above mentioned types of people frequently seek answers to all such occurrences in a superficial manner. They do not know how to fundamentally solve these problems. Thus, when a great fire occurs in a certain mountain and forest region after continuous dry weather, they think they can do nothing to help the situation. The only thing to do is let the fire burn strongly for a few months or even a few years. They think that if an earthquake occurs, then all they can do is let the earth quake. All they can do is let the fire fighters rescue people from the rubble. This is all they can do. Everyone is helpless. Since they think the course of events cannot be reversed, they do not take precautions beforehand. Of course, with such mentality, the only thing for everybody to do is let the situation go unchecked and suffer hardships.

However, the basic reason for all such suffering lies in the inability of living beings to understand that it is a scientific process that brings about their karmic retribution. The Buddha Dharma is magnificent and profound. It is the life order of another world and dimension.

For a cultivator to place himself among the ranks of ordinary people is pitiable. People of the world do not understand the principle of cause and effect, or karmic retribution. Therefore, they commit foolish acts without any fear of the consequences. Yet, there are cultivators who do understand some principles of cause and effect but who nevertheless follow worldly people in doing evil. They allow the external circumstances to sway them. They regard their karmic obstructions and ignorance as very normal things. To put it in unpleasant terms, this is rather ignorant!

Therefore, these cultivators treat their "amnesia" as an extremely unimportant and ordinary matter. As an excuse to cover up their own ignorance, they even say that everybody in the world is like this, since everybody suffers from "amnesia." Is this not somewhat self-deceiving? Is this not a case of the more one tries to make excuses, the more one is exposed?

Because of delusion and ignorant views, some cultivators think that their family members in this life are their only true family members. They think that only those live people who now appear before them are their family members. They do not regard their family members over many lives as being their dearest family members.

Suppose an ordinary person in one lifetime has only a father and a mother, a pair of brothers or sisters, a wife, and a couple of children. After 1,000 generations, these flesh and blood family members will have increased to several thousands of people. If one attempted to calculate the progeny of these close family members starting from many lives and eons ago, would such progeny not be countless?

Any of the strangers who casually pass right by you on the street at any given time may have been your son, daughter, father, mother, brother, or sister in a previous life. This is true even though ignorance obstructs your vision and shrouds your consciousness, causing you not to recognize them. It is just that you cannot penetrate this truth due to karmic obscurations, the causes of which were planted over many previous lives.

As such, if you mistreat a certain living being, perhaps you are abusing your previous father or mother, a family member whom you sincerely loved in a previous time! This includes a small ant walking on the ground. If you take your bow and arrow or your gun and aim it at the small bird flying in the sky, you might be aiming at your previous playful son whom you dearly loved in your last life or your previous cute little daughter in your last life!

If you ask someone to aim his gun at his own children in this life, he would definitely not do it. If he really did it, people would say that he had lost his mind, that he is crazy, and that he is an evil demon. Yet, when someone aims his gun at a hawk flying in the sky or at a wild animal running on the ground and shoots it dead, people praise him as being a hero. They do not say that he is a butcher! This shows the ignorance of modern day people. This also shows the pitiable aspects of modern day people.

Of course, you can say that such people know nothing about such prior relationships. Nevertheless, they cannot use this as an excuse to absolve themselves. This is because living beings in the three spheres and the six realms of existence have all been our dearest family members at one time or another from beginningless time. One must make amends for all karmic offenses!

Sakyamuni Buddha said that sentient beings in the three spheres and the six realms of existence have all been our family members – our fathers, mothers, brothers, and sisters – at one time or another in our many previous lives spanning over eons of time. This means that if the cultivator loves his family members in this life, he must also love his family members from many previous lives spanning over eons of time. If he is only willing to pay a price for his family members in this life, whom he loves, and ignores his dearest family members from many previous lives, then one can truly call into question the sincerity of the love he has for his family members in this life. It can be affirmed that his love is definitely one-sided and incorrect!

How can one's love for one's family members justifiably be called correct? How should one love one's family members? Should one love them in a broad and rational manner according to the Buddha Dharma or should one blindly love in a conniving and indulging manner? These are questions that cultivators should deeply ponder!

There is something that I can clearly tell all cultivators. If you want to truly love your family members in a faultless manner, then you must act according to the principles laid out in the Buddha Dharma. You must act according to the teachings of the Master and not according to the wishes of other living beings. (Of course, this refers to a Vajra Master who truly meets the standards of the Dharma rules, who is thoroughly conversant in both exoteric and esoteric Dharma, who has mastered the Five Sciences, and who has attained a state of Dharma virtue.) You must act according to the meaning of the Buddha Dharma rather than submitting to the wishes of a certain family member. You must act according to correct ways rather than yielding to erroneous and evil ways. You must cultivate yourself well, in the proper and correct manner, rather than engaging in self-deception and deception of others. You must act according to the principles of the Buddha Dharma rather than worldly principles.

Only by acting in this manner will you be able to attain accomplishment. Only by acting in this manner will you also be able to save and transform your dearest family members! Only by acting in this manner will you truly forever love your dearest family members!

Chapter Eleven

CONFUSED VIEWS CONCERNING SCHOOLS AND BIASED THOUGHTS THAT OBSTRUCT THE PURSUIT OF ENLIGHTENMENT

THERE ARE MANY SCHOOLS OR SECTS WITHIN Buddhism nowadays. They cannot be enumerated in just a few sentences. Besides the orthodox schools, there are the heterodox schools, splinter schools, schools founded upon the views of a certain person, etc. Because of the differences in these schools, the views for which they stand are often not totally the same. Given this situation, some practitioners are unable to clearly distinguish between schools that uphold correct understanding and those that do not. They mix up the relationships between the schools and the ideas of each of the schools. They even make seriously irresponsible remarks by maligning a certain Master, a certain founder of a school, etc. They commit various serious offenses.

There are some Dharma Teachers with biased thoughts. Because of their confused views, they make irresponsible remarks. This causes people from all walks of life in society who do not understand the principles of the Buddha Dharma, plus some reporters who also do not understand Dharma principles, to add fuel to the flames. As a result, these people and reporters slander the Buddha Dharma and many of the different schools. At all kinds of occasions, they freely express their false theories and spread their ignorant views.

They say, for example, "Cultivators must be totally poor and own nothing. They must sit alone on a rush cushion, cut off their hair, and not eat after noon. Those who wear splendid and beautiful clothes and jewels, who have a fancy hairdo and put on eyebrow makeup, are definitely not cultivators."

People who hold such erroneous and evil views are truly quite pitiful! They have not yet heard that an Arhat saves himself, cultivates himself in poverty, lives humbly, wears coarse clothes, eats simple food, and is troubled by clinging to the Hinayana Dharma. A Bodhisattva enlightens others. A Bodhisattva practices Dharma to bring about both wisdom and good fortune. Precious gems give a Bodhisattva's body a dignified appearance. A Bodhisattva is happy to bestow enlightenment upon others.

Of all the many Mahayana Bodhisattvas, such as Kuan Yin Bodhisattva, Manjughosa Buddha Mother, Ding Ji, and the Dakinis, which one does not wear jewels and necklaces, flowers and green jade, giving their bodies a dignified appearance and manifesting their good fortune and wisdom? Actually, one cannot differentiate between who is a true and who is a false Great Virtuous One from appearance alone. Rather, one must determine whether such being understands the methods of cultivation, whether such being holds the correct Dharma of the Tathagata.

Someone's entire body may be adorned with brilliant jewels and pearls and her face may have makeup. If this person holds the Buddha Dharma, then she is still a true practitioner. Someone may have an appearance of total poverty. He may only eat one meal in the middle of the day and meditate day and night. If this person does not hold the Buddha Dharma, then his basic character is still that of an ordinary person. Therefore, those who maintain the above quoted opinion concerning the appearance of cultivators are ordinary people devoid of understanding!

Additionally, there are people who say, "Those who follow Vajrayana Buddhism are mantra chanters. They only chant mantras. Those of us who learn exoteric Dharma should not mingle with them."

There are those who say, "Vajrayana Buddhism is high-level Buddha Dharma. We who learn Vajrayana Buddhism should not mingle with those who learn the low-level exoteric Buddha Dharma."

There are people who say, "Those of us who learn esoteric Dharma are high-level cultivators. Those who learn exoteric Dharma are low-level practitioners. I look down upon them...."

People like those just quoted are all people of shallow understanding. Essentially, their nonsensical words are due to the differences in their learning. It is a problem involving their different levels. Their shallow knowledge prevents them from having correct understanding and correct views. On the contrary, they are burdened with biased views and mistaken thoughts. On the light side, the consequences of their conduct will be that they will not attain accomplishment. On the heavy side, if they delay others from attaining accomplishment and wisdom, the consequences will be endless trouble in the future – they will, of course, descend into hell!

There are people like this among those who are by my side. They also speak in the manner I just described. This is truly regrettable!

A few days ago, I conducted a few Nectar Dharma Assemblies. My Rinpoche and Dharma Teacher disciples were seated below the dais, and other Rinpoches and attendants were seated on the dais. They all saw certain Buddhas transform into light, certain Buddhas exhibit supernormal states, and certain Buddhas manifest their solemn and holy appearance. The Buddhas bestowed true nectar from the sky. Therefore, although these holy Dharma Assemblies were not unprecedented, nevertheless, they were rare and hard to come by! All of those who attended the Dharma Assemblies increased their Dharma powers several-fold.

Of course, in conducting these Dharma Assemblies, I completely relied upon the great assistance of the holy Buddhas, holy Bodhisattvas, and holy Dharma Protectors. Additionally, all of the disciples in attendance were people of model virtue. In response to this, the various powers in the Dharma realms formed a state of accomplishment. Only because of these conditions did the Buddhas personally come and bestow nectar. If these various conditions had not come together, what merit and virtue would I, Pamu, alone have to raise the banner of the Dharma and invoke the Buddhas to bestow nectar? Without these various conditions coming together, I am afraid that water would have had to be substituted for real nectar! Thus, I have no merit or virtue.

All of you saw with your own eyes nectar from the land of the Buddhas. The Buddhas bestowed nectar, which was produced out of nothingness and which truly does not exist in the human realm. It is a precious, lustrous substance that resembles liquid. It constantly changed inside the golden bowl. It is incomparably wonderful!

However, during the assembly, a very excited Rinpoche disciple surprisingly expressed the following strange viewpoint: "The ability to successfully invoke the Buddhas to bestow nectar can only be found in our Vajrayana Buddhism. Those who follow exoteric Buddhism do not have the qualifications and good fortune to see such true Buddha Dharma!"

After hearing this, I felt deeply sad for him. I tell all of you now that this statement is not the statement of a benevolent follower of the Vajrayana. What is this "those who follow exoteric Buddhism" and "our Vajrayana Buddhism"? What is this "openly taught Buddhism" and "secretly taught Buddhism"? What is this "Buddha Dharma taught by the Han Chinese" and "Buddha Dharma taught by the Tibetans"? What is the difference between these statements and the statements made by those so-called scholars in society who are engaged in Buddhist studies or the statements made by some monks who have biased views?

The above-quoted statements reflect confused views with respect to schools. Such people have not yet understood the correct principles of logical reasoning. They are people of shallow knowledge who do not study the various treatises and commentaries. In Buddhist circles throughout the world today, biased and erroneous thoughts such as these commonly exist. They basically stem from a lack of clarity concerning what is meant by exoteric Buddhism, what is meant by Vajrayana Buddhism, and what the relationship is between exoteric Buddhism and Vajrayana Buddhism.

Actually, exoteric Buddhism and Vajrayana Buddhism are not two separate schools. They are together one and a half schools. What is meant by a one and a half schools? All of you practitioners should carefully listen to my teaching.

What is called exoteric Buddhism is half of a Dharma system. What is called Vajrayana Buddhism is one Dharma system. Everybody seated here today – you Rinpoches, Geshés, and Khenpos – which one of you did not start out learning exoteric Buddhism? Which one of you has not studied and learned the ten common schools within Buddhism? You have learned the Pure Land school wherein one chants the name of Amitabha Buddha and visualizes the image of Amitabha Buddha. As for Zen, you have meditated upon the answers to koans and have engaged in practices that lead to sudden or gradual enlightenment. As for the Hua-yen school, all of you understand Dharma realm contemplation states. You are also thoroughly familiar with the Mind-Only school (Yogachara) and the Dharma-Laksana school. Practicing the Water and Land Dharma or the Dharma to Save Flaming-Mouth Pretas[74] are simple matters to you, as is daily sutra chanting. You practitioners of the Vajrayana must learn and practice such things. This is your responsibility as a Vajrayana practitioner.

Why did this disciple who is a Rinpoche forget this? Before one penetrates the Dharma, one must learn at least 5 to 13 different schools and their treatises, or even 100 different schools and their treatises. These constitute a summary of the complete works of exoteric Buddhism. The average practitioner of exoteric Buddhism has not learned many of the aspects of exoteric Buddhism that all of you have learned, yet he can still be called a person of great virtue. Therefore, all of you practitioners of the Vajrayana have actually learned and applied each of the schools of exoteric Buddhism! Because of these conditions, it is not the case that you have no connection at all with exoteric Buddhism. Rather, you deserve to be called Great Virtuous Ones of exoteric Buddhism.

If one only practices exoteric Buddhism, then one is practicing only a part of Vajrayana Buddhism. This comes from the principle of first learning the various schools of exoteric Buddhism along with their treatises and then learning the practices of Vajrayana Buddhism. This sequence is a Dharma rule of Vajrayana Buddhism. First, one learns the various schools of exoteric Buddhism and all of their treatises. As for the practices of Vajrayana Buddhism, this includes (1) chanting mantras, (2) mudras, (3) visualization, (4) mandala offerings practiced either in a group or alone, and (5) inner and outer tantric initiations.

Those who are Masters in Tibet must first learn the various schools of exoteric Buddhism and their treatises. Only after this can they begin to learn the tantric (esoteric) practices by entering the Vajrayana Institute. There they will be trained in the profound tantric Buddha Dharma. All practitioners of Vajrayana Buddhism in Tibet know this. This is a rule of Tibetan Buddhism.

Therefore, the first part, which involves learning exoteric Buddhism, is half of a Dharma system. The second part, which involves learning the tantric practices, is half of a Dharma system. When these two parts are combined, the result is the complete Dharma system of Vajrayana Buddhism. Simply put, Vajrayana Buddhism can roughly be divided into six parts: exoteric Buddhism, mantras, mudras, visualization, mandala offerings, and inner and outer tantric initiations.

Hence, Vajrayana Buddhism is the complete and perfect whole composed of these two parts. That is, it is the complete Buddha Dharma. Those who only pursue exoteric Buddhism are pursuing half of a Dharma system. When Vajrayana practitioners thoroughly understand the relationship of exoteric Buddhism to Vajrayana Buddhism, they then understand that exoteric Buddhism is merely the foundational part in one's learning of the complete Buddha Dharma. They therefore regard the relationship between exoteric Buddhism and Vajrayana Buddhism as different levels in one's learning of the Dharma. This is rather similar to different levels in education. It is like the sequence of education, which begins with kindergarten and then progresses to grammar school, middle school, high school, college, or even higher levels of education.

Although Vajrayana Buddhism and exoteric Buddhism are on different levels, they are indispensable Dharma to living beings. They were established in response to the different levels of capacity possessed by living beings in order to eliminate their negative karma. The true Vajrayana is definitely not that which is practiced by those mantra chanting teachers in society who do not belong to Vajrayana Buddhism, exoteric Buddhism, or any particular school or teaching. They can only speak a few common Vajrayana Dharma sayings or chant a few dozen mantras. They know nothing about the schools of exoteric Buddhism and their treatises. They do not become deeply immersed in the study of exoteric Buddhism. Of course, they cannot be mentioned in the same breath with the part of Vajrayana Buddhism known as exoteric Buddhism. They do not understand at all Vajrayana Buddhism, which is magnificent. They are not followers of Vajrayana Buddhism.

Those who only practice exoteric Buddhism frequently regard Vajrayana Buddhism as another separate, outside school. Actually, these people are not clear about the Dharma of the Vajrayana. They have not studied true Tibetan tantra. They mistakenly consider those so-called mantra teachers to be practitioners of Vajrayana Buddhism. They do not know that true practitioners of Vajrayana Buddhism must be proficient in exoteric Buddhism. They do not know that these true practitioners must go through debates on the various treatises of exoteric Buddhism and successfully graduate from this phase before they can deeply enter a higher level of learning – the level which contains the esoteric practices. They do not understand that exoteric Buddhism, which they themselves learn, is the first part of Vajrayana Buddhism.

There are also some practitioners who are involved with Vajrayana Buddhism and who do not have clear and thorough knowledge of exoteric Buddhism. They are not very conversant in exoteric Buddhism. This causes some disciples of exoteric Buddhism to mistakenly think that all practitioners of Vajrayana Buddhism just chant mantras. Based upon this misconception, there have been many instances in which followers of exoteric Buddhism wrongfully malign the Buddha Dharma of Vajrayana Buddhism! With respect to this matter, practitioners of Vajrayana Buddhism who are not conversant in the Dharma principles of exoteric Buddhism must truly bear a certain degree of responsibility!

Some followers of exoteric Buddhism have not yet deeply penetrated into the advanced levels of the Buddha Dharma. Because of this lack of understanding, they draw arbitrary conclusions about things, separate out different schools, and give rise to biased thoughts that obstruct their pursuit of enlightenment. However, it is a strange thing that one who is a Rinpoche also gave rise to ignorant, biased thoughts today. Your school is one that requires thorough mastery of exoteric Buddhism and the tantric practices. As such, how could you say that those who learn exoteric Buddhism are no-good? If exoteric Buddhism is no-good, why must you first learn exoteric Buddhism before you are allowed to enter the Esoteric Dharma Institute to learn the tantric practices? Exoteric Buddhism is part of your school!

Another Rinpoche said that Vajrayana Buddhism is high level Dharma and exoteric Buddhism is low level Dharma. This is also quite wrong! The Buddha Dharma is not divided into high and low. All 84,000 Dharma methods came into being in response to the different innate faculties of living beings. It is like attending school. Some people attend primary school. Some people attend college. As long as the education corresponds with the student so that the student's performance is successful, then the education is good. For this reason, the Buddha established different types of Dharma methods and used various skillful means in order to transform and save living beings. Hence, no matter how many schools there are, the Buddha Dharma has only one truth. It is the truth of the universe: the Dharma of ending the cycle of birth and death!

No matter what school it is, only if the Dharma of the school corresponds with the practitioner will the practitioner be able to progress smoothly and end the cycle of birth and death. If one does not live according to Buddhism, then even if one practices the highest Dharma within Vajrayana Buddhism, it will still not be possible to become accomplished. No matter how great the innate faculties of someone may be and no matter what school of exoteric Buddhism that person may belong to, that person must still have faith, make vows, and engage in cultivation. That person must still cultivate morality, concentration, and wisdom. No matter what particular school of Vajrayana

Buddhism one may belong to, that person likewise must constantly practice the six paramitas.

My goal in writing various books is to have all of you practice according to the Dharma, as well as to educate future practitioners, in order to eliminate biased viewpoints that obstruct the pursuit of enlightenment. Sakyamuni Buddha and the Great Bodhisattvas did this. I, as one with a heart of humility, emulate them. I hope that all of the Rinpoches, Geshés, Khenpos, and great cultivators in attendance here today will emulate the Buddhas and Bodhisattvas!

You absolutely must not look down upon exoteric Buddhism. The Buddha Dharma of exoteric Buddhism is part of the Buddha Dharma of Vajrayana Buddhism. Mahavairocana Buddha said, "Without the foundation of exoteric Buddhism, Vajrayana Buddhism could not exist. However, without the tantric practices, exoteric Buddhism could still exist on its own." I, Pamu, am clearly telling everybody today that whoever only learns exoteric Buddhism and does not learn the tantric practices is one who learns the Dharma of exoteric Buddhism. Whoever only learns the tantric practices and does not learn exoteric Buddhism is an ignorant mantra teacher. Whoever learns both exoteric Buddhism and the tantric practices is one who follows true Vajrayana Buddhism!

If all of you do not thoroughly understand this, you might make fools of yourselves. This would be a minor incident. However, if because of this lack of thorough understanding you misguide others and thereby damage their pursuit of enlightenment, then this would be committing a serious offense for which you must bear the karmic consequences. If one has confused views and mistaken understanding concerning schools, this will naturally produce karmic obstructions on one's path toward enlightenment. Therefore, all of you good people seated here today – you who are people of exemplary virtue – must thoroughly understand this matter!

You are not merely experts in Buddhist studies. Rather, you are Rinpoches, Geshés, and Khenpos. To put it in a bit more worldly terms, you are experts in the three aspects of Buddhism, Buddhist studies, and the Buddha Dharma all put together. You are not researchers engaged in Buddhist studies who only know empty theories. Rather, you are liberated ones who truly put into practice the Buddha Dharma! Worldly scholarly viewpoints should not be maintained by you.

Take, for example, those researchers engaged in Buddhist studies. No matter how kind they may be and no matter how much theoretical knowledge they may have, nevertheless, during their entire lives they will never be able to attain your deep states of realization. It will be even more impossible for them to see the Buddhas actually bestow from the sky true nectar, which comes from the land of the Buddhas. This is because they engage in Buddhist studies and have not deeply entered the Buddha Dharma. From the perspective of the Buddha Dharma, the word *study* is called emptiness.

You have deeply entered the Buddha Dharma and are able to enter into Dharma states. However, you cannot become arrogant because of this. Although tantra is the advanced level, nevertheless, exoteric Buddhism is, after all, part of this advanced level. It is only because of the existence of exoteric Buddhism that Vajrayana Buddhism, which is the advanced level, can exist. We should respect and praise those good people who only follow exoteric Buddhism. They are also part of us!

Basically, with respect to those who only practice exoteric Buddhism, the most accomplished ones are Arhats. Those who have attained the level of Bodhisattva are rare. This is because the highest level within exoteric Buddhism is the prajna state and the Dharmakaya state. However, those who learn Vajrayana Buddhism already have exoteric Buddhism as their foundation in their cultivation of the Dharmakaya. At the same time, those who learn Vajrayana Buddhism cultivate the Sambhogakaya and the Nirmanakaya.[75] Hence, those who learn exoteric Buddhism do not understand at all how to cultivate the Sambhogakaya, not to mention how to cultivate the Nirmanakaya. If practitioners who only follow exoteric Buddhism want to cultivate the Sambhogakaya and the Nirmanakaya, they must practice a more advanced Buddha Dharma – namely, Vajrayana Buddhism – which combines exoteric Buddhism and the tantric practices.

However, all of you must understand something. Within exoteric Buddhism alone, there have been Great Bodhisattvas who came to this world in response to its needs and who propagated the Dharma. An example of this was Hui Neng, that illiterate monk from the Nanhua Temple in China. Although the Dharma that he propagated was the sudden enlightenment method, he actually was a Vajra Bodhisattva who came to this world again. This is like the worldly principle of division of labor. His coming to this world again was due to the fortunate karmic destiny of living beings. Of course, such Buddhas and Bodhisattvas coming to this world again is also the result of their own vows.

In short, practitioners who only practice exoteric Buddhism should not be like those common worldly people who do not understand Buddha Dharma principles and who go around recklessly voicing their ignorant ideas, thus producing negative karma born of ignorance. Such practitioners should abandon their misconceptions and biases that lead them astray. They should deepen their understanding of Dharma principles. In so doing, they will naturally come to a sudden, great understanding.

I suggest that those practitioners who do not understand Vajrayana Buddhism go to Tibet and visit a normal Vajrayana temple. They will then immediately understand. Those who make such a visit will see Lamas who are young and Lamas who are children learning nothing but exoteric Buddhism. These Lamas learn exoteric Buddhism in a very real way. Each of them is trained in debating the exoteric sutras. Only after they graduate from this phase, having thoroughly understood the schools of exoteric Buddhism and their writings, are they allowed to enter the Esoteric Dharma Institute to practice tantra. You should now be clear about what is meant by exoteric Buddhism and what is meant by Vajrayana Buddhism.

Those who practice Vajrayana Buddhism should understand that the first half of the Dharma that makes up Vajrayana Buddhism is the exoteric Buddha Dharma. Thus, such practitioners should not have any sense of superiority. They should maintain a heart of humility. They should practice as humble practitioners. They should consider themselves to be humble practitioners. They should not only totally master exoteric Buddhism, they should also advance further and strive for the realization of the Three Bodies and the four forms of wisdom of a Buddha[76] in order to carry out the great vow of an enlightened being to save all living beings. This is what an enlightened being views as his responsibility. You must remember not to maintain biased thoughts or confused views about schools. Such thoughts and views only obstruct your pursuit of enlightenment!

⇒ *Chapter Twelve* ⇐

FALSELY CLAIMING TO BE A DHARMA KING OR RINPOCHE

One Who Falsely Claims to Be a Dharma King or Rinpoche
Will Certainly Descend into
One of the Three Lower Realms of Existence

IN TODAY'S EARTHLY REALM, THERE ARE many cultivators who are learning Buddhism. This is especially true with respect to those Buddhists who learn and practice tantra. It can be said that such Buddhists can be found in every country in the world. In every corner of the world, the Dharma is being propagated. Both Tibetan Tantric Buddhism and Japanese Tantric Buddhism are being spread far and wide and are growing day by day.

However, most cultivators who are learning Buddhism often place a great deal of blind faith in those so-called "Great Dharma Kings," "Great Rinpoches," and "Great Dharma Teachers." Of course, respecting Great Rinpoches and Great Dharma Teachers is a very good and wonderful thing. It is also the basic morality a cultivator should have. It is the correct way of behaving. However, there is something that these people do not know. Having blind faith in those false "Dharma Kings," false "Rinpoches," and false "Dharma Teachers" will cause them to descend into one of the three lower realms of existence!

In Tibetan Buddhism, most Rinpoches are not very conversant in the teachings of the sutras. Thus, such Rinpoches often gradually accumulate negative karma. This lack of conversance causes them to produce negative karma out of ignorance. They make preposterous claims about themselves. They extol themselves and unjustifiably raise their status. They describe themselves as being so amazing. For example, some Rinpoches are average

Rinpoches, yet they claim to be Great Rinpoches. Some Rinpoches are small Rinpoches, yet they claim to be Great Dharma Kings.

What is even more frightening is that some boast that ages ago they became one of the first few Buddhas of this present Bhadrakalpa.[77] Without a doubt, these people will descend into hell. Their suffering will be indescribably horrible! They have in fact committed the offense of stating that they have attained realization and accomplishment when they have not. This is extremely serious conduct whereby they are violating the precepts and committing offenses!

In cultivating oneself and learning Buddhism, the first thing one must understand is to be humble and cautious. It is this principle that one must rely upon in one's daily conduct and cultivation. If one is conceited and self-righteous, if one cannot correctly measure oneself, then one cannot face oneself with a clear mind. One will then think that one is a Great Bodhisattva. In the end, this person will not only fail to become accomplished, he will also fall into degeneration. Suffering will closely follow him wherever he goes.

Look through Buddhist history from ancient times until the present and you will see that all Great Virtuous Ones and Bodhisattvas were humble and were cautious in their practice. None of them ever said that they were Great Bodhisattvas. Only those who are not Great Bodhisattvas claim to be Great Bodhisattvas! Hence, I now remind practitioners that you must pay attention to this.

Precisely because of this type of phenomena, precisely because he saw that the moral discipline of Vajrayana Buddhism practitioners had fallen into disorder, Master Tsongkhapa of the Gelug school took birth in Tibet. He put back into order the precepts and disciplinary rules of Vajrayana Buddhism. Thus, I very much praise the Gelug school for having straightened out these rules of moral discipline!

The precepts and disciplinary rules are extremely important. If these rules of moral discipline were not straightened out, then there would be even more Rinpoches who would make absurd claims about themselves, recklessly teach the Dharma, and exaggerate matters. Although such Rinpoches clearly know that something may weigh an ounce or two, they will say that it weighs a half pound. If something weighs a half pound, they will boast that it weighs 10 pounds or 100 pounds. Those worldly people who just took up Buddhism and who lack understanding of the principles of Buddhism are very easily deceived by such people.

It can be said that these deceivers, who are false Rinpoches, are not true Buddhists. Although they wear the robe of Buddhism and drape over their shoulders the clothing of tantra, they nevertheless do diabolical things. This is extremely serious. I therefore again remind everybody that you must cautiously practice. All genuine Great Rinpoches and Dharma Kings are cautious and humble. They are not boastful!

We will now use the example of the position of Dharma King. Many Buddhist books and Dharma writings set out in very clear, definitive, and strict terms that only one who has mastered both exoteric and esoteric Dharma, who is thoroughly conversant in the Five Sciences, who is successor of a true Dharma lineage, who teaches and transforms living beings, and who can perform all five Inner-Tantric Initiations can be called a Dharma King. Only this person is qualified to be acclaimed as a Dharma King. However, frequently the phrases "mastered both exoteric and esoteric Dharma" and "thoroughly conversant in the Five Sciences" have become common expressions for some Dharma Teachers and Rinpoches. It is as if all they have to do is say words like these and they can become just like a Dharma King!

Actually, if we do a little comparing, we will know. We will not discuss for now the matter of mastering both exoteric and esoteric Dharma. Since they label themselves as Dharma Kings, they should at least understand the 13 treatises. Do they understand *The Hetu-Vidya Treatise*? Do they understand *The Precepts and Discipline Treatise*? Do they understand *The Prajna Treatise*? If they do not understand any of those three treatises, if they do not understand *The Middle View Treatise*[78] and are totally unfamiliar with *The Abhidharmakosa Treatise*,[79] then they actually do not even meet the qualifications of an ordinary Rinpoche. How could they even speak of being a Dharma King?

Yet, in the present world, there are many false Rinpoches who claim to be Dharma Kings. Of course, there are some real Rinpoches who claim to be Dharma Kings. Nonetheless, it may well be asked, if they do not understand those five treatises, how could they teach the correct Dharma to Rinpoches and correct the misconceptions of Rinpoches? Since they claim to be Dharma Kings, then they must answer the questions and solve the problems of Rinpoches. Yet, if they do not understand those five treatises, how could they teach Rinpoches and clear up the puzzlement of Rinpoches?

Therefore, everybody must remember not to believe the beguiling words of these wildly arrogant people. Anyone who is a Dharma King must be proficient in the treatises. Besides the above-mentioned five standard treatises, a Dharma King must also understand *The Treatise on Impermanence*, *The Treatise on the Path to Liberation*,[80] *The Treatise on the Method for Understanding all Dharma*, etc.! Without such understanding, one would not be able to write even one book on Buddhism. If such a one were to write a spurious book on Buddhism, he would need to copy from others. It would not be his own work and would be full of mistakes. This being the case, can such a person be called a Dharma King? Can such a person be called the successor of a true Dharma King?

These people are truly pitiable. Yet, pitiable living beings who are even more confused often become attached to such people and have blind faith in them. Actually, even if one understands those few treatises and can clear up the puzzlement of Rinpoches, one still does not have the qualifications to call oneself a Dharma King. This alone is not enough. It will still depend upon whether one can perform the five Inner-Tantric Initiations.

If one calls oneself a Dharma King, then one must manifest one's Dharma Wheel. The Dharma Wheel must be able to sing, talk, predict life and death matters for people, fly, jump, move, and transform itself. Do those people have such a Dharma Wheel? This is what must be relied upon to practice great Dharma!

Some Rinpoches will say, "At the present time, I still do not have such a Dharma Wheel. However, I am successor of the position of Dharma King." All right, for the time being we will assume that they are successors of the position of Dharma King and that they do not have a Dharma Wheel. Nonetheless, do they understand the treatises? Please briefly expound for us *The Hetu-Vidya Treatise*. Please briefly describe for us *The Prajna Treatise*.

If they do not understand even the five treatises, not to mention other various Dharma writings, then it is obvious that they are not successors of the position of Dharma King! This is because they lack even the most basic qualifications. They do not even meet the qualifications of a Great Rinpoche! All they can do is deceive those who are not in the know, those who are ignorant. Yet, astute people will be absolutely clear about them at first glance!

Of course, some Rinpoches commit only these offenses, while in other areas they have performed deeds of great merit, such as seriously cultivating themselves, building temples, spreading the Dharma, saving living beings, etc. Their merit is great! However, the merit that they planted is often totally destroyed by their committing the offense of stating that they have attained realization and accomplishment when they have not. Thus, I want to especially instruct all of you practitioners seated here today that you must not follow in the footsteps of these ignorant Rinpoches.

Now then, is this type of situation common or not? It is common, very common. Each school has this type of person. The previous Panchen Master also had this type of person under him. Jiang Yang Qin Zhen likewise had this type of person under him. The same with the Venerable Chiming. What will surprise everybody to hear is that even the holiest and most virtuous Dharma King in today's earthly realm, Great Dharma King Yangwo Yisinubu, does not lack this type of person by his side! The number of this type of offending disciple under other Dharma Kings and Rinpoches is so much greater that they cannot even be counted. One can thus imagine the degree of disorder that exists in this present Dharma-Ending Age!

Although I do not know Great Dharma King Yangwo Yisinubu and have not yet seen him in this lifetime, nevertheless, due to the truth of Dharma nature, I deeply understand him. I can affirm that Dharma King Yangwo Yisinubu is the topmost leader among all Dharma Kings in this world! He is the true incarnation of Dharma King Qian Ba. Yet, he has always considered himself as a humble practitioner. Since ancient times, he has practiced in a humble and cautious manner. He truly has the state of realization and the state of virtue of the future Lion's Roar Buddha. He has always been one of tremendous virtue. He has always been a paragon of virtue. He is the leader of Buddhism in this earthly realm!

In order to clarify just how disorderly the present state of the Buddha Dharma is in this world, I have decided to use the example of truly the most magnificent Dharma King of great virtue in today's world. This Dharma King has indeed achieved a high level of realization in the Five Sciences. He is not lacking in any one of them. With respect to each one of the Five Sciences, if judged in worldly terms, he has at least surpassed the highest international standards. He has achieved perfect mastery of the five Inner-Tantric Initiations. He has unhindered understanding of exoteric and esoteric Dharma. One can say that there is no difference between him and those such as Master Padmasambhava, Master Marpa, the Selfless Mother, and the Venerable Atisha. He is a Great Holy One on the same level of realization as these others. Who is he? He is Great Dharma King Yangwo Yisinubu, who can successfully invoke the Buddhas to bestow nectar from the sky!

Yet, even the Great Dharma King Yangwo Yisinubu does not lack such offending disciples under him. Surprisingly, there are ordinary practitioners under him who falsely claim to be one of the Eight Great Rinpoches. They do not understand at all how high the position and state of realization are of any of the Eight Great Rinpoches! Attaining the position of a Great Rinpoche means that one has already reached a certain Bodhisattva stage. These people who wrongly think that they have attained such a position do not examine their conscience. They do not ask themselves whether they are, after all, a Bodhisattva and whether they indeed have the skills of a Bodhisattva! This type of problem is not limited to only ordinary disciples of Dharma King Yangwo Yisinubu. Even a disciple who is one of the Four Great Dharma Princes has made a false claim concerning himself.

I will now use the example of one of the disciples of Great Dharma King Yangwo Yisinubu in the hope that all practitioners will be careful and vigilant. There is a disciple like this even under him, not to mention disciples under other Dharma Kings! It can be said that there are a great deal of such disciples. I am afraid that they are as numerous as rocks, that there are so many of them in the world.

This type of phenomena should not occur among disciples of the Great Dharma King Yangwo Yisinubu, who is most wonderful. Now then, what are the causes of this? In this time of demonic Dharma, in this Dharma-Ending Age, demonic power has obscured and covered up the minds of some practitioners who were clearheaded, causing them to engage in distorted, dreamlike thinking. With the arising of ignorance and obscurations, they commit these offenses.

I do not want to belittle Great Dharma King Yangwo Yisinubu. I very much respect and love him. Yet, as a cultivator, I must speak sincere words. I use him as an example to show that this type of phenomenon exists even more among disciples of other Dharma Kings in this world. This is a matter of utmost importance to practitioners and a matter from which practitioners can draw lessons. It is a significant problem that has to be solved urgently.

Since the Yuan Dynasty[81] until the present, the disciples of Great Dharma King Yangwo Yisinubu can be divided into five main categories. (The disciples of ordinary Dharma Kings can be divided into four main categories. However, under Great Dharma King Yangwo Yisinubu, there are two disciples who are on the level of a Dharma King.) Simply put, his disciples can be divided into five levels or ranks. The first category is the highest level. The disciples in this category have the greatest accomplishment. Their roots of kindness are the deepest. They are practitioners whose state of realization and state of virtue have almost reached perfection. In ordinary Dharma language, they are called Great Masters.

Great Dharma King Yangwo Yisinubu has two such disciples. One of them is an elderly man over 100 years old. The other is an elderly man who is now close to 90 years old. Within the group of disciples under Great Dharma King Yangwo Yisinubu, these two are called the white general and the black general. The black general is Elder Dharma King Gama Dorje Losang. The white general is Elder Dharma King Jiang Yang Qin Zhen. Both of them have the status of Dharma King. This is due to their karmic destiny. In the past, they were already founders of major schools, that is, Dharma Kings.

The second category of disciples is below the first category. They cannot compare with the first category of disciples in terms of state of realization and cultivation. Disciples of Dharma King Yangwo Yisinubu in this category are called the Four Great Dharma Princes. These four people have or had a rather high position in the world. They are or were illustrious, noble people. They are or were Great Rinpoches with extremely high reputations. They have already entered the higher stages on the Bodhisattva path.

The first one is Gama Puba Fajian Rinpoche. This Rinpoche already passed away while sitting in meditation. The level of his practice was very amazing. His body has already become indestructible sharira. The second one is a Dharma King of the Xueba sect whose name is Gama Dege Gyatso Xila Rinpoche. He is presently still in Tibet propagating the Dharma and benefiting living beings. The third one is Kang Qin Rinpoche. He is presently cultivating the advanced Buddha Dharma at the side of the Great Dharma King. The fourth one is Gama Dun Zeng Zhuo Ga Rinpoche.

These four Rinpoches are also called the Four Great Dharma Princes of Vajrayana Buddhism. They are called Mind Princes as well. They are or were amazing people of great virtue. Among disciples of the Dharma King, their authority and position are or were quite high. Furthermore, the remaining three are all people of immense virtue who are over 60 years old. Their position is just one level below the Dharma Kings known as the black general and the white general.

Everybody should bear in mind that the Four Great Dharma Princes whom I just described are the Four Great Dharma Princes of Vajrayana

Buddhism. The Kagyu school also has four Rinpoches who are called the Four Great Dharma Princes. You must not get them mixed up.

The third category of disciples, of course, cannot match the Four Great Dharma Princes with respect to state of realization, mastery of the Dharma, innate faculties, and cultivation. They are lower than the Four Great Dharma Princes. These are eight great disciples of Great Dharma King Yangwo Yisinubu who are called the Eight Great Rinpoches. Of these Eight Great Rinpoches, five of them are from Tibet. The other three were incarnated in the land of the Chinese (Han) people and propagate the Dharma there.

Although their positions are merely Rinpoches on the third level, nevertheless, they enjoy an extremely high reputation in the world. One of them received the highest academic degree in the world with respect to the Buddha Dharma, that is, a doctorate in the Buddha Dharma. Some people mistakenly called them Dharma Kings. Actually, they do not have the status of Dharma King. They are spread all over the world. All of them are engaged in saving living beings. They might empower others on a regular basis through practicing the Dharma, or they might conduct huge Dharma Assemblies. The skills of ordinary Rinpoches in the world cannot be compared with the skills attained by the Eight Great Rinpoches!

Each of them has reached the position of being one of the Eight Great Rinpoches. From the perspective of the Buddha Dharma, there is a gap between them and the two elderly Dharma Kings and between them and the Four Great Dharma Princes. This is a disparity in rank. This signifies a disparity in positions. This disparity in positions is actually a disparity in states of realization. Of course, if any of the Eight Great Rinpoches exert great effort, perhaps he will quickly attain the level of realization of a Dharma Prince and thereby become a Dharma Prince.

In the fourth category of disciples are cultivators who have extraordinary roots of kindness but who are not on the level of a Rinpoche. Perhaps they are Vajra Acaryas. Their cultivation is also very good. Their state of virtue and state of realization are quite outstanding. As long as they continuously cultivate themselves according to the teachings of Great Dharma King Yangwo Yisinubu, and in addition propagate the Dharma and benefit living beings, then in the future their positions will gradually rise higher and higher. It is possible for them to reach the level of the Eight Great Rinpoches. It is also possible for them to reach the level of the Four Great Dharma Princes.

However, I must unequivocally state that this is not an easy thing. The accomplishment of the Four Great Dharma Princes is not something that the ordinary cultivator can achieve. Reaching this level of accomplishment requires exerting enormous effort and undergoing untold hardships. It requires cultivation spanning many lives and eons. If this fourth type of disciple cultivates himself in accordance with the teachings of Great Dharma King Yangwo Yisinubu, then he will, just as the others, attain a considerably high position.

However, it would be extremely difficult for those of tremendous virtue in the world today, such as the Four Great Dharma Princes or the Eight Great Rinpoches, to attain the position of Dharma King. To attain the position of Great Dharma King would be even less possible!

It can be said that the Four Great Dharma Princes have a slight possibility of attaining the position of Dharma King. However, with respect to the Eight Great Rinpoches, this is extremely remote! If one of the Four Great Dharma Princes were to attain the position of Dharma King, then he would have had to cultivate himself to a considerably high level. He would have had to attain the state of realization of a higher than tenth stage Bodhisattva. He would have had to enter the state of realization of a Dharma King. Only then could he attain the position of Dharma King. An example of this would be the position and state of realization attained by Elder Dharma King Dorje Losang. Nevertheless, there is not the slightest possibility for one of the Four Great Dharma Princes to succeed to the position of Dharma King. (This is because this is a firm Dharma rule.)

Therefore, not even one of the Four Great Dharma Princes has the qualifications to say that he will succeed to the position of Dharma King. Thus, all practitioners in the world today absolutely must not believe those Tulkus or Rinpoches who say that they are successors of the position of Dharma King within their spiritual lineage. You must not believe that this is true. This in fact is an extremely absurd and unrealistic joke. They are deceiving those who do not know the inside facts!

Everyone must understand that the position of Dharma King is not succeeded to. This position is not subject to succession. Rather, the Dharma King himself comes to the world again to assume the position.

Take, for example, the Dharma King of the Gelug school, Panchen Rinpoche. After he passed away, who succeeded to his position? There is nobody with the qualifications to succeed to his position! Even if there were such a qualified person, such person still could not succeed to this position. Panchen Rinpoche must come to this world again to assume the position.

Take, for example, the 17th Karmapa. After he passes away, people will have to wait for him to come to this world again. Only then can there be a successor who becomes the 18th Karmapa. It was the same thing with the 16th Karmapa. After he passed away, he came to this world again to succeed to the position and thereby became the 17th Karmapa.

Another example is Dorje Losang, the incarnation of the Venerable Vimala-prabha. After he passed away in a former life, who succeeded to his position? Other people could not succeed to his position. He himself must succeed to the position. Frankly speaking, Dorje Losang is Vimala-prabha. Vimala-prabha is Dorje Losang. This is how it has been life after life without change.

The same is true for Jiang Yang Qin Zhen, who has come back to this world life after life. A great many years ago he attained the position of Dharma King.

The same is true for Great Dharma King Yangwo Yisinubu. A great many years ago, he was Dharma King Qian Ba. In this life, he succeeded to the position formerly held by Dharma King Qian Ba. Nobody could possibly take his place! His Dharma Wheel cannot be transmitted to anyone else. (According to my understanding, each of the four major schools has a Dharma Wheel with great supernormal powers.) If he were to transmit his Dharma Wheel to someone else, the Dharma Wheel would crush the recipient to pieces, since the recipient would not be qualified to bear the heavy responsibility of having such Dharma power!

Of course, it is not possible that any of the Four Great Dharma Princes who are disciples of Yangwo Yisinubu are qualified to bear such responsibility. This is even more true with respect to the Eight Great Rinpoches. The position of the Four Great Dharma Princes is lower than that of their Buddha Master and that of the black and white generals. It is even less possible to place the Eight Great Rinpoches on par with their Buddha Master and the black and white generals!

However, what is most unfortunate is that one of the Four Great Dharma Princes, Dun Zeng Zhuo Ga Rinpoche, unexpectedly announced publicly that he will succeed to Great Dharma King Yangwo Yisinubu's position. Furthermore, he stated that among the 1,000 Buddhas to appear in this present Bhadrakalpa, he will be considered as one of the foremost! Honestly speaking, he is an elderly man who is over 60 years old. He is a Great Rinpoche who, after coming to this world, has cultivated himself for so many years. Yet, he surprisingly uttered such preposterous words.

What is even more pitiful is that not a small number of people unexpectedly believed what he said. These people blindly follow him and spread confusion. Together with him, they stir up trouble. They believe him when he says that he is on the list of the 1,000 Buddhas of this present Bhadrakalpa. They think that he is so amazing. They, of course, believe that it is natural and right that he should succeed to the position of Dharma King.

He absolutely should not utter the nonsense that he has uttered. He committed the offense of stating that he has attained realization and accomplishment when he has not. This will result in descending into the hell of uninterrupted suffering! Actually, smart people should understand that, at the very most, Dun Zeng Zhuo Ga is one of the Four Great Dharma Princes. Even if he were higher than this, he would still not reach the level of the black and white generals who are Dharma Kings. Yet, he went so far as to claim that he will succeed to the position of Great Dharma King.

What's more, even if we do away with the historical rules, thus allowing him to succeed to the position of Dharma King, the successor of the position of Great Dharma King should be one of the two generals. No matter what, the successor would not be one of the Four Great Dharma Princes!

Let us leave aside for the moment the fact that hair has grown in between the eyebrows of the black general, Elder Dharma King Dorje Losang. Let us just speak of his meditative skills and his solemn and virtuous face. I empowered his beard, which grew quickly after it had basically stopped growing. How can the meditative skills and facial appearance of any of the Four Great Dharma Princes be put on par with the meditative skills and facial appearance of Elder Dharma King Dorje Losang?

Even though the Elder Dharma King has already been approved by Yangwo Yisinubu as a Dharma King, even though this further accomplishment was prophesied by Yangwo Yisinubu, and even though the Elder Dharma King is now firmly established as a Dharma King, nevertheless, it would be sheer nonsense to say that he will succeed to the position of Great Dharma King left behind by Yangwo Yisinubu. The Elder Dharma King does not have the qualifications. This is all the more true for one of the Four Great Dharma Princes. Is it not just as impossible for one of the Four Great Dharma

Princes to succeed to the position of Great Dharma King as it is to catch fish by climbing trees? Is this not like a child pretending to be indestructible?

Everyone knows that a tree only bears fruit; it does not grow fish. Of course, this can be likened to saying that one of the Eight Great Rinpoches is successor of the position of Dharma King. In the same way, this is pure fiction, like the Arabian Nights!

A dragon is a dragon. A shrimp is a shrimp. After a dragon passes away, it must have another dragon's body before it can become a dragon again. How could a shrimp become a dragon? Of course, a shrimp indeed can become a dragon, but it must go through many lives to complete such transformation. This process is definitely not so easy.

People with ordinary roots of kindness must engage in a great deal of cultivation whereby they live according to Buddhism and must go through many lives before they can become Rinpoches. Ordinary Rinpoches must likewise engage in arduous and diligent cultivation before they can attain the status and state of realization of the Eight Great Rinpoches. The Eight Great Rinpoches must likewise exert great efforts in their cultivation before they can reach the status of the Four Great Dharma Princes. The Four Great Dharma Princes must likewise engage in a great deal of cultivation, must go through many lives, and must save many living beings before they can become Dharma Kings like the two Dharma Kings, Chin Zhen and Dorje Losang.

Thus, if someone says that he will take over the Great Dharma King position of Dharma King Yangwo Yisinubu, this would truly be a most absurd thing. It would be sheer boastfulness! Zhuo Ga Rinpoche has committed the great offense of stating that he has attained realization and accomplishment when he has not. If he continues like this, he will descend into the Vajra Hell realm. He must deeply repent. He must practice the highest level Dharma. Furthermore, he must practice the Dharma of Vajrasattva. Otherwise, it will be extremely difficult to wash away his negative karma!

Honestly speaking, in this present world, the most magnificent is Great Dharma King Yangwo Yisinubu. Yet, he is so humble and cautious. He never considers himself as a Great Dharma King. He also never considers himself as a Great Virtuous One. He has always been one who quietly transforms and saves living beings. With a heart of humility, he saves living beings.

Jiang Yang Qin Zhen also never boasts of or flaunts his position of Dharma King. Dorje Losang always calls himself a humble monk. He has always cultivated himself in an earnest and down-to-earth manner. He thinks that he is not qualified to be a Dharma King.

Thus, how could one of the Four Great Dharma Princes be compared with the black and white generals? They are far from the level of the black and white generals! I would like to remind each of the Eight Great Rinpoches that your position is only that of one of the Eight Great Rinpoches. You still cannot match the Four Great Dharma Princes. However, if you seriously cultivate yourselves and truly learn, then in the future it is possible for you to attain the position of Dharma Prince! Hence, everybody must bear in mind that if, on your path of cultivation, you state that you have attained realization and accomplishment when you have not, then you will descend into the Vajra Hell realm. By no means can you commit such an offense.

All of you here today, no matter if you are a Great Rinpoche or a Great Dharma Teacher, no matter if you have cultivated yourself by following me over many lives, no matter if your cultivation has reached a very high level, and no matter if your state of realization is deep, nevertheless, you must always remember to cautiously practice. You must not break the precept of stating that you have attained realization and accomplishment when you have not. Otherwise, you will be sorry when it is too late! Furthermore, you must teach your disciples not to break this precept in the slightest.

I also want to remind lay cultivators that you must attain wisdom and clear away from your mind the obstacles of delusion. You must clearly see and clearly understand. You should not think that someone who boasts he is a Great Rinpoche is in fact a Great Rinpoche. When you hear someone say that he is the head of a certain temple and that he is a Great Dharma King, you should not automatically believe that he is truly a Great Dharma King. All of you must strictly examine such people.

No matter whether someone claims to be a Dharma King, a Great Rinpoche, or the head of a great temple, you must properly measure such claims. What is the level of this person after all? Has he mastered both exoteric and esoteric Dharma? Is he conversant in the sutras? Is he conversant in the 13 treatises? Is he proficient in the five initiations? During his performance of the Vajra Samadhi Initiation, does the weight of his Vajra scepter increase to thousands of pounds? Can his Vajra scepter emit the true fire of samadhi? During his performance of the Auspicious Selection Initiation, are miraculous states manifested? At the Buddhist altar area, are auspicious miraculous states truly manifested and does selection truly occur? During his performance of the Dharma Wheel Communicates With the Holy Ones Initiation, does his Dharma Wheel truly move around on the ground, move around in water, speak, jump, and make predictions? During these initiations, have you personally seen him use samadhi Dharma water that has seeped through the wall of a bowl? Did he practice this Dharma himself? Is he truly able to successfully invoke the Buddhas and Bodhisattvas to bestow nectar from the sky in front of his disciples? Only if he can do all of these things without exception does he truly have the state of realization of a Dharma King! Otherwise, no matter how amazing he may be, he has not reached the level of a Dharma King.

All of you disciples here today must bear in mind that achieving the state of realization of a Dharma King is no trivial matter. A Dharma King can successfully invoke nectar from the sky. If one is unable to successfully invoke nectar, then this shows that he does not possess the state of realization of a Dharma King, since he does not have the ability to commune with the Buddhas.

Nowadays there are many people who claim, "I am successor of the position of Dharma King, but I have not yet attained the corresponding state of realization." Of course, even if someone has not attained this state of realization, he still must understand the various treatises. Even if it is not demanded of him that he be proficient in all five initiations, he should at least be proficient in three initiations, including the Picking Slips From a Golden Vase Initiation! Does he truly possess such skills? All practitioners must ponder this deeply!

Thus, you should scrutinize such people from many angles to determine if they are true Dharma Kings or true Great Rinpoches. Based upon the Dharma state of Great Dharma King Yangwo Yisinubu and his disciples, one can see that Dharma King Yangwo Yisinubu is a true Great Dharma King. He is the magnificent Lion's Roar Buddha Tathagata. He is a Holy Virtuous One who is respected by sacred spirits and living beings in all of the Dharma realms – even by the countless Buddhas who have existed since beginningless time. That among his disciples there are such offenders shows that living beings are so pitiable!

Thus, one can see how pitiable those practitioners are who claim to be Dharma Kings or Great Rinpoches. Can they compare with the two Dharma King disciples of Great Dharma King Yangwo Yisinubu? They are far behind those two!

I believe that after Dun Zeng Rinpoche reads this Dharma book, he will give rise to a sufficient amount of awakening and will become very remorseful. As a result, I believe he will truly walk the Bodhisattva path and engage in correct practice. Of course, I ask him to forgive me for having used him as an example. In this present world, there are truly so many other Buddhist disciples whose conduct is worse than that of Dun Zeng Rinpoche just described and whose conduct is even of a diabolical nature. Everybody should use this as a lesson!

In summary, practitioners should remember that cultivation means correcting one's practices. It does not entail boasting about oneself or viewing oneself as being amazing. It does not entail becoming a Buddha just because one speaks of oneself as a Buddha. If one engages in such ways, not only will one be unable to attain accomplishment, one will simply descend into one of the three lower realms of existence to experience endless suffering!

One must cultivate oneself humbly. This is exactly reflected in the words of Dorje Losang, who said that he is a humble practitioner. Dorje Losang is quite good. Because he is like this, his meditative skills continue to grow, and his state of realization reaches new heights day by day. I empowered his state of realization and his beard. His beard, which had basically stopped growing, truly grew again rapidly. In the future, it will grow to be four or five feet, which can represent the state of realization of a Dharma King. Yet, he never considers himself to be a Dharma King. This is quite good!

However, I would like to give a piece of advice to Dorje Losang. When your beard grows to be a few feet long, the long hair in between your eyebrows will at the same time become a wonder for people in the world. At that time, due to your extraordinary appearance, you will be worshipped as a holy person by a myriad of people in the world. The number of Rinpoches, Dharma Teachers, and living beings who respect and worship you will be countless. At such time, you must bear in mind not to be carried away with your own importance. You should always remember the Dharma teachings of Great Dharma King Yangwo Yisinubu to always be a humble practitioner, to diligently and cautiously cultivate yourself, to strive to become a Buddha in this lifetime, and to shoulder the highest responsibilities of a Tathagata. In so doing, the education and support provided to you by your Master, by Pamu, and by the Buddhas in the ten directions will not have been in vain!

Thus, practitioners should learn from Dharma King Dorje Losang and from Elder Dharma King Jiang Yang Qin Zhen. Practitioners should emulate the conduct of three of the Four Great Dharma Princes. Of course, practitioners should emulate the good aspects of Dun Zeng Zhuo Ga Rinpoche. They should never again emulate any of his bad aspects.

Disciples of other Dharma Kings and Great Virtuous Ones have even more negative habitual tendencies that violate the Dharma and engage in even more evil conduct. I will not speak about this or mention their names at this point. In short, everyone should use these people as a lesson. One's cultivation should be down-to-earth. One should practice in a humble manner. One must not state that one has attained realization and accomplishment when one has not. One's three karmas must correspond with the teachings of the Master. One must cultivate oneself in accordance with the Dharma. One must be humble and cautious. One must be constantly content with self-purity. One must maintain a heart of humility. One must not falsely claim to be a Dharma King or Rinpoche.

Only by practicing in this manner will one be able to truly attain the state of realization of a great practitioner! Otherwise, if one violates the rules I have just enunciated, then one will certainly be heading toward hell or another of the three lower realms of existence. After one descends into any such realm, it will already be too late to repent!

At this point, I would like to especially request the magnanimous forgiveness of Great Dharma King Yangwo Yisinubu. Although we have not yet seen each other in this life, nevertheless, I have deeply looked into the mind of the Dharma King and future Buddha. It is a mind that exists for the benefit of living beings. If you would not have been used as an example, who else could have served as a ready example? I think that Master Padmasambhava would also have been willing to be used as an example. Everything we do is for the benefit of living beings!

Chapter Thirteen

INHIBITING DISCIPLES; CONTACT WITH THE MASTER

Those Who Inhibit Their Disciples from Following Elder Virtuous Masters Will Certainly Descend into the Hell Realm; One's Cultivation Will Be in Vain and One Will Not Attain Wisdom and Good Fortune if One Does Not Often Come in Contact with the Master

AMONG PRACTITIONERS OF BUDDHISM, especially among Rinpoches who are Vajra Acaryas, one often sees people whose cultivation deviates from the correct way. The deviation I speak of now relates to certain Rinpoches who are Vajra Masters. Once they enter a certain level of realization, they often become negligent and violate the Samaya Precepts! They are especially inclined to inhibit their disciples from following elder virtuous Masters or other virtuous Masters. This way of acting is not in furtherance of saving living beings. It is not the conduct of a Bodhisattva. Therefore, Vajra Masters should be especially cautious and should carefully examine themselves to see whether they are committing such an offense.

To put it frankly, this means that in the course of propagating the Dharma and benefiting living beings, some Vajra Masters do not truly have as their purpose the saving of living beings. They do not truly act from a Bodhisattva state of mind. Quite the contrary, they superficially save living beings. What they are really doing is building up their own power and their own places of worship, as well as expanding their own personal prestige.

Such conduct is totally motivated by the desire for personal gain. It is selfish conduct designed to destroy others and is no different from the conduct of an ordinary person. People who engage in this type of conduct are called ordinary Acaryas. This kind of person will be unable to save others.

Furthermore, since during the course of their so-called "propagating the Dharma" they accepted offerings from their followers and were worshipped and respected by their followers, they will suffer a great loss of good fortune. They will lose the good seeds (good causes) that they have planted and the merit that they have accumulated. Thus, these good seeds, which have not yet ripened into good fruit, will totally disappear. They are planting bad seeds (bad causes) that will ripen into the fruit of retribution. Hence, these Rinpoches are engaging in a futile and superficial propagation of the Dharma. More important, due to such conduct, they will certainly descend directly into hell!

For the most part, this type of practitioner engages in disputes over different views among the many sects. Most of these practitioners commit this offense out of ignorance. If they could discern the empty nature of things and naturally enter the Dharma state, they would be able to avoid karmic retribution. In so doing, they would attain the realization that karmic hindrances are originally empty. Those who have not yet attained such realization must first repay worldly karmic debts.

However, it is frequently the case that those Rinpoches who have attained this state of realization have not yet understood the Bhutatathata.[82] Because they have not yet understood this ultimate reality, they do not have true realization. Thus, they have the consciousness of an ordinary person. They are motivated by the desire for gain and do not care about saving living beings and spreading the Dharma. It can be said that, for the most part, this type of Rinpoche is a false Rinpoche. They are not truly walking the Bodhisattva path. They are not Mahayana practitioners who truly possess the Bodhisattva state of mind!

Therefore, I often instruct you that it is extremely difficult to find even a few true Rinpoches among 1,000 Rinpoches. All practitioners must scrutinize Rinpoches according to the standards laid out in *How to Recognize the Vajra Tantra* and *Know the True Doctrines*. We must make things clear for future generations of students so that they will not be deceived. Otherwise, they will be ruined for their entire lives and will not attain accomplishment!

A minority of Rinpoches act in this offending manner since they have biased views. They have insufficient knowledge of a certain other sect, or they have inadequate understanding of a certain person of great virtue. Thus, they give rise to extreme views. They are then unwilling to let their disciples learn from others. This type of person is likewise committing an offense. However, his offense is much lighter than the offense committed by a false Rinpoche!

Those Masters who purposefully inhibit their disciples from making progress, who use various means to prevent their disciples from learning from elder virtuous Masters, will surely descend into the hell realm. They are committing a most heinous offense! They lack bodhicitta. Furthermore, in a diabolical way, they are destroying the foundation upon which living beings can attain enlightenment. They are preventing other people from becoming accomplished and enlightened. In order to build up their own prestige and reputation, they are willing to destroy other living beings. One can thus see how great their offense really is! They will definitely bring about the total destruction of their good fortune and will lose all of their good merit. They will become one of the pitiful living beings in the Vajra Hell realm.

There is another type of Rinpoche who is a Vajra Master. He will only allow his disciples to learn from him. He does not allow his disciples to learn from elder virtuous Masters. For example, he does not allow his disciples to bypass him and seek the Dharma from his own Master or from his own Grand Master.[83] He will all the more not allow his disciples to follow elderly virtuous Masters of his own sect or eminent monks and Great Virtuous Ones of other sects.

As soon as he discovers that certain of his disciples are following and learning from these people of great virtue, or are thinking of doing so, or only want to worship and make offerings to them out of respect, he will take measures to stop such disciples. He will not allow these disciples to fulfill their wish to seek the truth. Rather, he immediately uses certain means to inhibit them or even attack them. He prevents them from learning the Dharma and seeking the truth from a good teacher. Actually, this person is already someone who is not a cultivator. This conduct is totally demonic!

All Buddhas and Bodhisattvas are rooted in great compassion and regard the saving of living beings as their responsibility. We should support that which enables living beings to become liberated and attain great accomplishment. We should support disciples in learning from any person who truly holds the correct Dharma. Whether another person of virtue saves a disciple or whether I save a disciple, it is in fact totally the same. It is the same thing.

If my disciples can follow and learn from my Master, then I should be very happy and supportive. We should be as happy as if we had drunk nectar. This is the way to walk the Bodhisattva path! Any Master who is not happy and supportive in such case is a Master who is violating the Samaya Precepts or a Master who has already become diabolical. One can no longer follow such a Master!

Everything that Great Bodhisattvas do is for the benefit of sentient beings. Great Bodhisattvas do not think of fame and gain, and they are not attached to reputation. They have already cut off all attachment to the concept of self and to the Buddha Dharma by which they obtained liberation from the cycle of birth and death. They only differentiate between the correct and the evil, not between themselves and others. Everything Great Bodhisattvas do is for the benefit of living beings, not for the benefit of themselves!

Master Marpa was a magnificent Master of Vajrayana Buddhism. When he began to learn the Buddha Dharma, he journeyed from Tibet to India. On his way there, he came to a certain place in Nepal where he heard that two tantric Masters were preaching the Dharma. He then went to see them so that he could become their student and follow them. These two people were disciples of Master Naropa, whose names were Pentapa and Kantapa. Master Marpa first learned the Dharma by following these two.

Later on, these two Masters told Marpa that their Vajra Master is a true Great Dharma King and a Buddha. They sincerely and joyfully urged Marpa to visit their Master, Naropa, and learn the Dharma under him. They told Marpa that if he did so, he would certainly become accomplished. While Marpa was learning the Dharma under Master Naropa, Master Naropa urged Marpa to learn the Dharma under many other Masters, such as Serlingpa, Shiwa Sangpo, and Maitripa. Later on, after Marpa finished learning the Dharma under these other Masters, he returned to the side of Master Naropa and continued to learn the Buddha Dharma under Master Naropa. He went on to become a magnificent Master within the Kagyu school of Vajrayana Buddhism.

These Great Virtuous Ones and Great Masters were true Bodhisattvas. Therefore, the prospect of their disciples becoming enlightened made them extremely happy. They did not care whether other Masters taught their disciples or whether they themselves taught their disciples. They had only one goal. As long as their disciples were able to learn the Buddha Dharma and become accomplished, they did not object. This is how a true Great Bodhisattva should act. This is the breadth of mind that practitioners of Mahayana Buddhism should have. This is a manifestation of the truly enlightened mind! How can the actions and mentality of those ordinary Rinpoches or those false

Rinpoches be mentioned in the same breath with the actions and mentality of such Great Virtuous Ones and Great Masters!

Since the above-described Rinpoches only act to further their own power, this proves that they are ordinary people and not Holy Virtuous Ones. They are totally unqualified to be Rinpoches. Why would anybody continue to follow them? If their followers do not quickly leave them, then these followers will never attain liberation!

There is another type of Rinpoche. They think, "If my disciples follow my Master, then in the future, won't they only respect my Master and not respect me?" It can be said that Rinpoches with this mentality already lack the state of realization of a Rinpoche. I would like to ask them, what is meant by respect? What, after all, is the worth of respect? Can so-called respect substitute for the great undertaking of propagating the Dharma and saving living beings? What can make you happier than causing your disciples to attain accomplishment and end the cycle of reincarnation? Do you mean to say that your personal prestige is more important than saving living beings by leading them to liberation? Since you still hold on to such mundane and defiling concepts, which hinder your attainment of enlightenment, there is no need for you to attempt to save living beings.

When you attempt to save living beings and carry out your bodhicitta vows, you should know that one does not save living beings in order to fish for fame and credit. In the quest to save living beings, one does not put one's own benefit before the benefit of living beings. Living beings are always first. One's own personal interests come after the interests of living beings. If you do not understand even this point, then how could you save living beings?

These people fully hold on to the concept of self. Their minds are completely filled with the thoughts of an ordinary person. They regard their own prestige as being more important than the accomplishment of other people. It is obvious that they do not regard the saving of living beings as being of any importance! They have not yet cut off their attachment to the concept of self and to the things of the world. One can say with certainty that they cannot even save themselves. It is truly a case where they cannot even save themselves, let alone others!

I will give such people a piece of advice. You must understand that all that we do is for the benefit of living beings and not for anything else! If you use improper methods, such as repression, criticism, being domineering and imposing, etc., in order that your disciples respect you, then it will be impossible for you to achieve this goal! This is because your disciples follow you in order to seek the ending of the cycle of birth and death and in order to learn the Buddha Dharma. If you exhibit in various ways the mentality and conduct of an ordinary person, will your disciples continue to seek knowledge from you and respect you? Definitely not!

If you want to be respected, then you, as a Master, should cultivate yourself according to the Dharma and benefit living beings according to the Dharma. You should cut off your attachment to the concept of self and to the things of the world. You should establish a moral mindset. Your disciples will respect you only when they know that you deserve to be in the same category as the Great Virtuous Ones and that you are able to save them!

Hence, these Rinpoches must act according to the Dharma. Otherwise, there is no difference between them and demons! Of course, going back to what I said before, with respect to disciples within Vajrayana Buddhism, once your Master has truly attained the state of a Great Virtuous One, then your three karmas must correspond with his teachings, and you must respect him according to the Dharma. Otherwise, you are also violating the Samaya Precepts!

There is something else that must especially be borne in mind. Those disciples who have been initiated by the Master should strive to be by the Master's side whenever and wherever possible. They should place emphasis upon furthering Buddhist matters. As soon as they have spare time, they should come in contact with the Master.

There are disciples who have spare time but constantly find excuses not to be by the Master's side. They place emphasis upon worldly matters. There might be as much as ten days or half a month that goes by without ever seeing them. They cling to worldly things, which they view as being more important than the Buddha Dharma.

This type of disciple has already violated the Samaya Precept that proscribes leaving the side of the Master and the Samaya Precept that proscribes viewing one's own matters as more important than Buddhist matters. Having violated the precept that proscribes leaving the Master's side, it will not be easy for them to attain supernormal powers. It will be even more difficult for them to attain liberation! For them, increasing good fortune and avoiding disasters is out of the question.

Of course, the Dharma prescribes that if a disciple truly must perform worldly matters or if a disciple lives more than one thousand "li"[84] away from the Master, then he can cultivate himself away from the Master. However, when he has time, he must do all he can to proceed to the side of the Master. Otherwise, he is still violating the Samaya Precepts!

Since the Master is the total embodiment of the Three Jewels, he emits Vajra Seeds Empowerment Force[85] several times a day. If at this time the disciple is at the side of the Master, then the disciple's blessings and wisdom will naturally increase immeasurably. Thus, when the Master is sitting in meditation, if the disciple sits close to the Master facing the Master, then the disciple will receive extraordinary benefits. The more the disciple can do this, the better! This is due to the Close Accomplishment Empowerment Force.[86]

There is also another aspect of tantra that is wonderful and mysterious. A Master will often suddenly and without any prearranged design impart teachings to disciples, causing them to suddenly attain realization. This can include attaining the Wu Xiu Natural Vision of Wisdom, the Brightness Wisdom Vision, the Great Perfection Wisdom Vision, the Prajna Wisdom Vision, etc. Most of such Wisdom Visions will be suddenly attained by disciples sometime in the course of their being together with the Master on a daily basis. The Master must engage in observation and will occasionally determine that the underlying conditions are ripe, whereupon he will impart to the disciple certain tantric teachings or certain pith-instructions[87] or will perform an initiation for the disciple.

However, if the Master has made a special arrangement for the disciple, if the Master has orally instructed the disciple that he should leave the Master to cultivate himself, or if the Master has gone somewhere and has left the disciple, then the disciple's not being by the side of the Master will not be considered a violation of the precepts. Otherwise, in all circumstances, the disciple should not be separated from the Master for several days!

Ga Ma Yang Zong was practicing the Dakini Dharma and entered the state of ascending into space while chi energy enters the mind. It can be said that she entered into this state faster than any other disciple. For a little more than a year, her body levitated more than six feet over the ground. In 1993, she left me to return to Tibet in order to pay reverence to certain holy people there. She was away for more than two months. After she returned from her trip, she was only able to elevate her body more than two feet over the ground. This was due to the fact that when I allowed her to return to Tibet, she was supposed to go quickly and come back from her trip quickly. However, she went quickly and came back from her trip slowly. During this period of time, she could not partake of the empowerment that comes from being close to the Master. Although Yang Zong has very good moral discipline and is very diligent in her cultivation, if she is separated from the Master too long, her skills will decrease.

There is also the example of Changdu Rinpoche. He learned the Dharma by following his Dharma King Master for twelve years. During this period of time, generally speaking, every two or three days he could be seen at the Master's place. One day when the conditions had ripened, the Master suddenly imparted to him a Secret-Tantric Dharma teaching – The Mind Seal Pith-Instructions. This disciple thus received a supreme Dharma treasure. Within seven days, he realized the five great supernormal powers.[88] At that time, his Master said to him, "You have already realized supernormal powers. However, you must be careful and exert great effort!"

This disciple thought that he had already cultivated the miraculous powers of going through walls, flying through the air, and being omniscient. He also knew that he was a Tulku who had come to this world again voluntarily. Thus, he decided to leave his Master. He decided to travel to a far away place for recreation. After a month, he returned to his Master. His supernormal powers were just as before. He was quite happy about this. He felt that the continuity of his miraculous powers was ensured.

He then again left his Master and returned after two months. Around half a year went by and he was not to be found. One day he suddenly returned to the place of his Master. He was weeping with extreme regret. He said that four of his five supernormal powers had disappeared and that they could not be revived! The only supernormal power left was the divine ear.

His Master said to him, "I told you long ago that you must be careful and exert great effort. However, you did not heed such advice at all. You had not yet realized all of the six supernormal powers. You had not yet realized the sixth supernormal power, which is knowing that your defilements are extinguished and that you have attained liberation from the cycle of reincarnation. Notwithstanding this, you went so far as to violate the precept that proscribes leaving the side of the Master. What's done is done. You should now cultivate yourself from the beginning!"

All practitioners should deeply ponder this story! I will not elucidate its subtle meaning in this book, since it involves the profound and great Dharma of Vajrayana Buddhism. Each of you should deeply reflect upon this story so as to reach understanding!

In summary, disciples must be careful and cautious in order to prevent their practice from becoming futile. Those who are Masters must not, out of selfish concerns, inhibit their disciples from following elder virtuous Masters or from following Holy Virtuous Ones of other sects. They must not inhibit their disciples from learning the Dharma under these other people or from showing respect to these other people. If they inhibit their disciples in such manner, they will not be benefiting themselves at all. More importantly, their conduct might result in their descending into hell to experience endless suffering.

Chapter Fourteen

HOW TO OBTAIN SUPERNORMAL POWERS

SUPERNORMAL DHARMA POWERS ARE skills that will inevitably appear during the course of a Buddhist's cultivation and his striving for enlightenment. These powers are also a type of realization that the cultivator must naturally possess.

This is especially true with respect to practitioners of Vajrayana Buddhism. When the Vajra Acarya Master manifests the Dharma at the Buddhist altar area, these skills will provide empowerment that is an indispensable part of the Buddhist altar area state. Those who are Rinpoches, Dharma Teachers, and Great Virtuous Ones desire and require such skills.

Even ordinary cultivators who have just begun to follow Buddhism want to possess a few supernormal Dharma powers! Because of such ignorant thinking, these practitioners will not only cultivate themselves for their entire lives without attaining any supernormal powers, they will also never have the opportunity to even meet up with a teacher of great virtue who does possess supernormal Dharma powers! What is the reason for this result? Can it be said that desiring supernormal Dharma powers is blameworthy and produces hindrances?

Desiring supernormal powers can be a proper desire for the Dharma. The desire for supernormal powers can be divided into two types: blameworthy and non-blameworthy. It is blameworthy if one desires supernormal Dharma powers primarily for one's own use. This would include desiring to appear impressive and awe-inspiring by showing off one's Dharma powers. It would also include using one's miraculous powers to subdue people, reap fame and gain, cheat people out of money, hoodwink people into sexual misconduct, further one's worldly selfish and evil intentions, and do all kinds of bad things.

These people do not know that the Dharma Protectors in space are inspecting and can see their evil minds. The Dharma Protectors will then immediately exercise their samadhi obstructive powers. These Dharma Protectors will seal up the chakras in the bodies of these ill-intentioned people. Their chakras will be confined to this earthly realm. As a result, for their entire lives, these people will only be able to manifest the state of an ordinary person. It will be impossible for them to obtain supernormal powers.

This is because if these evil people were ever to obtain supernormal Dharma powers, they would immediately become sorcerers. That would be horrible. Wouldn't the three spheres of the universe thereby fall into great chaos?

The Buddhas and Bodhisattvas in the various Dharma realms look back into beginningless time and look forward into the eternal future. They know all living beings in the three spheres of existence like the palms of their own hands. They specifically designate certain conditions under which they will bestow supernormal Dharma powers. Additionally, they dispatch Dharma Protectors, who keep watch on all practitioners, to manage the miraculous powers of living beings.

Even if a Great Virtuous One is momentarily deceived by a person with such evil intent and consequently transmits the Buddha Dharma to him, as long as this person's evil intentions still remain, it will be impossible for him to obtain supernormal Dharma powers no matter how diligently he may practice. This is because the Dharma Protectors inspecting from above do not dare to violate the precepts! They see that evil person's preposterous ideas and immediately cease his miraculous Dharma powers. They block his chakras to prevent his chakras from developing. This is the responsibility of these Dharma Protectors.

There is a second type of person. Their desire to obtain supernormal Dharma powers is not blameworthy. The main reason why this type of person desires miraculous powers is to enlighten themselves and others. The practice of this type of person is based upon the four limitless states of mind. They constantly carry out the six paramitas. They have taken the great bodhicitta vows. They cultivate themselves in order to liberate all living beings.

They want to obtain miraculous Dharma powers in order to liberate living beings from the suffering connected with samsara. They desire to obtain supernormal powers in order to benefit all living beings. They themselves clearly believe in the law of cause and effect. They even often fear that obtaining supernormal powers will bring about karmic hindrances and will cause them to go against the law of cause and effect. Thus, they are frightened of miraculous powers and maintain a heart of humility. They are Great Bodhisattvas, yet they always consider themselves to be ordinary living beings.

The practice of this type of person is entirely in accordance with Buddhism. Since their practice is in accordance with what I am now lecturing on – *Dharma That Every Buddhist Must Follow* – the Dharma Protectors inspecting from above will provide them with the most wonderful assistance. These deities will untie the knots in the energy channels of these practitioners and will cause the supernormal Dharma powers of the Buddhas and Bodhisattvas to suddenly turn into light and enter their chakras. At that time, the mandala in each practitioner's body will respond well and will accept these powers. As a result, miraculous powers will naturally appear and Dharma powers will open up!

Now then, how does one obtain supernormal Dharma powers after all? Those who are smart might already know the answer. However, perhaps those ignorant people who fantasize about learning miraculous Dharma powers do not yet understand. Hence, I, Pamu, will now clearly tell all of you! How should we obtain supernormal Dharma powers?

There are methods to obtain miraculous Dharma powers. There are mantras, mudras, and visualization techniques. When one's three karmas unite into one body and correspond with the teachings, supernormal Dharma powers will come into being. One can then exhibit power and light. The uniting of one's three karmas into one body and their correspondence with the teachings will be manifested in the state of realization and state of virtue one has attained through practice of the Buddha Dharma. When one's state of realization and state of virtue have reached the level where it is appropriate to obtain supernormal Dharma powers, then as soon as one practices according to the Dharma, supernormal Dharma powers will appear. If one's state of realization and state of virtue have not yet reached the level where it is appropriate to obtain supernormal Dharma powers, then even if one recites mantras until one's lips crack, and even if one practices mudras until one's wrists fall off, one will still not obtain the slightest Dharma power.

The ordinary practitioner of exoteric Buddhism knows that without moral discipline, one cannot develop concentration. Without concentration, one cannot attain wisdom. One also cannot attain supernormal powers. Without concentration, one cannot master the Dharma.

I am telling this to all of you here today in the hope that you will pass these instructions on to all of those people who fantasize about having limitless Dharma powers and great supernormal powers. If one does not learn the Tripitaka well and does not live according to Buddhism, or if one does not deeply study and truly practice the teachings contained in the books I have written, such as *The Prajna of Ultimate Reality, Entering the Door of the Dharma, Dharma That Every Buddhist Must Follow, Brief Commentary on the Precepts and Discipline Treatise*, etc., then one will not be able to obtain supernormal Dharma powers! This is because the great door leading to supernormal Dharma powers is opened by living according to the teachings of Buddhism and by possessing a high state of realization and a high state of virtue. There are no other means by which one can obtain supernormal Dharma powers!

Supernormal Dharma powers are arranged by the Buddhas and are managed by the Dharma Protectors who patrol and inspect in the sky. Since the beginning of Buddhist history, not one Dharma Protector has bestowed supernormal Dharma powers upon any cultivator who does not live in accordance with the teachings of Buddhism and who does not have a high state of realization and a high state of virtue. Since the beginning of Buddhist history, not one Dharma Protector has opened up the energy channel knots of any cultivator who does not live in accordance with the teachings of Buddhism and who does not have a high state of realization and a high state of virtue.

Chapter Fifteen

HOW DIFFICULT IS IT TO BECOME ACCOMPLISHED?

FROM ANCIENT TIMES UNTIL THE PRESENT, there have been countless disciples who cultivated themselves through learning Buddhism. Practitioners who became accomplished and ended the cycle of birth and death are as countless as the sands of the Ganges River. They are too numerous to be listed. This serves to greatly increase the confidence of those practitioners who are cultivating themselves and striving for enlightenment!

Nevertheless, from ancient to modern times, there have also been many Buddhist disciples who vigorously cultivated themselves in the hope of ending the cycle of birth and death, including those who wholeheartedly devoted themselves to cultivation, yet who were unable to reach their goal. In the end, reality did not accord with their hopes. The results were entirely contrary to their expectations. Instead, some of them even descended into one of the three lower realms of existence. This truly is a matter of great regret within Buddhism!

Based upon these circumstances and responding to the order of my Buddha Master, I, Pamu, gave these discourses entitled *Dharma That Every Buddhist Must Follow*. These discourses were written by me. The principles contained herein were expressed in an ordinary manner yet are broad and lofty. These principles were expressed in an ordinary manner because they were expounded in oral talks. These principles are lofty because they are difficult to put into practice. These discourses pull together the experiences of the Buddhas and Bodhisattvas from their past cultivation and explain such experiences in ordinary language. Therefore, these discourses are easy to read and difficult to practice.

However, this book is truly a supreme Dharma treasure. These discourses were given in order to provide a bright light for all practitioners who desire to leave the cycle of birth and death and realize accomplishment. This light can illuminate the path of cultivation! It can be said that all cultivators who cultivate themselves according to *Dharma That Every Buddhist Must Follow* will definitely become accomplished without hindrance. There are no exceptions!

Why do I say that *Dharma That Every Buddhist Must Follow* has such great effect? In making such a statement, I am not in any way deceiving the multitudinous Buddhist disciples who devoutly and truly cultivate themselves. It has such great effect because it truly is the crystallization of how the countless Buddhas and Bodhisattvas in the ten directions attained enlightenment! It is a Dharma treasure that explains how the Buddhas and Bodhisattvas ended the cycle of birth and death and realized enlightenment!

From the top level of the ancient Buddhas and Mahasattvas, to the medium level of first stage through tenth stage Great Bodhisattvas, to the lower level of Pratyeka Buddhas and Arhats who realized the various fruits of the supramundane path through the practice of Hinayana Buddhism, it can be said that all of their accomplishments are inextricably related to the principles explained in *Dharma That Every Buddhist Must Follow*. To put it more clearly, the practices that practitioners must follow as described in this book must have been followed by all those who already attained accomplishment and enlightenment.

There are also practices that the multitude of Accomplished Ones did not practice. These are the practices which *Dharma That Every Buddhist Must Follow* warns practitioners against. These practices run counter to the Buddha Dharma. Practitioners absolutely must not engage in them.

Without exception, all of the Great Accomplished Ones within Buddhism attained accomplishment by following the Dharma principles described in *Dharma That Every Buddhist Must Follow*. Even the magnificent Sakyamuni Buddha is no exception. The same is true for Kuan Yin Bodhisattva!

Conversely, if those Great Accomplished Ones within Buddhism had not practiced according to the principles described in *Dharma That Every Buddhist Must Follow*, then they would not have been able to attain their present state of realization and virtue. That is, it would have been impossible for them to have attained any accomplishment or to have received any beneficial effect.

To this day, they would still not be Buddhas or Bodhisattvas. Rather, they would be ordinary living beings just like some of you practitioners here today!

Actually, getting to the bottom of the matter, *Dharma That Every Buddhist Must Follow* is a Dharma treasure that collects and summarizes the experiences of the Great Accomplished Ones. It summarizes the various erroneous practices that cultivators striving for enlightenment have engaged in throughout many lives spanning over eons of time. It contains the essence of how to practice the Buddhist scriptures. It contains the mind-essence summed up by the Buddhas and Bodhisattvas in the ten directions while in their state of enlightenment.

Dharma That Every Buddhist Must Follow goes straight to the heart of the matter and lists the specific extremely serious erroneous practices that exist in the actual cultivation of many cultivators. After entering into the clarity of samadhi, I have seen that many of these erroneous practices are serious problems for modern day cultivators! *Dharma That Every Buddhist Must Follow* prescribes a medicine specially for the particular disease. It addresses the various mistakes that cultivators tend to make. It explains profound theories in simple language. It teaches students in accordance with their aptitudes.

Since cultivators generally cannot discover their own shortcomings and negative karma, they do not know in what respect they are not living in accordance with the rules of the Buddha Dharma. They do not know what mistakes they make. Although some practitioners hear the Master or another person point out the mistakes they commit in their practice, they nevertheless do not know how they should correct such mistakes. Perhaps they do not have a clear conceptual understanding of their predicament. This causes them to have insufficient awareness of their own faults and misdeeds. This is harmful to their practice of the Buddha Dharma. In the end, this prevents them from becoming accomplished!

Dharma That Every Buddhist Must Follow can solve this extremely serious problem of cultivators. By and large, it lists one by one the mistakes often committed by cultivators and the evil practices in which cultivators tend to engage. It allows practitioners to easily compare and contrast their own practices against these listed mistakes and evil practices. In this way, they can determine whether or not their practices conform with the practices of a true cultivator.

If the cultivator's practices do not conform with the teachings in *Dharma That Every Buddhist Must Follow*, then he must carefully examine himself and correct his erroneous ways. Otherwise, he will not be able to become accomplished! This is because this book contains the experiences of the Buddhas and Bodhisattvas since beginningless time. Furthermore, the Holy Ones, using their great supernormal powers, penetrated into the minds of living beings and saw that the Dharma contained in this book is the Dharma that living beings must follow in order to advance. If one's practice totally conforms with the Dharma principles expounded in this book – principles that must be practiced by every Buddhist – then clearly one will not have difficulty in becoming accomplished.

This is due to the special Dharma conditions underlying *Dharma That Every Buddhist Must Follow*. It is precisely because this book is the crystallization of the wisdom of the Accomplished Ones within Buddhism that cultivators can, with minimal effort, practice correctly and, in the shortest possible time, become accomplished and end the cycle of reincarnation! Those who practice the contents of this book are clearly in an especially advantageous position.

The Dharma principles explained in *Dharma That Every Buddhist Must Follow* are suitable to be learned by every cultivator who follows Buddhism! All Buddhist disciples in the three spheres of existence can practice according to the teachings in this book. This includes disciples of the Three Jewels, practitioners within one of the seven classes,[89] Buddhists who desire to become accomplished, and Buddhists who are already accomplished. As long as their practices do not violate the teachings explained in this book, then they will definitely become accomplished without hindrance!

This book can help cultivators to avoid taking wrong paths in the course of their cultivation. It is a true Dharma treasure that leads Buddhists to the goal of accomplishment! As long as one acts in accordance with the principles taught in *Dharma That Every Buddhist Must Follow*, as long as one definitely does that which one should do, as long as one absolutely does not do that which one should not do, and as long as one strictly follows all of the provisions in this book, then ending the cycle of birth and death will be as easy as turning over one's hand. There will be no difficulty!

I am absolutely not exaggerating in the slightest in saying such things. I am not boasting. I say these things because *Dharma That Every Buddhist Must Follow* is true and dependable. Its importance to cultivators is immeasurable. Other general Dharma books cannot take its place! I say these things because it was not only Sakyamuni Buddha who attained perfect Buddhahood by following the Dharma principles contained in this book. Kuan Yin Bodhisattva also attained enlightenment by following such principles. Master Padmasambhava also attained the highest accomplishment by following the Dharma expounded in this book.

Furthermore, my Supreme Vajra Master, Piluzhena Buddha Mahavairocana, agrees with this. His Holiness approved of my work *Dharma That Every Buddhist Must Follow*. His Holiness approved of the Dharma principles explained in this book! Additionally, the magnificent future Lion's Roar Buddha, Yangwo Yisinubu, also agrees with this!

Today, I, Pamu, hereby say the same thing. Those practitioners who rely upon *Dharma That Every Buddhist Must Follow* will definitely be able to attain enlightenment. Furthermore, in an easy and relaxed manner, they will be able to learn the Buddha Dharma, end the cycle of reincarnation, and save living beings. Thus, what *Dharma That Every Buddhist Must Follow* provides to cultivators so that they can attain accomplishment cannot be matched by any other Dharma book! General Dharma books cannot provide such a guarantee!

Practice of the Buddha Dharma has spanned over countless eons. This practice has continued from ancient times all the way up to modern times. There have been so many cultivators. Yet, in comparison to the total number of cultivators, there have been few who attained accomplishment. There have been so many who cultivated themselves but who did not attain accomplishment. There has also been no shortage of people who not only failed to end the cycle of reincarnation, but who instead descended into one of the three lower realms of existence!

The ultimate reasons for this are none other than as follows: They knew true Buddha Dharma principles, yet they did not follow them. They heard true Buddha Dharma principles, yet they did not contemplate and internalize them. They clearly understood true Buddha Dharma principles, yet they did not practice them. They came in contact with the Dharma, yet they did not abide by it. They read writings on the Dharma, yet they did not practice the contents of such writings. They saw what is good, yet they did not follow the good. Instead, they rushed toward evil ways, like a flock of ducks rushing to water!

Thus, practitioners not only must understand the importance of the teachings contained in this book with respect to ending the cycle of birth and death and becoming accomplished, they must also practice according to these teachings. They must consider this book as something that they can correctly rely upon in order to realize enlightenment and become a Buddha. They must practice its contents. Only then can they save themselves and others from the fire wheel by which living beings revolve in the six realms of reincarnation!

To give an analogy, *Dharma That Every Buddhist Must Follow* is just like a bronze mirror. It clearly reflects the karmic hindrances and deluded conduct of Buddhist cultivators who seek enlightenment. It openly reveals their ignorant, obstructive, and defiled ways before everybody. They cannot hide from this! Those practitioners who truly want to become accomplished should use this book as a mirror. They should often look at themselves in this mirror. They should examine each principle in this book against their own practices. As a result, they will be able to discern their ignorant, negative tendencies and will be able to think and act in a correct manner.

In so doing, they will cause the hindrances to enlightenment to never resurface. When one cultivates oneself according to these Dharma principles, one engages in correct practices, walks the correct path, and truly carries out correspondence of the three karmas with the teachings of the Master. Relying upon this book is like holding the most precious treasure: the crystallization of the experiences of the countless Buddhas and Bodhisattvas. If one follows the teachings in this book, what difficulty is there in cultivation? What difficulty is there in becoming accomplished?

Why is *Dharma That Every Buddhist Must Follow* so awesome? All of you should know, what did Sakyamuni Buddha teach? What did Master Padmasambhava teach? What did Master Marpa teach? What did the ancient Buddhas rely upon in order to attain supreme enlightenment? Many cultivators will respond by saying, "They taught great Dharma. They relied upon great Dharma in order to reach Buddhahood." I will tell all of you that they indeed taught and relied upon great Dharma. However, any great Dharma is only useful if it is practiced. There is no other way except practice. There is nothing one can rely upon except practice. What these Great Accomplished Ones taught and relied upon was cultivation. This is the main theme of *Dharma That Every Buddhist Must Follow*!

Notes

1. Although Amang Nopu is female, she is still called *Dharma King* rather than *Dharma Queen*.

2. A description of nectar will be provided below. At this point, suffice it to say that it has nothing to do with any substance found on earth.

3. The author often refers to herself by simply using the last two syllables of her name, *Pamu*. Others also often refer to her as simply *Pamu*.

4. The Chinese term *tan cheng* can be translated as either *Buddhist altar area* or *mandala*.

5. The word *sharira* is usually described as relics of a Buddha or Holy One after they are cremated, such as bones, hair, teeth, etc., which are preserved and venerated in temples, stupas, etc. As the text indicates, in this case the shariras bestowed were not the result of any cremation.

6. The Chinese term *mi fa* can be translated as *tantra* or *esoteric Dharma*. See glossary entry for *tantra*.

7. The term *roots of kindness* or *roots of goodness* refers to one's natural capacity to realize enlightenment through learning Buddhism. These "roots" can deepen over many lives and eons.

8. The Chinese term *fan nao* can be translated as *defilements* or *afflictions*. The Sanskrit word is *kilesa*, which refers to the passions and ignorance that cause one to wander in samsara and hinder one from attaining enlightenment. Six of the basic defilements are greed, hatred (anger), ignorance (delusion), conceit, doubt, and wrong views. Use of the word *afflictions* emphasizes the effects of the defilements.

9. Throughout this book, the word *Master* is synonymous with the word *Guru*.

10. This is Dilgo Khyentse Rinpoche (1910-1991).

11. The rest of this preface was written in the classical or ancient Chinese literary style, whereas the first part of this preface was written in modern Chinese.

12. A Bodhisattva cannot be distinguished as being either male or female. The translator uses the male gender here for purposes of convenience only.

13. The two attachments are: (1) attachment to the concept of self, i.e., the concept that there is a real, permanent ego entity; and (2) attachment to things of the world or to the concept that things of the world and worldly phenomena in general are real.

14. Also known as the five corruptions: (1) The turbidity of views. This is when incorrect, perverse thoughts and ideas are predominant. (2) The turbidity of passions. This is when all kinds of transgressions are exalted. (3) The turbidity of the human condition. This is when people are usually dissatisfied and unhappy. (4) The turbidity of the life span. This is when the human life span generally decreases. (5) The turbidity of the world-age. This is when war and natural disasters are rife.

15. Also known as Kuan Yin Bodhisattva. See glossary.

16. For definitions of *exoteric Dharma* and *esoteric Dharma*, see glossary.

17. This would take place during a particular initiation. The piece of paper may contain vows written by the disciple being initiated or it may contain the Dharma that is to be transmitted to the disciple.

18. The Four Great Dharma Princes have attained a state of realization beyond that of the Eight Great Rinpoches.

19. In Buddhism, the phrase *the other shore* refers to liberation and accomplishment.

20. Vajra Acarya is also written as Vajracarya. See glossary entry for *Acarya*.

21. Zhang Guo Lao was a celestial being with supernormal powers.

22. Sichuan is a province in Mainland China.

23. The word *greed* here connotes selfish desire, lust, avarice, and the like.

24. The term *Buddhist resources* in this book means invisible resources, such as merit and wisdom. It also refers to visible good fortune and wealth. Of course, such wisdom and wealth should be used in furtherance of Buddhism and for the benefit of others.

25. The Small Vehicle is Sravaka-yana or Hinayana, which leads one to become an Arhat. The Middle Vehicle is Pratyeka Buddha-yana or Midhyama-yana, which leads one to become a Pratyeka Buddha. Pratyeka Buddha literally means "solitary awakened one." It refers to one who has attained enlightenment on his own and only for himself. The Great Vehicle is the Bodhisattva-yana or Mahayana, which leads to supreme Buddhahood. Vajrayana is part of Mahayana Buddhism.

26. The term *arouse bodhicitta* has several levels of meaning. For the unenlightened, it is the determination to become enlightened in order to liberate all living beings from samsara. However, in a deeper sense, bodhicitta means the enlightened mind, Buddha-nature, non-dual wisdom, or primal awareness.

27. This means the conducting of tantric rituals and ceremonies.

28. In this context, the word *monastics* refers only to Buddhist monks and nuns.

29. These are the desires for forms, sounds, smells, tastes, and touch sensations.

30. The fruits are the four levels of the supramundane path within Hinayana Buddhism. They are (1) the stream enterer, (2) the once-returner, (3) the non-returner, and (4) the Arhat. The stages are the twelve stages through which a Bodhisattva advances.

31. In the Vajrayana, this means taking refuge in the Four Jewels. Those Buddhists who do not practice Vajrayana Buddhism generally take refuge only in the Three Jewels. Taking refuge is done during a ceremony in which the person taking refuge recites the appropriate refuge formula. For definitions of the terms *Three Jewels* and *Four Jewels*, see glossary.

32. That is, his subject of meditation.

33. This applies to deep meditation that would be distracted even by the thought of strengthening concentration.

34. This means that one must make up one's mind about which of two things one wants.

35. The mountains are cold and the lake is warm.

36. Also translated as "Afflictions are bodhi." This is a Mahayana teaching of the highest level. The defilements are inseparable from Buddhahood. Enlightenment is achieved only when one realizes that the defilements themselves have no real, independent existence. When one sees the empty nature of the defilements, one realizes that there is, in essence, nothing to eliminate in order to enter into enlightenment. This phrase is often used in conjunction with the phrase "Samsara is the same as nirvana."

37. Koans are words, phrases, questions, riddles, or statements used as objects of meditation. Essential to a koan is paradox, i.e., that which is beyond thinking, which transcends the logical or conceptual. Through contemplation of the koan, the student is brought to great awareness of reality.

38. That is, it originated from worldly truth or worldly affairs.

39. With this particular viewpoint, which is one of the two extreme viewpoints, one views things (such as a self or soul) as being eternal. That is, one views things as being real in themselves rather than existing conditionally. The other extreme viewpoint rejected by Buddhism is that of nihilism whereby one views things – even the delusory manifestations of the world – as not existing in any sense. One also believes that nothing continues after death. That is, nihilists deny the doctrines of reincarnation and cause and effect.

40. The eighth consciousness is the alaya consciousness. All karma created in the present life and previous lives is stored in the alaya consciousness. It is regarded as that which undergoes the cycle of birth and death.

41. The external objects corresponding to the six bases (i.e., corresponding to the eyes, ears, nose, tongue, body, and mind) are visible objects, sounds, odors, tastes, body-impressions (tactile objects), and mind-objects (thoughts or ideas).

42. That is, when one saves living beings, one should not be attached to the undertaking of saving living beings.

43. They would enter into nihilism because they would know the principle of emptiness yet would not have directly realized the true state of emptiness.

44. This refers to everything that comes into existence only through the occurrence of certain conditions.

45. This refers to everything that is completely beyond conditioned existence; beyond arising, dwelling, and passing away.

46. That is, being patient and tolerant when insulted or disgraced.

47. Master Milarepa here is referring to himself as the person before Gampopa. In other words, when Gampopa can treat his Master as being no different from Sakyamuni Buddha, then he can expound the Dharma to living beings.

48. That is, they think that what they know is the whole truth and thus do not open themselves up to new and different ideas and concepts.

49. Powerful Masters are able to raise or deliver the consciousness of the dead or dying to higher realms through the practice of what is called *Phowa*. This is sometimes referred to as transference-of-consciousness. Often, the consciousness of the deceased is raised to a Buddhafield, i.e., a paradise reigned over by a particular Buddha.

50. Vidya-Raja literally means "Knowledge King."

51. These are the Ten Precepts. See glossary entry for *Ten Precepts*.

52. See glossary entry for *Tripitaka*.

53. More wonderful in the minds of disciples.

54. Here, the author is using the word *Dakinis* metaphorically as a substitute for the word *women*.

55. The sixth heaven is the highest heaven in the Desire Sphere (Kamaloka). The Desire Sphere is the lowest of the three spheres that constitute the universe.

56. Also known as the three poisons. They are the first three of the five poisons. See glossary entry for *five poisons*.

57. The Eight Winds can be divided into four pairs: (1) gain and loss; (2) honor (fame) and disgrace (dishonor or infamy); (3) praise and ridicule (censure, blame, or criticism); and (4) pleasure and suffering (pain).

58. That is, one can obtain beautiful women and wealth from becoming a successful scholar.

59. Alternative translations would be *desire* or *thirst*.

60. These are the precepts for male and female Buddhist novices who are often children over the age of seven.

61. This can also be interpreted as enduring or bearing humiliation, disgrace, or contempt.

62. For a definition of the term *five poisons,* see glossary.

63. An alternative translation would be *meditation.*

64. The Sanskrit word for morality is *shila,* which can also be translated as moral discipline or moral practice. It is abstaining from all unwholesome actions. The Sanskrit word for concentration is *samadhi,* which can also be translated as meditation. The Sanskrit word for wisdom is *prajna,* which basically means purifying insight into emptiness – the true nature of reality.

65. These mantras contain wording that is to be intoned by the practitioner over and over again during his meditation or sadhana practice.

66. The term *mantra teacher* has a pejorative connotation.

67. That is, he will be unable to successfully practice Phowa, or transference-of-consciousness.

68. These are (1) the prajna obtained through the written word, (2) the prajna obtained through contemplating reality, and (3) the prajna of ultimate reality.

69. In other words, it is better for the doer to undo what he has done. Let the mischief-maker undo the mischief. Since one has caused the trouble, it is up to him to fix it.

70. The four great elements are earth, water, fire, and wind. They correspond, respectively, to the principles of solidity, liquidity, heat, and movement. They are the first four elements of the six great elements that make up a human being.

71. Also known as the seven treasures. They are traditionally listed as gold, silver, lapis lazuli, crystal, agate, red pearl, and carnelian. They represent the seven powers of faith, perseverance, sense of shame, avoidance of wrongdoing, mindfulness, concentration, and wisdom.

72. That is, good companions have good influence, while bad companions have bad influence. In this case, one is negatively influenced by constant contact with these ignorant family members.

73. The Chinese term *gong ye* can be translated as *common karma, collective karma,* or *group karma.*

74. Such Dharma is practiced for the benefit of living beings in the preta (hungry ghost) realm.

75. See glossary entry for *Three Bodies.*

76. The four forms of wisdom of a Buddha are (1) the great mirror wisdom of Aksobhya, (2) the universal wisdom of Ratnaketu, (3) the profound observing wisdom of Amitabha, and (4) the perfecting wisdom of Amoghasiddhi.

77. A Bhadrakalpa is said to last 236 million years during which 1,000 Buddhas arise. The present Bhadrakalpa is called the Fortunate Age or Good Age.

78. This is *The Madhyamika Treatise.*

79. Literally, "Treasure Chamber of the Abhidharma." It was composed in the fifth century and contains two parts: a collection of 600 verses and a prose commentary on these verses. It is considered one of the highest authorities on dogmatic questions.

80. This is *The Vimoksamarga Treatise.*

81. The Yuan Dynasty began in 1271.

82. This is the immutable, eternal, absolute, and ultimate reality, as opposed to forms and appearances that arise, change, and pass away.

83. The term *Grand Master* refers to the Master of his own Master.

84. A *li* is a Chinese unit of length. One thousand li equals about 312 miles.

85. Vajra seeds are the origin of enlightenment. They are planted by the Master into the practitioner during initiation. The Vajra Seeds Empowerment Force is a type of empowerment that causes these seeds to grow into the fruit of enlightenment more quickly.

86. That is, everything that is close to the Master falls within his empowerment.

87. Pith-instructions are whispered oral teachings from Master to disciple.

88. The five great supernormal powers are (1) the ability to fly through the air; (2) the ability to hear sounds that normally cannot be heard, such as the sounds of ants walking or sounds emanating from a far away place, even in another realm of existence (called *the divine ear*); (3) the ability to read the minds of other beings; (4) the ability to recollect previous existences; and (5) the ability to see things that occur outside one's presence, such as things happening at a far away place, even in another realm of existence (called *the divine eye*).

89. The seven classes of practitioners are (1) the monk (bhikshu); (2) the nun (bhikshuni); (3) a novice or observer of the six precepts (siksamana); (4) a male youngster, generally over the age of seven (shramanera); (5) a female youngster, generally over the age of seven (shramanerika); (6) a male lay adherent who vows to observe the Five Precepts (upasaka); and (7) a female lay adherent who vows to observe the Five Precepts (upasika).

⚞ Glossary ⚟

accomplishment - Common accomplishments can be simply supernormal powers. However, in this book, the word *accomplishment* almost always refers to the supreme accomplishment, namely, liberation from the cycle of reincarnation and complete deliverance according to the Mahayana point of view.

Abhidharma - A collection of commentaries and treatises on Buddhist psychology and philosophy. *See* Tripitaka.

Acarya - Literally, "teacher" or "master." It refers to one who is an eminent master.

Arhat (Pali: Arahat) - Literally, "foe-destroyer." It refers to one who has destroyed his mental defilements and thus become liberated from the cycle of reincarnation. In Mahayana Buddhism, an Arhat is below the level of a Bodhisattva.

bodhi - Literally, "awakened" or "enlightened." It has come to generally designate enlightenment. *See* enlightenment.

bodhicitta - Literally, "mind of enlightenment." An altruistic determination or intention on the part of the practitioner, or vow made by the practitioner, to realize enlightenment for the purpose of enlightening all sentient beings.

Bodhisattva - Literally, "enlightenment being." In Mahayana Buddhism, a Bodhisattva is a being who seeks Buddhahood through the systematic practice of the perfect virtues (paramitas) but who renounces complete entry into nirvana until all beings are saved. A Bodhisattva is above the level of an Arhat.

Bodhisattva Precepts - The Bodhisattva Precepts are 58 in number and are listed and explained in the Brahma Net Sutra.

Buddha - Literally, "awakened one." One who has attained enlightenment and is thereby released from the cycle of reincarnation (samsara). One who has attained complete liberation. Such a one has removed all obscurations veiling the mind and has developed all of the perfect virtues (paramitas) to perfection. According to the Mahayana perspective, there are innumerable Buddhas, with Sakyamuni Buddha being a single example.

chakra - Literally, "wheel" or "circle." It is a term for the centers of subtle or refined energy in the human body. These centers of energy are considered to be sources for psychic or spiritual powers.

concentration - Meditative absorption; a state of mind without any distraction.

cultivation - This refers to self-cultivation whereby the practitioner trains his mind and thereby corrects his erroneous ways.

Daka - *See* Dakini.

Dakini - Literally, "female sky-goer." A female figure that moves on the highest level of reality. They are usually depicted as wrathful or semi-wrathful deities. A Dakini is a feminine personification of wisdom. They are particularly associated with transmission of secret teachings to tantric practitioners. The male form is called *Daka.*

Dharma (Pali: Dhamma) - This word has several meanings. Its two main meanings are (1) the cosmic law underlying the universe, especially the law of karmically determined rebirth; and (2) the teachings given by the Buddha and other enlightened beings that express the universal truth and show the way to enlightenment.

Dharma-Ending Age - The present spiritually degenerate era, 26 centuries since the demise of Sakyamuni Buddha. Generally speaking, during the Dharma-Ending Age, a diluted form of the Dharma exists and enlightenment is rarely seen.

Dharma Prince - A Bodhisattva who is on the path leading to becoming a Dharma King.

Dharma Protectors (Sanskrit: Dharmapala) - Literally, "guardians of the Dharma." For the protection of its teachings and institutions, the Vajrayana called upon this group of beings, who can also be invoked by the individual practitioner. Dharma Protectors are sometimes emanations of Buddhas or Bodhisattvas, and sometimes spirits, celestial beings, or demons who have been subjugated by a Great Master and bound under oath.

Dharma Teacher - In Mahayana Buddhism, an honorific title for a Buddhist monk or nun of maturity and high standing.

Eight Precepts - These are the five basic precepts that all Buddhists should observe (the first five of the eight) plus three precepts that lay Buddhists should observe on certain days or retreats. They are (1) not killing; (2) not stealing; (3) not engaging in sexual misconduct; (4) not engaging in wrong speech; (5) not drinking intoxicants; (6) not eating after noon; (7) avoiding music, dance, plays, and other entertainment; and (8) not using perfumes or ornamental jewelry.

Eight Winds - Eight situations that normally preoccupy and sway unrealized people. The Eight Winds are gain and loss, honor (fame) and disgrace (dishonor or infamy), praise and ridicule (censure, blame, or criticism), pleasure and suffering (pain). To be unmoved by these Eight Winds is a mark of a true practitioner.

enlightenment - Full awakening; Buddhahood. This is a state wherein all obscurations have been removed from the mind, and one lives in unlimited compassion and wisdom.

esoteric Dharma - Tantric teachings that are not open and that are only revealed to certain qualified practitioners.

exoteric Dharma - Buddhist teachings that are open, not secret.

five aggregates - Also known as the five skandhas. They represent the body and mind. They are (1) form or corporeality, (2) feelings, (3) perceptions, (4) mental formations, and (5) consciousness. All five aggregates are intrinsically empty. There is no self underlying them. However, the ignorant person thinks that there is a self underlying them or that one or more of the five aggregates are the self.

five poisons - The five poisons are (1) greed, which also includes selfish desire, avarice, craving, etc.; (2) hatred, which also includes anger, ill-will, aversion, resentment, etc.; (3) ignorance, sometimes referred to as delusion; (4) pride, which also includes arrogance and conceit; and (5) doubt, which is basically limited to doubt about the Buddha, the Dharma, the Sangha, and the Master.

Five Precepts - These precepts apply to all Buddhists, whether lay or ordained. They are (1) not killing, (2) not stealing, (3) not engaging in sexual misconduct, (4) not engaging in wrong speech, and (5) not drinking intoxicants.

Five Sciences - Also known as the Five Vidyas, Five Studies, Five Brightnesses, or Five Knowledges. They are mastery of (1) speech, grammar, and composition; (2) the arts, mathematics, science, and technology; (3) medicine; (4) logic; and (5) philosophy, which in this context means knowledge of the ultimate truths of the universe as taught by the Buddhas.

Four Jewels - Also known as the Four Gems. They are the Master, the Buddha, the Dharma, and the Sangha. In this particular context, the sangha usually refers the noble members of the order of Buddhist monks and nuns who have attained one of the four fruits of the Hinayana supramundane path (i.e., stream enterer, once-returner, non-returner, or Arhat) or who have reached the higher level of a Bodhisattva.

four limitless states of mind - Also known as the four boundless states of mind, the four immeasurable states of mind, or simply the four immeasurables. They are limitless loving-kindness toward all beings, limitless compassion toward all beings who are suffering, limitless sympathetic joy over the success and happiness of others, and limitless equanimity toward friend and foe.

Geshé - The highest academic title one can attain in the Gelug school of Tibetan Buddhism, corresponding to a doctor of divinity. One must memorize a vast amount of Buddhist material and must pass certain debates before one can attain such title.

Great Perfection (Tibetan: Dzogchen) - Also known as ati-yoga, it is considered by its adherents as the definitive and most secret teaching of Sakyamuni Buddha. The Great Perfection consists of meditative practices closely associated with the Nyingma school. Within it are methods to realize the rainbow body.

Hetu-Vidya Treatise - The Treatise on Logical Reasoning.

Hinayana - Literally, the "Lesser Vehicle"; also known as Therevada Buddhism or Southern Buddhism. It is prevalent chiefly in countries in Southeast Asia, such as Sri Lanka, Burma, Thailand, Kampuchea, and Laos. The Hinayana practitioners' motivation for following the Dharma path is principally their intense wish for personal liberation from suffering and its causes. The goal of the Hinayana practitioner is the attainment of Arhatship.

initiation (Chinese: guan ding; Sanskrit: abhisheka) - Literally, "sprinkling" or "anointing." This is a ceremony in which the disciple is empowered by the Master to carry out specific meditation practices relating to a particular tantric deity.

karma - Literally, "action." It refers to the universal law of cause and effect whereby positive actions produce happiness and negative actions produce suffering. *See* three karmas.

Khenpo - The chief instructor or spiritual authority in a monastery. This title is also accorded to Lamas of great learning.

Kuan Yin - Also known as Kuan Shih Yin. Kuan Yin is the Chinese version of Avalokiteshvara. As the Bodhisattva of compassion, Kuan Yin is one of the four great Bodhisattvas of Buddhism and is the object of particular veneration.

Lama - *See* Rinpoche.

Mahamudra - Literally, "Great Seal," i.e., the seal of emptiness on all phenomena. This is a profound system of meditation upon the mind and the ultimate nature of reality. Mahamudra is closely associated with the Kagyu school. It is comparable to the Nyingma school teachings of Dzogchen, but is not entirely the same as Dzogchen.

Mahasattva - Literally, "great being." Refers to Great Bodhisattvas, often at the level of seventh Bodhisattva stage (bhumi) or higher.

Mahavairocana - Literally, "He Who Is Like the Sun." Also known as Vairocana. Mahavairocana is one of the five transcendent Buddhas.

Mahayana - Literally, the "Great Vehicle." It is one of the two general divisions of Buddhism, the other being Hinayana. It is the tradition of Buddhism practiced in northern Asia, China, Japan, Korea, Mongolia, Tibet, and the Himalayan regions. The Mahayana practitioners' motivation for following the Dharma path is principally their intense wish for all sentient beings to be liberated from suffering and its causes. To this purpose, the goal of the Mahayana is the attainment of the supreme enlightenment of Buddhahood, and the path consists of the practice of the six paramitas (perfect virtues). Vajrayana is a branch of the Mahayana.

mandala - This word has several levels of meaning, such as the following: (1) A circular diagram symbolic of the entire universe. (2) The abode of a meditational deity. (3) The arrangement of an offering, which is a powerful means of accumulating merit. (4) A place where tantra is practiced.

mantra - Syllables or formulas that are recited during tantric meditation and that protect the mind of the practitioner.

Mara - Literally, "the killer." He is often called "the Evil One" or the "non-liberator" since he is the opponent of liberation. He appears in the Buddhist texts both as a real being (i.e., as a deity who is lord of the sixth heaven in the desire sphere) and as a symbol of everything that hinders progress on the path of enlightenment.

Marpa - Marpa lived from 1012-1097. He was a renowned yogi from southern Tibet, who was also called Marpa the Translator. He is a principal figure in the lineage of the Kagyu school of Tibetan Buddhism. By making three trips to India, he brought back to Tibet certain tantric teachings. He was the Master of Milarepa.

merit - Good karma; the positive energy generated by wholesome actions of body, speech, and mind.

Milarepa - Milarepa lived from 1040-1123. The most famous Tibetan yogi and poet. After he underwent trials of the utmost difficulty imposed on him by his Master, Marpa, he received Marpa's highest teachings. He is famous for his intense practice, devotion to his Master, attainment of enlightenment, and his many songs of spiritual realization.

Mt. Sumeru - Also known as Mt. Meru. A mountain thought to stand at the center of the universe according to ancient Indian cosmology.

mudra - A symbolic hand gesture used in meditation related to a particular meditational deity.

nirvana - The state of liberation from the suffering of cyclic existence. The goal of spiritual practice in all branches of Buddhism. However, the concept of nirvana differs in Hinayana, Mahayana, and Vajrayana Buddhism.

Padmasambhava - Literally, "lotus-born." He is the Indian Master who is said to have been born miraculously, appearing in a lotus flower. He was predicted by Sakyamuni Buddha in several sutras and tantras. In the eighth century, at the invitation of King Trisong Detsen, he quelled the local demons and gods who resisted the spread of Buddhism into Tibet. He introduced into Tibet the teachings of the Vajrayana and is one of the historically identifiable founders of Tibetan Buddhism.

prajna - Understanding, knowledge, wisdom, or insight. It is an intuitive wisdom that cannot be conveyed by concepts. It is insight into emptiness, which is the true nature of reality.

preliminary practices - Usually done 100,000 times each. The four main ones are recitation of the refuge formula, mandala offerings, prostrations, and Vajrasattva mantra recitation.

rainbow body - A subtle body composed of pure light.

Rinpoche - Literally, "precious one." It has the same meaning as Lama. In Tibetan Buddhism, it is a person who is a religious master or guru, venerated by his students, since he is an authentic embodiment of the Buddhist teachings.

sadhana - A tantric meditation practice involving visualization of a deity and the recitation of the associated mantra. Performing this type of practice requires initiation by a Master.

Sakyamuni Buddha - The Buddha of our time, who lived around the fifth century B.C. He was born into the Sakya clan in what is now Nepal. He taught the way to liberation and full enlightenment and is the historical founder of what came to be known as Buddhism.

samadhi - Generally, collectedness of the mind on a single object through the calming of mental activity.

Samaya - Literally, "promise." In Vajrayana Buddhism, this refers to the sacred link between the Master and the disciple and also the sacred links between fellow disciples of the same Master. It can also refer to the pledges and commitments made by disciples concerning their practice of tantra.

samsara - Cyclic existence within the six realms of conditioned existence. It is the beginningless, recurring cycle of death and rebirth sustained by greed, hatred, ignorance, and the power of karma. It is fraught with suffering.

sangha - Usually defined as Buddhist order or community of monks and nuns. It is also sometimes broadly defined as all practitioners of Sakyamuni Buddha's teachings.

sastra - Commentaries or treatises on Buddhism that augment, explain, and expand upon the primary texts.

sharira - The relics of a Buddha or Holy One after they are cremated, such as bones, hair, teeth, etc., which are preserved and venerated in temples, stupas, etc.

six bases - The eyes, ears, nose, tongue, body, and mind.

six great elements - The elements that make up a human being. They are earth, water, fire, wind, space, and consciousness.

six paramitas - Also known as the six perfections, six perfect virtues, or six transcendent perfections. They are generosity, moral discipline, patience, energy (diligence), concentration, and wisdom. These represent the fundamental practices of Mahayana Buddhism. They are the virtues perfected by a Bodhisattva in the course of his development.

six realms (Sanskrit: gati) - Also known as the six paths, six courses, or six modes of existence. In brief, they are the hell realm, the animal realm, the hungry ghost (preta) realm, the human realm, the realm of the asuras (demigods), and the heavenly realm (gods or devas). These are the realms within samsara, that is, cyclic existence. The first three are bad or lower realms (sometimes also called the three evil realms), while the last three are good or higher realms.

stupa - A Buddhist monument frequently containing the relics (sharira) of an enlightened being and varying in size. It often has a square base, a rounded midsection, and a tall conical upper section.

sutra - The discourses of Sakyamuni Buddha and his eminent disciples.

tantra - The esoteric texts of Vajrayana Buddhism. Often used to refer to the teachings and practices contained in such texts.

tantric Buddhism - *See* Vajrayana Buddhism.

Tathagata - Literally, "thus-gone one." Refers to one who has attained supreme enlightenment. It is one of the ten titles of Sakyamuni Buddha, which he himself used when speaking of himself.

ten directions - The four cardinal points, the four intermediary ones, the zenith, and the nadir.

Ten Precepts - These are the ten basic prohibitions binding on monks and nuns. They are (1) not killing; (2) not stealing; (3) not engaging in sexual misconduct; (4) not engaging in wrong speech; (5) not drinking intoxicants; (6) not eating after noon; (7) avoiding music, dance, plays, and other entertainment; (8) not using perfumes or ornamental jewelry; (9) not sleeping on raised beds; and (10) refraining from coming into contact with money or other valuables.

Three Bodies (Sanskrit: Trikaya) - Three kinds of bodies possessed by a Buddha according to the Mahayana view: the Dharmakaya (the body of reality), the Sambhogakaya (the body of delight or the reward body), and the Nirmanakaya (the body of transformation). The basis of this teaching is the conviction that a Buddha is one with the absolute and manifests in the relative world in order to work for the welfare of all sentient beings.

Three Comprehensive Precepts - Also known as the Three Bodies of Pure Precepts, Three Kinds of Pure Precepts, and Three Cumulative Precepts. They are three groups of precepts that form the basis for all Bodhisattva practice: (1) Do not what is evil. (2) Do what is good. (3) Be of benefit to all sentient beings.

Three Jewels - Also known as the Three Gems. They are the Buddha, the Dharma, and the Sangha. In this particular context, the sangha usually refers to the noble members of the order of Buddhist monks and nuns who are on one of the four stages of the Hinayana supramundane path (i.e., stream enterer, once-returner, non-returner, or Arhat) or who are on the higher level of a Bodhisattva.

three karmas - All of one's bodily actions or conduct, all of one's verbal actions or speech, and all of one's mental actions or thoughts. *See* karma.

three lower realms - *See* six realms.

three spheres - (Sanskrit: triloka) The three spheres or worlds into which the six realms of existence are divided. These three spheres are as follows: (1) The material sphere of desire where sexual and other forms of desire predominate. Within this sphere are the hell realm, the animal realm, the preta realm, the human realm, the asura realm, and the first six levels of the heavenly realm. (2) The sphere of desireless corporeality or form where desire for sexuality and food falls away, but the capacity for enjoyment continues. This sphere is inhabited by the gods dwelling in the four dhyana (meditation) heavens. (3) The immaterial sphere of bodilessness or formlessness, which is a purely spiritual sphere. The inhabitants of this sphere are free from both desire and the restrictions of matter. It has four non-substantial heavens.

Tripitaka - Literally, "three baskets." The first basket, the Vinaya-pitaka, contains accounts of the origins of the Buddhist order of monks and nuns as well as the rules of discipline regulating the lives of monks and nuns. The second, the Sutra-pitaka, is composed of the discourses of Sakyamuni Buddha and his eminent disciples. The third, the Abhidharma-pitaka, is a collection of commentaries and treatises on Buddhist psychology and philosophy.

Tulku - Literally, "transformation body." In Tibetan Buddhism, it refers to a person who, after passing certain tests, is recognized as the reincarnation of a previously deceased person, usually a Lama.

Vinaya - *See* Tripitaka.

Vajra (Tibetan: Dorje) - Literally, "diamond" or "adamantine." In general, it is that which is beyond arising and ceasing – hence, indestructible. It is a symbol of unchanging and indestructible wisdom capable of penetrating through everything. Vajra is also a small implement used in conjunction with a bell during tantric rituals.

Vajra Acarya (Sanskrit: Vajracarya) - Refers to one who is accomplished in the Vajrayana teachings and capable of transmitting them to others. *See* Acarya.

Vajravarahi (Tibetan: Dorje Phagmo) - Literally, "diamond sow." Vajravarahi is a female yidam deity who is a Dakini. She is usually depicted with a sow's head protruding from the crown of her head. The sow represents basic ignorance, which is transformed into highest wisdom.

Vajrayana Buddhism - Literally, "Diamond Vehicle." Basically synonymous with Esoteric Buddhism, Tibetan Buddhism, Tantric Buddhism, Tantrayana, and Mantrayana. It is a branch of Mahayana Buddhism. As the author explains in this book, Vajrayana Buddhism includes all of exoteric Buddhism. It also includes the study and practice of the secret or esoteric teachings of Buddhism, known as tantra. It is the quickest vehicle within Buddhism, as it allows the practitioner to attain enlightenment in this very lifetime.

Western Paradise (Sanskrit: Sukhavati) - Literally, "the Blissful." Also called the Pure Land of the West. It is reigned over by Amitabha Buddha, who created it by his karmic merit.

yidam - Refers to a deity representing enlightenment in a male or female, peaceful or wrathful form, who corresponds to the individual psychological makeup of the practitioner. Yidams are manifestations of the Sambhogakaya. They are visualized during meditative practice and are regarded as being inseparable from the mind of the meditator. In short, a yidam is the practitioner's personal or main deity for tantric practice; i.e., the deity with which the practitioner has the strongest connection. Yidam is sometimes referred to as one's meditational deity or one's tutelary deity.

Index